To Fred —
In honor of our coun

Malcolm too
10/13/92

FREDERICK LEONG, PH.D.
THE OHIO STATE UNIVERSITY
DEPARTMENT OF PSYCHOLOGY
142 TOWNSHEND HALL
1885 NEIL AVENUE MALL
COLUMBUS OHIO 43210-1222

CHINATOWN

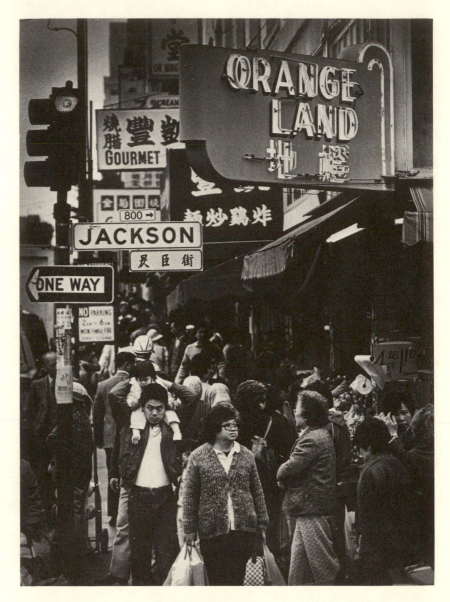

The heart of Chinatown, this scene depicts the contrasts of the neighborhood: shopping conveniences poised against crowding that runs three-persons deep. On weekends, pedestrians maneuver to a slow and jagged crawl. In 1985, Orangeland, the buildings on this corner that housed 195 Chinese immigrant families and elderly, was slated for demolition. Market-rate condominiums were to take its place. In order to preserve the existing housing, the San Francisco Board of Supervisors voted against the zoning change required for the condominium development. 1985. (Photograph by Craig Lee, courtesy of the *San Francisco Examiner*, copyright © *San Francisco Examiner*/Craig Lee.) Reprinted by permission.

CHINATOWN
MOST TIME, HARD TIME

CHALSA M. LOO

PRAEGER

New York
Westport, Connecticut
London

Copyright Acknowledgment

The author and publisher are grateful to the San Francisco Department of City Planning for allowing the use of portions of their Chinatown Master Plan of February 19, 1987 to be printed in this text.

Library of Congress Cataloging-in-Publication Data

Loo, Chalsa M.
    Chinatown : most time, hard time / Chalsa M. Loo.
        p.   cm.
    Includes bibliographical references and index.
    ISBN 0-275-93893-X (alk. paper)
    1. Chinatown (San Francisco, Calif.)—Social conditions.
  2. Minorities—California—San Francisco—Social conditions. 3. San
Francisco (Calif.)—Social conditions.   I. Title.
    F869.S36C475   1991
    979.4′61—dc20   91-27984

British Library Cataloguing in Publication Data is available.

Library of Congress Catalog Card Number: 91-27984
ISBN: 0-275-93893-X

First published in 1991

Praeger Publishers, One Madison Avenue, New York, NY 10010
An imprint of Greenwood Publishing Group, Inc.

Printed in the United States of America

The paper used in this book complies with the
Permanent Paper Standard issued by the National
Information Standards Organization (Z39.48-1984).

10 9 8 7 6 5 4 3 2 1

To all who helped to make this book possible

Depicting the starkness of some of Chinatown's interiors, this girl's play area consists of a broom, broken chair, garbage pail, crate, and paint cans. Conspicuously absent are toys, curtains, or pictures to grace the windows and walls. 1976. (Photograph courtesy of Pok-Chi Lau.) Reprinted by permission.

Contents

Tables and Figures

TABLES

FIGURES

Vignettes of Interviews

Acknowledgments

This work represents an effort to put the study of ethnic minorities within the vortex of empirical study and to reduce the myopia of traditional research with regard to cultural and ethnic diversity. I am grateful to those who worked for the Chinatown Housing and Health Research Project (CHHRP) and to those who helped me on this odyssey of three phases: (1) the research and field work, (2) data analysis and write-up, and (3) completion of the text. Different persons contributed to each phase.

A grant from the Center for the Study of Work and Mental Health of the National Institute of Mental Health funded the project from 1979 to 1982. I would like to acknowledge Elliot Liebow and Maury Lieberman of that center for their support. Faculty and staff at the Survey Research Center at the University of Michigan gave generously of their consultant skills; thanks go to Carlos Arce, Gerald Gurin, the late Steven B. Withey, Robert Groves, Robert Santos, Robert W. Marans, and James Jackson. Connie Young Yu, Ben Tong, Fae Ng, and Reiko True contributed to portions of the grant proposal, and Judy Woo was indispensable to the entire functioning of phase one. I am very grateful to our Board of Community Directors—Dr. Rolland Lowe, Dr. Cecilia Johnson, Dr. Ernest Wu, Henry Der, and Dan Richardi for their advice and support. An additional mention for Dr. Cecilia Johnson, who generously provided us with office space in our first year, when we had no funds for rent; without this, our project could not have been community based. I would also like to acknowledge the help of David Tong, Leung Yee, Jeanne Kwong, Angela Jeong, Elizabeth Harvey, Valerie Wong, Tony Lam,

Kam Wong, Kathy Fong, Philip Fisher, Philip Choy, Linda Wang, Lulu Mebelitini, Lois Scott, and the staff at the San Francisco Department of City Planning.

A special acknowledgment is due to the interviewers, without whom the survey could not have been carried out: Lincoln Lin, Salome Tong, Angie Lee, Layton Doung, David Tong, Winnie Suen, Kitty Tsui, Andrew Lau, and Angela Jeong. Their descriptive impressions of selected interviews introduce each chapter. Authors of these vignettes include: Angela Jeong for "Death of a Candy Store," Lincoln Lin for "Immigration Laws Ruined My Life," Layton Doung for "From Teacher to Seamstress" and "Very Bitter," Winnie Suen for "To Start All Over," Andrew Lau for "His Parents' Dream," Kitty Tsui for "His Health Problem," Salome Tong for "Lost Almost Everything," Lincoln Lin for "To Be a Man in My Next Life," and Angie Lee for "My Fate to be Unmarried." At the interviewers' request that I experience what they had to brave, I conducted one interview: "Noisy, Crowded Neighborhood" was written by this author. I edited the vignettes for clarity and, where necessary, to disguise respondents' identities.

For phase two, I'd like to give special thanks to Don Mar, who handled the data analyses and contributed invaluably to the spirit and functioning of CHHRP; I am particularly grateful to Don, whose years of patient commitment and help on this project were essential to the completion of this work. I also wish to thank Connie Young Yu and Paul Ong who, with Don, were important contributors to the write-up and interpretation of portions of the research. All three read through early chapter drafts and offered helpful suggestions. A grant from the San Francisco Foundation in 1986 helped provide funding support for the write-up of two sections of this text, and a grant from the Asian American Studies Research Center and the Institute of American Cultures at the University of California at Los Angeles in 1985–1987 provided clerical and research assistant funds. I'd like to thank Jane Bitar, Judy Chan, and UCLA's Social Science Manuscript Typing Service.

For phase three, I wish to thank Stephen Haynes for his encouragement and editing suggestions; to Steve Owyang, Robert Bechtel, Martin Wong, Lowell Chun Hoon, Maria Root, and Ron Johnson, I am most grateful for their helpful editing suggestions and insightful comments. Steven G. Doi provided me with the rare books needed for writing chapter two; Richard Wada helped me with photograph selections; Crystal Huie and Pok Chi Lau offered descriptive captions for their stunning photographs; Jody Carpenter was helpful in securing photograph permissions from the *San Francisco Chronicle;* Sharaine Lum and Julie Minami assisted in the clerical tasks of the write-up; and John Liu and librarians at the Chinatown branch of the San Francisco Library, Asian American Studies library at UC Berkeley, and the Social Science reference desk at the University of Hawaii library helped me secure obscure reference citations. Finally, thank you to Gary Okihiro and Mari Matsuda for their encouragement and Wes Senzaki for creating our CHHRP logo.

Approaching a neat, orderly room in one of the low-income residential hotels, this is the home of a dignified man in his 90s who lives alone. Even with no place to go, this well-groomed man dresses in a three-piece suit, a behavior that is characteristic of many men in his generation. From his sole window he has a full view of a brick wall, quite common for many rooms in Chinatown. With the natural light from his window, he reads the daily Chinese newspaper. This man is proudly self-sufficient and is content to live in Chinatown. 1984. (Photograph courtesy of Crystal K. D. Huie.) Reprinted by permission.

Death of a Candy Store

I walked in sight of my assigned address, then realized this was no stranger's home but a familiar place from my past. Not less than seven years ago, this address represented every child's dream—an unthinkable variety of gum, candy, and affordable toys. Better yet, it was all within a kid's arm's reach. The candy store was a very small cubicle, crowded and overstocked with every conceivable type of cavity-creating edible. It had the latest in candy, baseball card packages, and an unrelenting count of water pistols.

I approached the doorway only to see that much had changed. Its faded, peeling green exterior, and the rusted and outdated "Things Go Better With Coke" sign were not reminiscent of the flourishing candy shop I once knew. I knocked because I could find no doorbell. Quickly, a middle-aged man came to the door dressed in his mein knop *(cotton jacket),* tall hi *(Chinese slippers), and extremely worn-out pants.*

I identified myself and asked if he had received our letter. He said "yes," then immediately asked if the Chinatown Housing and Health Research Project (CHHRP) had anything to do with preventing private businesses or corporations from buying out the "little people." He was fearful that his residency might be in jeopardy. I said that this interview could indirectly help him but that CHHRP was not directly involved in preventing corporate buy-outs. Curious about our study, he welcomed me in anyway.

While entering, I noticed two walls still lined with shelves. But no candy now occupied the space. Instead, canned goods, old clothing, boxed games, and other storage materials appeared. A bunch of fabric lay in a pile by a sewing machine. The floor was concrete, showing little attempt to make the converted home cozy. I wondered if this was a candy shop converted into a home or a home awkwardly pieced together by remnants from the candy shop.

This respondent was an educated man who felt he was constantly waging an uphill battle. He didn't know what to do. Calling his job a "treadmill existence," he felt in a rut. Life had become too much of a routine; it lacked purpose or meaning.

He and his wife couldn't communicate. He only understood Chinese but couldn't speak it. She only spoke Chinese. He was extremely Americanized, while she was traditionally Chinese. He felt his wife expressed only disappointment in him and in the grim life they faced. He was forced to close down his store because of a triple increase in rent over a 10-year period. With the income he and his wife brought in, they could barely pay the bills and had nothing to save. Inflation and rent hikes were his unbeatable foes.

Upon concluding the interview, I thanked him for being so candid and open. He looked down at the floor, shook his head, and said, "I didn't think it would be such a grueling experience."

1

Researching Ethnic Minority Populations

Chinatown, San Francisco stands as the birthplace of Asian America and is one of the longest standing ethnic communities in the United States. This crowded, low-income community exists in the midst of abundant wealth and is visited by roughly 5,000 tourists per day. Within this community live 31,000 Chinese Americans, only part of some 60 million persons of color in this nation. This book provides social science research data about this historic community and its people. The portrayal, which combines scholarly and personal contexts, provides an understanding of the life problems, concerns, perceptions, and needs of a major segment of the Chinese American population. The research tests existing hypotheses about Asian Americans, corrects erroneous stereotypes, enlarges our empirical base of knowledge in order to train human service professionals to work with persons of color, and provides relevant data for policy planning and service delivery. By addressing key research issues relevant to Chinatown residents, the book also raises issues that are relevant to other low-income and ethnic minority populations.

This work documents a distinctive American community from an interdisciplinary perspective that incorporates psychology, sociology, urban studies, ethnic studies, community studies, history, women's studies, and linguistics. Within the field of psychology, this work bridges clinical, environmental, community, and social psychology. Methodologically, the work represents a model of quantitative, multidomain interview sample survey research, a form of scientific inquiry that is well suited to assessing the beliefs and perceptions of a population.

This chapter covers five topics: (1) the need to study U.S. ethnic minorities; (2) the Chinese American population and community of interest; (3) the sociopolitical context for the research; (4) the research method; and (5) the plan of the book. In the first section, we note that persons of color have been a neglected dimension of American history; that increases in anti-Asian violence and demographic increases in the population of ethnic minority groups accentuate the need for research on Chinese Americans; that there exists a need for research on the quality of life of Asian Americans and for research to test the validity of ethnic stereotypes; and finally, that there is a need for research on ethnic minority groups in the clinical and counseling psychology fields. In total, this study of Chinese Americans is an attempt to partially rectify the general neglect of social science research on ethnic minorities in the United States.

THE NEED TO STUDY ETHNIC MINORITIES

A Neglected Dimension of American History

The study of ethnicity has been a neglected dimension of American history and the study of immigration an underdeveloped field of historical inquiry. This state of affairs has left social scientists to charge that historians have failed to do their job in conducting historical research on ethnic groups (Vecoli, 1970). American historians were accused of either neglecting Asian immigrants or treating them as inflowing hordes of alien scabs or pawns, rather than as persons to be celebrated for their accomplishments (Daniels, 1966). A contemporary example of this neglect is the celebration of Ellis Island in New York as the immigrants' "Gateway to America" (Kinney, 1990, pp. 26–27). As seen in *Life* magazine, the new National Park Service museum, which commemorates four centuries of U.S. immigration, contains portraits of "America's immigrants"—Swedish, Italian, Russian, Hungarian, Norwegian, Romanian, and Austrian. Photographs of Asian immigrants or Mexican immigrants are conspicuously missing. These non-European newcomers arrived largely on the West Coast and from the South; however, no comparable memorial exists for them. Their absence from such memorials underscores the continued disregard of Asians and Hispanics as legitimate Americans.

The value of studying ethnic minority groups (or persons of color) has not yet been appreciated (Reid, 1988). To rectify this state of affairs requires acknowledging a history of racist rejection, which has been described as "too painful an experience to remember" (Nee and Nee, 1972, p. xi) and "one of the deepest ills of American society" (Surh, 1974, p. 168). Yet such study is critical to our need for new visions, interpretations, and conceptualizations of America's cultural plurality. Such analyses permit us to understand poverty, alienation, powerlessness, and the effects of a culturally monolithic society on its excluded groups.

Anti-Asian Violence

The need for research on Asian Americans has been accentuated by the rise of anti-Asian violence during the 1980s. There have been assaults on Asian refugees in Massachusetts; fire-bombing of Korean businesses in Washington, D.C.; assaults and intimidation of Vietnamese fishermen in Florida, Texas, and California; an assault on a Laotian American perceived to be a Japanese; a killing of a Vietnamese high school student in Davis, California by a white classmate after weeks of racial harassment by white students; and the shooting of Asian and Vietnamese American children in a California schoolyard by a white assailant.

While anti-Asian attacks have involved various Asian American groups, the murders that have received the widest press have involved two American-born Chinese—Vincent Chin, who was bludgeoned to death in Detroit by white assailants who blamed Japan for unemployment conditions within the U.S. automobile industry; and Jim Loo, who was murdered in North Carolina by an assailant who believed Loo was of the same race as those who had killed his brother in Vietnam. In a less publicized case, Gary Moy, another Chinese American, was stabbed in Brooklyn in 1986 by a youth who told him that Chinese "don't belong in this neighborhood" (Howe, 1986). These and other cases of anti-Asian attacks led to the formation of the Coalition against Anti-Asian Violence and to a report on Violence against Asians published by the U.S. Civil Rights Commission in 1986. If racial violence emerges out of ignorance about race and ethnicity, studies that educate the general American public about Asian Americans are needed.

Demographic Increases in the Population of Ethnic Minorities

The need for research on ethnic minorities is also highlighted by dramatic shifts in the proportion of the U.S. population they represent. Moreover, as our society faces striking demographic changes, empirical research on ethnic minority populations becomes vital for planning in the fields of education, health, mental health, public housing, immigration, and legal policy.

The proportion of persons of color in the United States in 1990 was estimated to be 24%, representing an increase from 16% a decade earlier. This 1990 total includes 28.4 million blacks, 22.3 million Hispanics, 7.3 million Asian/Pacific Islanders, and 2.0 million American Indian/Eskimo or Aleutians. These calculations take into account the fact that Hispanics may be of any race, that approximately 40% of the Hispanics were in the "white" race category, 5% in the "black" race category, and the remainder in the "other" race category. By the year 2000 it is estimated that one-third of all school-age children will be ethnic minority, and by the year 2010 one-third of the nation is expected to be of ethnic minority heritage (Commission on Minority Participation in Education and American Life, 1988).

The dramatic increase in the ethnic minority presence in this society is partly due to the increased proportion of immigrants from Asia, Mexico, and Latin America. In 1950, newcomers from these countries amounted to 30% of all immigrants to the United States. From 1981–1985, newcomers from these countries amounted to a full 83% of all immigrants to this nation (Bouvier and Gardner, 1986). In 1990 in California, the state with the largest population of immigrants, there were 16,923,632 Californians of color compared to 20,524,327 whites. By the year 2000, California's population is expected to be roughly balanced between whites and persons of color. By 2003, ethnic minorities will become the "new majority," constituting over one-half the state population (California State Department of Finance, 1988). With the increase in percentages of Hispanic and Asian American students, whites will become a minority in the California public schools for the first time.

In 1990, the number of Asian/Pacific Islanders in the United States (7,273,662) was more than double the number (3,500,439) counted in 1980. Asian/Pacific Islanders constituted 3% of the country's total population. Chinese Americans, who numbered 1,645,472, were the largest Asian or Pacific Islander group, as they were in 1980. Filipino Americans, who numbered 1,406,770, were the second largest Asian or Pacific Islander group, as they were a decade earlier. These groups were followed by Japanese Americans 847,562, Asian Indians 815,447, Korean Americans 798,849, Vietnamese Americans 614,547, Hawaiians 211,014, Samoans 62,964, Guamanians 49,345, and other Asian or Pacific Islanders 821,692 (which included Laotian and Cambodian—each with over 140,000—and Hmong, Thai, and Pakistani—each with over 80,000). From 1980 to 1990, the changes in percentage of the population for these groups were Chinese 104%, Filipino 82%, Japanese 21%, Asian Indian 126%, Korean 125%, Vietnamese 135%, Hawaiian 27%, Samoan 50%, and Guamanian 53% (1990b U.S. Bureau of the Census, Summary Tape File 1A, Tables 1 and 2).

The state with the largest Asian/Pacific Islander population in 1990 was California, with 2,845,659 Asian/Pacific Islanders (see Table 1.1). Thirty-nine percent of all Asian/Pacific Islanders lived in California (1990b U.S. Bureau of Census, Table 6B), and 10% of that state's population was Asian/Pacific Islander (1990b U.S. Bureau of Census, Table 6C). An estimated 3.3 million Asians are expected to reside in California by the turn of the century (Ong, 1988).

Reflecting the rising populations of ethnic minorities overall, the population of Chinese Americans has grown dramatically. The population of Chinese Americans increased by 700% from 1940 to 1980 and increased 104% from 1980 to 1990 (see Figure 1.1). In 1990, 43% of all U.S. Chinese lived in California. California's Chinese population increased by 90% from 1970 to 1980, and increased by 216% from 1980 to 1990. In 1990, there were 704,850 Chinese living in California. The largest concentration of California Chinese resided in Chinatown, San Francisco. Asian American/Pacific Islanders constituted 29% of San Francisco's 1990 population.

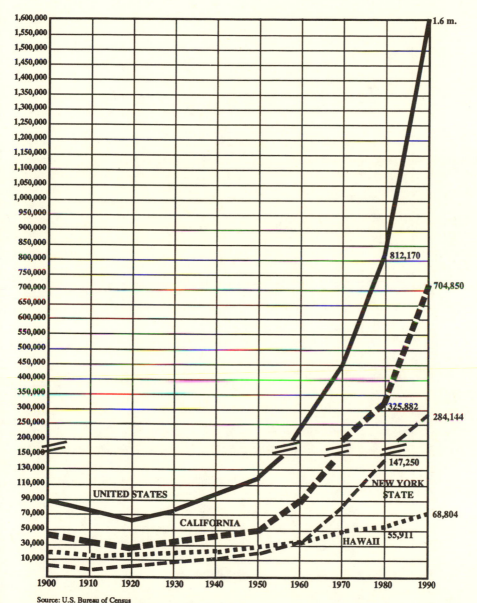

Source: U.S. Bureau of Census
1980: Census: PC 80-2-IE, C 223/10:80-2-IE/SEC.1
1990: Census Population Area Housing Summary Tape File IA. California, New York, Hawaii, respectively

Figure 1.1
Chinese Population: United States and by State, 1900–1990

Table 1.1

Asian or Pacific Islander Resident Population by State: 1990 and 1980

1990 Asian or Pacific Islander Population Rank	State	1990 Asian or Pacific Islander Population	1990 Percent of State Population	1980 Asian or Pacific Islander Population*	1980 Percent of State Population	Number Change 1980 to 1990	Percent Change 1980 to 1990
1	California	2,845,659	9.6	1,253,818	5.3	1,591,841	127.0
2	New York	693,760	3.9	310,526	1.8	383,234	123.4
3	Hawaii	685,236	61.8	583,252	60.5	101,984	17.5
4	Texas	319,459	1.9	120,313	0.8	199,146	165.5
5	Illinois	285,311	2.5	159,653	1.4	125,658	78.7
6	New Jersey	272,521	3.5	103,848	1.4	168,673	162.4
7	Washington	210,958	4.3	102,537	2.5	108,421	105.7
8	Virginia	159,053	2.6	66,209	1.2	92,844	140.2
9	Florida	154,302	1.2	56,740	0.6	97,562	171.9
10	Massachusetts	143,392	2.4	49,501	0.9	93,891	189.7
11	Maryland	139,719	2.9	64,278	1.5	75,441	117.4
12	Pennsylvania	137,438	1.2	64,379	0.5	73,059	113.5
13	Michigan	104,983	1.1	56,790	0.6	48,193	84.9
14	Ohio	91,179	0.8	47,820	0.4	43,359	90.7
15	Minnesota	77,886	1.8	26,536	0.7	51,350	193.5
16	Georgia	75,781	1.2	24,457	0.4	51,224	208.6
17	Oregon	69,269	2.4	34,775	1.3	34,494	99.2
18	Colorado	59,862	1.8	29,916	1.0	29,946	100.1
19	Arizona	55,206	1.5	22,032	0.8	33,174	150.6
20	Wisconsin	53,583	1.1	18,164	0.4	35,419	195.0
21	North Carolina	52,166	0.8	21,176	0.4	30,990	146.3
22	Connecticut	50,698	1.5	18,970	0.6	31,728	167.3
23	Missouri	41,277	0.8	23,096	0.5	18,181	78.7

24	Louisiana	41,099	1.0	23,779	0.6	17,320	72.8
25	Nevada	38,127	3.2	14,164	1.8	23,963	169.2
26	Indiana	37,617	0.7	20,557	0.4	17,060	83.0
27	Oklahoma	33,563	1.1	17,275	0.6	16,288	94.3
28	Utah	33,371	1.9	15,076	1.0	18,295	121.4
29	Tennessee	31,839	0.7	13,963	0.3	17,876	128.0
30	Kansas	31,750	1.3	15,078	0.6	16,672	110.6
31	Iowa	25,476	0.9	11,577	0.4	13,899	120.1
32	South Carolina	22,382	0.6	11,834	0.4	10,548	89.1
33	Alabama	21,797	0.5	9,734	0.2	12,063	123.9
34	Alaska	19,728	3.6	8,054	2.0	11,674	144.9
35	Rhode Island	18,325	1.8	5,303	0.6	13,022	245.6
36	Kentucky	17,812	0.5	9,970	0.3	7,842	78.7
37	New Mexico	14,124	0.9	6,825	0.5	7,299	106.9
38	Mississippi	13,016	0.5	7,412	0.3	5,604	75.6
39	Arkansas	12,530	0.5	6,740	0.3	5,790	85.9
40	Nebraska	12,422	0.8	7,002	0.4	5,420	77.4
41	District of Columbia	11,214	1.8	6,636	1.0	4,578	120.3
42	Idaho	9,365	0.9	5,948	0.6	3,417	57.4
43	New Hampshire	9,343	0.8	2,929	0.3	6,414	219.0
44	Delaware	9,057	1.4	4,112	0.7	4,945	120.3
45	West Virginia	7,459	0.4	5,194	0.3	2,265	43.6
46	Maine	6,683	0.5	2,947	0.3	3,736	126.8
47	Montana	4,259	0.5	2,503	0.3	1,756	70.2
48	North Dakota	3,462	0.5	1,979	0.3	1,483	74.9
49	Vermont	3,215	0.6	1,355	0.3	1,860	137.3
50	South Dakota	3,123	0.4	1,738	0.3	1,385	79.7
51	Wyoming	2,806	0.6	1,969	0.4	837	42.5

Source: 1990 U.S. Bureau of the Census, Summary Tape File 1A, Table 5A.

Need for Research on Stereotypes and Life Quality

Because erroneous stereotypes may contribute to anti-Asian violence and racial misunderstanding, there is a need to study the validity of commonly held stereotypes as well as the general well-being of Asian Americans. Since the 1960s, the U.S. media has portrayed Asian Americans as a successful "super minority" (Ramirez, 1986, pp. 150–161; "Success Story of One Minority Group in U.S." *U.S. News and World Report*, 1966, p. 7–8). Yet 14% of the Asian/Pacific Islander population was below the poverty level in 1989, compared to 10% for whites and 31% for blacks (U.S. Bureau of the Census, 1989, Table C). The validity of this "model minority" claim needs to be tested, for the attribution has been advanced against a backdrop of violence against Asians in the United States (see U.S. Commission on Civil Rights, 1986) and a backlash of anti-Asian discrimination in admissions to specific institutions of higher learning (Chan, 1987; Mathews, 1987). Suzuki (1977) and others have been critical of this "success" attribution, citing how many Asian Americans do not fall into this category and how it has a politically strategic effect of causing friction between Asians and other minorities by suggesting to other ethnic groups that it is individual effort rather than systemic discrimination that affects a minority group's success or failure.

Kitano and Sue (1973) have noted the lack of substantive empirical studies on Asian Americans, the virtual nonexistence of studies on nonstudent Asians in the community, and the need for empirical work to test the validity of the "successful" stereotype of Asian Americans. Reflecting the need for research on quality of life, Sue and Kitano (1973) noted: "Asians have made enormous strides in society, but the notion that they are satisfied and successful is questionable" (p. 9). While survey researchers have scrutinized the quality of life of Anglo-Saxon Protestants, much less research has been conducted on the well-being of America's minorities (Nandi, 1980).

In addition to the stereotype of the "successful" Asian, other stereotypes or assumptions need to be tested, including the following: (1) the notion that Chinese prefer crowding and can live in crowded conditions without ill effect; (2) assumptions held by advocates of the English as the Official Language movement that Asian immigrants are unwilling to acquire white American ways, are unaware that acquisition of the English language is key to socioeconomic mobility, that acquisition of the English language should not be difficult for immigrants, and that there is no justification for language assistance to certain language groups but not to others; (3) assumptions that Chinese Americans do not report mental health problems, believe mental disorders arise from organic causes, and use culturally based forms of mental health support such as acupuncturists or herbalists rather than mental health professionals; and (4) assumptions that Chinese Americans resort to Eastern forms of medical treatment rather than Western forms.

Finally, in the area of mental health, professionals need data on life satisfaction and life concerns of ethnic minority populations. Clinicians who need to rate a patient's global functioning on Axis V of the Diagnostic and Statistical Manual of Mental Disorders (American Psychiatric Association, 1987), taking into account the individual's general satisfaction with life and extent or number of everyday problems or concerns, cannot validly rate an ethnic minority patient without having some norms of satisfaction and concerns for that particular ethnic group.

Research on Ethnic Minorities in Clinical and Counseling Psychology

Since the 1970s there has been a growing awareness that the fields of clinical and counseling psychology have failed to meet the mental health needs of ethnic minorities and the poor. Several psychologists have criticized the human service professions for not adequately training their graduates to work with ethnic minority populations and for not conducting research on these populations (Atkinson, Morton, and Sue, 1989; Bernal and Padilla, 1982). Others have emphasized the need to take ethnic variables into account in planning intervention strategies (Acosta, Yamamoto, and Evans, 1982; Marsella and Pedersen, 1981; Sue, 1981).

At three conferences for clinical psychology training (the 1973 Vail Conference, the 1975 Austin Conference, and the 1978 Dallas Conference), it was noted that mental health professionals have been inadequately trained to work with ethnic minority groups, and recommendations were made to rectify the situation. In 1978 the President's Commission on Mental Health identified ethnic minorities as unserved or underserved populations and highlighted the need to prepare mental health professionals to provide services to these populations.

Korchin (1976) has noted that "there has been great concern with the role of social class and minority racial membership as variables in psychotherapy. . . . Not only is there greater need but also great inequities in the deliveries of services to the poor" (pp. 481–482). Research on lower socioeconomic class clients had demonstrated that they were less likely to be referred for psychotherapy than middle-class clients (Hollingshead and Redlich, 1954); if treated, lower-class clients were more often sent for medical treatment than for psychotherapy or were less likely to be accepted for psychotherapy—or, if seen, were usually assigned to lower status, less experienced therapists (Cole, Branch and Allison, 1962; Galagher, Sharaf, and Levinson, 1965; Hollingshead and Redlich, 1954; Kahn, Pollack, and Fink, 1957; Rosenthal and Frank, 1958; Schaffer and Myers, 1954); and that lower-class clients were more likely to break off therapy prematurely (Frank, Gliedman, Imber, Nash, and Stone, 1957; Imber, Nash, and Stone, 1955; Rubenstein and Lorr, 1956; Yamamoto and Goin, 1966). Furthermore, therapists were more likely to regard lower-class clients as less interesting, less cooperative, and more pathological than middle-class (Carlson, Coleman, Errera, and Harrison, 1965; Haase, 1964; Lee, 1968).

The major explanation offered for the aforementioned findings was that lower-class or ethnic minority clients were being treated by white therapists of middle-class status and values. This condition was thought to result in the following:

1. incongruence of expectations, with middle-class clinicians expecting more participation from clients in therapy and lower-class clients expecting more directive advice and a briefer course of treatment;
2. incongruence of concerns, with middle-class clinicians being more concerned with internal experiences and lower-class clients more concerned with external conditions such as income, jobs, or housing;
3. misconceptions, trepidations, and bias on the part of middle-class therapists when working with those of a different social class or ethnicity;
4. ignorance of the life problems of the ethnic minority or lower-class client, causing the therapist's concerns to seem irrelevant to the client;
5. fewer opportunities for ethnic minority or lower-class clients to find therapists of similar qualities due to a lack of professionals of a similar background;
6. distrust of mental health institutions by lower-class or ethnic minority persons due to their perception that these institutions are unresponsive to their needs.

Research on all accredited clinical psychology programs has revealed that preparation to work with minorities received minor attention (Bernal and Padilla, 1982). Although half of the directors of these training programs regarded the preparation of clinical psychologists to work with minorities as "somewhat important," only 20% of the programs offered a course on ethnic minorities or cross-cultural issues. Half of these courses were offered on an irregular basis. Half of the programs reported no faculty engaged in minority research. Summarizing the situation in the 1980s, Bernal and Padilla (1982) stated that (1) minority groups are underserved by the mental health field, (2) there is a severe shortage of ethnic minority professionals in the mental health field, (3) this shortage is not sufficiently addressed at the graduate level through active recruitment programs, (4) there is a dearth of ethnic minority faculty, (5) there is a shortage of applied behavioral scientists interested in and prepared for the scientific investigation of problems that affect the mental health of ethnic minority groups, and (6) most of the nonminority graduates of training programs have had little or no preparation in understanding the sociocultural determinants of mental illness or in identifying key minority research issues and thus are ill prepared to provide services to minorities.

Solutions that were proposed included:

1. making psychotherapy more responsive to the needs of the underserved by broadening the forms of intervention to include multiple human problems and the effects of social institutions;

2. abandoning verbal psychotherapy in favor of behavioral methods, which were proposed to be more relevant to lower-class clients;

3. providing professionals with greater knowledge about ethnic values, the effects of interacting in a racially hierarchical society, treatment by the larger system, and the barriers that prevent them from using mental health services (Bales, 1985; Sue, Akutsu, and Higashi, 1985; Sue, Bernier, Durran, Feinberg, Pedersen, Smith, and Vasquez-Nuttall, 1982); and

4. abandoning individual psychotherapy in favor of community-oriented interventions because of community psychology's greater stated commitment to the study of underserved communities.

However, in regard to solution number four, community psychology has yet to achieve its mission of researching and serving ethnic minority populations. Heller (1988) has complained that few psychologists study community phenomena and that little social planning occurs for and in communities. Loo, Fong, and Iwamasa's (1988) survey of all articles published in three community mental health journals from 1965 to 1985 (the life span of community psychology at that time) revealed that only 11% of the articles pertained to U.S. ethnic minorities. Notable was the finding that Asian Americans and Native Americans were particularly ignored.

With regard to Asian Americans, Sue (1978) called for empirical studies on Asian American communities to better assist policy makers and service deliverers in their planning efforts. Berk and Hirata (1973) and Sue and Morishima (1982) noted the need for research on the mental health of nonpatient Asian American populations and the importance of valid indicators of emotional disturbance in the larger population. Kim (1978) criticized the social sciences for having insufficiently determined the service needs of any Asian American group and for its lack of useful comparative data to the general population, all of which made it difficult to draw meaningful conclusions for service delivery. Moreover, very little is known about how to conduct culturally appropriate therapy with Asian American clients. While underutilization of mental health services by Asian Americans is widely held and documented, research is needed to identify means of increasing the rate of use (Leong, 1986).

In summary, this book contains data on quality of life, life satisfaction, and life problems for a nonstudent Asian American population. In so doing, the findings lend light to the question of whether these Asian Americans are "satisfied" and "successful" as the stereotype suggests. It also provides needed norms by which to assess life satisfaction and life concerns for this subgroup of ethnic Americans.

THE POPULATION AND COMMUNITY

The Chinese and Asian American Population

There were over 1.6 million Chinese Americans in the United States in 1990, representing .7% of the U.S. population. The median age of Chinese Americans was 30 years, the average persons per household was 3.14, and the average number of persons per family was 3.65 (U.S. Bureau of the Census, 1980b, Tables 18 and 20). One demographic characteristic that particularly distinguishes Chinese Americans from most Americans (although it is similar to certain other Asian American groups) involves the high proportion of foreign-born. While only 6% of the entire U.S. population are foreign-born (U.S. Bureau of the Census, 1990, No. 46), close to two-thirds of the Chinese Americans in 1980 were foreign-born (514,389); slightly over one-third (297,789) were American-born (U.S. Bureau of the Census, 1980b, Table 1). This represents a substantial rise in the percent of immigrants in the Chinese American population over the 1970–1980 decade; in 1970, the percentage of foreign-born was 47%. The high proportion of immigrants among Chinese Americans was similar to the Korean, Asian Indian, and Filipino American populations, for whom the percent of foreign-born were 82%, 70%, and 65%, respectively. Japanese Americans, in contrast, were primarily native-born; only 28% were immigrants in 1980.

In 1980 the majority of Chinese Americans (59%, or 155,241 persons) were U.S. citizens, either born in the United States or naturalized here; the remaining 41% (or 105,022 persons) were not citizens—most of them had immigrated recently, between 1975 and 1980 (U.S. Bureau of the Census, 1980a, Table 22). Naturalization was positively related to length of time in the United States; the largest number of Chinese who became naturalized were those who had entered this country before 1970.

Related to place of birth, two-thirds of the Chinese American adults could not speak English very well. Seventeen percent of the Chinese Americans (or 141,655 persons) spoke only English at home; the vast majority (70%, or 588,604 persons) spoke some Chinese dialect at home (U.S. Bureau of the Census, 1980a, Table 19). The proportions of Korean Americans who could not speak English very well (three-quarters), who spoke only English at home (18%), and who spoke Korean at home (67%) were similar to the Chinese. Consequently, functioning in the white American society was more difficult for these groups than it was for Japanese, Filipino, and Asian Indian Americans, groups that had smaller proportions who could not speak English very well (56%, 42%, and 32%, respectively). However, even for these ethnic groups, 57% of the Filipino, 53% of the Asian Indian, and 39% of the Japanese American adults spoke a non-English mother tongue in the home (U.S. Bureau of the Census, 1980a).

The U.S. Chinese constitute a particularly urban population; 98% of its members live in urban settings and only 2% in rural areas (U.S. Bureau of the Census, 1990, Table 1). In 1990, the largest number of Chinese Americans lived in the states of California (704,850), New York (284,144), and Hawaii (68,804) (see Figure 1.1). In 1980, the largest number of American-born Chinese resided in California (122,805), Hawaii (43,576), and New York (38,256). The largest number of immigrant Chinese lived in California (203,077), New York (108,994), Illinois (19,969), and Texas (19,089) (U.S. Bureau of the Census, 1980a, Tables 2–5). In terms of their concentration in specific Standard Metropolitan Statistical Areas (SMSAs), the largest number of Chinese lived in the San Francisco–Oakland SMSA (143,551), followed by the New York, N.Y.–New Jersey SMSA (133,074).

Asian Americans had a higher average number of workers per household (1.67) than white, black, or Hispanic Americans (1.29, 1.29, and 1.49, respectively); this must be taken into account when comparing mean or median household income by race. In 1979 the median household income for Chinese Americans was $19,561 (the mean was $23,657), and the median personal income was $8,133 (the mean was $11,738). The median and mean incomes for Chinese Americans were lower than the rates for Japanese Americans, Filipino Americans, and Asian Indian Americans but were higher than the rates for Korean Americans and Vietnamese Americans. Of the income-earning Chinese Americans in 1979, 53% made less than $10,000 and only 2% made $50,000 or more (U.S. Bureau of the Census, 1980a, Table 23).

Chinese Americans have a distinctive bimodal distribution with regard to occupational prestige. One-third of the Chinese Americans who were employed worked as managers or professionals, while another third fell in the lowest prestige occupations of service work and operatives (U.S. Bureau of the Census, 1980a, Table 21).

The Chinatown Community

It was here in Chinatown, San Francisco that the first Asians to come to America, the Chinese, began their journey to Gum San (Gold Mountain, or California), forging a livelihood amidst barriers of racial discrimination. Chinatown is the oldest Chinese community in the United States and its lifeline is a dynamic saga of Asian American legacy. Enduring for over 140 years, it is a living monument to the heritage of Asians in America. As the oldest part of San Francisco, its history also forms a major part of the city's heritage. When its history is combined with its contemporary residency, Chinatown stands as a symbol of forbearers fused with generations of immigrants and elderly.

Many residents of this community live much of their lives in this one neighborhood. Workplace, residence, recreation, shopping, educational services, banking institutions, cultural associations and social, health, and mental health services are contained within one defined area. While Bernard (1973) claimed that people no longer live their lives (work, play, shop, service) in neighborhoods, Chinatown in San Francisco is a rare exception. Furthermore, residents here have characteristics that often define a "community"; here live persons who are largely drawn together by a common ethnicity and, to some extent, by common interests, history, fate, experiences, and constraints. While Toennies (1887/1957) and others predicted that urbanization and industrialization would cause the death of "community" as defined by close-knit ties, Chinatown is proof that community by this definition still exists, although probably not with the close-knittedness found in some non-urban communities.

There were 127,140 Chinese in the city and county of San Francisco in 1990 compared to 82,480 in 1980. San Francisco's Chinatown is one of the two largest Chinese communities in the United States. Throughout its history, it has been referred to by at least three different names. In the nineteenth century, the community was called "the Chinese Quarter" by outsiders and "Tong Yun Fow" by insiders. By the twentieth century, it was referred to as "Chinatown." Although Nee and Nee (1972) claimed that Chinatown was a blind spot of American interest and concern, the media has portrayed this enclave in diverse and distinctive ways. Portrayals of this community were, at first, literary exercises in propaganda for Chinese exclusion (Kim, 1982). Chinatown was described as "a disgrace to the city, the State, the nation, and to civilization . . . most abominable and intolerable. . . . a concentration of crime, vice, filth, lechery, disease, and slavery" (Report of the Senate Committee on Chinese and Chinese Immigration, 1887, p. 3). Portrayals also were somewhat contradictory. McLeod (1948) described the Quarter as "a thousand Chinamen and a million smells . . . the most picturesque quarter of San Francisco . . . [containing] gloomy, ill-smelling, uninviting alleys" (p. 123). Leong (1936) portrayed Chinatown's exterior in Fu Manchu fashion and its interior as "nothing but a slum" (p. 20).

Other less sensationalistic descriptions attempted to capture the more humane aspects of the community. Dobie (1936) depicted Chinatown San Francisco as the most significant expression of every Chinatown in the United States. Kung (1962) referred to it as the most important of all U.S. Chinatowns. Dillon (1962) called this "a place that came to suggest the mysterious and sinister," "the most colorful district of a colorful city," "not merely an ethnic enclave [but] truly China in San Francisco," and "a long suffering, patient community [whose image] assaulted and captured the tourist imagination" (pp. 16, 63, and 263). Lowe (1937) depicted its potpourri of social contradictions, as did Hoexter (1976), who summarized its multiple portrayals as "either quaint and charming or poor and miserable" (p. 52). Finally, in a somewhat emotional attempt to characterize the collective feelings of a people, Allard (1975) described Chinatown as "a gilded ghetto [where] old men live out their lives in lonely rooms. . . . [A place that] is finding its voice, a voice that cries out in both anguish and hope. It is a voice of many dedicated men and women, and they wage a desperate battle" (pp. 627–643).

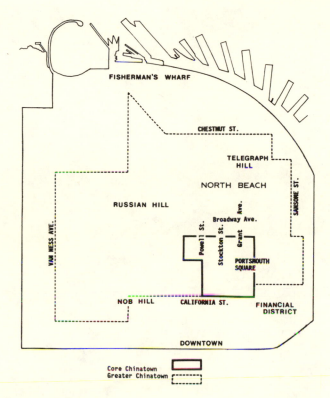

FISHERMAN'S WHARF

CHESTNUT ST.

TELEGRAPH HILL

NORTH BEACH

RUSSIAN HILL

Broadway Ave.

SANSOME ST.

VAN NESS AVE.

Powell St.

Stockton St.

Grant Ave.

PORTSMOUTH SQUARE

NOB HILL   **CALIFORNIA ST.**   **FINANCIAL DISTRICT**

DOWNTOWN

Core Chinatown
Greater Chinatown

Figure 1.2
Major Neighborhoods and Landmarks

Physical and Population Characteristics

Chinatown consists of 224 city blocks that constitute 428 acres. Based on the 1970 census, the Department of City Planning distinguished a core and a noncore area of Chinatown, which together comprised greater Chinatown (see Figure 1.2). Core Chinatown, a 17-block area bordered by Kearny, Pacific, Powell, and California streets, contains the heaviest concentration of restaurants, shops, and Chinese residents. In 1980, 7,439 persons resided in the core area; of these, 92% (or 6,829 persons) were Chinese. The core area consisted of three census tracts. In the southwest corner of core Chinatown is Portsmouth Square, the only park in the community. For old-timers living in eight by ten foot rooms, this "corner of the garden" serves as a living room.

Grant Avenue is the street most tourists traverse, while Stockton Street, which runs parallel to Grant, is alive with local residents. Small Chinese markets, grocery stores, and restaurants, interspersed with financial institutions, jewelry stores, and professional offices, line the vibrant street. Crates of

Sidewalk shopping on Stockton Street amidst crowds of shopping pedestrians. A woman scrutinizes a head of broccoli while a man converses with a shopkeeper. Chinatown is a very self-contained neighborhood where small ethnic businesses are in close proximity to residences. 1979. (Photograph by John Storey, courtesy of the *San Francisco Chronicle*.) Reprinted by permission.

bok choy, winter melon, and other fruits, vegetables, and produce crowd the sidewalks as shoppers select the choicest items.

The noncore area of Chinatown consists of 10 census tracts. According to the 1980 census, the area contained a total of 44,070 persons at that time. The noncore area consists of the residential area (which in 1980 contained 21,389 persons, of whom 62% were Chinese) and the expanded area (which contained 22,681 persons, of whom 39% were Chinese). Each of these noncore areas consists of five census tracts.

The Broadway strip cuts through the noncore area just north of Chinatown's core area (see Figure 1.2). Broadway's culture of topless nightclubs and sex-acts form no part of Chinatown residents' lives or livelihood. Yet, like the expensive neighborhoods that surround the community, they form a strange juxtaposition of contrast with Chinatown.

The Upper Grant area, once called "Little Italy," contains a mingling of small hardware stores, bars, cappucino cafes, boutiques, and Italian restaurants at the ground level and modestly priced apartments above. Chinese currently rent most of these apartments.

While detailed demographic data on the Chinatown population that were derived from this study will be presented in subsequent chapters, it is important to note that residents of Chinatown are not an advantaged lot when compared either to city residents as a whole or to Chinese Americans overall. Looking only at the proportion in the poverty level, one-fourth of the Chinatown residents were below the poverty level in 1980 compared to 14% of all San Franciscans and compared to 13% of Chinese Americans overall (U.S. Bureau of the Census, 1980b). In summary, this book represents a study of the less advantaged San Franciscan and the less advantaged American.

A City within a City

This low-income ethnic enclave is encircled by expensive, white neighborhoods and the expanding Financial District, which presses its southeast border. The Financial District is visually identifiable by its skyscrapers like the Transamerica Building, Holiday Inn, and the Bank of America building, all of which loom more than twice the height of the three- to four-story Chinatown structures.

The residential valley of Chinatown—west of the core area—consists of medium-height, bland-looking apartment buildings and is sandwiched by two exclusive, largely white neighborhoods perched on hilltop sites. Russian Hill stands stately to the north, Nob Hill majestically to the south (see Figure 1.2). Their upper-crust architectural quality distinguishes them from the drabness of Chinatown's residential area. Situated to the north of Chinatown are the upper-income, residential neighborhoods of North Beach and Telegraph Hill, which face the picturesque bay. Chinatown lies midway on the

Ten of the seventeen blocks that mark Chinatown are bordered by the massive highrises of the Financial District. The expansion of the Financial District is a constant threat to the existence of Chinatown. Pacific Avenue (lower left) and Stockton Street (lower right) converge at one of the Ping Yuens (public housing projects). 1985. (Photograph by Steve Ringman, courtesy of the *San Francisco Chronicle*.) Reprinted by permission.

tourist corridor that runs from downtown Union Square to Fisherman's Wharf. From the Union Square shopping district, cable cars jolt uphill through Chinatown and then breeze downhill toward the windy wharf.

In a city heavily dependent on tourism, Chinatown is a vital link in this industry. At least three out of every four of the three million visitors to San Francisco each year visit Chinatown (San Francisco Department of City Planning, 1984). Thousands of tourists pass through this urban village daily.

Chinatown also serves as "capital city" for the larger Chinese American population. The enclave is a shopping hub for Chinese goods and services. It also functions as a cultural center for Chinese institutions for the entire Bay Area and beyond (San Francisco Department of City Planning, 1985).

SOCIOPOLITICAL CONTEXT FOR THE RESEARCH

A contextual paradigm is a conceptual approach to scientific inquiry that involves the study of multiple domains of life and takes into account the larger social, cultural, historical, political, and economic context in which behavior occurs. Variables are not studied in isolation; instead, multiple variables are studied in order to enlarge the lens by which we view populations. Frequently, a contextual paradigm involves a multidisciplinary approach insofar as an analysis of multiple forces often requires concepts and methods from more than one discipline. Science is viewed as embedded in the history, politics, and culture of society (Maracek, 1989), and the scientist views individuals as affected by the history, politics, and economic conditions of their own subculture as well as those of the larger society. Values play a constructive role in shaping research, for research is not seen as an aseptic process executed in a social-political vacuum (Warwick and Lininger, 1975).

The orientations of feminist theory and community psychology exemplify this paradigm. Feminist philosophy has reflected this perspective in its attempt to turn psychology's focus on the individual to larger, external social and institutional forces. The focus of community psychology has also been contextual in nature, particularly its ecological orientation and emphasis on interventions linked to social reform and political action (Levine and Perkins, 1987). One of the governing principles of community psychology has been to take into account the historical, social, economic, environmental, and political contexts when seeking to solve social problems (Sarason, 1974, 1981, 1982; Levine and Perkins, 1987).

Scholars who have criticized their disciplines for taking too narrow a perspective have advocated a larger contextual framework. Nakanishi (1988), for example, criticized the field of race relations for its failure to fulfill its goal of an interdisciplinary focus. Bender (1978) criticized the field of community studies for its lack of historical analyses. Yamamoto (1990) criticized the traditional values analysis in law for its tendency to focus too narrowly on the individual, thereby ignoring social variables and social effects. Modern psychology has also been criticized for being too decontextualized in its approach, for analyzing the individual as an isolated entity (Gergen, 1973, 1985; Giorgi, 1970; Harre, 1984, 1986; Sampson, 1988), for not developing a historically situated perspective on its discourse and practices, and for being inadequately attendant to the cultural conceptualization of self that is formed by the economics and politics of the times (Cushman, 1990). Following the thinking of Levin (1987) and Rieff (1966), Cushman (1990) pointed out that psychotherapy has inadequately addressed the sociohistorical causes for the emptiness and fragmentation of patients. Heller (1988), who also noted the liabilities of psychology's traditional focus on the individual, encouraged the field to expand the conceptual templates through which it viewed the world and to recognize the multifaceted conceptions of community.

Because such a paradigm delineates the sociopolitical values underlying scientific inquiry, the values that frame this study are defined here. The study of ethnic minorities, ethnic immigrants, and women—subgroups of this study—is an outgrowth of five social movements of the 1960s. First, this research has been influenced by values of the civil rights movement, which sought to effect changes that would promote greater racial equity and self-dignity for blacks and, in so doing, brought race to the center stage of American politics (Omi and Winant, 1986). Second, this text is heavily influenced by values of the ethnic studies movement, which sought academic credibility for the study of persons of color (Murase, 1976), made communities the bastion of cultural identity and history and the base from which to intervene in the struggle against racial and ethnic oppression (Loo and Mar, 1985), and encouraged research that would illuminate the forces that bear upon the destiny of ethnic communities (Nakatsu, 1974). Third, this research is influenced by the values of the feminist movement, which sought to eliminate gender discrimination and establish academic credibility for research on women. Fourth, the domains of study of this text are influenced by the human ecology movement, which alerted our society to the environmental harm created by pesticides, technological wastes, and overpopulation and which led to a burgeoning research interest in the effects of crowding and other environmental stressors. Finally, the method used in this study is a reflection of the social indicators movement, which sought to provide socially significant measures and statistics of direct normative interest to facilitate concise, comprehensive judgments about the condition of major aspects of society. The advantages of social indicators research are the following: (1) they serve as a potentially powerful tool in the development of social policy, (2) they guide choices at several levels of decision making, and (3) they focus attention on current social problems (Andrews and Withey, 1976; Sawhill, 1969; Sheldon and Freeman, 1972; U.S. Department of Health, Education, and Welfare, 1969; Warwick and Lininger, 1975).

The contextual framework of this text involves the study of multiple domains of life, all of which are assumed to interact. The study uses multiple measures where possible and a multidisciplinary perspective in order to understand phenomena in as full a manner as possible. The topics of study parallel the social movements mentioned previously. The domains investigated included community, neighborhood, crowding, language and cultural shift, physical and mental health, employment, gender differences, and quality of life. While these are areas of concern for all Americans, they hold particular importance for low-income, immigrant, and ethnic Americans, persons for whom residential crowding, poor health status, prevalence of mental health problems, low occupational status, low wages, language and cultural barriers, and lower quality of life are common constraints. Thus, the inquiry raises major issues that face low-income or ethnic communities, including the status of mental health and physical health of its residents and their use of existing services, the factors contributing to low use of services, the preservation of the residential and cultural-serving functions of the neighborhoods, the effects of environmental stresses such as crowding and commercial intrusion on residents' neighborhood satisfaction, the means by which America assists or deters the integration of ethnic minority immigrants into its society, and the psychological, social, and economic conditions of women as compared to men.

Research application is part of the social responsibility of psychologists, for as the revised draft of the Ethical Principles states: "Psychologists have a responsibility to the societies in which they work and live. They apply . . . their knowledge of psychology to contribute to human justice and welfare" (American Psychological Association, 1990, p. 30). As a contemporary study, this research illustrates how informed decisions of planning and intervention can be driven by quantitative data as applied to housing, city planning, mental health assessment and intervention, health, employment, language training, immigration, political participation, and overall quality of life. Survey data also can help us understand how individuals of a particular ethnicity and socioeconomic class react to various stressors. In a more general sense, empirical studies of the status of America's ethnic minorities or low-income communities present a challenge of what this society must do to eliminate the problems that face its less advantaged members.

THE RESEARCH METHOD

Interview Sample Surveys

In the late 1970s, research among racial and cultural minorities was in its infancy (Montero and Levine, 1977), and scholars were noting the problems and pitfalls of conducting survey research among ethnic minority populations as indicated in an entire issue of the *Journal of Social Issues*, (1977) devoted to these issues. The necessity of gaining the acceptance of the community under study and responding to the concerns of minority communities was becoming evident (Montero and Levine, 1977). In addition to conducting research that could provide policy recommendations or generate interventions of benefit (Park, 1980; Platt, 1972; Price and Cherniss, 1977) came a concern for a more reciprocal and collaborative relationship between researcher and community, particularly with ethnic minorities (Bengston, Grigsby, Corry, and Hruby, 1977; Bevan, 1980; Blauner and Wellman, 1973; Fishman and Neigher, 1982; Guzman, 1967; Kasschau and Kessel, 1980; Sarason, 1976; Trimble, 1977). Studies on ethnic minorities were known to fail where community participation was neglected (Josephson, 1970) or where a hierarchical relationship between researcher and community led ethnic minorities to become skeptical of academic research (Williams, 1981).

Interview sample survey research can impact human service and planning needs in a beneficial way. Such research can also be conducive to a reciprocal relationship between the researcher and residents, provided that community leaders and groups are invited to contribute to the research objectives, that community members be involved as an advisory group regarding interpretation of the findings, that interviewers be indigenous persons, and that there be some form of remuneration provided to both the respondent and the community.

This Chinatown research project established a Community Board of Advisors, the principal investigator hired indigenous Chinese Americans, remuneration was provided to each respondent in the form of a Chinatown Resource Book of free and low-cost services, research findings were published in the local newspapers (both in the community and city) for public interest and benefit, and some of the research questions were derived from leaders in the community who were consulted prior to conducting the survey.

This study sought answers to the following questions, some of which originated in the community:

1. How satisfied are residents with their housing and are there differences by age that need to be taken into account in planning?

2. In a community as crowded as Chinatown [the second most crowded community in the United States], what are the effects of crowding on physical and mental health?

3. Are there differences in reactions to crowding as a function of age, household size, perceived alternatives, nativity, or past experiences?

4. To what extent does the U.S. Census definition of crowding match human perceptions of crowdedness?

5. To what extent are neighbors alienated from each other and from the world outside of Chinatown?

6. What proportion of the community residents want to leave and what proportion want to stay and for what reasons?

7. What is their level of neighborhood satisfaction and how does this compare to Americans overall?

8. How valid are the assumptions made by the advocates of the English as the

Official Language movement regarding immigrants' willingness and ability to learn the English language?

9. How health educated are these low-income residents?

10. To what extent do they rely on Western as opposed to Eastern forms of health care?

11. What is their health status?

12. What is their mental health status and what variables impact their use of services?

13. How do these compare with Americans overall?

14. What are their mental health beliefs?

15. How reluctant are these Asian Americans to seek help for personal problems?

16. What is the nature of their life concerns?

17. How do these ethnic Americans evaluate their quality of life and how does this compare with other Americans?

Combining the opinions of several leaders in this community, it became clear that no one variable could be studied in isolation, for crowding, housing, neighborhood, health, mental health, cultural dislocation and language skills, employment and occupation were all interrelated. Many community professionals simply concluded: "You really have to study the entire life quality of these residents." This reality was a validation of Moore's (1977) observation that the dynamics of research in minority communities seem inevitably to draw in broader issues than most academic researchers and funding sources are willing to acknowledge.

Closed-ended questions and scales provide data on the status, perceptions, and attitudes of a collective population. Open-ended questions permit the researcher to uncover qualitative data, which convey the richness of individual experiences and perceptions. Both types of questions were used in this survey. In addition to quantitative results, individual responses to open-ended questions are included in the text.

The quantitative nature of survey research also permits the social scientist to test theories and hypotheses. This demonstrates that, contrary to Stein's (1960) belief that studies of communities cannot be theoretical because the process of weaving the scattered strands of a community is itself a difficult task, theory and application can be joined in the same study. In this text, theories of residential location, residential satisfaction, residential safety, environmental adaptation, effects of crowding, cultural differences in attitudes and reactions to crowded conditions, and assumptions regarding low use of mental health services and low life satisfaction were tested.

Sample, Response Rate, and Sampling Method

Chinese American adults (18 years of age or older, racially 50% or more Chinese) who resided in San Francisco's Chinatown for more than one month comprised the population of interest. Eligibility screening was conducted for place of residency, adulthood, percent of Chinese ancestry, and length of residency. Screening for Chinese ancestry among 259 selected addresses revealed that there were no Chinese of mixed race; all were pure Chinese. Of the 151 eligible listings sampled, 108 interviews were completed. The response rate was 72%, a rate above what Babbie (1973) considered acceptable for face-to-face interviews.

Because evidence suggests that ethnic matching results in more honest responses (Schuman and Converse, 1971; Williams, 1964), all interviewers in this study were Chinese, with various Chinese dialects represented among them. The interviews averaged three hours in length. Seventy-three percent of the sample chose to be interviewed in Chinese, 27% in English.

Three sampling methods were used to select a representative sample of the greater Chinatown area (core and noncore); area sampling, the address telephone directory, and the Polk City Directory. The unweighted data more closely approximated the demographic data from the 1980 census than the weighted data; thus, analyses presented in this text are the unweighted data (where there were significant results using weighted data, these were noted).

PLAN OF THE BOOK

Each chapter begins with a photograph of Chinatown life and a vignette of one interview. The photographs and vignettes are intended to present perspectives of the research and population of interest that supplement or illuminate the data presented in the text. To preserve confidentiality, the photographs do not depict any respondent in the study.

Chapter 2, "Heartland of Gold: A Historical Overview," analyzes the major social and political forces that impacted Chinatown and Chinese Americans from 1849 to the contemporary period. This chapter forms the historical context for the survey data that are contained in subsequent chapters.

Chapter 3, "The Nature of Community and Desired Residential Mobility," addresses an issue central to all studies of neighborhoods—their fate over time. Chinatown's endurance makes it a unique laboratory to examine competing theories of community change. To understand the dynamic tension of life and death of communities, this chapter explores the salient characteristics of the residency, goodness of neighborhood, and residents' desire to move or stay.

Chapter 4, "Neighborhood Satisfaction: Development versus Preservation," deals with the controversy of development versus preservation, a dilemma encountered when residential displacement is threatened by gentrification, urban renewal, land speculation, or the invisible hand of the market. In this chapter, theories on neighborhood satisfaction are tested and data are brought to bear on community planning.

Chapter 5, "Crowding: Perceptions, Attitudes, and Consequences," continues the exploration of ecological issues by examining a facet of living that has long distinguished Chinatown and has been attributed to the Chinese—crowding. This survey represents the first effort to gather empirical data on Chinese attitudes and perceptions of crowding, which permits us to test the cultural assumptions that Chinese like crowding and reside in these conditions without ill effect. As Housing and Urban Development (HUD)-funded grants are a vital source of funding for low-income housing projects in ethnic communities, data on this topic are relevant to public planning and policy.

Chapter 6, "Language Acquisition, Cultural Shift, and the English-Only Movement," represents the first empirical effort to evaluate the validity of assumptions posed by English-Only advocates and to research the rationale for language assistance. The English as the Official Language movement most directly affects Asian and Hispanic immigrants in regard to multilingual ballots and bilingual education. However, there are larger implications. The issue of the bilingual ballot controversy affects educational and immigration policies, delivery of human services, race relations, the participation of ethnic minorities in the political process, the nature of cultural pluralism or ethnocentrism of this society, and even America's international trade relations.

Chapter 7, "Pulse on Chinatown: Health Status and Service Use," documents a particularly noteworthy history of change in the health delivery system and in health attitudes. Research in this area reveals the health status of the residents, their use of Western and Eastern forms of treatment, and the predictors of health status and health service use.

Chapter 8, "'Too Bloated with Misery to Eat a Salted Bean': Mental Health Status and Attitudes," empirically tests various cultural explanations regarding the mental health status, admission of mental health problems, reasons for low use of services, and methods of handling personal problems among Asian Americans.

Chapter 9, "Slaying Demons with a Sewing Needle: Gender Differences and Women's Status," contains an analysis of gender differences with regard to education, occupation, language, psychological attitudes, and satisfaction with job, marriage, and life. This chapter represents an integration of psychological, economic, and cultural variables in the study of ethnic minority women and men.

Chapter 10, "'Fook, Look, Sow': Quality of Life," integrates multiple domains of life that formed the focus of previous chapters into an overall comparative analysis of well-being, satisfaction, and happiness. Data on these ethnic Americans are compared to those of the nation as a whole on various scales and measures. Chapter 11, "Conclusion," contains a summary of the history, the research findings, and their implications for Asian Americans and the American society.

Appendix A contains the interview schedule, and Appendix B contains details of the research method—specifically, procedures used to optimize research participation, the sample selection, sampling procedures, screening and eligibility procedures, response rates, and the procedures and decision making related to the weighted and unweighted data.

The present, to have full meaning, requires a past. In the next chapter the reader is guided through the history of Chinatown, a journey that begins in 1849. At its close, the reader is left at the doorstep of the contemporary period, to which the remaining text is devoted.

Dedication of the first Ping Yuen housing project on Pacific Avenue, between Grant and Columbus streets. This was Chinatown's first HUD-subsidized, low-income public housing, the first significant outcome to meet a long-standing need. Six hundred applications were received for 234 apartments. These one-, two-, and three-bedroom units originally rented for $15 to $60 per month, depending upon income. The crowds attending the dedication attest to the victory this symbolized for the entire community. 1951. (Photograph courtesy of the San Francisco Public Library.) Reprinted by permission.

Immigration Laws Ruined My Life

My assigned address was in the basement of a two-story house in expanded Chinatown. Behind the thin side door, down a few steps, I slid through a long, narrow alley to a small apartment. Two small beds filled the living room. Clothes and objects were scattered about.

My middle-aged respondent looked much older than his stated age. Appearing physically weak, he moved slowly. His personal struggles had worn years off his life. Thirty years ago, he came to this country as a businessman with a visitor's visa. Later, his status changed to that of a permanent resident. Due to restrictive immigration laws, his girlfriend in Hong Kong was unable to enter the United States. After 18 years of waiting, they gave up. She married someone else. He also married and had two children, but the marriage was unhappy and ended in divorce. He married when close to 50 years of age. For a Chinese to marry at this age is uncommon, and for many Chinese, divorce is a disgrace.

For over 25 years this man lived on the first floor. Recently, when he and his wife divorced and his business went downhill, he was forced to move to the basement. He worried about his business, which went "in the red" last year. In terms of happiness, this respondent had felt much happier when he lived on the upper floor. Moving downward was symbolic of his financial problems and failure. He was facing an uncertain future.

This man placed himself at the bottom of the life satisfaction ladder. He saw his life as very empty, miserable, and disappointing. He presumed he'd have been happier had he married his Hong Kong girlfriend. He blamed former U.S. immigration laws for ruining his life. He'd been very angry and bitter at the U.S. government for a long time. It wasn't until the United States and China normalized relations that he wanted to become a U.S. citizen. This man was very sad and lonely. Nevertheless, when shown the ladder of life satisfaction for the next five years, he pointed to a higher level. He still clung to hope. His children were his only hope, satisfaction, and happiness. He constantly got up to check his children, who were in bed. He wiped away the sweat from the little boy's face and made sure his daughter hadn't kicked away her blanket.

2

Heartland of Gold: A Historical Overview

Chalsa M. Loo and Connie Young Yu

No ethnic American experience can be fully understood outside of its historic context. No community can be entirely documented without its historic setting. To these objectives, this chapter provides the needed background in which to frame contemporary conditions.

California was the heartland of Asian America, as Chinese pioneers, drawn by the Gold Rush, stepped foot into a world of relentless obstacles, racism, and exclusion. Hoexter (1976) called this history "no stranger than any other in the long uneasy history of racial tension in America. . . . only less well known" (p.xiii). Irony and conflict pervaded this saga—the irony of a people whose labor was indispensable to the development of the West Coast but who were persecuted, and the "impassioned conflict between stubborn white-racist hostility and the tenacious desire of the Chinese to survive and remain in the United States" (Tchen, 1984, p. 23). Based on the major characteristics of the community during various time periods, Chinatown's history is here reconstructed into the following periods: (1) Way Station (1849 to 1869), (2) Segregated Ghetto (1870 to 1919), (3) Base for Small Ethnic Businesses (1920 to 1940s), and (4) Growth, Crisis, and Advocacy (1950s to 1970s). The legacy was a long and tumultuous one. We now review Chinatown's history against the larger context of Chinese American history.

Both authors contributed equally to this chapter.

WAY STATION (1849 TO 1869)

In 1838, Yerba Buena was a trading post on the fringe of a muddy cove, a quiet Mexican port town by a foggy bay. A few Chinese, mostly merchants and traders, had been reported living there (Chinn, Lai, and Choy, 1969; O'Meara, 1884; McLeod, 1948). Records indicate that there were 54 Chinese living in California before 1849, the year that marked a turning point for the state (Coolidge, 1909).

Gold Rush and Mining

In 1849, shortly after the United States took California as spoils of the Mexican American war, gold was discovered on the American River. From a small Mexican village, Yerba Buena became San Francisco, transformed into a chaotic, cosmopolitan, frontier city. New saloons and lodging houses were hastily constructed for a society dominated by single men, mostly between the ages of 20 and 35. San Francisco drew thousands of profit-seeking Forty-Niners from all parts of the country and various parts of the world. "Fortunes were made in a week, all classes of conditions of humanity flocked to San Francisco, ruffians and cut-throats, thieves and gamblers. Convicts from Australia, scum from American and European seaboard cities . . . swooped down upon the infant city like a hideous brood" (McLeod, 1948, pp. 20–21). Just as European merchants and American seamen had traveled to China to seek its treasures of teas, silks, spices, and porcelain, so the Chinese, like other Forty-Niners, sought riches in California (Hoexter, 1976). Word of California gold and "good wages" reached the ears of Chinese peasants, who had been raked by political upheaval, rebellions, uprisings, floods, droughts, banditry, inflation, unemployment, and Western imperialist intrusions. Famine and failing confidence in the Manchu dynasty led thousands of Cantonese to leave the Kwangtung province in southern China for Gum San in search of *wun sick* (the means to eat). These pioneers emigrated despite an imperial decree that made emigration punishable by death.

Some of the Chinese borrowed money pooled from relatives for passage. Most contracted with Chinese merchant brokers, who advanced passage money to them under the condition of repayment with interest from future earnings. This, the most common method of entry, was called the credit ticket system (Barth, 1964).

Profiteering at Chinese expense began before their arrival on U.S. soil. Seeking to maximize profits, companies exceeded the passenger capacity of their vessels. The Chinese were packed into the ship's hold "as thick as herrings in a box. Although generally very clean in their habits, it is not possible for them under the circumstances to preserve health." (*Alta California,* 1851).

Unable to afford the means of transport to other parts of the city, the

Figure 2.1
The Chinese Quarter: 1850 and 1860

Note: Shaded area indicates the Chinese Quarter in 1850. By 1860 the Chinese Quarter had expanded to include the entire area shown.

Chinese established themselves close to the wharf where they landed—in what is now known as core Chinatown (Yu, 1981). The hub of the Chinese Quarter was Sacramento Street, or Tong Yen Gai (Street of the Chinese People), located between Dupont and Kearny streets (Tchen, 1984). In 1850, the Chinese Quarter comprised a five-block area. The stores spread down Dupont Street (now called Grant Avenue, the oldest street in San Francisco) between Kearny and Stockton streets (see Figure 2.1). Ten years later, the Chinese Quarter had grown to a ten-block area, bordered by Kearny, Pacific, Stockton, and Sacramento streets, reflecting the need to service the growing Chinese immigration population (Borthwick, 1857; Soule, Gihon, and Nisbet, 1854).

While San Francisco was the center of recreational diversion and a departure-supply point for white miners, the Chinese Quarter served as a provision stop for the Chinese en route to gold mines and later to agricultural and railroad sites. It was here that the Chinese dealt with district associations, family associations, and merchant middlemen and procured ethnic-specific supplies (rice, dried fish, ham, and Chinese clothes) and services (letter translators, tailors, apothecaries, herb doctors).

The California Chinese population grew as California's population grew. There were 791 Chinese in California in 1849; 4,018 in 1850; 7,370 in 1851; 25,116 in 1852; 40,730 in 1857; and 46,897 in 1860 (Coolidge, 1909). In 1860, the Chinese represented roughly 10% of the California population.

Like the rest of San Francisco's population, the Chinese society was predominantly male. Half of the early Chinese men who came were married.

Few brought their wives because respectable Chinese women were discouraged from leaving home. Only 14 Chinese women arrived between 1848 and 1853 (McLeod, 1948). In 1860, there were 33,149 Chinese men and 1,784 Chinese women in the United States. Women constituted only 5% of the U.S. Chinese population then. Many of these women had been sold into prostitution. Girls unwillingly sold for $50 in Canton brought $1,000 in San Francisco. Forced into four-year contracts of service with wages, required to make up one month's work for every 15 days sick, and compelled to pay for expenses incurred should they escape, these women led lives of slaves (Seward, 1881).

The Chinese appearance and dress—men's "dangling queue," "wide cotton pantaloons that extended to the knees and collarless blouse," "women's blouses and trousers and hair, arranged in knots and bows"—set them apart, making them objects of curiosity (McLeod, 1948).

For the first half of Chinatown's history, housing in this community reflected the needs of a working male society. Lodges, commonly simple, offered temporary bivouac for the majority of male workers. A few family-oriented, more economically advantaged Chinese merchants resided in Chinatown, often working in their place of residence.

The Chinese Quarter was not a major residential settlement, as only 8% of the Chinese in the state lived there in the 1850s and 1860s and the entire size of its population in 1860 was only 1,747. Eighty percent of the California Chinese lived in the outlying mining areas (Chinn, Lai, and Choy, 1969), where over 150,000 men of all nationalities roamed.

Lawlessness characterized the atmosphere in the mining districts. A total of 4,200 murders were committed in the state during those first years, and there were few legal convictions of killers (McLeod, 1948). As a fever of greed, violence, and vigilante behavior spread, the Chinese became unwitting targets.

As early as 1850, discriminatory legislation against the Chinese commenced with the Foreign Miners Tax, which marked the beginning of "a wholesale system of wrong and outrage practiced upon the Chinese population of this State." (Report of a Committee on Chinese Immigration of the Two Houses of the California Legislature, 1862, in Seward, 1881, p. 43). Under pressure from white miners, who represented the largest body of voters outside of San Francisco, the California legislature passed a law that required nonwhite men to pay a monthly tax for mining. Aimed at driving the Chinese from the state, this discriminatory law constituted "semi-legalized robbery" (Seward, 1881, p. 45). Politicians seized on anti-Chinese proclamations as a means of securing the miners' votes.

In the 20 years that the Foreign Miners Tax was enforced, the Chinese contributed 50% of the total revenues received from the tax in the first four years, then 98% during the final 16 years (Coolidge, 1909). The tax had originally been directed primarily against Mexican Americans, but by the end of 1852 they had been driven out. From 1855 on, the Chinese paid practically the whole of these taxes. Between 1851 and 1870, the amount collected from the Chinese by this tax alone totaled nearly $5 million (Coolidge, 1909), half of California's total state revenues from 1850 to 1870 (Lai and Choy, 1972). Mining counties and the state owed a tremendous debt to the Chinese, and in fact, many counties could not have survived without these revenues. Its effect on the Chinese, however, was devastating, driving many to other forms of livelihood, embittering them to the injustice against them, and making their dreams of Gold Mountain elusive.

Grave injustices attended the collection of the tax. Tax collectors were known to horsewhip, strike, stab, or shoot those who refused to pay, and they sometimes collected the tax two or three times a month, demanding payment from all Chinese, including cooks, traders, and those not engaged in mining (McLeod, 1948; Seward, 1881). A diary of one tax collector read: "Hunted Chinamen in the night" (Dobie, 1936, p. 50). The Chinese were victims of unprovoked attacks of robbery and murder (Seward, 1881), even by the hands of Indians and Mexicans (McLeod, 1948).

In 1862, with 30,000 Chinese engaged in mining, 88 Chinese had been murdered, 11 by tax collectors (Kung, 1962). In various counties several hundred Chinese were expelled from the mines, denied the right to hold claims, and driven from abandoned mines when they found diggings there (Dobie, 1936; McLeod, 1948; Chiu, 1967; Seward, in Chinn, Lai, and Choy, 1969). In one of many incidents, several hundred Chinese who had purchased claims were attacked by armed white men who stole their gold, plundered their stores, set fire to buildings, and then set themselves down as proprietors of the claim by right of possession (McLeod, 1948). Because the 1850 statute that prohibited Negroes and Indians from testifying for or against a white person was made applicable to the Chinese by the Supreme Court in 1854 (*People vs. Hall*), the Chinese could not bear witness against white men in court. Thus, the courts did not bring the thieves to justice. "Chinamen were beaten, robbed, and outraged without recourse to law" (Dobie, 1936, p. 50).

Racial disorders of the mining camps were repeated in the towns and cities. The Chinese became victims of both the discontented and portions of the San Francisco aristocracy, of whom at least a third were Southerners (Coolidge, 1909).

All other forms of taxation that followed had the intent of excluding the Chinese or segregating them into undesirable, less profitable occupations such as cooks or laundrymen. In 1852, masters of vessels who brought in Chinese passengers were taxed and required either to post a per capita bond of $500 as an indemnity against costs of medical and other relief of alien passengers or else to pay from $5 to $10 per alien passenger. While the revenues were apportioned among the principal California hospitals, the Chinese, who paid a total of $195,145 into state revenues as a result of this tax (Kung, 1962), were denied hospital care.

In 1855, the Head Tax forced owners of vessels carrying passengers ineligible for citizenship (Chinese) to pay $50 per passenger. In 1862, the Police Tax fined all Chinese adults who were not engaged in producing sugar, rice, coffee, or tea or who had not paid the Foreign Miners Tax. In 1858, the Chinese were forbidden to land on the Pacific coast except when driven by stress of weather. In 1860, the Chinese engaged in fishing were forced to pay a tax of $4 per month.

In return for taxation, "the Chinese received neither protection nor privilege—not even as much as the Negro," (Coolidge, 1909, p. 81). A joint committee of the legislature reported that about 50,000 Chinese in the state had contributed not less than $14 million in customs duties, fares, freights, taxes, and purchase of American property and products. The Chinese had received in exchange little more than the "privilege" of doing work that white men scorned (Coolidge, 1909).

Beginning in 1860, Chinese children were excluded from California public schools, a prelude to laws that supported school segregation. Between the California constitutions of 1849 and 1879, the state lawmakers passed numerous discriminatory acts against resident Chinese. While the U.S. Supreme Court was kept busy declaring most of these acts unconstitutional (Mears, 1972), California legislators heedlessly reacted by passing new laws.

Expulsion from the mines, the Foreign Miners Tax, and other discriminatory ordinances caused a drop in the population of Chinese immigrants. Compared to 16,084 Chinese who immigrated in 1854, only 3,329 immigrated to California the following year. In the 1860s California's Chinese population stabilized at 50,000 (Coolidge, 1909).

The Transcontinental Railroad

In the mid-1850s, while the state's economy was rapidly growing, the railroad barons of the West were determined to link California to the rest of the nation. By forging a coast-to-coast system of specialization and access of raw materials to markets through railroads, California could become part of the larger transportation revolution. But, for two frustrating years, Charles Crocker, General Superintendent of the Central Pacific Railroad, failed to secure the laborers needed. White workers were disinterested in the dangerous and merciless work of laying the railroad. In desperation Crocker hired Chinese men, who from 1865 to 1869 built the western portion of the transcontinental railroad.

Because development of the state's economy required thousands of workers at a time when Chinese immigration had dropped, the United States passed the Burlingame Treaty of 1868. This treaty facilitated the entrance of Chinese laborers into this country to work the railroads and recognized the right of free migration and emigration of the citizens of China and the United States, with the exception of naturalization.

The transcontinental railroad and other railroads could not have been built so cheaply or quickly without the Chinese (Seward, 1881). The economic effect was to increase California's land value for white landowners by 200% to 1000%. Shoveling through fierce snowstorms, losing lives while dynamiting through the High Sierras, 12,000 to 15,000 Chinese men opened up thousands of acres of California's land to settlements. The 20,000 pounds of bones that were sent back to China for proper burial, which represented some 1,200 railroad workers who had died, attested to the harsh risks of their labor (Lai and Choy, 1972).

The Chinese were aware of their exploitation. Chinese railroad workers laid down their tools for wages comparable to the Irish, who did the same work. Their strike demands were denied. Crocker cut off food supplies to the Chinese and wired east to inquire about bringing black workers in as strikebreakers (Chiu, 1967).

At the celebration of the completion of the Central Pacific Railroad, Crocker announced that "the early completion of this railroad has been in great measure due to that poor destitute class of laborers called the Chinese, to the fidelity and industry they have shown" (Chinn, Lai, and Choy, 1969, p. 46). Despite their vast contributions to the state, the Chinese railroad workers who tried to settle in towns at the railroad's end were stoned. Discouraged, many returned to the refuge of Chinatown. San Francisco's Chinese population increased to 8,128 by 1870, then to 14,688 persons by 1880. Of those who did not return to the enclave, some returned to China, others worked spur railroads, and some dispersed to the valleys. The latter Chinese transformed California's swamp lands into the nation's premier agricultural state.

Agriculture

Beginning in the 1870s, the Chinese played an indispensable role in California's agricultural development. An estimated five million acres of swamp and tule lands lay wasted without reclamation. White landowners' associations hired the Chinese to reclaim the land only after white labor rejected such work as distasteful (Seward, 1881).

The Chinese irrigated and built levees, dikes, and ditches, making thousands of acres available for production. In short, nothing could have been cultivated in California without Chinese labor. Their efforts allowed for the planting and plowing of every part of these lands. The Chinese provided much of the labor needed to harvest, bound, pack, preserve, and sell crops in almost every major agricultural region of California (Chan, 1986). In the 1880s the Chinese comprised 75% of California's farm workers. Between 1870 and 1890, California's fruit growers were almost totally dependent on Chinese workers (Hoexter, 1976). Wheat grain, the leading commercial export from California at the time, could not have been raised or exported without Chinese labor, nor could California's fruit industry have been developed or her winery businesses maintained (Seward, 1881). As fruit farmers, the Chinese brought their skills in planting, cultivating, and garden-harvesting of orchard crops to California horticulture (McWilliams, 1939/1969). Their work engorged the prosperity of the state, as reclamation gave landowners $60 to $90 million a year in wealth. Chinese labor on railroads and reclamation of tule lands alone had an estimated value then of $289,700,000—"wealth owned, held and enjoyed by white men and not Chinamen" (Seward, 1881, p. 36).

The Chinese were responsible for doubling the material wealth of the state but were hired at one-half the wages of whites (see testimony of Sneath in Seward, 1881, p. 66). As an anti-Chinese movement mobilized in the rural areas and as farm producers felt pressured to replace the Chinese with white workers, many Chinese left agricultural jobs and retreated to Chinatown. Simultaneously, two severe and successive droughts materially lessened the demand for agricultural labor (Coolidge, 1909).

Light Manufacturing Industries and Laundries

Chinese who did not work on the railroad spurs or in agriculture took jobs in San Francisco's light manufacturing industries (in woolens, jute, boot, shoe, slipper, and cigar making). Many of these enterprises would not have emerged without the Chinese or would not have continued without them (Cronise, in Coolidge, 1909; Seward, 1881; Tuthill in Coolidge, 1909). Previously, boots and shoes had to be imported from Massachusetts. Until the Chinese began making nearly half of all the cigars manufactured in San Francisco (Seward, 1881), cigars also were formerly imported from outside the state or country. Chinese businesses and labor in the tailoring and clothing industry had the added effects of lowering retail prices and providing greater convenience for Californians by making the importation of these products unnecessary.

As the city's population increased, laundry facilities were inadequate. The Chinese were "gap fillers" in laundries and domestic service (Coolidge, 1909), which contributed greatly to the convenience and comfort of California's people (Seward, 1881). The entry of the Chinese into the laundry business also led to lowered consumer prices.

In this, the first period of Chinese American history, historians are in unanimous agreement that the Chinese contributed immensely to California's prosperity (Lloyd, 1876), were of great benefit to the state (Coolidge, 1909) and were an absolute necessity to California's material advancement and development of her resources (Brace, in Coolidge, 1909; Kung, 1962; Lloyd, 1875). The wealth of California was dependent upon the Chinese (Seward, 1881), but their exploitation by white managers, intent on competing aggressively against East Coast producers, did nothing to endear them to white labor. The next period would see the implementation of stronger anti-Chinese agitation.

SEGREGATED GHETTO (1870 TO 1919)

The 1870s saw vast economic dislocations produced by the industrial revolution. The country was swept into an economic depression between 1873 and 1889. Half a million Americans were unemployed. Businesses failed. Financial firms went under. The Eastern panic of 1873 caused unstable market conditions, leading the unemployed in the East to search for jobs in the West. In 1874, California was on the verge of political and industrial upheaval. The San Francisco stock market was paralyzed as the disaster extended to California. In addition, the completion of the transcontinental railway had thrown 10,000 white and Chinese laborers into the labor market. Thus began "a rising tide of popular discontent, intensified by panic and unemployment, that expressed itself in attacks upon railway subsidies, monopoly, and cheap labor" (Tow, in Mears, 1927, p. 152). Ill-feeling centered on corporations and the Chinese, with the latter experiencing the brunt of this antagonism.

The period from 1870 to 1919 marked the escalation of the anti-Chinese movement, culminating in the Chinese Exclusion Act. Exploited by capital, victimized by labor, and prevented from assimilating, the Chinese became the "indispensable enemy" (Saxton, 1971). While capital found Chinese labor necessary for the production of cigars, shoes, and clothing, the emerging labor union movement, under the Irish-led Workingmen's Party, unified its ranks by scapegoating the Chinese as the "enemy" of white labor. "The general editorial consensus was that while the Chinese were not biologically suitable for America's melting pot, it would be foolish not to exploit their labor before shipping them back to China" (S. Miller, 1969, p. 159).

Anti-coolie clubs, formed during this period, instigated riots against the Chinese and Chinese-owned businesses. In 1871, for example, 21 Chinese, including a child and a doctor, were hanged in a mob killing in Los Angeles (McLeod, 1948). In that same year, 50 Chinese miners landing from a Sacramento boat in San Francisco were beaten, stoned, and robbed. For the next decade, no San Franciscan Chinese nor his property were safe from hoodlums. In 1877, 25 Chinese washhouses were burned as their owners and workers fled into Chinatown for protection (McLeod, 1948). In town after town, Chinese laundries and entire Chinatowns were burned.

Echoing the Workingmen's Party cry "Discharge your Chinamen!" boycotts of Chinese-made goods forced managers to stop hiring the Chinese in order to resolve conflicts with white labor (Jacobs and Landau, 1971). "Although the much-hated monopolists were a main target of organized agitation, the Chinese were increasingly made the scapegoats for social problems" (Tchen, 1984, p. 7).

The Workingmen's theme "The Chinese Must Go" rang throughout the state. Yet "the Chinese had not caused the drought, nor decline of mineral production, nor speculation and panic in stocks and real estate, nor land monopoly, nor even the labor movement" (Coolidge, 1909, p. 116).

Ironically, the occupations having the largest number of unemployed white men were not the ones in which the Chinese were chiefly engaged. Where Chinese and white workers did compete (in specific manufacturers), the degree of competition was slight and affected a very small number of white wage earners (Coolidge, 1909). Nevertheless, Chinese labor was the standard of efficiency by which other labor was measured.

City ordinances singularly discriminated against the Chinese. Aimed at crowded living conditions in the Chinese Quarter, the Cubic Air Ordinance of 1870 made it illegal for anyone to let or rent rooms with less than 500 cubic feet of air per person. This made just about all the sleeping areas of the Chinese illegal. Reportedly, enforcement of this statute led to the arrest of so many Chinese that the city jails were in violation of the ordinance (Dillon, 1962; McCunn, 1979).

In 1873 the city's Board of Supervisors passed a queue ordinance that permitted jail officials to cut off a "Chinaman's queue" to one inch from the scalp. Although Mayor Alvord vetoed the ordinance, calling it "a degrading punishment inflicted upon the Chinese residents for slight offenses and solely by reason of their alienage and race" (Dillon, 1962, p. 57), the ordinance was revived and ultimately passed. In a rare instance of justice, Ho Ah Kow, the first Chinese so victimized, sued, and in 1876 a U.S. Circuit Court judge declared the ordinance unconstitutional. A $10,000 judgment was awarded to the plaintiff against the sheriff and the city and county of San Francisco (Dillon, 1962; McLeod, 1948).

No other ethnic group but the Chinese carried their vegetables and clothes on poles; thus the Pole Ordinance, which prohibited persons from walking on sidewalks while using poles to carry goods, was yet another discriminatory law. Also, excluding the Chinese from a graduated tax structure, the 1873 and 1876 Laundry License Ordinances taxed those who had no vehicle (the Chinese) the equivalent sum as (white) owners who employed more than two vehicles, while (white) laundry owners with one or two vehicles paid less tax than either of the aforementioned groups.

In 1876 a committee of the California senate was appointed to hear testimonies regarding the social, moral, and political effect of Chinese immigrants and means of exclusion (should the committee determine that the presence of the Chinese was detrimental to the nation's interest). One year later, the California legislature conducted an investigation on the Chinese question and sent to Congress a petition for an end to Chinese immigration.

In 1878 the California constitution authorized residential segregation, which prevented the Chinese from living outside of the Chinese Quarter. In 1879 California's second constitution prohibited corporations and state, municipal, or county governments from employing Chinese, with a penalty of $10 to $1,000 or imprisonment. Upon the second violation of this law, the president of the Sulphur Bank Quicksilver Mining Company took this to court. The U.S. Circuit Court held that the law was unconstitutional.

The "Chinese question," defined by labor union leaders as the central political issue of the day, was as significant an issue as the "Negro problem" was in the South after the Civil War (Hoexter, 1976). Those with political aspiration were so dependent on the labor vote, that none would speak on behalf of the Chinese. "Anti-Chinese agitation was incorporated into a web of local, regional, and state politics" (Tchen, 1984, p. 7). Hostility against the Chinese became a political platform on which hundreds of campaigns for public office were launched (Lyman, 1974). Throughout the 1870s and 1880s, both political parties adopted anti-Chinese clauses in their national platforms.

In 1880 California Governor Perkins declared March 4 a legal holiday for public, anti-Chinese demonstrations (Chinn, Lai, and Choy, 1969), a most inappropriate treatment of the one ethnic group whose tax contributions to the state far overrepresented their population size and economic status relative to other groups. Humiliation and hostility were the rewards meted out to an ethnic group whose labor made it possible for California to become a full player in the nation's transformations.

Political and economic motivation fueled a xenophobic media campaign aimed as portraying Chinese as inferior, diseased, morally degenerate, and a peril to the purity of the white race—all with the objective of running the Chinese out of business. Referred to as "the yellow peril," the Chinese were included in the Anti-Miscegenation Law, which made it unlawful for persons of color to marry a white.

Pixley, representing San Francisco before the Congressional Committee of 1876, made the moral proclamation that "The Chinese have no souls to save and if they have, they are not worth saving" (Seward, 1881, p. 225). Physicians in San Francisco testified that the Chinese had nerve endings farther from the surface of the skin than whites, thereby making them less sensitive to pain—a justification for why Chinese workers could labor under terrible circumstances without complaining (Tchen, 1984).

The purported threat of Chinese "hordes" and "inundated floods . . . pouring forth into the United States" (see debate before the 1879 Congressional Commission in Seward, 1881, p. 294) had no validity in fact. In the 1880s and 1890s, the Chinese made up only 1% of the immigrant population, whereas Europeans comprised 95% or more of that population (Coolidge, 1909).

In 1882 anti-Chinese agitators in the West finally won national support for their movement. The Chinese Exclusion Act was passed, which suspended the immigration of Chinese laborers into the United States and prohibited the naturalization of Chinese.[1] Thereafter no state court or court of the United States shall admit Chinese to citizenship. This dramatic piece of legislation was the first national law to restrict immigration into this country on the basis of race. It was the first time the United States had repudiated its policy of welcoming immigrants regardless of race, religion, or national origin (Hoexter, 1976).

The Exclusion Act was amended in 1884, then renewed in 1888 as the more restrictive Scott Act. The Scott Act shut out any Chinese laborer who had left the United States from returning, prohibiting the issuance of more reentry certificates, and made those heretofore issued void. This act broke the Burlingame Treaty, insulted officials in the Chinese government, and invalidated the return certificates issued to 20,000 Chinese laborers, 600 of whom were on the ocean in the process of returning and were refused admission.

In 1892 the United States passed the Geary Act, which extended the Exclusion Law for 10 more years and required all Chinese laborers to register with the government and to purchase certificates of residence. After one year, those without certificates would be liable for deportation. The Geary Act violated the guarantees of the Bill of Rights and forbid the Chinese any writs of habeas corpus when arrested. The Chinese Six Companies[2] raised money to test the case before the Supreme Court, but to their dismay the Geary Act was upheld. The 1880s were punctuated with riots against the Chinese in various states (Nevada, Colorado, Montana, and Oregon), forceful evictions (in Seattle, Tacoma, Truckee, Antioch, Eureka, Juneau, and other cities), and mass killings (the most noted being in Rock Springs, Wyoming). With the passage of the Exclusion Act, hope for a future in the United States died for many Chinese, as reflected in their numeric decline. Between 1880 and 1920, close to 50,000 Chinese left the United States, a population decrease of 40%. With each succeeding year, the U.S. Chinese population shrank, bottoming in 1920 at 61,639. From 1908 to 1943, the number of Chinese who left was larger by 37,738 than the number of immigrants admitted (Kung, 1962).

The year 1904 marked the first time in the history of California's Democratic party that its platform had no anti-Chinese plank (Coolidge, 1909). It was unnecessary, for "by 1910, the bulk of Chinese were isolated, neglected, and demoralized" (Lyman, 1974, p. 84).

San Francisco Chinatown's Chinese population followed the national shifts. A population of 8,128 in 1870 that increased to 14,688 in 1880, then to 25,833 in 1890, plummeted to 11,000 in 1900 (Coolidge, 1909). To many U.S. Chinese, the laws were not aimed at their exclusion as much as their extermination (see Chan Kiu Sing, in Coolidge, 1909, p. 302).

Summarizing this period, Kung (1962) described this early history as:

one of sad struggle against apparently relentless obstacles. Early immigrants were ambitious workers willing to labor tirelessly at any trade to make a living. Their sacrifices were heavy. Their sufferings were great. Prejudice against them was widespread, discrimination against them came not only from American laborers, politicians, and a host of others but from the very law of the land, for the Chinese were the first race to be singled out for exclusion, and therefore not eligible for naturalization. (p. 253)

The Chinese Quarter became a refuge from the burnings of businesses and the beatings of Chinese outside the boundaries of their quarters.

Tong Yun Fow was the spiritual, if not actual, home of tens of thousands of Chinese who, because of a tidal wave of racist hostility, were forced to live in a segregated section of the city. Chinatown had been shaped by the swirling cross-currents of an epic three way struggle between industrial capitalists who sought to remake the West as they saw fit, Chinese merchants and workers who sought work and survival, and an often racist, yet class conscious, white working class driven by anger and fear for their livelihood." (Tchen, 1984, p. 3).

From 1870 to 1919, the Chinese Quarter functioned as a "ghetto prison" (Tchen, 1984, p. 19). The migration from mining, railroad, and agricultural sites to the Chinese Quarter caused severe overcrowding. Lodges were turned into more permanent quarters. Additional housing was built, much like dormitories and small sleeping rooms. The Chinese Quarter was no longer a way station as it took on the attributes of a crowded slum.

By 1890, the Chinese Quarter was an area of 12 city blocks housing 20,000 persons, or 26% to 30% of the Chinese in the state at that time (*all* blocks contained in Figure 2.1). In 1906 the Quarter comprised 15 blocks all below Mason Street and south of Sacramento Street. Farwell (1885) reported that there were 930 buildings in Chinatown (based on first floor occupants only); 30% were retail stores, 20% lodging residences, 18% light manufacturing industries, 11% prostitution houses, 10% gambling saloons, 7% services, 2% opium resorts, and 1% joss houses. A breakdown of the manufacturing industries listed 974 clothing makers, 599 boot and shoe makers, 427 cigar makers, 255 underwear makers, and 71 "miscellaneous," totalling 2,326 employees in the light manufacturing industries.

While tax revenues obtained from the Chinese helped transform San Francisco from a frontier town to a metropolitan city, discrimination and exploitation stunted the Chinese Quarter into a blight on an emerging American city (Yu, 1981). While Chinese labor enlarged the coffers of the state and all who employed them, Chinese laborers only made enough to survive. Consequently, the San Francisco Health Officer's Report for 1869–1870 reported that Chinese workers could not afford better than to rent crowded, "rickety, filthy, dilapidated tenement houses" (*Chinese Press*, in Yu, 1981, p. 97). A family of five or six persons occupied a single room, eight by ten feet in dimension (Lloyd, 1875). The economy of space that so amazed outside observers took on the character of a cultural attribute: "The ultimate problem of Mongolian existence seems to be how to get the greatest number of human beings into the least possible space" (Williams, 1875, p. 35).

Chinatown's reputation was decidedly unsavory, as disease and immorality were attributed to the place and race. Farwell's report, although admittedly "unusually sensational and misleading" (Coolidge, 1909, p. 189), was the document upon which the city's Board of Supervisors relied. "All great cities have their slums and localities where filth, disease, crime, and misery abound; but in the very best aspect which Chinatown can be made to present, it must stand apart, conspicuous and beyond them all in the extreme degree of all these horrible attributes, the rankest outgrowth of human degradation that can be found upon this continent" (Farwell, 1885, p. 5). With regard to their behavior, "The Chinese brought with them and have successfully maintained . . . the grossest habit of bestiality practiced by the human race" (Farwell, p. 5). Dramatizing the prostitution, opium smoking, and gambling, Farwell attacked Chinatown as "moral purgatory" and a "menace to the welfare of society" (p. 5, 65). He described their Quarter as "a slumbering pest . . . the filthiest spot inhabited . . . on the American continent" (p. 4). While the San Francisco Health Officer's Report of 1869–1870 called the Chinese mode of living the most abject in which it is possible for human beings to live (*Chinese Press,* in Yu, 1981), much of Chinatown's squalor was due to poverty and the city's failure to provide Chinatown with the benefits of sanitary services, health services, and police protection that were granted to the rest of the city (Trauner, 1978). San Francisco made no attempt to clean the Quarter's streets (see testimony by Brooks in Dillon, 1962, p. 165). While the Chinese paid more than their due share in city taxes, they gained few of its benefits. In summary, Tow (in Mears, 1927) stated the Chinese condition: "The general public in the country, unfortunately, do not know or understand the Chinese. . . . [they are] directed to misunderstand us . . . induced, led and taught to dislike, despise, and hate the Chinese, who have suffered public humiliation which they do not deserve." (p. 152)

During this period of Chinatown's history, the Chinese Six Companies lost its power in the defeat of its second efforts to test the constitutionality of the Geary Act. The power of the tongs grew.[3]

Initially, City Hall left the Chinese to settle their own quarrels. However, in two brief years (1873 and 1874), the casual attitude of the police turned active. With the insistence of Donadina Cameron (who led a crusade to rescue Chinese girls from brothels) and Chinese merchants (who pressed for an end to tong wars), police made vigorous arrests (Dillon, 1962), which helped to reduce the influence of the tongs.

In 1906 the San Francisco earthquake and fires spelled an end to the Chinese Quarter and nearly all of San Francisco. Chinatown burned to the ground. While some white San Franciscans hoped this would forecast the eradication of the Chinese ghetto, ownership of Chinatown real estate by the Chinese Six Companies foiled such dreams. Structures were rebuilt on the original site. The decision to allow the Chinese to stay was largely determined by economics. The city would have lost revenues from taxes paid by the Chinese if they moved to another city (Yu, 1981). Seven years later, however, the Chinese were prevented from further land ownership by the 1913 Alien Land Law, which prevented "aliens ineligible for citizenship" from buying or leasing property.

Lodging houses that had been destroyed were replaced by tenements, called residential hotels, which were designed for the working-class bachelor society. Chinatown was still primarily a male-dominated enclave, as discriminatory laws restricted non-merchant immigrants from bringing their wives. From 1870 to 1910, women represented no more than 7% of the Chinese population in the United States.

Unexpectedly, the earthquake created a legal loophole for Chinese entry into this unwelcoming land. As all U.S. customs immigration records were destroyed in the fires, it was now impossible to determine the number and identity of those Chinese who were legal citizens. Thousands of Chinese entered this country as "paper sons"—that is, sons by paper, not by birth—taking advantage of the ruling that children of U.S. citizens were permitted entrance into the United States. One unfortunate impact of this "illegal" entry was the ill-treatment of all Chinese as suspects by immigration officers (Coolidge, 1909).

Laundries and the Emergence of Merchants

Driven from nearly all desirable and profitable occupations, the Chinese were funnelled into laundries and garment work. In 1870 there were 3,653 Chinese launderers in the United States. By 1900 this number had risen to 25,483. For the next two decades, laundries were the leading source of employment for the Chinese. As a counterforce to the hostility of the outside world, mutual support organizations and trade guilds provided collective solidarity within the enclave. The Chinese Quarter had little basis for economic self-support and could not maintain its population through families because of the unbalanced ratio of men to women. Therefore, these associations and guilds were critical to survival.

Although merchants and laborers shared the dream of Gold mountain, success was largely attainable for the merchant alone. Chinese merchants in California collaborated with American companies in contracting labor for industries and imported luxury goods from China for the city's social elite (Tchen, 1984). In addition, the merchants made profits from selling supplies and services to the laborers. Since the exclusion law permitted merchants but not laborers to enter, the power of the merchants swelled. Moreover, only merchants could legally bring over their wives, which afforded them the chance to have families and a future in this country.

The emerging power of the merchants led to the establishment of the Chinese Chamber of Commerce. This central organization set the stage for the emergence of small ethnic businesses that dominated the next phase of Chinatown's history.

BASE FOR SMALL ETHNIC BUSINESSES (1920 TO 1940s)

Restraining legislation did not dissipate. In 1924 the Immigration Act was passed, which excluded all Chinese and Japanese from immigrating into this country, setting their quota at zero. Wives of U.S. citizens were now admissible because aliens ineligible for citizenship were denied entry. However, this period saw a general waning of discriminatory legislation.

In 1930 an act was passed that permitted Chinese wives who were married to U.S. citizens prior to 1924 to enter the United States. The result was an increasing presence of Chinese women. The male-female ratio of 19:1 in the previous period shrank to 7:1 in 1920, then to 3:1 in 1940 (see Table 2.1).

The percentage of Chinese women in the United States grew from 12% to 26% during this two-decade period. Women signified the emergence of a family society in Chinatown and also led to the sizable presence of family-run ethnic businesses, whose viability was largely due to the unremunerated work participation of wives. The major transformation of Chinatown in this third historic period was the emergence of an economic ethnic marketplace that signaled the beginning of a larger tourist industry.

Meanwhile, following the 1929 stock market crash, the nation staggered through its worst economic depression and recession. The safest occupational shelter lay within the enclave. As neither laundry nor garment work provided a strong economic base for the community's labor force, the number of Chinese working in laundries dropped to 12,550 in 1920 (Kung, 1962). The demand for laundries declined further due to the economic depression and the invention of home laundry machines in the 1930s. By 1940, only a small proportion of Chinese were in the laundry business.

As for the garment industry, white subcontractors made extensive use of Chinatown's factories because of the high profit margin gained from the low wages meted out to sweatshop workers. In 1932 there were roughly 30 sewing factories operating in Chinatown. However, the garment industry could not function as a major enterprise for the general labor force of the Chinese because of the gender-segregated nature of its employment, and, without union backing, operatives' jobs were precarious.

Light manufacturing industries declined, falling in number from 169 to 55.[4] The greater delineation of retail/sales businesses, indicated in Wong's 1929 map, signified the emergence of this trade, while the absence of prostitution houses, gambling saloons, and opium resorts reflected the demise of these industries. Hotels, benevolent association buildings, and specialized professional services (such as doctors and optometrists) appeared where they had been previously largely absent.

This period was marked by an increase in the number of Chinatown restaurants that were family-run enterprises catering to a tourist trade. In 1920, 11,438 Chinese worked as cooks, waiters, or restaurant keepers. The power base of the merchants was strengthened. Merchant efforts to alter the Quarter's notorious reputation served to promote the tourist industry. Chinatown's image was now more appropriately under the control of the community itself.

Table 2.1
Sex and Nativity of the Chinese Population in the United States, 1860–1970

	Total	%	Gender				Nativity			
			Male	%	Female	%	Native	%	Foreign	%
1860	34,933	100.0	33,149	94.9	1,784	5.1	0	0	34,933	100.0
1870	63,199	100.0	58,633	92.8	4,566	7.2	517	0.8	62,682	99.2
1880	105,456	100.0	100,686	95.5	4,779	4.5	1,183	1.1	104,282	98.2
1890	107,475	100.0	103,607	96.4	3,868	3.6	787	0.7	106,688	99.3
1900	89,863	100.0	85,341	95.0	4,522	5.0	9,010	10.0	80,853	90.0
1910	71,531	100.0	66,856	93.5	4,675	6.5	14,935	20.9	56,596	79.1
1920	61,639	100.0	53,891	87.4	7,748	12.6	18,532	30.1	43,107	69.9
1930	74,954	100.0	59,802	79.8	15,152	20.2	30,868	41.2	44,086	58.8
1940	77,504	100.0	57,389	74.0	20,115	26.0	40,262	51.9	37,242	48.1
1950	117,629	100.0	77,008	65.5	40,621	34.5	45,301	38.7	71,839	61.3
1960	237,292	100.0	135,549	42.6	101,743	60.5	142,796	60.5	93,288	39.5
1970	435,062	100.0	228,565	52.5	206,497	47.5	229,237	52.9	204,232	47.1
1980	812,178	100.0	410,936	50.6	401,242	49.4	297,789	36.7	514,389	63.3

Sources : Li, P. Occupational Mobility and Kinship Assistance: A Study of Chinese Immigration in Chicago. 1978. San Francisco: R & R Research Associates, pp. 43-44. U.S. Bureau of the Census (1975). Historical Statistics of the United States, Colonial Times to 1970 (Bicentennial Edition, Part 1), p.4; U.S. Bureau of the Census (1980a).

The Housing Movement

With the emergence of a family society, Chinatown's housing problem was glaring. Since Chinese were legally barred from buying land, only 25% of the real estate in Chinatown was owned by Chinese during this period. Housing discrimination had locked the Chinese into the enclave (Yu, 1981), exacerbating the housing crisis. There was a serious need for low-cost housing for families in the community:

The congestion in Chinatown has so aroused the ire of social welfare and public health officials that many of the tenement houses have been legally condemned and the tenants forced to vacate. As many as eight to ten members of one family have been reported to be living in a single room without bathing or cooking facilities other than public lavatories and community kitchens. (Lee, in Yu, 1981, p. 104)

Of the 3,830 dwelling units in Chinatown in 1951, approximately 3,000 were without heating and only 447 were classified as meeting acceptable standards (Coleman, 1945). The typical resident had to share a bath with 20 other persons and a kitchen with 12 other persons. One consequence of Chinatown's crowding and substandard housing was a tuberculosis rate that was three times that of the city (Coleman, in Yu, 1981).

In the 1930s the Chinatown Housing Project Committee, representing a variety of organizations, was formed for the purpose of securing funds for low-cost public housing. Through their efforts, President Roosevelt signed Chinatown's Housing Bill in 1939, which allocated one million dollars toward a public housing project. Tragically, the advent of war deterred the realization of this dream, as appropriated funds were used for war emergency housing instead (Yu, 1981). Housing conditions worsened as crises were put "on hold."

Normalization Begins

The alliance between the United States and China during World War II helped normalize the status of the U.S. Chinese. In 1943, in an effort to bolster Chinese morale in the interest of winning the war, the United States repealed the Chinese Exclusion Act (Kung, 1962; Riggs, 1950). This made the Chinese eligible for immigration and made the U.S. Chinese eligible for naturalization. Sixty years of American history had elapsed from passage to repeal of this racially discriminatory act.

A 1943 amendment to the Immigration Act of 1924 raised the quota for Chinese immigrants from zero to 105 per year. Although the annual quota for the Chinese was still discriminatory,[5] the amendment ended exclusion and permitted foreign-born Chinese wives and offspring to enter this country as nonquota immigrants. Also, the War Brides Act of 1945 permitted wives of members of the U.S. armed forces to enter the United States, which enhanced the emergence of family life. To add to this normalization, the restrictive covenant on real estate was lifted in 1947. In 1948, anti-miscegenation laws were nullified.

Previously, discrimination kept Chinese American professionals out of the mainstream occupational niches, but now, jobs in the war industries provided job opportunities for numerous educated Chinese Americans. After the war, these engineers and scientists found employment in government agencies and in U.S. companies. The opportunity of citizenship, which brought with it a sense of belonging, increased the civic consciousness of residents. Members of the growing native-born generation began to advocate for better housing and recreational facilities.

In all, no other period was witness to such a reversal in the perception and status of Chinese Americans. The "aliens" became citizens. Chinatown's reputation was substantially enhanced. The social character had changed. Chinatown was becoming a neighborhood of families, with an increasing presence of native-born and a decided presence of merchants. The reduction of indignities and racist legislation lifted an oppressive weight from these ethnic Americans.

GROWTH, CRISIS, AND ADVOCACY (1950s TO 1970s)

The social, economic, and political progress of the postwar era benefited all Americans, with the exception of Japanese Americans. This prosperity provided stability and optimism from which the social and political movements of the 1960s and the urban, economic, and social programs of the 1970s evolved.

With citizenship now an option, 14,133 Chinese were naturalized between 1954 and 1960 (Kung, 1962). Chinese Americans gained greater residential, social, and economic mobility in this period than before. The repeal of the Alien Land Law in 1959 permitted them to purchase land, which led to two major phenomena. First, those with economic means moved out of Chinatown. Second, owing to their improved social and economic status, Chinese Americans owned a full 80% of Chinatown's real estate in the core area by 1968.

Immigration Reform and Influx

In the midst of a healthy economy, the U.S. government liberalized laws that affected overseas Chinese and refugees. The McCarran-Walter Act of 1952 admitted 27,502 Chinese immigrants between 1951 and 1960. In 1962, a presidential directive under John F. Kennedy permitted Hong Kong refugees to enter the United States; over 15,000 refugees immigrated to this country within four years. The watershed was the 1965 Immigration Act, which abolished the 1943 quota of 105 Chinese per year. Instead, each country outside of the western hemisphere had a quota of up to 20,000 persons per year. With their quota now based on country of origin rather than race, Chinese would finally be treated like all other immigrants (Nee and Nee, 1972).

Hundreds of thousands of Chinese foreign-born entered the country. Between 1965 and 1970, roughly 100,000 Chinese immigrated to the U.S. and from 1971 to 1978, another 190,105 Chinese entered the country from China, Taiwan, and Hong Kong. The numbers of foreign-born Chinese in the United States grew from 93,000 in 1960 to 204,000 in 1970; 260,455 in 1976; and 394,337 in 1978. From 1970 to 1978, the foreign-born Chinese in the United States had doubled in only eight years. In 1970, close to half of all the Chinese in the United States (47%) were foreign-born. From 1970 to 1976, the Chinese foreign-born population in the San Francisco–Oakland SMSA increased by 35% and in the city of San Francisco by 39% (representing increases of 48,824 and 37,273, respectively).

Freed of legal obstruction to the entry and reunification of families, the community's lifeblood was renewed. With the exit of economically mobile residents, Chinatown's endurance required new immigrants. These newcomers provided the social, economic, and cultural nourishment that allowed Chinatown to grow. In fact, in terms of importance, Fang (1984) likened immigration reform for Chinese Americans to civil rights for blacks.

From 1940 to 1970, Chinatown's population increased by roughly 25% per decade: from 16,000 in 1940 to 20,000 in 1950; 25,000 in 1960; then 31,000 in 1970. Thousands of Chinese San Franciscans moved out of Chinatown into adjacent neighborhoods or to other parts of the city. With each succeeding decade from 1940 to 1970, an increasing proportion of Chinese lived just outside the core area. Some moved west into the nondescript urban valley between Nob Hill and Russian Hill. Some moved north into Little Italy. The net effect was the expansion of Chinatown's boundaries from 30 city blocks in 1940 to 224 city blocks in 1970. Chinatown grew from 40 to 428 acres.

In 1970 this altered demography lead the Department of City Planning to designate the core, residential, and expanded areas of Chinatown. Of the 31,726 Chinese in Chinatown in 1970, 8,073 lived in the core area, 15,070 in the residential area, and 8,483 in the expanded area. The proportions of the population in each area represented by Chinese were 89%, 68%, and 35%, respectively (see Table 2.2 and Figure 2.2).

Services, Advocacy, and Crisis

Sudden waves of immigrants severely pressed community resources to crisis proportions, creating glaring problems regarding housing, health, and youth. All was not well. In the late 1960s and 1970s, Chinatown became the topic of newspaper exposés of a gilded ghetto, depicted as a community of poverty and an "impoverished prison . . . behind the picturesque and colorful Grand Avenue facade" (Conant, 1967, p. 1).

Table 2.2
Asian/Pacific Islander and Total Population in San Francisco Chinatown: 1970 and 1980

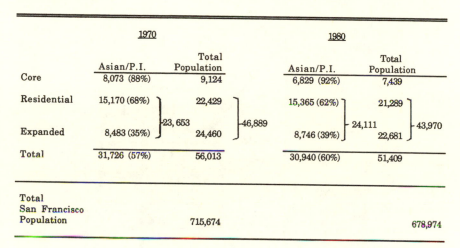

	1970		1980	
	Asian/P.I.	Total Population	Asian/P.I.	Total Population
Core	8,073 (88%)	9,124	6,829 (92%)	7,439
Residential	15,170 (68%)	22,429	15,365 (62%)	21,289
Expanded	8,483 (35%)	24,460	8,746 (39%)	22,681
Total	31,726 (57%)	56,013	30,940 (60%)	51,409

Residential + Expanded 1970: 23,653 and 24,460 → 46,889
1980: 24,111 → 43,970

Total San Francisco Population		715,674		678,974

Born of a generation of political activism, a new generation of Asian Americans met the challenges of this crisis. Making use of government-sponsored grants, an increasing number of Chinese American professionals and paraprofessionals brought their training and social-ethnic commitment to bear on the community's problems. They served as administrators, physicians, health and mental health workers, and attorneys in roughly 30 new service agencies that evolved during the 1960s and 1970s.

Chinatown served as headquarters for agencies such as Chinese for Affirmative Action, Asian Law Caucus, On Lok, Self Help for the Elderly, Chinese Newcomers Service Center, Chinatown Resource Center, Chinatown Youth Center, Chinese Hospital, Northeast Mental Health Center, and Chinatown Child Development Center. These agencies provided civil rights advocacy, free or low-cost legal services, social-medical services or general social service assistance for frail elderly or needy elderly, assistance to immigrants, community planning with regard to housing needs, services for gang members, bilingual health and mental health services, day care and developmental evaluation services.

In 1960 the proportion of second-generation Chinese in the United States increased to 61%. The male-female ratio narrowed to 2:1 in 1950 and reached parity in this same year. As the population of Chinatown swelled after the equalization of immigration laws, the housing crisis reappeared, made acute by the presence of families. Between 1960 and 1970, the elderly population in core Chinatown increased by 45%, and a majority (63%) of the households in the core area were low income (San Francisco Department of City Planning, 1977). Housing for the poor, elderly, and new immigrants was sorely inadequate.

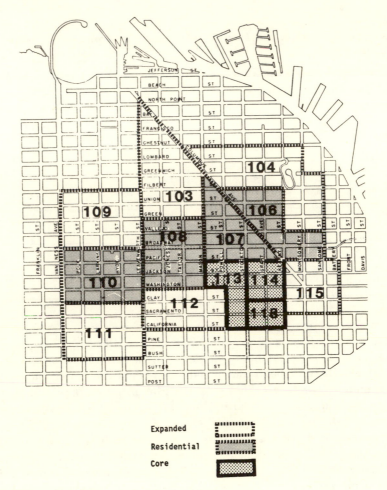

Figure 2.2
Census Tracts within Greater Chinatown

Miraculously, the advocacy work of the Chinatown Housing Committee finally reached fruition. In 1951, the housing crisis was attenuated by the construction of three six-story buildings, called the Ping Yuen projects. Chinatown had its first HUD-subsidized, low-cost, public housing project— a total of 234 units in fire- and earthquake-proof buildings located on Pacific Street. The community rejoiced: "Ping Yuen is a strong, handsome, living memorial to a dream and its happy realization after more than fifteen years of blood, sweat, and tears" (*Chinese Press*, in Yu, 1981, p. 105). "For the first time in the history of Chinatown there will be real homes. Families . . . will have a real living room. . . . Each home will have its own kitchen and bath, and enough bedroom space for all the family." (*San Francisco News*, in Yu, 1981, p. 105). For days, queues of applicants waited in line. There were 600 applicants for 234 available apartments.

In 1961 the efforts of the Housing Committee materialized into another Ping Yuen constructed on Pacific Street between Stockton and Powell, an 11-story building containing apartments. This Ping Yuen had a waiting list of 200 qualified applicants and 1,500 potentially eligible families waiting to apply. Many needy families without housing priority were locked out.

Yes, Chinatown proudly pointed to the addition of new low-cost housing, but the cry for more low-cost housing would not be stilled. This was perhaps best dramatized by the struggle to save the International Hotel (I-Hotel), a residential hotel that housed 196 tenants, most of whom were elderly. Located on Kearny Street across from Portsmouth Square, I-Hotel bordered Chinatown and the Financial District. In 1968, while in the process of selling the building to a development corporation, the owner of the I-Hotel issued eviction notices to all tenants. "We won't move!" was the tenants' rallying cry, a protest joined by thousands of demonstrating supporters. For nine years, demolition was forestalled. Finally, on August 4, 1977 at 3 A.M., with clubs and on horseback, the sheriff's police rushed the human wall of protection, several persons deep, that surrounded the building. The remaining tenants were physically removed to make way for demolition. Although the effort to save I-Hotel was lost, the outcry for low-cost housing for the elderly became a nagging memory for the city and the community.

With Section 8 HUD funds, an additional 53 units of public housing for the elderly, disabled, and handicapped were added at On Lok. The YWCA converted 98 units, of which 80 were for elderly. In the 1980s, Mei Lun Yuen, with 180 units of public housing for elderly and families, opened at Sacramento and Stockton. In 1985, Self-Help for the Elderly obtained HUD funds to construct the Lady Shaw Senior Center, a 70-unit housing project for the elderly. Then, in 1986, the Chinatown Housing Corporation secured a HUD-subsidized grant for a housing project for senior citizens.

Advocacy during this period took one other form—a rent strike to obtain better security measures in one of the Ping Yuen buildings where a grotesque murder had been committed by an outsider. With the assistance of the Asian Law Caucus and other community activists, the rent strike was successful. The community demonstrated that power could be had by those often thought to be powerless.

The city's garment industry profited from the large influx of new immigrant women who found employment there as seamstresses in sweatshops. From 1960 to 1968, employment in the industry increased from 8,000 persons to 9,500 persons, and the value added to the city's garment industry grew from $48 million to $98 million (Shribner, 1969).

Chinatown's tourist industry was flourishing by the late 1970s. Chinatown's commercial district became one of the largest business neighborhoods in San Francisco, paying more in business taxes (gross receipts and payroll expenses) than any other major commercial district in the area outside of downtown and the financial area. For comparison, in 1974 Chinatown had 591 gross receipt accounts compared to 239 for Fisherman's Wharf. Chinatown had 335 payroll expense accounts compared to 225 for Fisherman's Wharf (San Francisco Department of City Planning, 1975).

This "success" created two problems. First, the economic necessity of projecting a safe and healthy image of Chinatown for the sake of tourist dollars meant that city leaders and community merchants were hard pressed to acknowledge community problems without simultaneously scaring away tourist business (Light and Wong, 1975; Takagi and Platt, 1978). Second, ethnic enterprises that originally evolved to protect the Chinese from racist attack isolated these immigrants from the benefits of the open labor market. In essence, the industry's success limited immigrant labor to low-wage jobs in the ethnic labor market. Segregated into low-wage, dead-end jobs working as restaurant help or sweatshop laborers, immigrant workers in the tourist industry and garment subcontracting system perpetuated a non-integrated immigrant population, held hostage by the whites and Chinese who profited from these industries.

SUMMARY

The purpose of this chapter was to describe the history of a distinct group of Americans, the realities of these periods of history, and the process of change and transition. The saga of a nation's persecution of an ethnic minority group, particularly Asian Americans, is largely unknown. In general, the heritage of Chinese Americans from 1849 to the 1940s was a sad chapter in America's treatment of its nonwhite ethnic members. Into the twentieth century, the Chinese were victims of labor exploitation and discriminatory legislation. Contradictions stand out in relief: (1) while treated as an enemy, Chinese labor was indispensable to the development of California; (2) while contributing to the vast wealth brought to the state by their labor, the Chinese gained little from this prosperity; (3) while the Chinese were accused of not being assimilable, various laws and attitudes purposefully prevented the Chinese from assimilating; and (4) immigration legislation affecting the Chinese would reverse itself depending upon the social-political mood and economic needs of white America. The history of America's treatment of the Chinese has been a shameful contradiction of what America purports to be— a place where all persons have the right to justice and equal opportunity.

In terms of changes in the community itself, Chinatown has evolved from a jumping-off point for Chinese labor in the mid-1800s to a key commercial nexus of San Francisco and Northern California in the 1970s. For purposes of this text, the community's history was divided into four periods: (1) Way

Station (1849–1869); (2) Segregated Ghetto (1870–1919); (3) Base for Small Ethnic Businesses (1920 to 1940s), and (4) Growth, Crisis, and Advocacy (1950s to 1970s). The transformations during these times were dramatic. For sixty years the Chinese were prevented from buying or leasing property (the 1913 Alien Land Law) and their quota of persons permitted to immigrate into this country was set at zero (the 1924 Immigration Act). Six decades passed before the Chinese Exclusion Act of 1882 was eliminated and the 1924 Immigration Act was amended to permit a quota of 105 Chinese per year to immigrate into this country. In the 1940s the restrictive covenant on real estate was lifted and the anti-miscegenation laws were nullified. In 1959 the Alien Land Law was repealed, making it possible for Chinese to purchase land. Then, in 1965, the Immigration Act abolished the quota of 105 Chinese per year. Finally, the Chinese were freed of legal obstruction to the entry and reunification of families. The lifeblood of the community was renewed. Permitted citizenship, these ethnic Americans were no longer excluded from membership in this society.

There is no way to estimate how much longer the Exclusion Act would have remained in effect were it not for the fact that China and the United States were allies during World War II. Still to this day, portions of white America associate Asian Americans with foreigners, extensions of Asians abroad. Citizenship does not eradicate discrimination. The murders of Vincent Chin and Jim Loo in the 1980s illustrate this. There are white Americans today who clearly consider the names Chin or Loo un-American.

Throughout the early history of their presence in this country, Chinese Americans were subject to discrimination in the labor market and were restricted to the least desirable jobs. Against this backdrop of history, it is interesting to note that President Bush vetoed the Civil Rights Act of 1990 purportedly because the legislation would introduce quotas in the workplace. First of all, the legislation was not about quotas; it was about reversing or modifying recent Supreme Court rulings that made it more difficult for minority groups to win job discrimination suits. The Civil Rights Act of 1990 also would have expanded monetary remedies available to victims of job discrimination. Basically, the act would have better safeguarded the rights of women and minorities in the workplace. Yet even if the legislation had been about quotas, it is telling that quotas, intended to work against minorities (as in the 1924 Immigration Act and the Chinese Exclusion Act) have not been vetoed, but that when legislation is suspected to work against whites or white businesses, they have been vetoed.

There has been another major message of this chapter, namely, the endurance of a community for over 140 years. The reader can look upon this survival in one of two ways. First, we can view it as proof that an ethnic culture, people, and community can endure, given renewed population, cultural assertions of self-determination, resistance, and community commitment. After all, Galton (1908) had stated that immigrants were, on the whole, persons of considerable force of character—not the quiet type to succumb, but rather the type with energy to transplant themselves. The Chinese may be one example of this. Second, we can look upon Chinatown's endurance as evidence of the perpetuation of America's underclass, who live without most of the majority's advantages. We can interpret Chinatown's survival as an indication that this nation has not yet made racial and class equity a priority in its agenda.

Our overview of Chinatown serves as the historical context for the survey findings that are presented in subsequent chapters. While shadows of history will reappear where relevant, from here on the lives of the residents will take center stage.

NOTES

1. Laborers were defined as the "skilled and unskilled and those engaged in mining" (Chinn, Lai, and Choy, 1969, p. 27). The following classes were exempted from exclusion: teachers, students, and travelers (who were limited to short stays); merchants, their families, wives, and minor children; government officials, their families, and employees; Chinese born in the United States and their children; and Chinese previously lawfully and permanently admitted to the United States returning from temporary visits abroad (see Lee, 1960). From 1925 to 1943, 4,659 Chinese students came to the United States, a number greater than that from any other country (see Senate Report 1515, Table 14, p. 896 in Kung, 1962, p. 95).

2. The Chinese Six Companies was an organization composed of members representing six districts of China. Functioning much as a supreme court of the Chinese in California, it spoke and acted on behalf of all the California Chinese in affairs affecting them. It was also the official board of arbitration for disputes that arose between various district groups and was spokesman for the Manchu government in relations with the Chinese in America.

3. Tongs were secret societies that controlled the prostitution and gambling businesses (see Dillon, 1962; Lyman, 1974).

4. This calculation is based on a comparison of data taken from J. P. Wong's 1929 map of Chinatown and W. B. Farwell's (1885) map.

5. The quota for Chinese was far from equal to that of Europeans. Great Britain, for example, had an annual quota of 65,721.

Children are the greatest source of life satisfaction for Chinatown residents, but the neighborhood is not deemed a desirable one for raising children. Waiting for a bus at Sacramento and Stockton Street, these children represent the next generation of Asian Americans. 1985. (Photograph by Steve Ringman, courtesy of the *San Francisco Chronicle*.) Reprinted by permission.

From Teacher to Seamstress

Our project's first Mandarin-speaking respondent represented a unique minority within the community. Although racially Chinese, her cultural background differed from the majority of Chinatowners. Where the vast majority of the Chinatown residents were from the Canton district, she had been brought up in rich and educated circumstances in Shanghai. Traditionally, the northerners of China looked down on the "barbaric southern Cantonese." She still carried traces of this tradition. Her parents were both teachers, and she and her sister had servants when they were growing up.

In China, this woman taught Russian. Upon moving to Hong Kong, she was forced to find a new profession. Sewing, which was once a hobby, became her source of income. Believing that her sons had no future in China, she and her family emigrated to the United States. Having no friends in Chinatown and no relatives in this country, she felt isolated. She had never met her neighbors. Burglarized six months earlier, she refused to stay in her apartment alone.

The social service agency in Hong Kong advised her against living in Chinatown, but lacking a car, her family was forced to live here. Her husband worked as a cook from 10 A.M. until 11 P.M. She hated her job as a seamstress and commented on how the fabric here was of such poor quality compared to fabric in Hong Kong. She wanted a better job, one outside of Chinatown, perhaps as a salesclerk at Macy's if she could improve her English. Otherwise, she hoped to save enough money so that she and her husband could own a restaurant.

Complaining about her living conditions, she noted how dark the room was and how garbage smells were unmistakable when she opened the front door. Also, the closeness of their rear window to the adjoining apartment gave them no privacy from their neighbors. Asked what she'd do differently if she could live her life over again, she remarked, "I wouldn't have left my mother nor gotten married." She has repeatedly tried to bring her mother and brother to America.

3

The Nature of Community and Desired Residential Mobility

The fate of community over time is central to the field of urban sociology and central to the study of ethnicity in American society. Assuming a unidirectional change from personal ties of community to impersonal societal ties, human ecologists have predicted the disappearance of ethnic neighborhoods as a result of assimilation and the invasion of business and industry (Stoneall, 1983). Later, researchers found empirical evidence that contradicted the theory of community breakdown (Bender, 1978). To the surprise of sociologists, certain communities persisted and survived (Bottomore, 1972; Foley, 1952; Lewis, 1952). Exceptions to the community breakdown model formed the theoretical focus of structural functionalism, a theory emphasizing the structures and functions that hold a community together and give it life. Community existed as a complex network of relations between place of residence, employment of adults, and schooling of children (Parsons, 1960).

Chinatown San Francisco represents the uniquely indelible nature of some communities, a point that Lee (1960) and Kuo (1979) have made. Because most Chinatowns are located in areas pressured by commercial and industrial expansion, there is continual tension between forces that maintain a community and those that threaten its future.

Community is best understood by examining the nature of the community and desired residential mobility. The nature of a community is defined by residents' motives for living there, salient resident characteristics, neighboring relations, involvement in locally based organizations, the "goodness" of the neighborhood as a place to live, and the identity that residents give to their neighborhood. Desired residential mobility is defined as residents' desire to move or stay; it can be a reflection of residential satisfaction. The wish to move is often associated with negative assessments of environmental characteristics, while the wish to stay is often associated with positive ones (Campbell, Converse, Rodgers, and Marans, 1976). Reasons for wanting to move often reveal the undesirable qualities of one's current neighborhood (the "push" factors) and/or the desirable qualities of other neighborhoods (the "pull" factors). Desired residential mobility also mirrors the extent to which there may be stability or instability in the resident population and the extent of constraints to mobility despite desire.

This chapter provides a brief historical review of the changing nature of mobility in the community, followed by survey findings. These findings are divided into several sections: (1) data on the nature of community, specifically why residents live where they live; (2) residency characteristics and perceptions regarding one's neighbors and the neighborhood; and (3) data on desired residential mobility, specifically why residents would want to move, why they would not want to move, and predictors of the desire to move.

MOBILITY IN A PERMANENT COMMUNITY

The changing saga of mobility and permanence in Chinatown is a rare case of societal inconsistency and ethnic resilience. Chinatown's permanence may suggest that Chinatown dwellers have had no desire to leave, but this has not been the case. Before World War II, racial discrimination against the Chinese on the West Coast largely forced the creation of a homogeneous Chinese neighborhood along ethnic lines. Restrictive covenants in title deeds were tightly enforced, specifying that each seller safeguard property values and maintain white neighborhoods. The more desirable the residential district, the more strictly the covenants were upheld (Lee, 1960). The alliance of the United States and China during World War II changed this. The nation's attitude toward the American Chinese turned positive. Racial hostilities relaxed and discriminatory laws were overturned. The demand for skilled labor in the war-related industries generated new job opportunities outside of Chinatown for educated Chinese Americans. These factors, along with the 1947 U.S. Supreme Court decision that declared restrictive covenants in title deeds non-enforceable, afforded some residents the opportunity to leave the enclave. Thereafter, while Chinatown was homebase for the majority of San Francisco Chinese, it was not the exclusive place of Chinese residency. Since the end of World War II, migration in and out of Chinatown has been substantial.

Along with post–World War II changes that allowed educated Chinese Americans to leave the community, changes in immigration laws increased the immigrant population. Congress replaced the policy of immigration exclusion with a policy of restricted control. Legislation was enacted that called for a token quota of 105 Chinese per year. Wives of American citizens and permanent residents, political refugees, and highly educated Chinese were allowed to enter this country.

Where discrimination had previously forced a homogeneous neighborhood along ethnic lines, after World War II homogeneity along class lines emerged. Those with better incomes moved into adjoining, outlying neighborhoods—which became known as residential and expanded Chinatown. Living outside the ghetto connoted higher socioeconomic status (Lee, 1960). As one respondent explained the move from core Chinatown to the noncore area: "We used to live in Ping Yuen. After my children grew up, they moved out of Chinatown, and we didn't need to stay in the housing project because our financial situation got better. So we moved here."

The poorest remained in the core area, where rents were cheaper. The pattern of geographic redistribution along socioeconomic lines was set. The process was maintained by the expansion of Chinatown's population. Then an interesting phenomenon emerged. Although out-migration into surrounding neighborhoods involved greater interracial mixing, ethnicity remained an important determinant of residential location. Ethnic ties to the community continued—witnessed by the close proximity of the neighborhoods into which Chinatown residents migrated. Despite the out-migration that was fueled by improved socioeconomic conditions, the community remained.

The gradual expansion of the postwar period gave way to rapid growth in the mid-1960s, brought on by major revisions in the immigration laws. In 1962 President Kennedy signed an executive order permitting Hong Kong refugees to enter this country. Within four years, over 15,000 persons entered. The 1965 Immigration Act, which went into full effect in 1968, dramatically increased the size of the Chinese population in America. The 1965 act increased the annual quota for Chinese from 105 to 20,000 persons. Between 1965 and 1970, over 100,000 Chinese immigrants entered the country. This immigration rate has continued at roughly the same rate since. By 1978, there were estimated to be over a third of a million foreign-born Chinese in the country.

San Francisco has always been a first port of entry for many Chinese, and Chinatown has been the first settlement area for tens of thousands of Chinese newcomers. Between 1965 and 1970, approximately 2,000 newcomers were added to Chinatown's core area and 8,000 to the greater Chinatown area. In 1970, one out of every five core residents was a newcomer. The composition of the core area population was increasingly foreign-born. The percentage of foreign-born increased from 55% in 1960 to 60% in 1970, then 74% in 1980. In 1980, three out of every four Chinatown residents were born outside of U.S. shores.

THE NATURE OF THE COMMUNITY

Why Live in Chinatown?

Convenience, ethnicity/language, and low rent were the primary motives for living in Chinatown (the number of mentions were 77, 51, and 29, respectively, with some residents citing more than one of the aforementioned reasons).

The enclave's residential-commercial mix provides convenient access to work, stores, public transportation, Chinese restaurants, and school and health facilities. The community forms a nearly self-sufficient urban village containing a network of residence, employment, and children's schooling. Moreover, it is the neighborhood-serving character of its commercial arena that forms such a valuable nexus. Small ethnic businesses like grocery stores, drug stores, Chinese restaurants, Chinese movie theaters, banking institutions, bilingual schools, Chinese Hospital, and doctors' offices dot the neighborhood. Residents voiced their feelings in this way: "I want to live in Chinatown because it's close to shopping and movies. I like living in Chinatown." "There's lots of conveniences here. . . . Chinese food, provisions, shops, [public] transportation, you can get anything you want."

Comments concerning ethnicity or language suggested that the enclave provided cultural security for many and language security for those who did not speak English: "It is because I am Chinese and I'd like to live where most of the Chinese live." "I can't speak English too well so I rather live in a place that has more Chinese- speaking people." For others, Chinatown represented roots and familial security: "My parents have a business in Chinatown. They don't speak English so we live in this neighborhood." "We started here, our roots are here. We're settled. We have close-knit relationships here and no other family elsewhere." "I grew up in Chinatown. I am familiar with the neighborhood and feel comfortable. My parents live here." Chinatown is also a last refuge for elderly who moved here when family was no longer an option: "I used to live in the Sunset. Because I can't speak English, I was so bored. Also, I couldn't get along with my son and his family. So, I moved out from the Sunset to Chinatown."

Low cost of housing was the third most often mentioned reason given for living in Chinatown. Comments expressing this included: "My children were young. My husband passed away. We didn't have enough money to support ourselves. The rent is low here." "The rent is cheap. It's not too far from work. It's close to shops and this building belongs to the Tam Association."

RESIDENT CHARACTERISTICS AND PERCEPTIONS

Chinatown's population characteristics are distinct from the rest of the city. The enclave is uniquely a first settlement area for immigrants. Data from the Chinatown survey indicate that 81% of the sample were foreign-born, which is consistent with the 1980 census data. This is a far greater proportion than for San Francisco as a whole, where only 28% of the city population is foreign-born (U.S. Bureau of the Census, 1980b). Among the foreign-born, both old-timers and newcomers are equally represented: 28% of the immigrants interviewed had resided in the United States for less than five years; 32% had lived in the United States from five to ten years; 10% from 11 to 20 years; 30% for over 20 years.

Chinatown is also recognizably a home for the elderly. The average age of the adult population in this community is 48 years, which is a full 17 years senior to the city-wide average.

By education, Chinatown's residents are more disadvantaged than San Franciscans overall. Only 37% of the residents graduated from high school, the smallest proportion of any city-wide neighborhood. Over half of the Chinatown adults aged 25 years and over had less than nine years of education.

Chinatown residents are also a distinctly disadvantaged segment of the Chinese American population. In 1979 the median personal income for Chinatown residents was between $4,000 and $4,999; the median family income for Chinatown residents was $8,000 to $8,999 compared to $22,559 for Chinese Americans overall. Only 12% of the Chinatown residents had a college degree, compared to 37% of all Chinese Americans nationally.

In Chinatown the mean household size was 2.7 persons. Single-occupied, nuclear, and three-generational households were all represented in this community. Twenty-three percent of the households were occupied by one person, 24% by a married couple, 33% by nuclear families (parents and child/children), and 20% by other combinations. Nearly half (46%) included parents and children, and in half of these households children were under the age of 18. The majority of families with children (70%) had one or two children living with them.

Chinatown is distinctively Chinese, an ethnic homogeneity that is preferred by most dwellers. Eight out of every ten residents reported that it was "somewhat important" (44%) or "very important" (34%) for them to live among other Chinese Americans. Nine out of every ten Chinatown residents reported that it was "very important" (60%) or "somewhat important" (31%) for their children to know the Chinese language. The desire for continuity of the Chinese culture and language was felt by nearly all.

A majority of residents had some acquaintanceship with their neighbors. Eleven percent of the residents said they knew their neighbors "very well," 22% said "pretty well," 41% said "a little," 22% said "not well," and 4%

Table 3.1
Neighborhood "Goodness" for Elderly, Teenagers, and Children

"For [elderly people/teenagers/a place to raise children under twelve years], how would you rate this neighborhood as a place to live . . . very good, good, OK, not so good, or poor?" (1 = very good, 5 = poor)

	Very Good	Good	OK	Not So Good	Poor	D.K.	Mean
Elderly	13%	57%	18%	8%	4%	2.3	2.3
Teenagers	3	19	37	21	12	8	3.2
Children	4	22	36	26	6	6	3.1

said "not at all." This mix of neighbor acquaintanceship is probably due to in- and out-migration of residency in the area. Some segments of this population were mobile, others were not. The ebb and flow consisted of the poor and elderly, who replaced those who could economically afford to leave.

A majority described their neighbors as friendly. Nineteen percent of the residents interviewed said their neighbors were "very friendly," 48% said "somewhat friendly," 32% responded with "neutral," 1% said "somewhat unfriendly," and no one reported their neighbors to be "very unfriendly."

A majority anticipated some neighborhood assistance in times of trouble. Asked "If you were in trouble, how likely would it be that a neighbor would come and help you to go and get help?" 18% said "very likely," 43% said "somewhat likely," 20% said "somewhat unlikely," 4% said "very unlikely," and 15% "didn't know." Residents desired neighbors who were helpful or friendly (57 mentions) or Chinese (31 mentions): "I'd want neighbors who are willing to help. Especially since I can't speak English well, I need help." "Chinese, especially quiet Chinese. I don't like noisy people."

While 70% of the sample thought their neighborhood was a "good" or "very good" place of residence for senior citizens, less than a third judged their neighborhood to be a "good" or "very good" place for teenagers or children (see Table 3.1). Residents mentioned convenience for shopping, transportation, and access to services or facilities as assets for the elderly: "It's convenient for them. They can do shopping themselves. There are some group activities for them to join. There is no language barrier." "There are services for them from Self-Help for the Elderly and On-Lok."

Respondents saw gang influence in the neighborhood as undesirable for teenagers: "They are easily exposed to bad influences of the street gangs." For children, the neighborhood offered "no playground," "not enough space," "noise," "too many businesses," and a restricted life view—"I felt I was raised in the ghetto. The person who lives there only sees a one-sided world, these kids grow up seeing only one race." Neighborhood attributes are important when the inside resources are so meager. Eight out of every ten households have no backyard; only 13% of the core residents and 35% of the noncore residents had this resource.

Compared to the nation overall, Chinatowners have less confidence in police protection. National findings indicate that 73% of Americans sampled rated police protection as "fairly good" or "very good" (Campbell, Converse, and Rodgers, 1976). In contrast, only 28% of the Chinatowners evaluated police protection in such positive terms. Specifically, 4% said police protection in Chinatown was "very good," 24% said "fairly good," 33% said "neither good nor bad," 26% said "not very good," 4% said "not good at all," and 8% "didn't know." Lack of confidence in police protection may contribute to the perception that Chinatown is less than ideal for children and teens.

Residents here were not actively involved in locally based organizations. Only 16% belonged to any clubs, organizations, or associations, but this phenomenon is not unusual for most neighborhoods.

DESIRED RESIDENTIAL MOBILITY

One indicator of residency permanence lies in the prevalence of desired residential mobility. Of those interviewed, 42% said "yes" to the question, "Would you ever want to move out of your neighborhood?" and 58% said "no." This proportion is comparable to the proportion of the nation wanting to move (Campbell, Converse, and Rodgers, 1976). Since national surveys have found that the desire to move is inversely related to age, the proportion of Chinatown residents who wanted to move would have been higher than 42% had the survey data been age-adjusted to national age norms. Surprising to some is how Chinatown residents have no greater desire to remain in their neighborhood than residents in other parts of the country. In fact, Chinatown residents' desire to leave is very characteristic of first settlement areas (Warner and Srole, 1945).

Why Move?

Crowding was the reason most often mentioned for wanting to move: "Because it's too crowded. I'd like to have a better house in a better neighborhood." "The crowded traffic is lousy. I don't like the parking. I don't like the streets so dirty. There are too many people around. There are so many things I don't like." "The landlord says we have too many members in the family [living here]. He allows only two of us to live here." Besides crowding, other undesirable environmental conditions were cited as reasons to leave: "It's very dirty. Once you open the window, the flies come in. It's unsanitary, not safe." "This area is not too quiet. Buildings are too old. I don't like the environment." "Mice. The landlord won't do much about it. The mice are chomping out the walls." Improved financial status that affords the chance for home ownership was another reason to move: "If I had enough money, I would buy a house outside of Chinatown."

Other reasons for wanting to leave included dissatisfaction with current housing or high rent, or the desire for a better life: "I guess I'm for the new generation. I want to get away from congestion, gangs, and slums. I should achieve something that my parents didn't get a chance to. I should set an example for my brothers and sisters to make a better life for themselves." "I see Chinatown as a barrier, an obstruction. If I move out of Chinatown, it's a chance for me to progress. I wouldn't want my kids to grow up in Chinatown and suffer the same way I did." Many of these reasons for wanting to leave Chinatown reflect Tong's (1971) synthesis of Chinatowners' life goals: "The order of the day was to work hard, make as much money as possible, and get the hell away from the rats and cockroaches" (p. 17).

Why Not Move?

For those who wanted to move, reasons for not having yet moved were financial: "I can't afford it." Persons who didn't want to move would consider moving under conditions of financial gain, deterioration of neighborhood or housing conditions, or life changes: "If, all of a sudden, there was money falling down from the sky, then I could have a large amount of money to buy a house . . . then I'd move."

Predictors of the Desire to Move

Investigating the predictors of the desire to move permitted us to test whether class or race is more powerful in determining residential location. The class-based theory, built on the work of Park (1923, 1936) and Burgess (1928), argued that ethnic groups follow an irreversible settlement process of contact, competition, accommodation, and assimilation. Social and class groups compete for various built environments in the city. Ethnic enclaves result from the competition among various racial groups for urban spatial location. The economically, politically, and socially advantaged locate in the more desirable locations. The competitive process of selection results in a certain homogeneity within urban neighborhoods. Ethnic groups are first segregated into the lowest grade areas of the city. Once they adapt to the new order, they break from their isolation and begin moving into the larger community (Warner and Srole, 1945).

The class-based theory assumes that residential mobility is the act of translating the aspiration for a higher status into movement to a higher status area. Economic mobility is indispensable for social class mobility. As Lieberson (1963) implied, residential desegregation of immigrant groups and their increasing socioeconomic status are intertwined. The class-based theory predicts that poorer residents would need to stay.

The race-based theory of residential location, on the other hand, argues that class alone does not explain where people reside because the desire for ethnic homogeneity remains a strong factor in residential comfort (Darroch and Marston, 1971; Kantrowitz, 1973). If the race theory prevails, we would expect that the more importance one attaches to living among Chinese, the greater would be the desire to stay.

Environmental factors also dictate the desire to move (Guest, 1971; Haggerty, 1971). Michelson (1977) found that among Toronto families, crowding was the most often mentioned reason for residential mobility. Similarly, in Chinatown, dwelling crowding was the most commonly mentioned reason for wanting to move. Dwelling crowding, along with persons per room and need for more space, were all significantly correlated with the wish to move.[1] Thus, it seemed reasonable to expect that in Chinatown dwelling crowding would predict desired residential mobility. Since other environmental variables, such as neighborhood crowding and noise, might also be correlated with the desire to move, these variables were examined as well.

Other variables tested included acculturation (using English-speaking ability as a proxy) and demographic variables (age, owner/renter, workplace in/out of Chinatown, and children in the household). Because relocation has been shown to be traumatic to the elderly, it was hypothesized that the desire to move would be inversely related to age.

All variables combined explained a majority of the variance and were statistically significant in predicting the desire to move (see Table 3.2). In terms of individual predictors, the desire to move or stay was significantly predicted by age, income, children, living in the household, and desire to live among other Chinese. Perceptions of dwelling crowding, neighborhood crowding, and neighborhood noise were also positively correlated with the desire to move, although they did not reach significance in the regression analysis.

All things being equal, younger adults wanted to move out of Chinatown more than older adults. It is assumed that younger adults have greater potential opportunity, energy, and aspirations to "move up" in life, while senior citizens, who are more settled and less capable of moving, prefer to accommodate to existing conditions. Having fewer resources and alternatives and being less able to cope with change, the elderly are more vulnerable to the harmful effects of forced relocation.

Poorer residents showed less desire to move, all other things being equal. One of Chinatown's drawing cards is reasonable rent, an especially compelling reason for the poor to stay. Those with greater financial capability anticipate the attainment of a better life and therefore want to leave.

Holding all other variables constant, those without children wanted to stay. Those with children were more desirous to leave; for them, residential

Table 3.2
Analyses for Desired Residential Mobility

"Would you ever want to move out of your neighborhood?"
(1 = yes, 0 = no)

Independent Variables	Standardized Beta Coefficient	F-value	r
Age	-0.3767	19.117***	-.60
Income	0.2903	13.185***	.35
Children in Household (1 = yes, 0 = no)	0.2623	11.099***	.42
Live Among Chinese (1 = v. imp, 4 = not imp.)	0.1680	4.649*	.38
Crowded Dwelling (1 = lots space, 4 = v. crd)	0.1544	3.371	.33
Owner (1 = own, 0 = rent)	0.0670	0.839	.09
Neighborhood Noise (1 = lots, 4 = never)	0.0596	0.529	.42
Neighborhood Crowding (1 = lots space, 4 = v. crowded)	0.0319	0.145	.29
Work Chinatown (1 = yes, 0 = no)	-0.0140	0.032	.03

$$R^2 = 0.5587$$
$$\text{Adjusted } R^2 = 0.5131$$
$$F = 12.2399***$$
$$df = 9,87$$

*$p < .05$.   **$p < .01$.   ***$p < .001$

Note: Weighted data: "Crowded dwelling" is also statistically significant (F = 8.72, p < .01) and level of significance for "live among Chinese" is higher (F = 16.80, p < .001). When "English speaking" and "live among Chinese" are both entered into the regression, neither was significant with the unweighted data, but with weighted data, "live among Chinese" was significant (F = 12.22, p < .001) but not English-speaking.

mobility was an opportunity to secure a higher living standard for their children and a means to provide more living space for them. Many of these residents considered Chinatown a ghetto and a slum. As such, moving out is status-conferring, representing upward mobility toward "the better life."

Those who attributed more importance to living among other Chinese were more interested in staying, all other things being equal. Alternatively, those who attributed less importance to living among other Chinese were less interested in staying. Substituting "English-speaking ability" for "desire to live among Chinese" resulted in a significant effect for language. "Since I can't speak and write English, I have to dwell with Chinese and live in Chinatown and work in Chinese restaurants. I can't step out of Chinatown because I'm afraid that I'll get lost and nobody will help me." "Language problems create a lot of problems like finding a job, going to the doctors or to government agencies." "I can't speak English, so I'm forced to stay in Chinatown all the time."

Perceived environmental stress—namely, a crowded dwelling, crowded neighborhood, and neighborhood noise—were additional variables that were related to the desire to move. However, because they were also correlated with the other predictor variables of life stage, economic status, family size, and need for ethnic homogeneity, they did not reach statistical significance in the regression analysis.

SUMMARY

This chapter has revealed the multiple factors that influence why people live where they live and why they want to move or stay. First, residential location is related to economic fit. Rent is more affordable in Chinatown than in most other San Francisco neighborhoods. Residents can function here without owning a car. Moving out is associated with a change in economic status. Those with higher incomes want to move. The poorest need to stay. The significant effect of income on the desire to move supports the class-based theory of residential location.

But class alone does not explain it all. Preference for ethnic and language homogeneity plays a role in residential location. Even with income held constant, those who attributed greater importance to living among other Chinese showed greater wish to stay. This supports the race-based theory of residential location.

Finally, life stage explained the desire to move. Younger adults showed greater wish to leave; the elderly showed greater wish to stay. Those with children showed greater wish to leave; those without children reported greater wish to stay. The community seems to serve a better fit for elderly and those without children.

With regard to the classic sociological debate between class and race, this research revealed how both factors were powerful determinants. The study also revealed that other variables besides class and race, such as life stage and environmental stress, predicted residential mobility.

Park's theory that ethnic settlements are occupied by immigrants who are less able to compete in the larger society is supported by the data. Chinatown is primarily a first settlement area for newcomers who do not yet have the economic resources or language skill to compete for better jobs and better living conditions. But it is also a residential niche for the elderly, which was a factor that Park did not really consider.

Immigrants, who have difficulties competing in the American mainstream, ease their process of acculturation by locating amidst language and cultural security. But this security exists along with crowding and adverse environmental conditions. As economic, language, and social constraints lessen, the need to live in the ethnic enclave gives way to the desire to move out in order to secure better housing, better opportunities, a better life. The push to leave is greatest among the younger adults and among those whose desire for social-economic mobility or need for more family space outweighs their preference to live among others of their own ethnic group.

Neighborhoods have a powerful tendency to become homogeneous with regard to class, ethnicity, and age. Thus, barring any major changes in housing, rent, immigration, and economics, the population composition of this enclave will become increasingly that of the poor, the elderly, and the immigrant.

One crucial question underlying the race versus class debate is whether socioeconomic mobility implies de-ethnization. The fact that so many Chinatown residents felt it was important to have other Chinese in their neighborhood suggests that the desire for ethnic homogeneity exists, but not at the expense of socioeconomic mobility. The emergence of the "second Chinatown" in the Clement Street area of the Richmond District illustrates the persistence of cultural and ethnic ties in spite of economic and residential mobility. Chinatown residents who can accumulate the capital to become homeowners have moved into the Richmond area, creating a distinct ethnic commercial and residential presence there. This invisible exodus trail between Chinatown and the Richmond District is fueled by socioeconomic mobility coupled with the desire for ethnic homogeneity in one's neighborhood.

In conclusion, this chapter has been devoted to a consideration of Chinatown's endurance, which required us to study the nature of the community and desired residential mobility. Chinatown has survived for various reasons. It serves as a first settlement area for Chinese immigrants—an entry point into American society and a nexus of residence and workplace. It is the focus for cultural identity and continuity of the Chinese language. Consistent with the theory of human ecology, these immigrants locate where the existence of a large population with similar language and culture eases their entry into the American society. For the economically disadvantaged immigrant who does not speak English, Chinatown offers a residence at low rent, bilingual schools for children, and an ethnic labor market where English facility is not required for employment. It is also a convenient place for low-income elderly. The cultural commercial-residential mix and central location make it an extremely convenient place of residence. Chinatown is a prime example of the factors that structural functionalists point to as key to a community's survival.

Chinatown has persisted for yet another reason—because many disadvantaged Chinese immigrants remain disadvantaged and unable to compete successfully in mainstream America. Employed in low-paying, nonadvancing jobs, segregated from the larger labor market, their jobs afford them no opportunity or time to learn English. It is not resistance to assimilation that causes Chinatown to survive, it is necessity—nearly half of the sample said they had little or no choice in their housing. Chinatown is an enclave for Chinese immigrants who have few resources and few choices.

Chinatown San Francisco has also survived because it represents more than language and housing necessity. Residents expressed the desire for ethnic homogeneity of residential location and the desire for cultural and language continuity, factors that are independent of socioeconomic class.

For some, Chinatown is a place to leave as soon as it is economically possible. For others, the community is a place of necessity; they have no hope for a better life. For still others, Chinatown represents cultural comfort, security, and convenience. In its broadest symbolic term, the community is heartland and refuge for Chinese America. Thus, one does not find a population entirely resigned to living here because of necessity, nor an entire population anxiously waiting to exit, nor a residency that is stable due to contentment. Rather, we find all of the above, which explains why there was no unanimity about moving or staying. Indeed, Chinatown is a classic example of the surviving ethnic settlement and the many factors that shape this phenomenon.

NOTE

1. $r = .33$, $p < .001$; $r = .35$, $p < .001$; and $r = -.47$, $p < .001$, respectively.

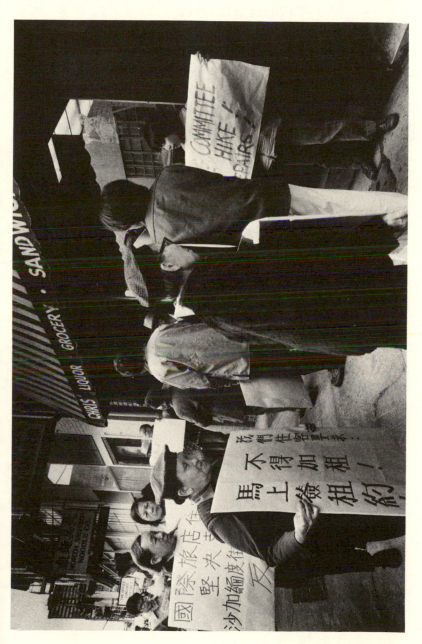

In 1977, these women engaged in a protest against rent hikes. The need for housing affects all Chinese immigrants, for without affordable rent this residential community would die. 1977. (Photograph by Joseph J. Rosenthal, courtesy of the *San Francisco Chronicle*.) Reprinted by permission.

To Start All Over

The building with its carpeted hallways was very well kept up. The elevator brought me to the assigned address. My respondent was in his 70s. His wife, who had difficulty hearing and speaking and whose legs were paralyzed, sat quietly on the sofa. They lived in this building because the elevator was convenient for his wife, who was wheelchair-bound. They resided in Chinatown because, not knowing how to drive, this neighborhood was convenient for shopping.

This man immigrated to the United States at age 19. Life was hard then. He had to start all over again. The education he received in China was useless here. He first worked as a janitor because of problems he had speaking and understanding English. Wiping floors and stairways at the Fairmont Hotel, his muscles were so sore that after one week of work he wanted to quit. To make matters worse, people treated him in a demeaning way. But he reminded himself that success required patience.

This man firmly believed that Chinese are discriminated against in the United States. He had tried to buy a home in Palo Alto but a neighbor objected to having a Chinese next door. This was one of several examples he gave.

Chinatown is getting too crowded with immigrants, he said. They gather here because of insecurity and fear in a foreign land. But due to their apprehension of whites, these Chinese become isolated, an undesirable outcome.

4

Neighborhood Satisfaction: Development versus Preservation

Most low-income ethnic neighborhoods in metropolitan areas inevitably face the threat of development, which can spell an end to existing housing. Chinatown San Francisco is no exception, but the lessons learned here provide a model for other neighborhoods. In 1985 the San Francisco Planning Commission proposed interim controls on Chinatown development in order to retain affordable housing and discourage the spillover of massive development from the adjoining Financial District into the community. The controls called for: (1) height restrictions on new nonresidential buildings higher than 40 feet (buildings in the core area currently average 35 feet, or 3½ stories); (2) additional public hearings for proposed new development projects; (3) a reduction in the floor area ratio (ratio of total floor space to lot area) in core Chinatown from 10:1 to 6:1 and a reduction in the floor area ratio in noncore Chinatown from 6:1 to 4.8:1.[1] Under interim controls, a developer could not construct any residential building higher than six stories in the core area or four stories in the noncore area.

Heated controversy arose. The Chinese Six Companies, other property owners, architects, real estate brokers, and some members of the community protested the proposed restrictions. These pro-development advocates affirmed their desire for "a first-class Chinatown," their freedom "to build to what the property here is worth," and their impatience with "living in a ghetto" (*Asian Week*, 1985, p. 13). In response, Mayor Dianne Feinstein and Planning Director Dean Macris cut the period proposed for these interim controls in half. On the other hand, community groups such as the Chinatown Coalition for Better Housing, Chinatown Resource Center, and Asian Neighborhood Design supported interim controls because of the need to curtail "overly liberal zoning rules that encourage owners to develop properties at the expense of housing" (*East West*, 1985, p. 1).

The controversy between those who favored and those who opposed controlled development raised two questions. First, who more accurately represented the residents and their interests—the Planning Commission and certain community groups or the Chinese Six Companies and pro-development advocates? In the mid to late 1900s, the Chinese Six Companies was empowered to speak and act for all the California Chinese (Chinn, Lai, and Choy, 1969). However, as the Six Companies acquired increasing portions of Chinatown real estate, the organization veered in a politically conservative direction. After the 1960s, community agencies replaced the Six Companies as progressive advocates for the community (Lyman, 1974).

The second question concerned the price of unchecked development. Can property values be maximized without sacrificing housing for low-income and elderly Chinese? What margins of choice exist? Can current residents afford the additional costs required in a "first-class Chinatown"? What effects would uncontrolled commercial development have on the quality of neighborhood life? Chinatown has historic significance as the oldest Chinese community in the United States. What effects would unchecked development have on its ethnic character and community?

Core Chinatowners are a vulnerable population, relatively helpless with regard to housing supply and rent demands; nearly all (97%) are renters, only 3% homeowners, which differs from the noncore area where 68% are renters and 32% homeowners.[2] While noncore residents are less vulnerable, the majority are still rather powerless to control their housing options.

In this chapter, survey data on neighborhood satisfaction and safety are applied to policy questions regarding development. The first section presents results related to the extent to which residents are satisfied with their neighborhood and how this compares with Americans overall. Section two contains findings regarding residents' perceptions of the undesirable and desirable qualities of their neighborhood. Section three contains the findings on the predictors of neighborhood satisfaction, and section four covers the level and predictors of neighborhood safety. In answering the questions of neighborhood satisfaction and safety, this author tests several urban theories. Section five is an abbreviated version of the Master Plan, adopted by San Francisco's Department of City Planning in 1986 two years after the implementation of interim controls. The final section addresses some visible problems that do not bode well for the community's future.

Neighborhood satisfaction is defined in this study as the degree of "fit" or congruence between one's neighborhood aspirations or ideals and one's actual residential circumstances, a definition similar to that put forth by Campbell, Converse, and Rodgers, (1976). Neighborhood satisfaction was measured by using satisfaction scales and by comparing descriptions of an ideal neighborhood with those of the present neighborhood. Using satisfaction scales similar to those used nationally permitted this researcher to compare the neighborhood satisfaction of Chinatown residents with those of a national sample.

LEVEL OF NEIGHBORHOOD SATISFACTION

How satisfied are Chinatown residents with their neighborhood and how does this compare with Americans overall? Chinatown residents were far less satisfied with their neighborhood than U.S. residents were overall (see Table 4.1).[3] On average, white Americans felt "pretty satisfied" with their neighborhood, while Chinatown dwellers felt "neutral" about theirs. Eighty percent of the American sample felt satisfied with their neighborhood compared to only 42% of the Chinatown residents. Close to half of the national sample felt "completely satisfied" with their neighborhood compared to a mere 2% of the Chinatown sample who felt "very satisfied" with theirs. Only 9% of the national American sample felt dissatisfied with their neighborhood compared to 29% of the Chinatown sample.

Campbell et al. (1976) asked a national sample of households from 60 metropolitan areas to describe their neighborhood as "excellent," "good," "fair," or "poor." Of this sample, 38% described their neighborhood as an "excellent" place to live. Chinatown residents evaluated their neighborhood less favorably. Residents were asked to rate their neighborhood in terms of its goodness for elderly, then for children, on a 5-point scale from "very good" to "poor." Only 13% of the Chinatown respondents considered their neighborhood a "very good" place for elderly, and only 4% considered their neighborhood a "very good" place to raise children.

UNDESIRABLE AND DESIRABLE
NEIGHBORHOOD QUALITIES

How do residents assess the undesirable and desirable qualities of their neighborhood? Residents felt that "quiet," "clean," and "uncrowded" describe their ideal neighborhood. These attributes were followed in frequency by location convenience, positive human qualities, natural environment qualities, quality of housing, and quality of services, in decreasing order of mention (see Table 4.2). How does Chinatown measure up to these ideals?

Table 4.1
Neighborhood Satisfaction for Chinatown and the United States

CT: ("How satisfied or dissatisfied are you with the overall living conditions in Chinatown?")

very satisfied	pretty satisfied	slightly satisfied	neutral	slightly dissatisfied	pretty dissatisfied	very dissatisfied
2%	11%	29%	29%	17%	8%	4%

US:[1] ("All things considered, how satisfied or dissatisfied are you with the neighborhood as a place to live?")

1 completely satisfied	2	3	4	5	6	7 completely dissatisfied
46%	21%	13%	11%	4%	2%	3%

1 Campbell, Converse, & Rodgers (1976) national distribution has not been age-adjusted to the age distribution of the Chinatown sample. Chinatown has a greater proportion of elderly and less educated than the national distribution but also a higher proportion of non-whites.

Table 4.2
Qualities of an Ideal Neighborhood

"Thinking about what an ideal neighborhood would be like for you, please tell me what things about it would make it an ideal neighborhood?"

	Frequency of Mentions	Percent of Total Mentions
Environmental Qualities (Quiet, clean, uncrowded)	93	37%
Location Convenience (Close to shops/stores, entertainment, public transportation)	54	21%
Human Qualities (Friendly neighbors, Chinese-speaking, neighborhood homogeneity by class, goals, culture, race, age)	39	15%
Natural Environment (Fresh air, scenic, good weather)	33	13%
Quality of Housing (New homes, lower buildings, larger homes, backyard)	12	5%
Quality of Services ((Lots of parking spaces, community services available)	11	4%
Other (Don't know, low/reasonable rent, don't care)	10	4%
Total	252	99%

Undesirable Neighborhood Qualities

The ideal neighborhood for Chinatown residents was quiet, clean, and uncrowded—qualities not found in Chinatown. Asked "What do you dislike about your neighborhood?" two-thirds of the respondents disliked something about their neighborhood and most often it was its "filth," "crowding," and "noise" (these accounted for 53% of all disliked aspects of the neighborhood that were mentioned). Remarks included: "Not enough space." "Traffic jams." "Parking is impossible." "No usable open space." "No fresh air." "Dirty roads." "Filthy environment." "Garbage in the streets." "Too many people crowded in a small area." "Like a slum, too crowded, not very clean."

"Too crowded and noisy. I don't like living in Chinatown." "Not as safe as before. It's changing all the time. All I see now are tourist places, banks, restaurants, shops." "Overcrowded, too many people in the street, and streets are too noisy and dirty." "What I hate the most is the cable car noise. Move the cable cars. Why don't they put them in front of the president's house—waking everybody up." "What I dislike about this neighborhood is the crowdedness, the filth, the gangs, and the old men spitting in the streets."

"Filth" is largely due to the commercial sector, specifically the tourist and food industries. Congestion in the streets and sidewalks cause restaurants, grocery stores, and meat and fish markets to leave refuse on pedestrian thoroughfares in the evenings.[4] "Air pollution" is directly connected with the traffic attendant to the tourist, restaurant, and commercial businesses.

"Crowding" is due largely to population density. In 1980 the population density of the core area was 744 persons per residential acre, ten times greater than that of San Francisco.[5] The population densities of the residential and expanded areas were four and two times greater than that of the city, respectively.

The daily influx of tourists and shoppers from outside the community exacerbates vehicle congestion and competition for parking spaces. Congested pedestrian traffic adds to the sense of crowding. During the midday of a weekday, over 1,500 persons pass through just one main intersection of Chinatown (the corner of Stockton and Pacific streets) within a 20-minute period, and pedestrian traffic during the weekend is nearly as high (Tudor Engineering, 1979). In 1987, in a move to alleviate sidewalk congestion, Supervisor Tom Hsieh authored legislation forcing peddlers to stop setting up shop on the sidewalks and curbs of Stockton Street, Chinatown's main thoroughfare. The peddlers were moved to spots around the corner on Pacific Avenue (*Asian Week*, 1988).

The noise factor was largely due to traffic, street, and commercial activity and less from uninsulated buildings. Asked how often they heard traffic and street noises, 34% of the Chinatown residents said "a lot of the time," 33% said "sometimes," 19% said "rarely," and 13% said "never." Complaints included: "[It's] noisy at midnight because there are two bars in this alley." "Streets are too noisy." "Traffic noises from outside, up and down the street, bother me when I'm watching TV. I don't want to turn the TV on too high so it will disturb the neighbors but if the sound is too soft, the noises from outside will distract me from hearing the TV." In comparison, half of the residents interviewed did not find noises of their neighbors to be a big problem (22% said they "never" hear neighbor sounds, 31% said they "rarely" hear neighborhood sounds, 29% said "sometimes," and 18% said "a lot of the time").

Adding "traffic jams" and "parking problems" to "filth," "crowding," and "noise" accounted for 64% of all disliked neighborhood attributes. Stockton

Street traffic spells "headache." A Tudor Engineering report (1979) stated: "Vehicle operations . . . can often be described as saturated flow, a stop-and-go situation that is considered to be the worst level of traffic service" (p. 42).

The major problem is traffic congestion, caused largely by city and tourist traffic. Local vehicle use is not a major causal variable. According to the 1980 census, three-quarters of the Asian/Pacific Islanders in core Chinatown and half of the Asian/Pacific Islanders in the noncore area did not own a vehicle.

The placement of the Stockton Street bus stops directly across the street from each other exacerbates congestion. The "30 Stockton," one of the most heavily traveled lines in the city, "turns to molasses as it flows through Chinatown" (*Asian Week,* 1988, p. 16). Congestion results when a northbound Stockton bus stops between Sacramento and Clay streets. Should a southbound bus on that block stop at the same time, traffic grinds to a complete halt in both directions. To alleviate gridlock, Supervisor Hsieh proposed eliminating one of the three bus stops and staggering the remaining two so they would not be directly across from each other.

Available parking is insufficient to accommodate persons from outside the community who are drawn to Chinatown's commercial sector. The search for parking invariably contributes to traffic congestion.

Adding "gangs" and "crime" to the list of disliked neighborhood qualities accounted for 82% of all undesirable traits mentioned. In the 1970s, the crime rate among the Chinese in San Francisco was highlighted by the murder of Barry Fong-Torres (director of a delinquency prevention project) and by the Golden Dragon massacre, in which five persons were killed and 11 wounded. Takagi and Platt (1978) attributed the increased incidence of crime among Chinese Americans relative to other ethnic groups to the increased population of Chinese, the increased proportion of adolescent Chinese, and capitalistic labor exploitation that has broken down family cohesiveness.

Desirable Neighborhood Qualities

Despite Chinatown's undesirable attributes, 90% of the respondents liked at least one aspect of their neighborhood. Chinatown's greatest assets included its "location convenience" and "ethnic quality," which together accounted for 70% of all desirable neighborhood qualities mentioned. "Ethnic quality" refers to Chinatown's racial, cultural, and language homogeneity. Because residents mentioned "location convenience" and "cultural homogeneity" as attributes of an ideal neighborhood, it can be assumed that Chinatown meets these needs. Residents voiced these assets in the following ways: "It's close to shopping. There's good transportation, and since I don't speak English, it's better for me to live here." "Good location, relatively low crime, near relatives, near Asians, accessible to shopping, downtown, transportation, an interesting place to live." "Chinatown belongs to the Chinese. I like to live with Chinese shops around, people to talk to, and it's convenient to see a doctor."

Chinatown's central location within the city makes it "very convenient for everything;" it's close to "shopping," "bus lines," "downtown," "services," "relatives or friends," and "Chinese restaurants." On a 4-point scale, dwellers said their residence was either "very convenient" (73%) or "somewhat convenient" (26%). Only 1% said their neighborhood was "somewhat inconvenient," and no one described it as "very inconvenient."

A vast majority preferred ethnic homogeneity in their neighborhood. Eight out of every ten residents felt it was "very important" or "somewhat important" to have Chinese in their neighborhood. Residents stated: "I want to be close with my people." "Most of the people here are Chinese. I feel more comfortable and close to them."

The necessity of convenient location and ethnic homogeneity stems largely from income, mobility, age, and language limitations, particularly for core Chinatown residents. Due to poverty, immobility, and age, core dwellers are dependent on public transportation and accessible services. Location convenience is essential for ease of life functioning. Eight out of every ten core dwellers do not own a car, twice as many residents as in the noncore area (a statistically significant difference).

For the Chinese-speaking, residence in Chinatown is a function of language necessity combined with preference for ethnic homogeneity. Said one resident, "I have to live here because I'm from Taiwan and my English is poor." Thirty-nine percent of Chinatown residents cannot speak any English, and another 24% speak English "rather poorly." Slightly over half (57%) of the Chinese cannot read English and an additional 8% do so "rather poorly." Overall, nearly seven out of every ten Chinatown dwellers are Chinese language dominant or dependent.

Thus, by virtue of location convenience and ethnic homogeneity, Chinatown is ideal. But its filth, crowding, noise, and traffic congestion make the community unappealing. In terms of neighborhood satisfaction, the balance of assets against liabilities probably accounts for the overall "neutral" rating given to the neighborhood by its residents.

PREDICTORS OF NEIGHBORHOOD SATISFACTION

What factors best explain neighborhood satisfaction? Analyzing the determinants of neighborhood satisfaction permits us to answer the question of why residents feel satisfied and dissatisfied. Three theoretical orientations—the urban scale, compositional, and quality-of-local-conditions—were tested in this process.

The urban scale theory, espoused by Lee and Guest (1983), presumes that increases in population size and density negatively affect neighborhood satisfaction. Core Chinatown has a higher population density and more commercial intrusion than noncore Chinatown. Consequently, this research hypothesized that core dwellers would be less satisfied with their neighborhood than noncore dwellers.

The compositional perspective, as put forth by Gans (1962), explains neighborhood satisfaction according to dweller characteristics. Normally, dweller characteristics include age, income, gender, children in the household, living alone or with others, and renter/owner status. Campbell, Converse, and Rodgers (1976) found that neighborhood satisfaction increased with age, a phenomenon that Simon (1955) attributed to the closing gap between aspiration and reality with age, which was due to either realized aspiration with age or a realistic reduction in aspiration. In this study, two other variables were added: English-speaking ability and self-reported social class.[6]

The quality of life perspective, described by Fernandez and Kulik (1981), Lee (1981), and Marans and Rodgers (1974), explains neighborhood satisfaction in terms of the influence of local conditions. Local conditions tested in this survey included: neighborhood crowding, neighborhood safety, neighborhood noise, and neighbor acquaintanceship.

These theoretical perspectives were conceptual guides by which to organize the variables. They were not intended to be mutually exclusive. In reality, the perspectives overlap, particularly in low-income immigrant communities. For example, high density areas (urban scale) where the poor reside (compositional) are more likely to have run-down housing, unclean streets, noise, and congestion (quality of local conditions).

Results of a multiple regression analysis for neighborhood satisfaction were statistically significant (Table 4.3). Together, the variables tested explained nearly half of the variance. Individual variables that predicted neighborhood satisfaction included age, core/noncore residency, and neighborhood crowding.

Among Chinatown adults, neighborhood satisfaction increased with age, a trend that parallels national surveys. This one compositional variable predicted neighborhood satisfaction, whereas the other compositional variables—income, gender, children in household, living alone, owner/renter, English-speaking ability, and social class—did not.

High population density along with high commercial intrusion was significantly related to lower levels of neighborhood satisfaction. Core dwellers were less satisfied with their neighborhood than noncore dwellers, holding all other variables constant. This finding supports the urban scale theory.

Residents who did not perceive their neighborhood as crowded were more satisfied with their neighborhood than those who perceived their neighborhood as crowded, all other things being equal. Perception of neighborhood as safe and home ownership were also correlated with neighborhood

Table 4.3
Analyses for Neighborhood Satisfaction

"How do you feel about your neighborhood? Do you feel very satisfied, somewhat satisfied, not too satisfied, or not satisfied at all?" (1 = "very satisfied" and 4 = "not satisfied at all")

Independent Variable	Standardized Beta Coefficient	F-value	r
Age (A41)	-0.380	13.93***	-.43
Core/Noncore (1 = core, 0 = noncore)	0.313	10.74**	.30
Neighborhood Crowding (A33) (1 = lots space, 4 = v. crowded)	0.190	3.98*	.37
Owner (1 = own, 0 = rent)	-0.154	2.36	-.30
Neighborhood Safety (A30) (1 = completely safe, 4 = not safe at all)	0.143	2.63	.30
Social Class (1 = upper, 5 = lower)	-0.119	1.69	-.08
Neighbor Acquaintance (A25) (1 = very well)	0.111	1.55	.23
Neighborhood Noise (B14) (1 = lot, 4 = never)	-0.109	1.21	-.26
English-Speaking (1 = Eng spk, 0 = not)	-0.107	1.05	.18
Live Alone (1 = live alone, 0 = not)	-0.106	1.19	-.14
Income	0.099	0.86	.16
Gender (1 = male, 0 = female)	-0.096	0.97	.05
Children in Household (1 = kids, 0 = none)	-0.088	0.81	.17

$$R^2 = 0.476$$
$$\text{Adjusted } R^2 = 0.393$$
$$F = 5.723^{***}$$
$$df = 13, 82$$

*p < .05.   **p < .01.   ***p < .001

Note: Using weighted data, four other variables were also significant: social class (p < .01), live alone (p < .05), know neighbor acquaintance (p < .05), and owner (p < .05).

satisfaction, although their correlations with the significant predictor variables meant they did not reach statistical significance in the regression analyses.

In summary, age, population density, and perceived neighborhood crowding were significant predictors of neighborhood satisfaction. Neighborhood satisfaction was therefore related to a combination of external and internal variables: urban scale, life stage of the resident, perceived neighborhood conditions, and home ownership.

LEVEL AND PREDICTORS OF NEIGHBORHOOD SAFETY

On a four-point scale from "completely safe" to "not safe at all," three-quarters of the dwellers felt that their neighborhood was safe. Specifically,

6% of the sample felt the neighborhood was "completely safe," 70% felt it was "usually safe," 21% thought it was "not too safe," and 2% said it was "not safe at all."

What variables best explain why residents do or do not feel safe in their neighborhood? One theory is that safety is a function of the degree to which residents feel anonymity in an urban environment; this is referred to as the urban anonymity theory. Advanced by Simmel (1950), Toennies (1957), and Wirth (1938), the urban anonymity theory proposed that persons in large urban areas feel more anonymous than persons who do not live in large urban areas. In our study, I hypothesized that urban anonymity can be (1) environmentally induced (e.g., from living in high density areas, in large multi-unit structures, rental of residence, perceived neighborhood crowding, or floor level), and/or (2) experienced as personal vulnerability or lack of protection (e.g., confidence in police protection, confidence in neighbor intervention in times of trouble, neighbor acquaintance, and neighbor friendliness) and/or (3) related to individual characteristics that might relate to feelings of vulnerability (e.g., living alone, age, gender, income, social class, English-speaking ability, number of children in the household). This survey permitted us to test the influence of these variables. Previous research by Newman (1972) found that the highest crime rates occurred in housing structures with the largest number of units and the poorest surveillance design. Newman's findings demonstrated the effects that physical environment had on feeling unsafe in one's neighborhood.

Results of the multiple regression analysis for neighborhood safety were statistically significant. The combined variables explained roughly 40% of the variance (see Table 4.4). In terms of individual variables, confidence in police protection and number of units in the building were significant predictors of perceptions of neighborhood safety. Of these two predictors, police protection was the more powerful. The lower their confidence in police protection, the less safe residents felt, all other variables being equal. Dwellers in larger multi-unit structures felt less safe in their neighborhood than dwellers in smaller-unit structures, all other variables held constant. This finding lends support to the urban anonymity theory and is consistent with Newman's finding.

Confidence in neighbor intervention, home ownership, and gender were also correlated with perceived neighborhood safety, but their simultaneous correlations with the significant predictor variables meant they did not reach statistical significance in the regression analyses. Residents who had more confidence in neighbor helpfulness, those who owned their home, and men reported feeling safer in their neighborhood than women, renters, or those with less confidence in neighbor altruism.

Apparently, feelings of safety in this neighborhood are most strongly predicted by feelings of protection by the city police. The city's effort in the 1980s to increase recruitment of bilingual/bicultural Chinese Americans on

Table 4.4
Analyses for Neighborhood Safety

"How safe do you think your neighborhood is? Is it completely safe, usually safe, not too safe, or not safe at all?" (1 = "completely safe" and 4 = "not safe at all")

Independent Variable	Standardized Beta Coefficient	F-value	r
Police Protection (A32) (1 = very good, 5 = not good at all)	0.374	9.867**	.43
Units in Building	0.250	3.762*	.23
Neighbor Intervention (A31) (1 = very likely, 4 = very unlikely)	0.219	2.882	.25
Owner (1 = owner, 0 = renter)	-0.177	2.301	-.27
Gender (1 = male, 0 = female)	0.189	2.033	.27
Neighbor Friendliness (A26)	-0.124	0.721	.03
English-Speaking (1 = Eng spk, 0 = not)	0.117	0.731	.23
Social Class (1 = upper, 5 = lower)	-0.106	0.781	.03
Floor	-0.106	0.606	-.02
Core	0.089	0.456	.14
Live Alone	-0.081	0.346	-.07
Age	0.081	0.365	-.17
Neighborhood Crowding (A33) (1 = lots space)	0.074	0.362	.18
Income	0.059	0.148	.12
Neighbor Acquaintance (A25) (1 = very well)	-0.037	0.063	.02
Children in Household	0.011	0.009	.05

$$R^2 = 0.417$$
$$\text{Adjusted } R^2 = 0.253$$
$$F = 2.543**$$
$$df = 16, 57$$

*$p < .05$.   **$p < .01$.   ***$p < .001$

Note: Using weighted data, four additional variables were significant--age, English-speaking, children in household, and owner of dwelling ($p < .05$). Residents who owned their dwelling felt safer in their neighborhood than those who rented, probably because home ownership provides a greater sense of control over one's physical environment and therefore less anonymity (it is a proxy for better housing and therefore better security) and ownership provides a sense of environmental identity, the antithesis of anonymity. Those with children in their household were less likely to feel safe in their neighborhood than those without children. Older residents felt less safe than younger adults, and English-speaking residents felt less safe than non-English speaking residents.

the force and to offer Chinatown merchants greater anonymity—and, thus, protection in cases of extortion by youth gangs—can be assumed to be important inroads to residents' sense of neighborhood safety. Also, while large multi-unit structures add needed housing to this already crowded community, a major drawback is that size of structure impacts feelings of safety of its residents. Thus, in planning for a sense of neighborhood safety, both environmental planning and police presence are vital.

In summary, findings supported the urban anonymity theory with both physical and social aspects predicting feelings of neighborhood safety. Living in large multi-unit buildings and lack of confidence in police protection significantly explained feeling unsafe in one's neighborhood.

THE CHINATOWN MASTER PLAN

In 1987 the Chinatown Master Plan was adopted (San Francisco Department of City Planning, 1987). The designers of the plan developed their objectives from data obtained from our Chinatown survey and from opinions raised in community forums, reactions to issue papers, and attempts to formulate compromises between community factions. The objectives of the plan were consistent with respondents' attitudes. The plan represented a model aimed at preserving the area's character, scale, residential value, neighborhood-serving commercial base, and multiple roles. There were seven objectives to the Master Plan.

Objective 1 was to preserve the distinctive urban character, physical environment, and cultural heritage of Chinatown. Policies aimed at implementing this objective included: (1) maintaining the low rise scale of Chinatown's buildings because 75% of the structures in Chinatown are three stories or less in height; (2) promoting a building form that harmonizes with the scale of existing buildings and the width of Chinatown's streets, because Chinatown is primarily composed of small-scale buildings that are relatively short in depth, the typical lot size being 3,500 square feet; (3) retaining Chinatown's sunny, windfree environment, which requires setback requirements for various streets and retaining lower height buildings; and (4) protecting the historic and aesthetic resources of Chinatown. There are over 250 historically and/or architecturally important buildings that date from Chinatown's early post-earthquake years. Insensitive alteration and dramatic shifts in scale threaten the character of the area.

Objective 2 involved retaining and reinforcing Chinatown's mutually supportive functions as neighborhood, capital city, and visitor attraction. Chinatown has three major roles: (1) a residential neighborhood with its own language and newspapers, groceries, fish and meat markets, and small shops; (2) a capital city and center of civic, religious, political, and social service organizations, as well as a specialized shopping center for the larger Chinese population of the Bay Area; and (3) a destination for most visitors to the city, where many Chinatown restaurant and gift store enterprises have a strong tourist trade.

Objective 3 was to stabilize and, where possible, increase the supply of housing. Policies to accomplish this objective included: (1) conserving existing housing because Chinatown's 6,500 housing units, with their moderate rent, are a virtually irreplaceable housing resource; (2) increasing the supply of housing through new zoning controls that insure that a substantial part of new buildings will consist of housing; and (3) seismically upgrading unreinforced masonry buildings without imposing undue financial burdens or permanent displacement of residents. Demolition of housing units should be allowed only if that is the sole way to protect public safety or if it is for a specific use for which there is a high degree of community need. Low-cost housing removed by new development should be replaced on a unit-for-unit basis and adequate relocation assistance for all displaced persons should be assured.

Objective 4 involved preserving the urban role of Chinatown as a residential neighborhood through policies that would protect and enhance the neighborhood-serving character of commercial uses in predominantly residential areas; controlling proliferation of uses that tend to crowd out needed neighborhood services; guiding a location of tourist-oriented uses away from predominantly residential neighborhood commercial areas; and expanding open space opportunities.

Objective 5 involved retaining and enhancing Chinatown's role as a visitor attraction by maintaining Grant Avenue as the traditional retailing area since an estimated one-third of the 20,000 jobs in Chinatown are related to visitors.

Objective 6 involved retaining Chinatown's role as a capital city; center of civic, religious, and political organizations; and a specialized shopping area for the larger Chinese population of the Bay Area. Policies that would advance this objective included incentives for the location and expansion of institutions and cultural facilities and provision for modest expansion of community business offices related to its capital city role.

Objective 7 was to manage transportation impacts to stabilize or reduce the difficulties of walking, driving, delivering goods, parking, or using transit in Chinatown through policies that would implement measures responsive to pedestrian needs such as scramble system intersections, increased duration of walk signals, and limits on auto use in alleys. Other measures included (1) making bus routes more reflective of and responsive to Chinatown ridership, including bilingual signage, schedules, and maps; (2) improving and increasing parking enforcement; (3) increasing public parking opportunities and setting rates to discourage long-term parking; (4) minimizing truck loading/unloading conflicts; and (5) implementing concentrated commercial loading zones and uniform truck delivery schedules.

THE FUTURE OF CHINATOWN

Unfortunately, the adoption of the Chinatown Master Plan did not eliminate the problems of Chinatown's future. In 1989 the face of Chinatown was visibly altered by the proliferation of tourist T-shirt shops, primarily owned or leased by non-Chinese. On Grant Avenue and Jackson Street, a T-shirt shop replaced what was once the "Italian Market," where Chinese roast ducks, squabs, *char siu* (roast pork), and chickens were sold. The new shop was so transient in appearance that the Italian Market sign had not yet been removed.

Cheap T-shirt stores dot the face of Chinatown—one on Washington Street across from Portsmouth Square, two on Grant Avenue and Washington Street, two on Grant Avenue near Clay Street, and one on Grant Avenue and Pacific Street. Camera and electronics stores also mar the ethnic character of the community; "Camera Express," "1 Hour Photo," and "Japan-U.S.A. Europe Connection" signs are obtrusive against the surrounding ethnic businesses.

Among its objectives, the Master Plan called for "retaining the urban role of Chinatown as a residential neighborhood" along with "retaining and enhancing Chinatown's role as a visitor attraction." The plan called for locating tourist-oriented uses away from predominantly residential neighborhood areas and maintaining Grant Avenue as the traditional specialty retailing area. The problem is that specialty retailing stores that cater to tourists can vary, ranging from stores that retail items of Chinese character to those that retail items of no cultural relevance. The proliferation of the latter saps Chinatown of its distinctive ethnic character, deprives the Asian American community of culturally appropriate retailing stores, and destroys ethnic consistency in the area.

The delicate balance needed to preserve Chinatown while also providing better housing presents another dilemma. The city's Landmark Advisory Board has recommended that all of Chinatown be declared a historic district. Most of the buildings, erected to house the early Chinese immigrants, are standing monuments to that history. At the same time, there is need for more and better housing, which often requires the demolition of existing buildings. Compatibility of housing needs and preservation needs, or some balance between the two, is the crucial goal that this and many other ethnic communities must achieve if they are to survive.

SUMMARY

Chinatown residents were much less satisfied with their neighborhood than residents in U.S. neighborhoods overall. Twenty-nine percent of the Chinatown sample were dissatisfied with their neighborhood compared to only 9% of a national sample. Only 42% of the Chinatown sample were satisfied with their neighborhood compared to 80% of the nation. Chinatown has the positive attributes of location convenience and cultural homogeneity.

But its other attributes of being dirty, crowded, noisy, and congested make the neighborhood far from ideal.

If this community is to thrive and survive, there is little margin for planning error. Considering how low neighborhood satisfaction is, attention must be focused on retaining those conditions that lead to neighborhood satisfaction while ameliorating those that cause dissatisfaction.

Residents who live in core Chinatown, where population density is greatest, were less satisfied with their neighborhood than residents living in the less dense, noncore area. One can deduce that development that leads to increased population density and perceived neighborhood crowding will lower the level of neighborhood satisfaction. Furthermore, since the core area is a mixed commercial-residential area, increased commercial zoning is likely to exacerbate Chinatown's unattractive environmental qualities of noise, dirt, and traffic congestion. The result of unplanned development will be a less livable, more stressful neighborhood for those who have little choice in housing.

Compared to younger adults, the elderly were more satisfied with living in Chinatown. However, this satisfaction can be expected to decline with increased density or commercial intrusion, while the dissatisfaction of younger adults will intensify. For younger adults, dissatisfaction may reach intolerable proportions contained only by the constraints of "no alternatives."

Although three-fourths of the respondents perceived Chinatown as safe, development that increases residential building density can be expected to lower residents' sense of neighborhood safety, all other things being equal. Police efforts to continue recruitment of Chinese Americans on their force and to increase their protective presence in this neighborhood will help to reduce residents' sense of vulnerability.

The pro-development perspective does not reflect the views of the majority of residents. The allowance of affordable error is small. Height and density limits and commercial zoning controls are necessary to preserve the residential community. Furthermore, efforts are needed to bolster resident confidence in the city police as protectors of the neighborhood.

Development of the community into a first-class Chinatown could easily transform the area into a commercial tourist center. Development at high market rates would eliminate Chinatown's ethnically homogeneous residential base by displacing Chinese immigrants and elderly. Low-income residents would be forced out by rising rents, condominium conversions, or commercial takeovers of residential areas.

Once an ethnic residential community, San Francisco's Japantown now functions largely as a commercial and tourist center. Chinatown will follow suit if a large population of Chinese immigrants are displaced from the community. Without controls on development, there may well be a loss of home and community to thousands of Chinese immigrants.

There are lessons here for other cities and other neighborhoods, for it is unlikely that the findings in this neighborhood differ much from others. Neighborhoods that serve important functions need a Master Plan if they are to be preserved, for one cannot rely on the invisible hand of the market to protect an area's ethnic character, scale, residential value to its current residents, neighborhood-serving base, and multiple roles. Indeed, this case example demonstrates that even with the highly detailed Master Plan designed by the San Francisco Department of City Planning, the nearly instant proliferation of retail stores that destroy ethnic consistency, dilute the ethnic character, and reduce the overall quality of an area were not curtailed.

On the issue of development versus preservation, uncontrolled development without planning has costs. Its costs are neighborhood satisfaction and, ultimately, the survival of the residential ethnic community.

NOTES

1. Barring other restrictions—such as setback requirements—a developer could, under the previous floor area ratio rules, construct a 10-story building over the whole lot or a 20-story building over half the lot in core Chinatown and a 6-story building over a lot in noncore Chinatown.

2. Differences between the core and noncore areas were statistically significant.

3. The national data were taken from the Campbell et al. (1976) survey. Both the national survey and the Chinatown survey used seven-point satisfaction scales, but the questions were phrased slightly differently. The distribution for the national survey has not been age-adjusted to the age distribution of the Chinatown sample. Campbell et al. (1976) found greater neighborhood satisfaction among the elderly, the less educated, whites, and married persons. Chinatown has a greater proportion of elderly and less educated than the national distribution of Americans, but Chinatown's population is primarily non-white with a higher proportion of unmarried.

4. Community efforts to clean up the streets have met with some success, but the problem remains. In the 1960s several cleanup campaigns were waged to control the deluge of garbage and litter. The Chinatown Litter Control Committee, working in conjunction with a citywide campaign, installed new, large cans on street corners and posted bilingual signs urging use of the litter cans for a more beautiful city. In 1977 the staff of a Comprehensive Employment and Training Act (CETA)-funded Chinatown Beautification Project swept sidewalks, tore down posters plastered on walls, painted lamp posts, and put "Make Chinatown Beautiful" posters in storefront windows; and lately, the Chinatown Litter Control Project is trying to introduce a street trash compactor.

5. Residential acreage does not cover secondary residential use (where housing is located above ground floor commercial activity). Since there are buildings in Chinatown where housing is located above ground floor commercial space, population

density based on total acreage may be a more valid indicator of actual population density, but, unfortunately, it underestimates actual population density because not all upper floors of commercial acreage are residentially used.

6. "Social class" was intended to be differentiated from "income," the former being a measure of aspired class, the latter a measure of actual financial resources.

These two Vietnamese Chinese families live in a five by eight foot room. They are part of a larger family of eighteen persons who occupy three rooms in this residential hotel. These women's parents were born and raised in China but moved to North Vietnam as fishermen during the civil war. After the war, they returned to China only to face the Japanese invasion. They escaped by boat to South Vietnam, then migrated to Thailand, then Guam, and on to Louisiana, where they worked on a dairy farm. Alarmed to find all nine of their working family members were together paid only $700 a month for 16-hour work days, they left for San Francisco. 1976. (Photograph by Pok-Chi Lau.) Reprinted by permission.

Noisy, Crowded Neighborhood

The address was on upper Grant. I crossed the Broadway strip, a culture of nudity so distinct from the Chinatown society. I walked through a street girdled with parked cars and suffocating buildings rising to either side of me.

The assigned address was situated between a bar and a hardware store. Four mailboxes marked this three-story building. Unable to go beyond the iron gate, I wrote a note to leave for my potential respondent. A young boy curiously observed me as he entered the locked front door. An elderly woman held out her hand, offering to deliver the note for me.

That evening, the resident called the office. We parried back and forth over a day and time to meet. His work hours being so irregular, he didn't know from day to day what his next day's schedule would be. And, he's "pretty busy." Finally, he offered to meet me that night at 8 p.m. I walked hurriedly around sex-act barkers, darting around lights of moving cars that glittered the congested streets.

This is a single, American-born male in his 30s, living with his mother, who is in her 70s. His father died when he was one year old. His mother, unable to speak English, was forced to work as a seamstress in a sweatshop. He distinctly recalled the repeated nights she brought work home.

This man disliked the tourists, outsiders, and winos that frequented the businesses in his "noisy, very crowded" neighborhood. "Not satisfied at all" with his surroundings, he wanted to move to a place of "peace and quiet." Neighbor and street noises bothered him. With resignation, he stayed because of the language barrier and the inconvenience that a move would pose for his mother. He felt he had little choice in housing.

This man worked as a grocery clerk in a white-owned department store. His irregular work schedule and night work hours nearly preclude any social or personal life. He has little time to see even his own mother.

This man felt "very comfortable" with American-born Chinese, Japanese Americans, blacks, Chicanos, and whites, but felt "pretty uncomfortable" with Chinese immigrants. He compared his life favorably to white Americans and Chinatown residents. Compared to whites, he felt that Chinese have a better upbringing. Compared to Chinatown residents, he felt his life had greater diversity. Yet he was dissatisfied with many things—his junior college education, his working conditions, his living environment, the inadequate community services, and his lack of leisure time and a personal life.

5

Crowding: Perceptions, Attitudes, and Consequences

Communities have salient defining qualities. Chinatown San Francisco is no exception. "Chinese" defines its social and cultural distinctiveness, "crowding" its environmental reputation. From the late nineteenth century, white observers were both awed and appalled at Chinatown's crowdedness, where "from four to ten [persons lived] in the space that one American would regard as essential to his health and comfort" (Report of the Senate Committee on Chinese and Chinese Immigration, 1887, p. 4). The San Francisco Health Officer's Report for 1869–1870 described Chinatown conditions in this way: "Apartments that would be termed small for the accommodation of a single [white] American are occupied by six, eight, or ten Chinese, with seeming indifference to all ordinary comforts. . . . the majority of them live crowded together . . . like so many cattle" (*Chinese Press*, in Yu, 1981, p. 97).

Chinatown residents were characterized as persons who "apparently delight to exist in their more dense conditions of nastiness" (Farwell, 1885, p. 4. "It is almost their universal custom to herd together as compactly as possible. [Having been] trained in centuries of stifling gregariousness . . . they like crowds and clamor and elbow-jostling" (Dobie, 1936, pp. 6–7). Overcrowding in the workshops and sleeping rooms was called "the great bane of the Chinese" (Editorial, in Coolidge, 1909, p. 415).

McLeod (1948) observed that despite the fact that "crowded conditions were universal in the Chinese Quarter," the Chinese appeared no less physically healthy than whites. "They seemed to think . . . that every cubic foot of space must be economically utilized and profitably occupied. A family of five or six persons would occupy a single room . . . apparently comfortable, and showing no sign of being cramped by the narrow limits that confined them" (p. 128). Noting that two or three Chinese businesses might occupy the same room, McLeod remarked on how the Chinese worked together "in utmost harmony" (p. 130). In these earlier years, only Dobie (1936) suggested that Chinatown crowding might be due to something other than cultural predilection. His statement that the Chinese "had to conserve space, conserve funds, conserve time" (p. 7) suggested that economic constraints caused this need to conserve.

Depicting conditions in the 1960s, Wolfe (1969) portrayed a Chinatown adolescent's reactions to white American living standards:

It was really the whole high school scene that first made you think about your father and your family and Chinatown in relation to the white status system. White kids might invite you over to their house or their apartment some afternoon—and you'd think these white kids must be millionaires. The *space* they lived in! Everybody had his own bedroom. They had dining rooms that weren't used for anything except meals! It was incredible . . . . Then you would find out that the kid's father was nothing but an insurance salesman or a construction foreman. This was just the way ordinary whites lived. It seemed like almost every kid in Chinatown had grown up in a household where everybody and everything was crowded into two or three little rooms. If a family has a twelve-by-twelve foot square of open floor space, that was *Sunset* magazine stuff by Chinatown standards.

Even today, most of the Hong Kong immigrants can't afford anything more. . . . Father, mother, two children, and the grandmother are crowded into a couple of little rooms. . . . There are twenty or thirty rooms to a floor and one bathroom and one kitchen. Fifteen families . . . on one floor . . . take turns doing the simplest things. They stand in line in the morning to go to the bathroom, holding their towels, toothpaste, toothbrush, razor, or whatever, in their hands and shuffle forward in the gloom to the tubercular beat of the toilet flushing. . . . A lot of people take turns sleeping "hot bedding," sleeping shifts. (p. 194)

THEORY, POPULATIONS, AND CULTURE

In the 1930s and 1940s, the Chicago School of Sociology pioneered a theoretical framework for crowding as part of a larger study on the effects of urbanization, poverty, and cultural patterns of cities. Plant (1937/1966) led the early inquiry into the effects of crowding. Wirth (1938) took this investigation further and theorized that urban crowding was related to psychological stress and social conflict.

In the 1970s and 1980s, empirical studies of crowding were generally detached from sociological theory, and disadvantaged populations were largely ignored. Social scientists (Baldessare, 1979; Booth and Cowell, 1976; Choldin, 1978; Freedman, 1975) who maintained that crowding was of no real harm had not examined the effects of crowding on vulnerable populations. Loo (1978) admonished crowding researchers for ignoring the poor, powerless, institutionalized, and minority populations, for in her view, social relevance made it imperative that researchers investigate the impact of crowding on the less advantaged. Simultaneously, Mitchell (1971) argued for greater attention to the study of high density in natural settings.

There has been no consensus on the cultural universality of crowding attitudes. Jacobs (1961) argued that "everyone hates crowding," but her view has not been shared by those who contend that the Chinese do not value space or suffer ill effects from crowding. Assertions similar to those made about San Francisco Chinatown residents have been made about the Hong Kong Chinese. Anderson (1972) suggested that the Hong Kong Chinese place little value on space: "Most of this crowding was voluntary [since] many of its richer citizens could have afforded far more space than they had. . . . The response to having a larger house has been not to give more space to each individual but to bring more individuals into the space" (p. 143).

Reacting to queries about the limited size of Hong Kong apartments, a construction supervisor stated that tenants there would sublet half of their floor space if contractors doubled the square footage of the apartments (American Institute of Planners Newsletter, 1967). Schmidt, Goldman, and Feimer (1976) assumed that Hong Kong Chinese had a cultural predilection for crowding—"a remarkable affinity for close quarters . . . which they ascribed partly to a natural gregariousness and partly to an inability to pay the transportation costs implicit in reduced densities" (p. 216).

Anderson (1972) surmised that even the most extreme crowding (among Hong Kong Chinese) did not lead to any particular increase in social stress. Schmitt (1963) concluded that the Chinese showed a "successful tolerance for high densities and overcrowding" (p. 216). Finally, Baldessare (1979) suggested that "the social and economic characteristics of some cultures make them better suited to function at high population densities" (p. 25).

Speculations about Chinese attitudes toward crowding have never been empirically tested. Claims have been based on outsider impressions, not on the voiced attitudes of the Chinese themselves. Thus, survey research in Chinatown brings data to bear on the debate concerning the cultural determinism of crowding attitudes and effects. The survey method provides for direct inquiry of environmental users, which Sommer (1969) considered the most valid measure of environmental effects. Similarly, Harrison and Howard (1972) noted that residents' perceptions of their environment are as important if not more important than the physical environment itself.

THE NATURE OF CROWDING AND DENSITY

Because researchers have not adequately investigated the nature of crowding, this investigation also examined the following: (1) differences in crowding attitudes and perceived benefits between primary and secondary environments; (2) predictors of crowding perceptions and attitudes; and (3) social and nonsocial determinants of perceived crowding. Hawley (1972) expressed surprise that few studies had explored differences between primary environments (homes) and secondary environments (neighborhoods), despite directives to assess residents' perceptions of assets and liabilities associated with these settings. Stokols (1972) suspected that crowding in the home leads to more stress and conflict than crowding in the neighborhood, and Baldessare (1979) postulated that residents attribute benefits to a crowded neighborhood but not to a crowded household. To test these hypotheses, this study examined the positive and negative attributes of crowding at the home and neighborhood levels. To evaluate the predictors of crowding perceptions, this study explored the following: (1) the relationship between subjective and objective indicators of crowding; (2) the relationship between need for space, persons per room, and the perception of crowding; and (3) which variables best explained the perception of crowding.

In this study, "density" was defined as an objective index. "Dwelling density" was measured by persons per room, and "population density" was measured by persons per acre. "Dwelling crowding" was defined as residents' perceptions of crowding in their dwelling, and "neighborhood crowding" was defined as residents' perceptions of crowding in their neighborhood. Deviation from these definitions was made only when citing the Census Bureau's unique indices.

Attitudes toward crowding refer to the extent to which one likes or dislikes crowding, that is, the values (positive or negative) assigned to crowding. Perceptions of crowding, on the other hand, refer to either the level of density at which an individual judges a situation to be crowded or the extent to which a setting is judged to be crowded or uncrowded.

The first section of this chapter contains the data on the density characteristics of Chinatown. Sections two and three contain a presentation of historical information on Chinatown crowding and survey results on crowding attitudes, respectively; both of these provide data to test a prevailing notion that crowding in Chinatown was due to cultural preference. Section four contains a test of the theory of environmental adaptation. Section five contains findings on the effects of crowding. The final section examines the nature and meaning of crowding and density through inquiry into primary and secondary environments, predictors of neighborhood crowding, analyses of the meaning of dwelling crowding, predictors of dwelling crowding, and the nonsocial and social components of dwelling crowding.

DENSITY CHARACTERISTICS OF CHINATOWN

By various indices, Chinatown is crowded. Greater Chinatown's population density of 240 persons per residential acre is enormously greater than the 35 persons-per-residential acre designation of a very dense neighborhood made by Baldessare (1979). The densities of each of the Chinatown subareas were greater than the city as a whole. In 1980, core Chinatown's population density of 186 persons per acre was six times greater than San Francisco's density. The population densities of the residential and expanded areas, 116 persons and 111 persons per acre, respectively, were both four times greater than San Francisco's (see Table 5.1).[1]

The preponderance of multi-unit residential buildings in the area creates much of the high density. In 1970, buildings containing five or more units accounted for 90% of the residential structures in core Chinatown. The percentage of units of the same size in residential and expanded Chinatown were 73% and 67%, respectively, as compared to 45% in San Francisco overall. In that same year, buildings containing 50 or more units accounted for roughly one-fourth of all the residential structures in core Chinatown, 20% in residential Chinatown, and 10% in the expanded area, as compared to 10% in San Francisco overall. There was a statistically significant difference in building size for core and noncore residents.[2] Core Chinatown residents lived in buildings that averaged 18 units, while noncore residents resided in buildings that averaged nine units (half this size). This compares with the 1980 city-wide average of four or less units per building. From 1970 to 1980, larger multi-unit structures replaced smaller ones in the core area. In 1980 the proportion of core area housing units in structures of 50 or more units jumped to 51%, a twofold increase over one decade.[3]

The proportions of dwellings that were crowded in core and residential Chinatown were higher than for San Francisco overall. Using the census index of 1.01 or more persons per room as the measure of "overcrowding," 31% of the dwellings in core Chinatown, 26% of the dwellings in residential Chinatown, and 7% of the dwellings in expanded Chinatown were "overcrowded" in 1980. The proportion of core Chinatown dwellings that were overcrowded (31%) was over four times greater than that of San Francisco (7%). The proportion of overcrowded dwellings in expanded Chinatown was comparable to that of the city overall.

Using the Census Bureau's index of 1.51 or more persons per room as the measure of "very overcrowded," 19% of the dwellings in core Chinatown, 15% of those in residential Chinatown, and 4% of those in the expanded area were "very overcrowded" in 1980, compared to 4% for San Francisco overall.

Between 1970 and 1980, dwelling crowding rose in the core and residential areas, while the expanded area, more parallel to the city as a whole, saw minimal fluctuation. From 1970 to 1980, dwelling "overcrowding" rose 5%

Table 5.1
Population Density in San Francisco Chinatown for 1970 and 1980

	1970 Population	Net Acreage	1970 Residential Net Acreage	1970 Density Per Net Acreage	1970 Density Per Residential Acreage	1980 Population	1980 Density Per Net Acreage[1]
Core	9,124	40	10	228	912	7,439	186
Residential[1]	22,429	184	78	122	288	21,389	116
Expanded[1]	24,460	204	137	120	179	22,681	111
	56,013	428	225	----	----	51,509	----
San Francisco	715,674	22,601	9,037	32	79	678,974	30

Source for 1970 data: Chinatown 1970 Census, San Francisco Department of City Planning, 1972.

Note: Residential net acreage was not calculated for 1980 by City Planning, although impressions are that it was reduced in the core area.

1 City Planning defines residential Chinatown to include the core area and defines expanded Chinatown to include the residential and core areas. However, for the calculations of this table and the analyses and sampling of this survey, the three areas are considered to be exclusive of each other.

in the core area and 10% in the residential area. The expanded area saw no change. In comparison, in 1970 the percentages of "overcrowded" dwellings in San Francisco as a whole, all central city households, and in all U.S. households were 7%, 8.5%, and 8.2%, respectively.

From 1970 to 1980, the percentage of "very overcrowded" dwellings rose 1% in the core area, 15% in the residential area, and 1% in the expanded area.

Crowding was not due to household size. The average persons-per-room ratios in core and noncore Chinatown were 1.28 and 1.19, respectively, a difference that was not statistically significant. Of those interviewed, 45% lived in dwellings with 1.01 or more persons per room. Of those who lived with others, 59% lived in dwellings with 1.01 or more persons per room.

HISTORICAL DATA ON CHINATOWN CROWDING

To test whether crowding in Chinatown was due to cultural preference, two pieces of historical evidence were analyzed in addition to the survey data. Data from the nineteenth century suggest that the Chinese lived in crowded conditions out of economic necessity. Stephens (1976) suggested that economic means determined one's level of dwelling crowding. Between 1870 and 1880, Chinese American merchants lived in households with an average of less than five persons, while Chinese American shoemakers lived in households of 15 to 20 persons. The merchants (who were those with economic means) paid for the luxury of not sharing their homes with large numbers of persons. By contrast, the shoemakers (who were those without economic means) were forced to share their quarters with many others.

Data from the twentieth century indicated a dramatic drop in the percentage of severely overcrowded dwellings in core Chinatown from 1940 to 1950. In 1940, 35% of the dwellings in core Chinatown contained 1.51 or more persons per room. A decade later, following world War II, only 19% of the dwellings in this area were as overcrowded. The cause for this decline excludes explanations of cultural predilection. Before World War II, racial discrimination against the Chinese was a major determinant of residential location. The Chinese in San Francisco were restricted from leaving their crowded enclave to secure better housing elsewhere. However, during and after World War II, discrimination against Chinese Americans waned. Restrictive covenants of title deeds were lifted, permitting those Chinatown residents with economic means to secure housing in outlying neighborhoods. When racial discrimination in housing diminished and Chinese Americans were permitted socioeconomic opportunities in the mainstream, dwelling density in Chinatown declined. In summary, historical evidence indicates that while San Francisco's Chinatown has almost always been a crowded community, the primary causes have been poverty and racism.

Table 5.2
Attitudes toward Crowding

"How do you feel about a crowded [neighborhood/building or housing project/room or apartment] . . . would you say a crowded [neighborhood/building or housing project/room or apartment] is very good, somewhat good, neutral, somewhat bad, or very bad?"

	Very Good	Somewhat Good	Neutral	Somewhat Bad	Very Bad
Neighborhood	4%	12%	27%	48%	9%
Building	0	4	15	65	17
Room/Apt.	0	0	8	57	35

SURVEY DATA ON CROWDING ATTITUDES

Crowding attitudes were measured in four ways in this survey. Respondents were asked to do the following: (1) rate a crowded dwelling, a crowded building, and a crowded neighborhood on a five-point scale; (2) indicate whether they felt that crowding caused problems; (3) indicate why they would want to move out of their neighborhood (if they had said "Yes" to the question, "Would you ever want to move out of your neighborhood?"); and (4) choose whether they would use or rent out extra space.

Chinatown residents viewed crowding as undesirable. A full 92% of the respondents rated a crowded dwelling negatively, 82% rated a crowded building negatively, and 57% rated a crowded neighborhood negatively. No one judged a crowded dwelling positively, only 4% viewed a crowded building positively, and 16% evaluated a crowded neighborhood positively (see Table 5.2).

Nearly all of the residents interviewed (95%) believed that crowding caused problems.[4] Only 4% of the residents stated otherwise. Moreover, residents who perceived their dwelling as crowded were more eager to leave Chinatown, a difference that was statistically significant.[5] Also, of the reasons given for wanting to move, 40% related to crowding. Crowding was the most often mentioned reason for wanting to move out of Chinatown.

A vast majority of Chinatown's residents (93%) said they would use extra apartment space. Only a small minority (7%) said they would rent it out. Those who would use the extra space cited functional rather than recreational uses: "For bedrooms. We had to convert the living room so that three-fourths of it is a bedroom and the other fourth a living room."

Virtually all of the core respondents (99%) said they would use extra space, compared to 81% of the noncore respondents, a difference that was statistically significant.[6] This supports the obvious: the greater the population density, the greater the need for more dwelling space. In summary, there was no empirical support in Chinatown for notions that the Chinese prefer crowded conditions, find it desirable, or give little value to space.

THEORY OF ENVIRONMENTAL ADAPTATION

Sommer (1969) and Dubos (1965) suspected that individuals accommodate to adverse environmental conditions over time. Chinatown offered a natural laboratory in which to test this assumption. To do so, we examined whether those who had been raised in very crowded areas (Hong Kong or San Francisco's Chinatown) had more positive attitudes toward crowding than those who grew up in less crowded areas (foreign-born who were not raised in Hong Kong). Since most American-born in our sample grew up in and around Chinatown, we treated American-born as a proxy for Chinatown-raised. Crowding attitudes toward two referents were examined: (1) dwelling and building crowding (the micro-environmental level) and (2) neighborhood crowding (the macro-environmental level).

Both American-born and Hong Kong–raised Chinese held similar attitudes—both evaluated crowded dwellings and buildings negatively (see Table 5.3), and both had more negative feelings about crowded dwellings and buildings than those who were raised in less crowded settings. There was no attitudinal difference among the foreign-born or between American-born and those raised outside of Hong Kong for neighborhood crowding.

No evidence of attitudinal accommodation to crowding was discovered among the Hong Kong–raised. Instead, greater exposure to crowding apparently intensified negative attitudes about crowding at the dwelling and building levels. Although individuals may behaviorally adapt to crowding while holding negative attitudes, the survey results offered no support for the adaptation theory with regard to attitudes.

Compared to those who were raised in Hong Kong, American-born Chinese felt less negatively about neighborhood crowding. Greater functions served by a crowded American Chinatown than by a crowded Hong Kong city may explain this. Chinatown is *the* Chinese village and "city" for the Bay Area Chinese who seek the security, goods, institutions, and services of their culture. The enclave is the only place in the city that provides such cultural and linguistic comfort for the Chinese American.

THE EFFECTS OF CROWDING

Those who felt that crowding caused problems (95% of the sample) were asked to describe these problems.[7] Residents cited three major effects of crowding: (1) environmental and health problems (108 mentions), (2) psychological problems (76 mentions), and (3) interpersonal problems (51 men-

Table 5.3
Attitudes toward Crowding by Place of Birth

"How do you feel about a crowded neighborhood . . . building . . . dwelling?"
(5-point scale, 1 = "very good" to 5 = "very bad").

| | American-born | Foreign Born | |
		Hong Kong-raised	Raised elsewhere
Neighborhood			
Crowding	3.1(a)	3.8(b)	3.5(c)
Building Crowding	4.2(d)	4.2(e)	3.8(f)
Dwelling Crowding	4.5(g)	4.5(h)	4.2(i)
n =	20	15	71

t-tests:

neighborhood	ab	t= -2.73, df = 36, p < .01
crowding	ac	t= -1.44, df = 89, ns
	bc	t= 1.27, df = 85, ns
building	de	t= 0.07, df = 36, ns
crowding	df	t= 2.21, df = 89, p < .05
	ef	t= 2.03, df = 85, p < .05
dwelling	gh	t= 0.03, df = 36, ns
crowding	gi	t= 2.19, df = 89, p < .05
	hi	t= 2.04, df = 85, p < .05

Note: Weighted data, ac, bc were significant (t = 2.20, p < .05 and t = -2.04, p < .05 respectively).

tions). With regard to environmental and health problems, residents reported that crowding caused "too much noise"; "no fresh air"; "air pollution"; and "breathing problems." Conditions caused by crowding were described as "unsanitary," "dirty," and "unhealthy." Comments like "Crowding gives me a headache" and "Crowding makes me sick" conveyed the potent impact of crowding.

With regard to psychological problems, crowding made Chinatowners "frustrated," "stressed," "uptight," "tense," "annoyed," "irritable," "impatient," "short-tempered," "uncomfortable," "in a bad mood," and "depressed." The following comments convey the potency of this stressor: "It makes me have a nervous breakdown." "Lack of privacy causes problems with self-identity." "Crowding kills your personality." "Crowding drives me crazy."

With regard to interpersonal problems, crowding was reported to cause "arguments," "conflicts," "fights," "unfriendliness," "distrust of others," and "unaccountability." Elaborations of the aforementioned included: "Crowding makes me yell at my kids." "I become unreasonable." "I leave no room for discussion." "Crowding made me hate my brothers."

Less frequently mentioned effects of crowding included: inconveniences (35 mentions), lack of privacy (19 mentions), insufficient living space (17 mentions), and difficulties in work or study (5 mentions). Remarks included: "It interferes with my sleep." "Sharing the bathroom with other tenants makes me late for work." "I'm unable to think." "It deteriorates my study habits." "It lowers productivity."

Residents' full remarks conveyed a more impassioned sense: "With crowding, you get on each other's nerves. There's no privacy. In a way, it's killing your personality. It's suffocating. I can't write, I can't do anything when it's so crowded." "Crowding makes me feel uncomfortable. It's so noisy. If possible, I'll get out of this place and come back in the evening." "Crowding causes too much friction between individuals. You have arguments and even fighting." "Crowding causes a great deal of fighting between kids. Their study habits deteriorate. Husband and wife fight more, too. There's no place for quiet thinking to solve problems." "No privacy. It slows down your daily work. It causes a lot of confusion and it's dirty." "People snap at each other and get on each other's nerves." "You can't concentrate if you want to study. You can't think on your own. You become dependent on the people you live with." "There's not enough fresh air for everybody, not enough space. More space makes people feel more relaxed." "It causes psychological strain and stress, frustration, noise, and problems with light and air." "Tempers fly between people. It's uncomfortable. No privacy. Conflicts cause fights over the use of the bathroom, television, and cooking." "It's too noisy, and I'll feel dizzy and uncomfortable." "Rodents. More people, then there's more germs." "It's not sanitized. People who live in these conditions are low income, barely surviving." "It causes crime, mental problems, and unsanitary conditions." "If conditions are too crowded, there is a higher possibility for people to get sick. It is because of not enough fresh air." "I cannot completely relax or take a rest when I'm tired. Since so many people live in the building and share the kitchen and bathroom, there is no privacy. I have to rush to cook all the time." "You never know your neighbors. Even if you do, you can't trust them." "It makes things noisy all the time. It's not good to raise kids in such an environment. It causes arguments." "Crowding causes lots of tension within a household. People can't be alone, and they don't have time for themselves. It's bad for teenagers and it breeds lots of illness."

When the two residents who did not believe that crowding causes problems were asked why they held this opinion, they said: "Because as long as I can use my space wisely, there's no problem," and "I like to live with all my family members even though it's crowded. I've gotten used to it. Sometimes crowding causes unity." In the minds of these two individuals, crowding was unpleasant but could be worked around or balanced by the positive quality of keeping one's nuclear family under one roof.

Responses to the open-ended questions on crowding elicited more elaborate and multiple mentions than any other item in the survey. This led us to conclude that crowding extensively impinges on the lives of these ethnic Americans, making them particularly tuned to its effects.

We found no empirical evidence for Anderson's (1972) belief that crowding does not lead to social stress among Chinese. Instead, the findings support Wirth's (1938) theory that crowding leads to social conflict and psychological stress with the added harm of environmental problems. While these findings do not prove that crowding is behaviorally related to social conflict and stress, they do indicate that the self-reported effects of crowding correspond to those hypothesized by Wirth.

While only comparative cross-cultural research on crowding can fully resolve the debate of whether or not there are cultural differences in behavioral and attitudinal responses to crowding, findings strongly indicate that poverty, not cultural predilection, accounts for residency in crowding conditions. For many Chinese, living in crowded conditions requires a tolerance born of necessity, but its impact is not without harm. The data suggest that American Chinese may be no better suited to function in high density conditions than non-Chinese, the only exception being their cultural value of retaining intact families under one roof.

THE NATURE AND MEANING OF CROWDING AND DENSITY

Primary and Secondary Environments

When comparing primary and secondary environments, Stokols (1972) and Baldassare (1979) hypothesized that a crowded household was more undesirable than a crowded neighborhood. The Chinatown survey data supported this hypothesis. A higher percentage of respondents judged a crowded dwelling to be "somewhat bad" or "very bad" (92%) compared to a crowded neighborhood (57%). Individual differences in desirability ratings between environmental domains were statistically significant for all comparisons. Residents regarded a crowded dwelling to be significantly less desirable than a crowded building and a crowded neighborhood, and they regarded a crowded building to be significantly less desirable than a crowded neighborhood.[8]

In addition, dwelling crowding and neighborhood crowding were both significantly related to the desire to move out of Chinatown.[9] Crowding was judged to be undesirable and an incentive to move, but crowding in the dwelling was a stronger aversive condition than crowding in the neighborhood.

A crowded dwelling was probably judged to be more undesirable than a crowded neighborhood because of the differing nature of activities that occur in each setting. Crowding in the neighborhood is more tolerable than crowding in the dwelling because neighborhood settings involve transitory and superficial social and market interactions. By contrast, crowding in a household setting affects continuous and intimate relationships. The more crowding infringes on personal functioning in a constrained condition, the more likely it will be considered undesirable and harmful. Thus, crowding in dwellings causes more stress because of the nonmobile, nonchoice nature of the interactions that take place there.

To test Baldassare's hypothesis that a crowded neighborhood provides some benefits to its residents while a crowded dwelling does not, the benefits of one's neighborhood and dwelling were assessed by asking, "What do you like about your neighborhood?" and "What do you like about your (room/apartment/flat/house)?" Convenience was the most frequently mentioned benefit of the neighborhood. Convenience of shopping, workplace, transportation, Chinese restaurants, or entertainment were mentioned by 63% of the respondents who liked something about their neighborhood, and 28% mentioned cultural and familial factors such as "being among Chinese" or "being close to relatives."[10] By contrast, no benefits were attributed to a crowded dwelling. The data lend support to Baldassare's hypothesis that a crowded neighborhood provides some benefits, while a crowded dwelling does not.

Predictors of Neighborhood Crowding

Subjective indices of crowding in Chinatown corresponded to objective indices on population density; that is, residents' perceptions of crowding in Chinatown corresponded to population density indices that depicted Chinatown as crowded. Ninety percent of the residents described Chinatown as "a little crowded" or "very crowded." Of the residents interviewed, 0% said that Chinatown contained "lots of space for everyone," 6% thought it had "enough space for everyone," 38% thought Chinatown was "a little crowded," 52% considered Chinatown "very crowded," and 4% "did not know."

To determine which variables best predicted the perception of crowding in Chinatown, a multiple regression analysis was conducted for the following variables: place of birth (United States or foreign-born, Hong Kong or non–Hong Kong raised); personal characteristics (gender, income, age, rich/poor background); past environmental frame of reference (size of city raised);

Table 5.4
Analyses for Perceptions of Crowdedness of Chinatown

(1 = "lots of space," 4 = "very crowded")

Independent Variable	Standardized Beta Coefficient	F-value	r
Core (1 = core, 0 = noncore)	-0.454	20.148***	-.29
American-born (1 = US born, 0 = foreign)	-0.464	17.752***	.29
Neighborhood Safety (1 = completely safe, 5 = not safe at all)	0.383	16.056***	.26
Size of City Raised	-0.167	2.711	.05
Hong-Kong Raised[a] (1 = HK raised, 0 = not)	0.143	1.809	-.01
Income	-0.134	1.536	.11
Rich-Poor Background (1 = rich, 5 = poor)	-0.114	1.391	.03
Traffic Street Noise (1 = lots of times, 4 = never)	-0.051	0.254	-.10
Age	0.046	0.171	-.16
Gender (1 = male, 0 = female)	0.028	0.077	.07
Units in Building	0.003	0.001	-.03

$$R^2 = 0.343$$
$$\text{Adjusted } R^2 = 0.257$$
$$F = 3.988***$$
$$df = 11, 84$$

*$p < .05$.   **$p < .01$.   ***$p < .001$

a: Substituting "Hong Kong born" resulted in no substantial difference in results.

population density (core/noncore Chinatown, number of units in building); and perceptions of neighborhood characteristics (safety, noise). These variables together accounted for one-third of the variance (see Table 5.4). Of the individual variables, population density, nativity, and neighborhood safety significantly predicted the perception of Chinatown as crowded. Size of city raised, Hong Kong–raised, income, rich/poor background, noise, age, gender, and units in the building did not predict perceptions of Chinatown crowding.

Perceptions of crowding were influenced by one's frame of density reference. Chinatown was judged to be more crowded by those who lived in an area of lesser density than by those who lived in an area of greater density, all things being equal. Thus, noncore residents more often perceived Chinatown as "very crowded," while core residents were evenly divided among those who perceived it as "a little crowded" and those who perceived it as "very crowded."

Crowding perceptions were also influenced by one's cultural frame of reference. American-born Chinese more often described Chinatown as "very crowded," all other variables held constant, while foreign-born Chinese described Chinatown as "a little crowded." Apparently, American standards involve a set of perceptual judgments about crowding that vary from the standards held by the Asian-born. Finally, those who perceived their neighborhood as unsafe were more likely to see Chinatown as crowded than those who judged the neighborhood to be safe.[11]

Nearly every Chinatown resident interviewed, regardless of place of birth or residency, saw Chinatown as crowded. However, the degree to which the community was judged to be crowded was influenced by one's environmental and cultural frames of reference and by environmental perceptions. Those born in the United States, those living in the noncore area of Chinatown, and those who perceived their neighborhood as unsafe were more likely to perceive Chinatown as very crowded.

The Meaning of Dwelling Crowding

In this study, three dwelling crowding variables were studied: (1) dwelling crowding, which was measured by asking residents to rate the crowdedness of their dwelling (1 = "very crowded" to 4 = "not crowded"); (2) persons per room, which was assessed by the ratio of number of persons to number of rooms in the dwelling; and (3) need for more space, which was assessed by asking, "Do you feel you need more space in the place you're now living?"

Of those interviewed, 23% described their dwelling as "a little crowded" or "very crowded," 45% lived in dwellings with 1.01 or more persons per room, and 50% expressed the need for more space. The rather low percentage that felt crowded in their dwellings may be due to small household size or to the popular notion that crowding implies large numbers of people. Twenty-seven percent of the core residents lived alone, and the average household size for the core area was 2.7. For the noncore area, 16% of the residents lived alone, and the average household size there was 3.0.

"Dwelling crowding," "persons per room," and "need for more space" were all significantly correlated.[12] But not all persons who lived among 1.01 or more persons per room needed more space; 64% of those who lived in dwellings with 1.01 or more persons per room expressed the need for more space. However, all residents who felt crowded in their dwelling felt the need for more space. Conversely, of those who needed more space, 46% said they felt crowded in their dwelling. Thus, the need for more living space is a necessary but not sufficient condition for feeling crowded in one's dwelling. Crowding implies more than insufficient space.

Table 5.5
Analyses for Dwelling Crowding

"What about the living conditions in your room/apartment/flat/house? Is there a lot of space, enough space, or is it a little crowded or very crowded?"

(4-point scale, 1 = "a lot of space" to 4 = "very crowded")

Independent Variable	Standardized Beta Coefficient	F-value	r
Number of People	0.5510	24.097***	.27
Number of Rooms	-0.5150	20.463***	-.19
American-born (1 = US born, 0 = foreign)	0.2132	4.319*	.08
Rich-Poor Background (1 = rich, 5 = poor)	-0.1511	2.692	-.03
Core (1 = core, 0 = noncore)	0.1412	2.389	.21
Gender (1 = male, 0 = female)	0.1405	2.265	.06
Income	-0.0934	0.825	-.09
Hong Kong-Raised (1 = HK-raised, 0 = not)	0.0773	0.690	.20
Home raised more crowded than present home (1 = much more crowded, 5 = much less crowded)	-0.0343	0.146	.02

$$R^2 = 0.333$$
$$\text{Adjusted } R^2 = 0.268$$
$$F = 5.098^{***}$$
$$df = 9,92$$

*p < .05.   **p < .01.   ***p < .001

Note: Weighted data: number of people, number of rooms, and gender (F = 7.09, p < .01) were significant.

Predictors of Dwelling Crowding

To ascertain the predictors of dwelling crowding, a multiple regression analysis was conducted in order to test for the effects of objective density indices (number of people, number of rooms); cultural background (American-born or foreign-born, raised in Hong Kong or not); personal characteristics (gender, income, rich-poor background); current environmental frame of reference (core/noncore); and past dwelling crowding referent (extent to which one's current home is crowded compared to the home in which one was raised). The combined effect of all variables was statistically significant and explained one-third of the variance for dwelling crowding (see Table 5.5). With regard to individual variables, number of persons, number of rooms, and nativity were significant predictors of dwelling crowding. Core residency and Hong Kong–raised were also correlated with perceived dwelling crowding but were not statistically significant in the regression analysis due to their simultaneous correlation with the predictor variables.

The objective density indices—number of persons and number of rooms—were very strong predictors of dwelling crowding. Residents of larger households felt more crowded in their dwellings than residents of smaller households, all things being equal. Residents with fewer rooms in their dwellings felt more crowded than residents with more rooms, all other variables held constant. In addition, American-born Chinese perceived their dwelling as more crowded compared to foreign-born, all things being equal. Thus, cultural frame of reference affects environmental perceptions.

Nonsocial and Social Components of Dwelling Crowding

The experience of crowding was not restricted to a social condition, for 24% of the respondents who lived alone described their home as crowded. Some people can feel crowded even without the presence of others. The implication of this finding is that the deletion of single-resident households in the Census Bureau's calculation of overcrowded dwellings underestimates the proportion of persons who actually feel crowded in their dwelling. However, we cannot understate the importance of the social component. "Number of people" accounted for a larger proportion of the variance for dwelling crowding than any other variable, including "number of rooms." The social component of crowding is the most critical, but not the exclusive, defining element of dwelling crowding.

SUMMARY

Chinatown San Francisco is one of the most crowded neighborhoods in the nation. In 1980 greater Chinatown had a population density of 240 persons per residential acre. A majority of the residents in our sample lived in structures of 50 or more units. This represented a twofold increase over a decade. Crowding figures dominantly in these residents' lives, as it does for many low-income ethnic immigrants. The perceptions and responses of these respondents offer important insights about crowding.

Historical and empirical data dispel beliefs that Chinese Americans prefer crowding or live in crowded conditions without ill effect. The effects of poverty and discrimination on the Chinese have been incorrectly interpreted as a cultural preference for crowding. Survey data offered even stronger evidence of this. Contemporary residents named crowding as one of the most undesirable attributes of their community and mentioned crowding most often as their reason for wanting to move out of the neighborhood. The data consistently demonstrated that nearly all of the Chinatown respondents viewed a crowded dwelling negatively. Nearly all of the residents interviewed considered crowding to be harmful. The major effects were environmental and health problems, psychological problems, and social problems. Given the option of additional space for personal use or economic gain, the vast majority chose the former. The findings support Wirth's theory that crowding is related to social conflict and psychological stress.

The findings revealed no evidence to support the belief that the Chinese are better suited to function at high density conditions, although conclusive proof requires comparative research. For example, comparative survey research on Hong Kong Chinese would be desirable in order to determine whether these findings are universal for all Chinese. Chinese may endure suffering stoically, but this does not mean that they prefer adverse living conditions or that they exist in them without negative impact. Because the Chinese seem to represent the group thought to be most amenable to crowding, the prevalence with which Chinatown residents felt negative about crowding suggests two things. First, certain cultural differences thought to exist may not really exist. Second, Jacobs's contention that "everyone hates crowding" may be correct.

Misleading notions about the Chinese and crowding may be due to one or more of the following: (1) failure to collect interview sample survey data on attitudes and crowding effects on the Chinese; (2) neglect in accounting for the constraints of poverty; (3) cultural misinterpretations arising from a white middle-class American perspective; or (4) misinterpretation of a preference for "a family under one roof" for a cultural preference for crowding.

Crowding perceptions were influenced by one's frame of density reference and cultural reference. The greater the population density, the greater the need for more space. The more Anglo-acculturated the resident, the more likely it was that the individual viewed the community and his or her dwelling as crowded. There was no evidence of attitudinal accommodation to crowding.

Results suggest that greater life exposure to crowding is related to greater dislike of crowding at the dwelling and building levels, evidenced by the more negative evaluations of the Chinatown and Hong Kong–raised persons compared to those raised in less crowded areas. Thus, greater exposure to crowding breeds greater distaste for this environmental stressor. However, there is something about being born and raised in Chinatown, compared to Hong Kong, that makes a crowded neighborhood less aversive, perhaps because of the cultural meaning and comfort provided in Chinatown that cannot be found elsewhere in the city.

In conclusion, this study reveals that many assumptions about the Chinese and crowding are either invalid or questionable. This closer focus throws new insight onto much of the existing literature and provides important data relevant to housing policies nationally. If HUD or legislative representatives misinterpret the intentions and meaning of Asian, Hispanic, or any other ethnic group living in crowded conditions, this can have serious consequences on the allocation of funds for adequate housing. Indeed, our housing policies depend on the accessibility of accurate data, particularly for those whose economic resources do not provide them with options.

NOTES

1. Population density per acreage underestimates Chinatown's density because not all commercial acreage contains residences on the upper floors. However, residential population density (calculated in Table 5.1 for 1970) is an overestimation of actual density because it does not convey secondary residential uses, which are very common in the core area where housing is often located over ground floor commercial activity.

2. $t = -2.79$, df = 105, $p < .01$.

3. The proportion of structures containing 50 or more units in the noncore area in 1980 was 13%. A mere 3% of the core Chinatown population resided in single-home dwellings.

4. The phrasing of this question may be prone to yea-sayer bias; however, the elaboration and multiple responses given to the probe questions that followed it (if "yes," ask, "In your opinion, what kinds of problems does crowding create?") strongly indicated that responses to the first question were valid.

5. $X^2 = 3.09$, df = 1, $p < .01$ or $r = .33$, $p < .001$.

6. $X^2 = 8.47$, df = 1, $p < .01$.

7. In addition, all respondents were asked, "What effects, if any, does crowding have on how you feel and what you do?" Responses to both questions were similar and, thus, were combined.

8. $r = .56$, $p < .001$; $r = .20$, $p < .05$; $r = .21$, $p < .01$.

9. $r = .33$, $p < .001$, and $r = .26$, $p < .01$, respectively.

10. With regard to other responses to "What do you like about your neighborhood?" 7% said "nothing" and 2% "didn't know."

11. $X^2 = 10.25$, df = 2, $p < .01$.

12. $r_{ab} = .41$, $p < .001$; $r_{bc} = -.43$, $p < .001$; $r_{ac} = -.56$, $p < .001$, respectively.

This photograph captures a typical Chinatown room—the thermos with hot tea, the plate and bowl, a black rotary phone, the American flag, Chinese American bilingual calendars, photos of family members, a picture of a Hong Kong movie star superimposed on the Parade of the Dragon, and the Deity of Fortune (which is often found in the homes of the poorer Chinese from southern China). Evidences of a bicultural experience are found in the list of names written in Chinese with their phone numbers in English, the American flag adjacent to a newspaper clipping about how the United States will not help Chinese Americans reunite their families, newspaper clippings of changing U.S. immigration laws that partially cover a map of China, the sample election voting ballot on which are handwritten Chinese translations, the abacus, and across the room a print of Marilyn Monroe alongside a print of Miss Chinatown. 1976. (Photograph by Pok-Chi Lau.) Reprinted by permission.

His Parents' Dream

This single man in his 30s immigrated from Taiwan because his parents sought greater opportunities in a "safer, wealthier country." To help actualize his parents' dream, he gave up his job, house, friends, country, future wife, and a satisfying and pleasant life.

Here he lives in a tiny apartment with poor facilities. The noise makes reading or thinking impossible. In this foreign land, loneliness is his only friend. He misses his girlfriend and has no one with whom to share his feelings.

Because his English is poor, he works as a waiter in a Chinese restaurant. His working hours are long. He feels alienated from his coworkers, whom he finds uneducated, socially inept, rude, and foul of language. Although his job is undesirable, he stays. His parents' plans—to buy a house, a car, save money—prevent him from quitting his job. He'd be the last to destroy his parents' dream.

His parents are old and make little money working in a Chinese restaurant. Asked why he doesn't go to school or a career training program to improve his English so he might secure a better job, he shakes his head in exasperation: "I can't just go to school to improve myself and leave the family in a financially difficult situation." As the oldest son of three children, his parents put most of the family responsibilities on his shoulders. This respondent feels trapped, unable to return to Taiwan and unenthused about remaining in the United States.

6

Language Acquisition, Cultural Shift, and the English-Only Movement

Chalsa M. Loo with Paul Ong

Second language acquisition and cultural shift are issues that are not only central to the non-English speaking immigrants' experience, they have become points of controversy within the larger American society. Such debate is perhaps most vividly depicted in the current discourse on the English as the Official Language movement and the bilingual ballot, issues of considerable social and political controversy that impact upon immigrants in this country. Multilingual ballots are part of the provisions of the Voting Rights Act, intended to increase the sociopolitical participation of citizens who are of certain language minority groups. In the 1980s, the English as the Official Language movement was an expression of strong ideological and emotional opposition to these provisions. Since 1981, a bill to declare English the official language has been introduced in the U.S. Congress yearly.

Events in California reflected this national movement to institute a constitutional amendment that would make English the official language of the United States. In 1983, 62% of the voting residents of San Francisco approved Proposition 0, a resolution that sought to repeal the bilingual election provisions of the Voting Rights Act. In 1984, 71% of all voting Californians approved Proposition 38, an initiative that urged an amendment of federal law so that ballots, voter pamphlets, and other official voting materials would be printed in English only. Two years later, 73% of voting Californians passed Proposition 63, a constitutional amendment declaring English as the state's official language. In 1988, voters in Florida and Colorado passed a constitutional amendment declaring English as their states' official language. The amendment was approved by 84% of the voters in Florida and 61% of the voters in Colorado. In Arizona, the amendment passed by less than 1%.

The bilingual ballot provisions arose out of the multilingual provisions of the 1975 amendments to the 1965 Voting Rights Act. The English-Only movement[1] was but one event in the rise of anti-Asian attitudes and restrictive legislation in the 1980s aimed against non-English speaking immigrants, particularly Asians and Hispanics. This movement coincided with a dramatic increase in the proportion of immigrants from Asia, Mexico, and Latin America. In 1950, newcomers from Asia, Mexico, and Latin America amounted to 30% of all immigrants to this nation. From 1981 to 1985, newcomers from these countries rose to 83% of the immigrants to the United States (Bouvier and Gardner, 1986).

This chapter begins with a review of the Voting Rights Act and the provisions of the 1975 amendments. Section two sets down the arguments offered both for and against the bilingual ballot provisions. Section three lays down the reasons why data on this issue are needed. Section four, which represents the bulk of this chapter, contains research findings that test assumptions about acculturation and second language acquisition. Section five contains data to test whether there is any empirical support for assisting certain language minorities and not others. The final section involves a consideration of English-Only and the U.S. trade deficit.

THE VOTING RIGHTS ACT AND PROVISIONS OF THE 1975 AMENDMENTS

The Voting Rights Act of 1965 prohibited the use of "voting prerequisites" ("literacy tests" and other barriers) in states and political subdivisions that had disenfranchised blacks from exercising their right to vote (Hunter, 1976). Impetus for amendments to the 1965 act came largely from evidence presented to Congress of acts designed to interfere with or abridge the rights of Mexican American voters in Texas, a state not covered by the 1965 act. The principles were generalized to provide coverage for other language minority groups in order to overcome possible objections of legislative narrowness (Hunter, 1976).

The 1975 amendments expanded the coverage of the special provisions to additional areas and required bilingual elections in certain areas (Voting Rights Act, 1975). Bilingual ballots were required of a state or political subdivision of a state not covered as a whole, where either of the following two conditions were present: (1) more than 5% of the citizens of voting age of the jurisdiction were members of a single language minority group ("persons who are American Indians, Alaskan natives, Asian Americans, or of Spanish heritage") and (2) either fewer than 50% of the voting age citizens of the jurisdiction voted in the 1972 presidential election, or the illiteracy rate of this single language minority was higher than the national rate (see U.S. Commission on Civil Rights, 1976, Section 55.1 and sec. 203, Section 55.6).

The amendments to the Voting Rights Act were intended to eliminate discrimination in voting against language minority groups whose denied voting rights were assumed to result partly from unequal educational opportunities afforded them, thus creating low voter participation and high illiteracy.

ARGUMENTS FOR AND AGAINST THE BILINGUAL BALLOT PROVISIONS

Supporters of bilingual ballots, who resent the "Anglo culture supremacy" of the English-Only proponents (Hussein, 1985, p. 5), argue that an enforced monolingual-monocultural society is contrary to democratic ideals. They maintain that the United States should be a multicultural society where there is no discrimination against those of a different mother tongue. Those who support bilingual ballots argue the following: (1) English-only ballots would unfairly prevent thousands of Americans who have difficulty with the English language from exercising their right to vote; (2) bilingual ballots encourage assimilation by encouraging all citizens to participate in their government; (3) Hispanic and Asian Americans want to learn English, for they recognize it as one of the keys to economic advancement and social integration; (4) bilingual ballots and bilingual voters' pamphlets provide the opportunity for citizens to cast intelligent, responsible votes while they perfect their English; and (5) although federal law requires a fifth-grade level of English to become a naturalized citizen, state and local propositions are often written in such complex language that they confuse even English-speaking college graduates. Supporters also contend that bilingual ballots are useful to new American citizens—particularly the elderly, whose English is often strong enough to pass the citizenship test but who feel the ballot choices facing them deserve careful study in the language they know best (*California Voters Information Pamphlet,* 1984).

By contrast, those who oppose bilingual ballots contend the following: (1) bilingual ballots remove an immigrant's motivation to learn the English language; (2) bilingual ballots work against integration of the foreign-born into the wider community; (3) Chinese and Hispanic Americans do not wish to learn English, preferring instead to resist assimilation; (4) bilingual ballots falsely imply that a full economic, social, and political life can be achieved in the United States without competence in English; (5) earlier immigrants who learned English resent special treatment for current immigrants; (6) bilingual ballots are costly;[2] (7) voters who have limited knowledge of English cannot understand the issues and, therefore, would not be informed voters;

(8) bilingual ballots are unnecessary since U.S. citizenship requires passing a test for literacy and proficiency in English; and (9) the nation needs to be unified by a common language.

Some officials and newswriters have declared that immigrants should not enjoy the privileges of this society if they are unwilling to assimilate. In 1979, Thomas Kearney, the former San Francisco registrar of voters, responded to a request to hire bilingual poll workers at the ballot booths in Chinatown with the remark, "Goddamn Chinks." Criticism from the Chinese American community over Kearney's racial slur and his uncooperativeness in complying with the Voting Rights Act led to Kearney's dismissal. In the wake of his departure, columnist Herb Caen (1979) attributed Chinese Americans' desire for language assistance to ethnocentricity and lack of motivation to learn English: "Why are the proud, intelligent Chinese so bent on ethnic speaking aids in the voting booth? Obviously the Chinese can learn English. Is the message that they shouldn't be asked to or that they can't be bothered?" (p. 25).

Bilingual advocates view English-Only advocates as un-American on legal and ideological grounds, while English-Only advocates consider it un-American to be non-English speaking. In all other ways, each side offers opposing claims (see Table 6.1).

THE NEED FOR DATA

Little empirical evidence has surfaced with regard to immigrant language acquisition and acculturation. Shuy (1981) claimed that bilingual education programs, multilingual social services, and multilingual voting procedures are viewed with suspicion because beliefs about the unwillingness or inability of Hispanics to learn English have not been successfully refuted.

There has also been little study of the language and acculturation issues underlying the bilingual ballot debate. Congress justified bilingual ballot requirements on the basis of other factors, namely, (1) educational disadvantage (illiteracy rates for people of Spanish heritage, Chinese Americans, and American Indians were 19%, 16%, and 15%, respectively, compared to 5% for white Americans); (2) racial disparities in the proportions registered to vote (44% of the Spanish-speaking and 67% of the blacks were registered to vote, compared to roughly 80% of the Anglo-Americans); (3) barriers obstructing equal opportunity for political participation among Mexican Americans; (4) past discrimination against Chinese Americans, American Indians, Alaskan natives, and Hispanic students in education; and (5) civil rights violations against Spanish-speaking, Asian American, and American Indian citizens (U.S. Congressional Records, 1975).

Chinatown represents a natural laboratory in which to test the validity of

Table 6.1
Claims of Bilingual Advocates and English-Only Advocates

Assumptions	Bilingual Advocates	English-Only Advocates
Bilingual Ballots	... encourage assimilation	... discourage assimilation
	... prevent discrimination	... represent reverse discrimination
	... assume more informed votes	... erringly permit the uninformed vote
	... are cost effective	... are costly
Immigrants	... want to learn English	... don't want to learn English
	... want to integrate	... don't want to integrate

assumptions made by those who oppose the bilingual ballot. These assumptions include that: (1) immigrants are unwilling to acquire American customs and ways and often choose not to adjust; (2) immigrants are unaware that English language acquisition is key to socioeconomic mobility; (3) acquisition of the English language should not be difficult for immigrants; and (4) no justification exists for language assistance to certain language minorities but not others. With regard to the last point, critics have argued that biliterate provisions are discriminatory because no equal right is afforded to other language minorities such as Italians, Greeks, Jews, Russians, French, Germans, and Poles (Committee for Ballots in English, 1983; Wright, 1983). Is it justifiable to provide language assistance to certain language minorities but not to others? If so, on what grounds?

Because some representatives maintained that documentation on Asian Americans was lacking in hearings on the Voting Rights Act (Voting Rights Act, 1975, pp. 85–89), this chapter will closely attend to data on Asian Americans. To address issues of bilingual-bicultural shift, we rely on the second-language acquisition literature and on data from the U.S. Census Bureau and the Chinatown survey.

Of the Chinatown sample, 63% were largely monolingual Chinese-speaking, 27% bilingual, and 10% monolingual English-speaking (see Figure 6.1).

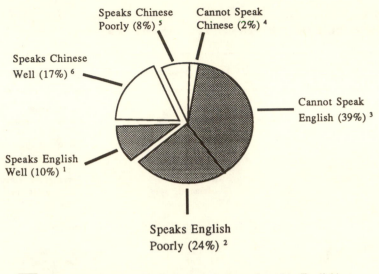

Figure 6.1
Language Use among Chinatown Residents

These proportions roughly approximate that of the U.S. Chinese foreign-born (see Table 6.2).

TESTING ASSUMPTIONS ABOUT ACCULTURATION AND SECOND LANGUAGE ACQUISITION

In this section we examine three areas: first, Chinese immigrants' willingness to acculturate and the variables that correlate with acculturation; sec-

Table 6.2
Language Shift Patterns of the U.S. Chinese: San Francisco Chinatown Chinese (18 Years and Over)[1] and U.S. Foreign-Born Chinese (14 Years and Over)

	English Usual Language			Non-English Usual Language		
	Mono-lingual	Bi-lingual	Total	English Competence		
				High	Low or No	Total
U.S.	6%	28%	34%	36%	30%	66%
Chinatown	10%[2]	17%[3]	27%	10%[4]	63%[5]	73%

(Source for national data: 1976 Survey of Income and Education, see Veltman, 1983).

[1] Statistics for Chinatown are for all respondents, native and foreign born.

[2] Those who were interviewed in English who either cannot speak Chinese or do so "very poorly."

[3] Those who were interviewed in English who said they could speak Chinese "pretty well" or "very well."

[4] Those who were interviewed in Chinese who said they could speak English "pretty well" or "very well."

[5] Those who were interviewed in Chinese who said they could speak English "rather poorly" or "not at all."

ond, immigrants' awareness of the English language as necessary for social mobility; and third, whether successive English language acquisition is difficult.

Willingness to Acculturate

De-ethnization is an unrealistic measure of acculturation because it involves the loss of original ethnic heritage and values (Weinstock, 1968). Willingness to acculturate is better determined by evaluating willingness to acquire aspects of the new culture while retaining aspects of the old. Cultural shift is easier when the values of both cultures are consistent and more difficult when the absorption of one cultural norm must be at the exclusion of the other (Mendoza and Martinez, 1981). Thus, in determining the ease with which acculturation can take place, researchers must consider the compatibility of values from different cultures.

In the nineteenth century, the press derided the Chinese as "unassimilable aliens" (Miller, 1969). But Coolidge (1909) asserted that arguments of non-assimilation were invalid because it takes two to assimilate and the larger society neither wished the Chinese to assimilate nor gave them opportunity to do so:

Had the first white immigrants to California found themselves met by a hostile population and hostile laws; had they been beaten in the streets, robbed, and plundered . . . had discriminating taxes enforced against them under the guise of law; had they been refused citizenship and their children admission to the public schools, chances are they would not have fallen in love with the people, country, religion or laws. (Becker, in Coolidge, 1909, p. 254)

Acculturation is generally found actualized in the next generation. "Among the few hundred men who have families in this country, not many care to vote themselves, but all are proud of the fact that their sons can vote" (Coolidge, 1909, p. 442). Kung (1962) observed that:

[Chinese Americans maintain] a hearty support of the free world, they believe in freedom and democracy. They are no less loyal to America than are the immigrants from other lands. They fully realize that they must adjust themselves to be integrated members of the American community. . . . they take the position that East and West, in many respects, should complement each other. (p. 262)

The survey findings support Kung's assertion. When asked, "What American ways should be taken and what ways should be rejected?" and "What Chinese ways should be retained and what ways should be rejected?" Chinatown immigrants held both praise and criticism for Anglo-American traits. Respondents valued American traits of "courtesy," "politeness," "honesty," "open-mindedness," and "friendliness." They also praised principles of the American political system or related outcomes or attributes: freedom, democracy, equality, government benefits, and the Protestant ethic. The following remarks demonstrate their weighing of the positive and negative aspects of the American culture: "We should learn to be friendly and honest like most of the Americans, but not take things for granted like some of the Americans." "We should act as courteously and with an open mind like most of the Americans, but reject their system of marriage—it's too easy to get married and too easy to get divorced." "We should retain American ways of honesty and practicality, but reject their liberal life-style—they show no respect to their parents or to elderly." "Most Americans don't gossip as much as Chinese, that should be retained. But we should reject how they're too loose with their kids. In the United States you're considered an adult when you reach 18, but many 18-year-old girls and boys aren't capable of making decisions. It's dangerous to allow them all those rights and freedom."

Immigrants also held both praise and criticism for Chinese traits. They commended Chinese values of "filial piety" and "close family ties" but disparaged Chinese traits of "introversion," "narrow-mindedness," "inability to enjoy life," "indulgence in gossip," and "selfishness." "Chinese are selfish, maybe because the country they came from was originally poor. . . . Nowadays, only the older people are helpful." "They are getting so selfish, maybe because they're new immigrants or because they're too worried about making a living." "They look at self-interest rather than group interest."

The aforementioned findings revealed two important points. First, Chinese immigrants do not resist the American culture in favor of unquestioned loyalty to their native culture; they see merits and liabilities in both cultures. Second, certain Chinese values are incompatible with certain American ones. Chinese loyalty to one's family is contradictory to the American focus on individualism. Chinese respect for elders conflicts with the American adoration of youth. Thus, Chinese emphasis on filial piety and family are in conflict with America's idealization of youth and ease of divorce. Consequently, we can assume that cultural shift among Chinese immigrants would be more difficult than for those whose native cultural values are more consistent with white American values.

To define whether Chinese immigrants saw the need to acculturate and to what extent they have acculturated, foreign-born respondents were asked, "Do you think that an immigrant needs to take on American customs in order to get along in this country, or do you think an immigrant can get along all right without changing old ways and customs?" and "Since coming to the United States, have you changed some of your old customs and ways to American customs and ways? Have you changed a lot, some, a little, or not at all?" (If respondent said "a lot," "some," or "a little," we asked, "What kind of changes have you had to make?")

Close to three-fourths of the Chinese immigrants believed an immigrant should make some cultural changes.[3] Half of the immigrants had made some cultural changes, the other half had not. Examples of cultural shifts included: wearing American attire, greater independence and friendliness, less conservatism in attitude and behavior, greater independence for their children, and acquiring American food and eating habits.

There was no statistical relationship between having made cultural changes and the belief that immigrants need to acculturate.[4] In other words, those who saw a greater need to adopt American ways were no more likely to have made cultural changes than people who saw little or no need to adopt American ways. I suspect that the opportunity to acculturate is more important than the individual's desire to acculturate, as suggested by the following findings. Parents' educational attainment was correlated with immigrants' ability to take on new customs and cultural habits; that is, acculturation was significantly greater for those whose mothers had a college education compared to those whose mothers had less than a college education.[5] Acculturation was also significantly greater for those whose fathers had a high school degree compared to those whose fathers had less than a high school degree.[6]

Defining employment in the ethnic labor market as those who work in Chinatown, acculturation was found to be significantly greater for those employed in the larger labor market than for those segregated in the ethnic labor market.[7] Over three-quarters of those interviewed who worked in Chinatown (in the ethnic labor market) reported having made no cultural changes, while only 31% of those who worked outside of Chinatown (in the larger labor market) reported having made no cultural changes. Those who worked in Chinatown were less able to speak English, were older when they immigrated to the United States, made less in wages, and had mothers who had less than a college education.[8]

Finally, those who perceived that Chinese Americans faced discrimination[9] were significantly more acculturated than those who did not perceive discrimination.[10] This suggests that immigrants may not be aware of unfair treatment until they begin to acculturate into the larger white society. There are indeed constraints to acculturation despite the immigrants' desire for acculturation.

Grosjean (1982) maintained that with the exception of elderly and invaded populations, most immigrants want to adjust. When ethnic immigrants are unable to adjust to their new culture, it is often because the larger society excludes or prevents them from full participation. Rejection can take the form of economic, occupational, cultural, and social isolation or segregation from the majority society (Blauner, 1971; Bonacich, 1972; Burawoy, 1976; Piore, 1979). Inadequate skill is a barrier to jobs outside the low-paying ethnic labor market. However, much of the barrier is due to discriminatory rejection by the larger system.

English Language Acquisition and Socioeconomic Mobility

Is there any validity to the claim by English-Only advocates that immigrants are unaware that acquisition of the English language is necessary for social mobility? No validity was found for this assumption in the Chinatown data. Chinese immigrants were not uninformed that English is necessary for social mobility. In fact, nearly all employed Chinatown residents who had difficulty with the English language believed that English-speaking ability would increase their socioeconomic mobility; 95% said they would feel qualified for a better job if they could speak English well.

Awareness that non-English language facility affects job status and ease of life functioning was widespread. Many were aware that the inability to speak English restricted their geographical mobility, leaving them captive in an ethnic enclave by virtue of language: "If my language problem could be solved, everything would be better." "Life is rather hard for me because I can't write or read in English." "I can't speak the language so I can't go to places beyond Chinatown by myself." "Language problems cause a lot of inconvenience." "Because I don't know English, it's so difficult for me to find a job."

English-Only proponents argue that immigrants do not learn English because they do not aspire beyond their menial, low-paying jobs. The survey data failed to support this argument. Eighty-two percent of the Chinatown immigrants said they would want another job if they could speak English well. Motivation was not the issue. Faster English language acquisition among Chinese immigrants is most often due to occupational segregation in the ethnic labor market and difficulties inherent in successive language acquisition. Veltman (1983) concluded that the fact that a minimum of one in three of these ethnic persons (Chinese, Vietnamese, and Spanish-speaking immigrants) born outside the United States speak English as their usual language indicates strong willingness to accommodate their language behavior to that of the American environment.

Difficulties of Successive Language Acquisition

Successive language acquisition is the condition whereby English is learned as a second language under stress as a consequence of immigration. In successive language acquisition, the dominance of the native language makes certain linguistic constructs harder to internalize (Grosjean, 1982). The stronger language interferes with the weaker one, thereby retarding differentiation.

Psychological and emotional conflicts resulting from second language acquisition compound the problem. When learning English as a second language, adult immigrants often feel like children, depending on others for communication of their needs (Anderson, 1982). Second language acquisition can also produce identity changes with resultant loss in self-esteem or emotional stability (Anderson, 1982; Castro, 1976).

Five areas will be discussed that elaborate on various difficulties of successive language acquisition: (1) biliterate skill lags behind bilingual skill; (2) acquisition is a function of current age and (3) age at time of immigration; (4) acquisition is affected by geographical concentration; and (5) acquisition is made more difficult under conditions of occupational segregation.

Biliterate Skill Lags Behind Bilingual Skill. The four language skills include oral comprehension, speaking ability, reading ability, and writing ability; among these, bilingual persons often have unequally developed skills in the newly acquired language (Anderson, 1982; Grosjean, 1982). Immigrants who have learned English in school in their mother country often have a reading comprehension that exceeds their oral comprehension. However, in normal language acquisition, facility in oral comprehension exceeds speaking ability, which in turn exceeds reading and writing skill (Veltman, 1983).

The hierarchy of speaking and oral comprehension over reading and writ-

Table 6.3
English Language Skills and Level of Competence of Chinese-Speaking Adults in Chinatown

	Total "Yes"	Level of Competence Among Those Who Said "Yes"		
		"Rather Poorly"	"Pretty Well"	"Very Well"
Understand Spoken English	52%	76%	20%	5%
Speak English	47%	70%	27%	3%
Write English	22%	35%	59%	6%
Read English	22%	53%	47%	0

ing English also holds true in Chinatown (see Table 6.3). Chinese immigrants reported greater skill in oral comprehension of English than in speaking ability, which in turn was more developed than their abilities to read or write English. Among the Chinese monolingual and Chinese-dominant speaking residents, twice as many have English receptive and speaking skills as have English writing and reading skills. Roughly half of those persons interviewed in Chinese could understand a conversation and/or carry on a conversation in English, although most of these persons could do so only minimally. By comparison, only one in five persons interviewed could write and/or read English (and here again, not very well). For Chinatown foreign-born, English reading ability was the most difficult of the four language skills. Furthermore, the proportion that read English poorly exceeded the proportion that wrote English poorly.

Since bilingual skill (the ability to speak English) exceeds and precedes biliterate skill (the ability to read English), low competence in reading English does not mean that an immigrant is unwilling to learn English or that the immigrant is non-English speaking. Furthermore, since reading competency is normally one of the most difficult of the four language skills, literacy assistance in election provisions targets the ability of greatest difficulty.

Current Age. Rates of language shift surge in the late teens and early twenties, then level off after the early to mid-thirties when work choice has been made and schooling has been completed (DeVries, 1974; Lieberson, 1965; Veltman, 1983). Among Chinatown immigrants, age was significantly related to English-speaking ability. The mean age of the English-speaking foreign-born was 38 years, while the mean age of the non-English speaking foreign-born was 53 years.

Age at Time of Immigration. Age at time of immigration was also significantly related to English-speaking ability. The average age at time of immigration

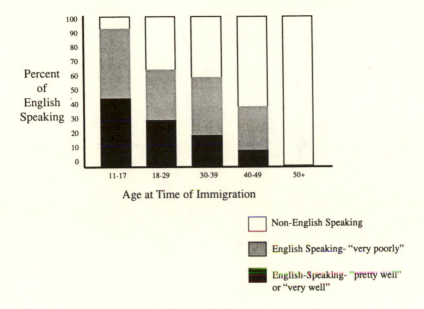

Age at Time of Immigration

☐ Non-English Speaking

▨ English Speaking- "very poorly"

■ English-Speaking- "pretty well"
or "very well"

Age at Time of Immigration	Non-English Speaking	Competence in English-Speaking		Percent English-Speaking
		Low	High	
11-17	8%	42%	58%	92%
18-29	33	56	44	67
30-39	40	67	37	60
40-49	61	71	29	39
50+	100	0	0	0

Figure 6.2
English-Speaking Ability by Age at Time of Immigration

for those who spoke English was 24, while the average age at time of immigration for those who could not speak English was 36. The younger the immigrant at the time of entry, the more likely it was that he or she spoke English and the greater was his or her mastery of that language. Nearly all Chinese immigrants who entered the United States at ages 11–17 spoke English. By contrast, none of those who entered this country at age 50 and over spoke English (see Figure 6.2).

Age at time of immigration was also related to English literacy. The younger the person at the time of immigration, the more likely it was that he or she could read English (see Figure 6.3). Two-thirds of those who entered the United States at ages 11–17 could read English. By comparison, none of those who entered at age 50 and over could read English.

Geographical Concentration. Acquiring English as a second language is a slow

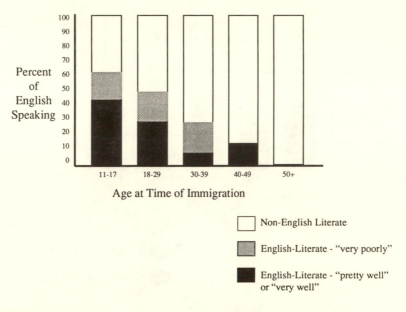

Age at Time of Immigration

Non-English Literate

English-Literate - "very poorly"

English-Literate - "pretty well" or "very well"

Age at Time of Immigration	Non-English Speaking	Competence in English-Speaking		Percent English-Speaking
		Low	High	
11-17	39%	25%	75%	61%
18-29	56	33	67	44
30-39	73	75	25	27
40-49	89	0	100	11
50+	100	0	0	0

Figure 6.3
English-Literate Ability by Age at Time of Immigration

process for populations that are highly concentrated geographically (Veltman, 1983). Over three-quarters of the Chinese in America live in urban areas. Due to poverty, language, and the difficulty of securing jobs outside the ethnic labor market, many of the foreign-born are concentrated in Chinatowns in large urban cities like San Francisco, New York, and Los Angeles.

Occupational Segregation. A relatively high percentage of Chinese in the United States are occupationally segregated. Nationally, minorities are segregated from the majority in the types of occupations they have (U.S. Commission on Civil Rights, 1978). Isolated from the larger labor market, most immigrants work in low-paying, low-status jobs in the ethnic labor market (Mar, 1985). With respect to U.S. Chinese, a majority of the Chinese immigrant labor force are employed in the Chinese restaurant business as service workers or operatives in the garment industry.

Among non-English speaking Chinese adults, lack of English remains a major cause of unemployment and underemployment, with many locked into a system whereby their lack of English forces them to work long hours in low paying jobs. . . . Their long working hours prevent them from taking advantage of English instruction opportunities . . . [and] opportunities for Chinese to learn English while working on a job are extremely limited. (Bay Area Social Planning Council, 1971, p. 8)

Mar (1985) found that employment in the ethnic labor market deterred English language acquisition because there was no incentive or need to use English in the workplace and because mobility out of the ethnic labor market was so difficult. Lack of English-speaking ability slowed socioeconomic mobility outside the ethnic labor market; however, the effect of English language ability on mobility was not as great as expected. Neither English language ability nor length of employment at one's workplace resulted in higher wages for Chinese immigrants in the ethnic labor market. Moreover, employment in the ethnic labor market explained more of the wage variance than English-speaking ability. Thus, it is the structure of the labor market and not just language that restricts Chinese immigrants.

Chinese immigrants need access to jobs in the larger labor market if they are to gain the exposure and better jobs necessary to acculturate. However, Takagi and Platt (1978) have pointed out that capitalistic exploitation within a U.S. profit-motivated economy constrains Chinese immigrants to low-paying, low-status, nonpromoting jobs as sweatshop workers or waiters and cooks. Chinatown residents in the ethnic labor market are less able to speak English, are older at time of immigration, make lower wages, and have less education than those who work outside the ethnic labor market. All of these factors put immigrants at a disadvantage.

Shuy (1981) argued that there were no economic or cultural incentives for Hispanic Americans in border communities to learn English. Similarly, Veltman (1983) reported that the better-prepared, English-speaking persons of Spanish language background were not receiving rewards that corresponded to their educational attainment, equivalent to those obtained by the white English language group. Thus, for Asian and Hispanic immigrants, it appears that the structure of the labor market, poverty, and racial discrimination in the labor market constrain ethnic immigrants to conditions that deter English language acquisition.

We conclude this section on the difficulties of successive language acquisition with the words of one immigrant.

I knew it was going to be tough. I knew it the minute I stepped out of the airplane with my two boys and wife. English! English everywhere. I walk in the streets of this new land, and I feel like a blind man stumbling along. I can't read the street signs! I can't understand what people are talking about! People say, "Why don't you learn English?" Yes, yes, learn English, but where? Some say there are free English lessons at X street, some say they're at Y street. Where should I go? How can I find out?

Well as I said, it's tough, it's tough! I'm forty years old and my tongue is getting stiff. You think I can learn English in a couple of months? No, no. And in the meantime what should I do if something happens?—Like the phone bill. The phone company keeps billing me for calls that we didn't make, but how can I tell them? Whenever I pick up the phone, I'd hear English. What else can I do except pay the bill?

Also, there is my job. I suppose everyone can guess. I work in a restaurant in Chinatown. Wages are low and hours long. I'd really like to try my luck somewhere else, but where? I walk into an American firm. The boss looks at me and I look at him. I can only say, "Job, job." They think I'm crazy.

People ask, "Why don't you go to your friends and relatives for help?" Well, I tell you, it's not good to bother people. My brother speaks English, but he's got a job and a family to look after. How can he look after me and my family too? I feel like a prisoner, locked in the blocks of Chinatown. How can I ever get out? I don't even know how to take a bus! (Huang and Wong, 1977, p. 56)

RATIONALE FOR ASSISTANCE TO CERTAIN LANGUAGE MINORITIES

Is there any empirical support for assisting certain language minorities and not others? Language shift rates were high among German, Scandinavian, Russian, and Yiddish immigrant groups—these being 92%, 95%, 88%, and 92%, respectively—and lower among Koreans, Chinese, Vietnamese, and Spanish language immigrant groups—47%, 34%, 33%, and 29%, respectively (Veltman, 1983). In this section we will examine factors that affect language shift rates for various language minority groups. These factors include: first, the pattern of immigration and population characteristics of the foreign-born; second, the percentage of those who do not speak English "very well"; and third, linguistic differences between one's native language (L1) and the acquired language (L2).

Pattern of Immigration and Population Characteristics

Populations with a high proportion of native-born have a higher English literacy rate than populations with a low proportion of native-born. This is because most first-generation American-born complete whatever anglicization their foreign-born parents did not achieve, and each successive generation evidences an increasing proportion of English monolinguals (Veltman, 1983). For example, 23% of the Chinatown foreign-born can speak English,

77% cannot. But among the native-born in Chinatown, 95% can speak English, leaving only 5% who cannot.

Compared to European immigrant groups, the Vietnamese, Korean, Filipino, and Chinese foreign-born have substantially higher proportions of foreign-born and higher proportions of non-English mother-tongued among their foreign-born. The proportions of minority language speaking foreign-born in the United States for Vietnamese, Korean, Filipino, and Chinese were 100%, 98%, 84%, and 87%, respectively. By contrast, the proportions of minority language speaking foreign-born for Yiddish, Scandinavians, Russians, and Germans were 55%, 37%, 51%, and 45%, respectively (Veltman, 1983, p. 46).

The population size of recent immigrants and the proportion of immigrants of that language group accounted for by recent immigrants affect the rate of English language shift, when age is held constant. Veltman (1983) demonstrated that for all language groups, immigrants who entered the United States earlier showed a higher rate of language shift to English than those who immigrated later. For example, of the Chinese and Spanish language groups who entered the United States before the 1950s, 43% of the Chinese mother-tongued and 42% of the Spanish mother-tongued acquired English as their normal language of use. Of those who immigrated during the 1960s, 34% of the Chinese mother-tongued and 29% of the Spanish mother-tongued shifted to English as their usual language. Finally, of those who enter the United States in the 1970s, 26% of the Chinese and 12% of the Spanish mother-tongued shifted to English as their principal language of use.

For immigrant groups characterized by a recent pattern of arrival, English language acquisition is more difficult because there are fewer anglicized members of the same ethnic group to ease their passage into the new society. Asian American and Spanish-speaking language groups constituted the largest proportion of language minorities among recent immigrants. Between 1970 and 1980, 70% of all immigrants who entered this country came either from Asia or Mexico and/or Latin America.

When the amendment to the Voting Rights Act was drafted and passed, the largest number of persons affected by English language difficulty were the Spanish-speaking and Asian American language groups—those with the largest numbers of recent immigrants (see Table 6.4). From 1970 to 1976, over one million recent immigrants were Spanish-speaking; close to 145,000 recent immigrants spoke one of the Philippine languages; and nearly 120,000 recent immigrants were Chinese-speaking. By contrast, among recent immigrants, only 1,900 spoke Yiddish and 12,000 spoke Polish.

More recent statistics (which include 1981 arrivals) reiterate that the largest proportion of recent immigrants are the Spanish-speaking and Asian American language groups. Immigrants from European nations accounted for fewer of the recent immigrants to this country. Immigrants from Vietnam,

Table 6.4
Percentage of Language Group Immigrants Arriving in Various Periods (Persons Aged 14 and Over, United States, 1976)

Language Group	Pre-1960s (%)	Period Arrival 1960-69 (%)	1970-76 (%)	Number of Recent Immigrants (1970-76)
All Spanish	27	36	36	1,150,290
Filipino	26	27	48	144,820
Chinese	29	34	37	119,343
Korean	5	20	75	86,857
Vietnamese	1	4	96	79,331
Italian	73	19	8	71,531
Portuguese	36	33	31	63,409
Greek	51	28	22	50,984
French	57	27	15	49,625
Japanese	56	18	27	40,229
German	81	15	4	37,307
Polish	82	14	4	12,057
Yiddish	98	2	1	1,943

Source: A reconstructed version of Table 3.4 in Veltman, 1983, p. 51 taken from the 1976 Survey of Income and Education. Number of recent immigrants was calculated from the weighted sample provided in Table 3.4, multiplied by the proportion of foreign born who arrived between 1970-76.

Korea, Hong Kong, Central America, and the Philippines have very recent immigration patterns (see Table 6.5). Nearly all Vietnamese immigrants and over 80% of all Korean immigrants to the United Stats arrived between 1970 and 1981.

Then there are groups with both recent and early arrivals. Immigrants from Portugal, Japan, China, and Mexico have a visible proportion of early arrivals concomitant with a larger proportion of recent arrivals. By contrast, immigrants from Italy, Germany, Poland, France, and the Soviet Union all have early immigration patterns. One-half to three-quarters of the foreign-born from these countries came to the United States before 1960. Only immigrants from Greece deviated from this pattern. Their immigration process was fairly steady.

Inability to Speak English "Very Well"

The 1982 amendment to the Voting Rights Act changed the provisions, such that eligibility for bilingual ballots subsequently required that the single language minority be unable to speak English "very well." The percentage of those who did not speak English "very well" was highest for the Asian

Table 6.5
Foreign-Born Persons in the United States by Country of Birth, Citizenship Status, and Period of Arrival

Country of Birth	Period of Arrival Pre-1960 (%)	Period of Arrival 1960-1969 (%)	Period of Arrival 1970-1980 (%)	Number of Immigrants 1981	Number of Immigrants 1970-1981	Percent by Citizenship Naturalized Citizen (%)	Percent by Citizenship Not Citizen (%)
Mexico	20	22	58	101,300	1,376,836	24	76
El Salvador	6	17	77	8,300	80,888 ⎫	14	86
Guatemala	6	24	69	3,900	47,499 ⎬ 1,505,163[1]	18	82
Philippines	14	23	63	45,300	359,682	45	55
Vietnam	9	2	98	55,600	282,078	11	89
Korea	3	13	84	32,700	276,216	35	65
China	25	27	47	25,800	160,267 ⎫ 215,019	55	50
Hong Kong	7	31	63	4,100	54,752 ⎬	38	62
Japan	32	23	46	3,900	156,700	43	57
Italy	70	18	12	4,700	104,528	77	23
Germany	69	21	10	6,600	91,540	79	21
Portugal	19	34	47	7,000	90,378	37	63
Greece	40	28	32	4,400	71,278	65	35
Poland	75	14	11	5,000	50,991	78	22
France	55	24	21	1,700	26,942	64	36
Soviet Union	70	5	24	9,200	18,944	73	27

Source: 1985 Statistical Abstract of the United States, U.S. Dept. of Commerce, Bureau of the Census, Table No. 127, p. 87.
[1]When immigrants from Central America are added.

Table 6.6

Number of Persons by Language Group Who Speak a Language Other Than English at Home, Number and Percent Who Speak English Less Than "Very Well"

Language Group	Total Number Who Speak a Language Other than English in the Home	Total Number Who Speak English Less than "Very Well"	Percent Who Speak English Less than "Very Well"
Vietnamese	194,588	146,945	76
Thai	84,961	60,604	71
Korean	266,280	176,123	66
Chinese	630,806	377,747	60
Portuguese	351,875	185,857	53
Japanese	336,318	175,080	52
Spanish	11,116,194	5,581,329	50
American Indian or Alaskan Natives	333,020	163,230	49
Philippine Languages	474,150	199,915	42
Greek	401,443	157,676	39
Polish	820,647	283,407	35
Yiddish	315,953	93,919	30
French	1,550,751	444,165	29
German	586,593	417,538	26

Source: PC 80-1 D1-A. Detailed Population Characteristics, U.S. Summary, 1980 Census of Population, Table 255 (A and B).

American language groups, Spanish language group, and American Indian or Alaskan natives (see Table 6.6). Except for the Portuguese, the other European language groups did not have as high a proportion unable to speak English "very well."

Linguistic Relationship Between L1 and L2

The greater the linguistic differences between L1 (native language) and L2 (acquired language), the greater the difficulty of acquiring the second language. Compared to learning a second language similar in structure to one's native language, learning a second language with a different structure poses a heavier burden. Learning a new writing system that differs from one's native language poses an additional problem.

Previous research on bilingualism and second language acquisition generally ignored the linguistic relationship between one's native language and the

Figure 6.4
Orthographic Examples for Indo-European and Asian Languages

second acquired language (Niyakawa, 1983) largely because most research on bilingualism had been concerned with Spanish and English or French and English, all of which are languages within the same "family."

What is meant by a language family? The major part of the Western world uses a language from the Indo-European family. Languages such as Greek, Portuguese, Italian, French, Polish, and English share similar grammatical structure and vocabulary (especially technical vocabulary). Asian American languages, on the other hand, are not of the Indo-European family. Moreover, while most Indo-European languages (Portuguese, Spanish, Italian, French, Polish, and English) use the Roman alphabet, most Asian languages have unique orthographies (Niyakawa, 1983). See Figure 6.4 for orthographic examples. Some Asian languages like Chinese are logographic. Japanese is written with a mixture of syllabic and logographic symbols. Other Asian language (Korean, Thai, Cambodian, Lao, Burmese) have entirely distinct non-Roman alphabetic writing systems. Vietnamese, with a Roman-based writing system, is an exception, but it is radically different from any European language in its grammar and vocabulary. In sum, there are legitimate linguistic reasons why Asians may have more difficulty learning English than would be the case for those of an Indo-European mother tongue.

ENGLISH-ONLY AND THE U.S. TRADE DEFICIT

Finally, we need to consider the English-Only position in relation to America's historically unprecedented trade deficit and trade imbalance under the Reagan administration. In Glick's (1988) words: "Whether here or abroad, whether to increase visible or invisible exports, more Americans must become competent in foreign tongues. . . . We have nothing to lose but a good part of our trade deficit" (p. 7b).

Even if Americans could better compete in international trade on the basis of product quality alone, "we still lose export sales because of our monolingualism and ignorance of other cultures. . . . our linguistic chauvinism is more than an educational eccentricity. It is now an economic liability that we can no longer afford and that we can reduce only by a total immersion of Americans into foreign languages" (Glick, 1988, p. 7B).

Similarly, Peters (1988) linked America's trade problem with Japan to the fact that Americans "steadfastly refuse to learn anybody else's language" (p. 1p). While the result has been rather nil in European trade, he argued that the same is not true for Asia. Many of the Japanese can read our technical journals, which gives them a decided advantage; by contrast, "very, very few of us can read theirs." The Eurocentered focus of our educational content has left Americans relatively uncomfortable, if not ignorant, of Asian culture and history. The solution, Peters suggested, lies in "forcefeeding Asian languages into our school curriculum." In an ironic statement of role reversal, he noted: "[for Americans,] Chinese and Japanese are devilishly difficult for Westerners, both the spoken and especially the written word." Yet if America does not make these changes, "we are in for tough sledding as the axis of American economic interests rapidly twists from Europe to Asia" (Peters, 1988, p. 5b).

Prestowitz (1988) attributed Japanese trade advantages over the Americans to the fact that Japanese diplomats have facility with English and have involvement and familiarity with the American educational, political, and sociocultural system. By contrast, 90% of the staff at the American Embassy in Japan cannot speak any Japanese. "As a result, the Japanese are full players in Washington, but Americans in Tokyo have difficulty even understanding what is said" (Prestowitz, 1988, p. 3E).

Thus, in the 1980s a new argument emerges for multilingualism. Initial impetus for biliterate ballots was to assist the linguistically disadvantaged. Now, it is the American who is disadvantaged internationally by English-Only ethnocentrism. Multilingual competence affects America's diminishing effectiveness in the international trade arena, particularly when so much of the trade activity has swung to Asia. The very irritation that English-Only advocates feel with regard to multilingual ballots may be the very self-imposed prison that prevents America from enhancing its economic effectiveness abroad.

SUMMARY

The aim of this chapter was to analyze widely held assumptions about language acquisition and acculturation of immigrants, with particular attention to Chinese Americans. English-Only advocates assume that immigrants are unwilling to acquire American customs and ways. Research data unveiled the inappropriateness of this assumption; two-thirds of the Chinatown foreign-born believed that immigrants should make cultural changes.

English-Only advocates assume that ethnic minority immigrants are not aware that English language acquisition can lead to socioeconomic mobility. But this was not found to be the case. Of those interviewed, 95% of the non-English speaking believed they would qualify for a better job if they could speak English well; 80% of the Chinese immigrants in the labor market said they would want another job if they could speak English well. Most Chinese immigrants demonstrated willingness to acquire aspects of the new culture. Most understood that English language facility would qualify them for a better job, ease their life functioning, and eliminate their dependence on an ethnic enclave.

Data from this survey revealed that acculturation was correlated with parents' education, employment in the larger labor market, and awareness of discrimination against Chinese Americans. Facilitating the acculturation of ethnic minority immigrants requires more than their learning the English language; acculturation requires eliminating immigrants' occupational segregation from the larger labor market, their educational disadvantage, and racial discrimination against them. These factors deter full and equal participation in the mainstream society for all ethnic immigrants.

Many English-Only proponents assume that acquisition of the English language by immigrants should be easy. This chapter has focused on factors that make second-language acquisition difficult for Chinese immigrants and certain other language minorities. First, biliterate skills (the ability to read English) normally lag behind bilingual skills (the ability to speak English). Thus, immigrants may be fluent in English but not yet fully literate in the language. Language assistance in the electoral process assists those who have not fully mastered English literacy, the most difficult of the language skills.

Second, language shift is affected by age at time of immigration, geographical concentration of the language population, and occupational segregation of non-English speaking immigrants. Language shift is harder for those who immigrate at a later age, for those ethnic groups that are more geographically concentrated, and for those that are occupationally segregated from the larger labor market.

Third, English language acquisition is harder for language minorities heavily comprised of recent immigrants. The Spanish-speaking, Chinese, Korean, Filipino, Vietnamese, and Thai immigrants have greater numbers and/or greater proportions of recent immigrants, and they have higher proportions of non-English speaking than European immigrants. The percentage of those who do not speak English very well is highest for the Asian American language groups, Spanish language group, and American Indian or Alaskan natives. Except for the Portuguese, the other European language groups do not have so high a proportion that are unable to speak English very well.

Last, learning English as a second language is more difficult if the language structure and written form of the native language differs substantially from English. In general, Asian languages have a grammatical structure that is very different from languages of the Indo-European family. Furthermore, while most Indo-European languages use the Roman alphabet, Asian languages are logographic or have unique writing systems, making it all the more difficult to master written English.

At the present time, there is justification for language assistance to certain language minorities and not others, but reasons differ for specific groups. For instance, the Spanish-speaking do not contend with large linguistic and orthographic differences between their native language and the English language, but the population size of their recent immigrants exceeds all other language minorities. Also, differences exist among Asian American language groups; data on Japanese Americans differ substantially from data on Korean or Vietnamese Americans in terms of need for biliterate ballot assistance. It may be more logical to consider the Asian language groups separately rather than cluster them as one generic category.

Finally, we examined the international trade deficit argument for a multilingual America. Here Herb Caen's attacks on Chinese immigrants can be reversed by asking, "Why are the proud, intelligent Americans so bent against non-English languages? Is the message that they shouldn't be asked to or that they can't be bothered?" The basic thrust of the trade deficit argument is this: As language use is intimately tied to economic trade and international relations, America has been and will be increasingly disadvantaged in the world trade arena unless attitudes and policies on non-English language use change.

In summary, data did not support assumptions held by the proponents of the English as the Official Language movement. Mistaken assumptions riddle the controversy of the bilingual ballot (which should more accurately be called the biliterate ballot, since the written rather than the oral form of language is at issue). Beneath the sound and fury of this controversy lies a reality that must replace myth if this country is to be linguistically and culturally inclusive.

With regard to the implications of these findings, there are strong arguments for making English language training available to all non-English speaking immigrants as a rite of passage to this country. To permit them to immigrate without also providing them with a ticket of language passage is to continue to exclude them from the advantages that this society offers. America cannot simultaneously justify marketing itself as a land of opportunity if it continues to segregate its non-English speaking poor into the ethnic labor market. Where is the opportunity if America merely exploits their labor in a profit-motivated economy that restricts farm workers or sweatshop workers to dead-end jobs, with wages lower than our minimum wage? Federal funding should be made available so that there are sufficient English language classes, thereby eliminating waiting lists entirely.

There is a victimized contradiction when a country attacks non-English speaking immigrants for using their mother tongue when that same country does not provide sufficient opportunity for these persons to actualize their desire to learn the English language. This society needs to provide the mechanisms by which the barriers to non-English speaking immigrants can be broken if they are to expect or hope for the quick acculturation of its newcomers. These immigrants want the American dream; if they did not, they would not have made the great effort required to leave their native land and start life anew.

To vote is one of the great privileges of this society. It is a symbol of what this country stands for. Those who originally fought to pass the bilingual election provisions of the Voting Rights Act surely knew this. And the provisions were passed with the intention of providing our citizens who have not yet fully mastered the English written language with the rights of political participation. Providing entry without opportunity is not much different from passing the Burlingame Treaty to permit Chinese workers to build the transcontinental railroad while simultaneously denying them the right of naturalization. This is still an item on America's future agenda.

NOTES

1. The English as the Official Language movement has been referred to in more colloquial circles as the English-Only movement; for simplicity both terms will be used in this chapter interchangeably.

2. The registrar of voters estimates bilingual voting costs $25,000 to $50,000 per election, whereas bilingual ballot proponents argue that bilingual elections accounted for less than 2% of county election costs in Los Angeles and in San Francisco, costing the average homeowner less than three cents annually.

3. Of those interviewed, 59% said "yes" unequivocally, 14% indicated an immigrant should take on "some" but not all American ways, 24% said "no," 2% said it "didn't matter," and 1% "didn't know."

4. $r = .00$.

5. $r = .54$, $p < .001$.

6. $r = .20$, $p < .05$.

7. $r = .44$, $p < .001$. Employment in the ethnic labor market was measured by the item, "Is your workplace inside or outside of Chinatown?"

8. $r = .40$, $p < .001$; $r = .26$, $p < .05$; $r = .23$, $p < .05$; $r = .23$, $p < .05$, respectively.

9. Items that measured perceived discrimination included: "Do you feel that in the United States, Chinese are treated better than, worse than, or the same as whites?" "Please tell me which statement best describes your opinion: (1) many Chinese don't do well in life because they haven't prepared themselves to make use of the opportunities that come their way, or (2) many Chinese have good training but they don't do well in life because they don't get as many opportunities as whites." "Please tell me which best describes your opinion: (1) the problem for many Chinese in America is that white society discriminates against them even when Chinese do what's proper and adapt to white American customs, or (2) the problem for many Chinese is that they refuse to adapt to white American customs. If they did adapt, they'd be accepted and would get ahead."

10. $r = -.26$, $p < .01$.

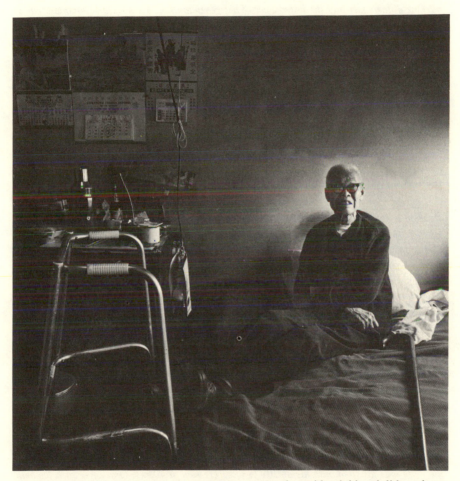

For all of 15 years prior to his death, this occupant of a residential hotel did not leave the building. Relatives and a maid brought him his food. His cane and walker were close at hand. The communal bath was just outside his door. His hot plate, thermos, *hau yau* (oyster sauce), cup, and bowl lie near his bed. A sheet of paper served as his lamp shade. 1976. (Photograph by Pok-Chi Lau.) Reprinted by permission.

His Health Problem

He lived in one of the many narrow alleys. I conversed with him in Chinese, explained the purpose of the study and the importance of his participation. He agreed to be interviewed. We set up a time. I explained that a Chinese-speaking interviewer would conduct it because my Chinese wasn't adequate. To this he said he thought my Chinese was fine. I said it wasn't. We argued back and forth. As I was speaking Chinese all the while, he didn't seem convinced. He said he couldn't speak English. I was somewhat doubtful, as he spoke Chinese with a heavy accent, but I did not dispute his claim. He didn't want to have the interview conducted in his apartment because "there's no space," so I invited him to the CHHRP office.

This man was in his 50s, with greying hair, glasses, and salt and pepper stubble on his face. He wore a light casual sports jacket and a dark-colored pair of pants. His hands were those of a worker, calloused and hard, the nails cut short with jagged edges. His fingers were yellow with tobacco. There was a smell of smoke about his person.

I offered him tea or coffee but he declined. Before we began, I showed him the Resource Book to break the ice. He flipped through it for the first hour or so, not because he was bored with the questions but because he seemed more at ease doing something while I was asking questions. He hardly ever looked directly at me, preferring to focus his attention on the book, the desk, or somewhere else.

This man was quite articulate. With his use of words like "centralized" and "influence" within the first few minutes, I had no doubt he had a good command of English. He seemed to be an intelligent man who was aware of political issues affecting the community. He also remembered dates of things that happened years ago—the time he was robbed and all the times he went to the hospital. Although articulate, he spoke slowly, sometimes with a slur. He was reluctant to talk about his health problem, just that he has "100% neuro-psychiatric disability."

The second time we met to complete the interview, he was more relaxed. As during the first interview, he didn't look at me but kept his eyes lowered on the desk.

This man was divorced and lived with several cousins. He said, "I have good friends and relatives who are supportive and help each other." He was proud of his son in college. He was not striving for anything and felt pretty satisfied that "life has been pretty good to me." He was satisfied with his ability to solve his own problems, sometimes with the help of a psychiatrist, whom he saw regularly.

7

Pulse on Chinatown: Health Status and Service Use

Health problems constitute a very central concern for low-income, immigrant, and elderly individuals in this society. Compared to the average American, their greater life stresses and vulnerability to health problems are exacerbated when they have limited access to health care services due to lack of transportation, financial constraints, or unavailability of services. Furthermore, for immigrant populations, both the language barrier and informational poverty deter them from obtaining proper medical and health care services.

Much can be learned from communities that have developed model health care delivery programs. When such programs involve service to low-income, ethnic immigrant populations, the lessons are all the richer because their challenges are so much greater. Yet, as identifiable communities continue to serve a function of housing incoming immigrants and elderly, the challenge is unending. This chapter chronicles one such model and one such community.

While crowded dwellings, substandard housing, and low-wage employment remain, Chinatown physicians point with pride to gains that have been made in health care and health attitudes. Since the 1960s, there have been major reforms in the health care delivery system for San Francisco's Chinatown. Moreover, federally subsidized medical care for the poor and elderly, implemented in the mid-1960s, made health service access more equitable for all Americans. To what extent have national reforms in health care costs and delivery led to improved health conditions for the Chinatown community? The answer lies with three factors: (1) the health status of the community's population; (2) the extent to which its population uses health services; and (3) the quality of the health care delivery system. While this chapter does not attempt to address the third factor, it does investigate the health status of these Chinese Americans, their health service use, and the predictors of both.

The first section of this chapter covers the history of health care in the community, which spans over 100 years. Section two presents the survey findings, which include the health status of the residents; variables that predict health status; dental health care; smoking; alcohol and drug use; health service use; use of Western versus Eastern forms of treatment; predictors of health service use; and health education.

To begin, the terms used throughout this chapter need to be defined. "Health status" is an indicator of need; it refers to the self-reported health of the residents. "Health service use" is an indicator of demand; it refers to the extent to which residents use health services. Health service use is affected by health attitudes, financial constraints to health care, and quality of the health care delivery system (Dutton, 1978).

THE HISTORY OF HEALTH CARE IN CHINATOWN

Three major periods define the history of Chinatown's health care: (1) the period of condemnation and self-sufficiency; (2) the period of transition; and (3) the period of crisis and expansion.

Condemnation and Self-Sufficiency

From the 1870s into the early 1900s, Chinatown was maligned as the most unsanitary and unhealthy section of San Francisco. Considering it a laboratory of infection, San Francisco's Board of Health formally condemned Chinatown as a health nuisance (Trauner, 1978). An 1885 report of the Special Committee of the San Francisco Board of Supervisors on the condition of the Chinese Quarter stated: "Here it may truly be said that human beings exist under conditions (as regards their mode of life and the air they breathe) scarcely one degree above those under which the rats on our waterfront and other vermin live, breathe, and have their being" (Farwell, 1885, p. 5).

Farwell (1885) claimed that Chinatown was likely at any time to generate and spread disease "should the city be visited by an epidemic in any virulent form" (pp. 4–5). His theme was resung two years later. In 1887, the Committee on Chinese and Chinese Immigration stated that "no other city in our Union has such a plague spot" (Report of Senate Committee on Chinese and Chinese Immigration, 1887, p. 3). Some even believed that disease was not caused by germs but by foul vapors arising from the filth of Chinatown (Hoexter, 1976).

Owing to this disease hysteria, the city's Board of Health in 1900 alleged that the Chinese had introduced the bubonic plague into San Francisco. The Chinese became medical scapegoats. Falsely blamed for the spread of disease, they were subject to discriminatory overreactions of quarantine and condemnation (Trauner, 1978) and were prevented from leaving the city (Armentrout, 1976). City authorities barricaded the community and passed an ordinance that forced the closure of Chinese-owned businesses. The Board of Health and the San Francisco Board of Supervisors resolved that all basements, cellars, and underground places in greater Chinatown be condemned and destroyed.

In a test case heard before the U.S. Circuit Court in 1900, the city quarantine was held to be illegal. Judge Morrow issued the following opinion: "If it were within the province of this Court to decide the point, I should hold that there is not and never has been a case of plague in this city" (Appendix to the Report of the Special Health Commissioners, 1900, p. 18).

As a result of a state investigation, 103 autopsies were performed. Not one case revealed death by bubonic plague. The report stated: "San Francisco is and has been absolutely free from the disease and those who said it existed were either mistaken or deliberately misrepresented the facts" (Report of the Special Health Commissioners, 1900, p. 11).

Despite this finding, the city and the federal quarantine officer refused to remove the quarantine. The governor telegrammed the U.S. secretary of state, stating that among 35,000 Chinese, 15,000 had been quarantined, causing 3,500 Chinese to have no means of financially supporting themselves. He added:

there has been no epidemic in Chinatown. . . . the municipal records show that the proportion of deaths in Chinatown has been no greater than that of any other portion of San Francisco since the date of the discovery of the alleged plague. . . . the medical gentlemen and experts of the City Board of Health and the Federal quarantine officers who have ventured the injurious opinions . . . have never seen a living case of plague, . . . [and the quarantine is] discriminating against the Chinese. (Appendix to the Report of the Special Health Commissioners, 1900, p. 17–18)

Three days later, the governor appealed to President McKinley, stating: "the Federal Quarantine Officer has unreasonably and unnecessarily quarantined this State in opposition to my report to the Secretary of State and in opposition to the opinion of Judge Morrow of the U.S. Court. . . . the rights of citizens as well as the rights of foreign subjects are outrageously impaired. . . . I protest against his actions" (Appendix to the Report of the Special Health Commissioners, 1900, pp. 16–17). On June 18, the president of the United States ordered the release of the state quarantine.

The absence of epidemic diseases among the San Francisco Chinese population amidst its unsanitary condition was a puzzlement to city officials and outside observers (Lloyd, 1875). The Farwell report raised the ridiculous proposition that Chinese immunity to epidemic diseases must be caused by opium smoking. In reaction, the *San Francisco News Letter* sarcastically remarked how it was a wonder that gambling was not lauded as the means by which the Chinese warded off diseases! (Editorial, 1886).

San Francisco showed no interest in providing health care to the Chinese. The city handled Chinatown's ills by isolating and condemning the area. Throughout the nineteenth century, city officials were reluctant to finance any health services for the Chinese and were hesitant to provide Chinatown with the sanitary services afforded to the rest of the city (Trauner, 1978). Although the Chinese had paid a hospital tax on arrival at port, they were denied admission to the city's hospitals (Kung, 1962). For a Chinese, going to a hospital meant leaving the protection of Chinatown, risking beatings or robbery only to be refused treatment (*East West*, 1974). The Chinese were left to take care of themselves.

Given the city's hands-off policy, Chinatown was forced to organize its own health care system. True, there were herbalists and pharmacists serving the community in the Chinese medical tradition. However, their sparse presence constituted no real system of health care. Each of the Six Companies maintained a hospital for its members, but these appear to have been "little more than bare places [in which] to die" (Coolidge, 1909, p. 415). The Chinese consul general and merchants raised money and bought land for a general Chinese hospital. However, the project was dropped when the city authorities refused to allow the Chinese to manage it (Coolidge, 1909).

Finally, in 1900, after more than ten years of planning by the San Francisco Chinese consul general and the Chinese Six Companies, the Tung Wah Dispensary was established. Taking its name from the Tung Wah Hospital in Hong Kong, the dispensary was the first Chinese medical facility in this country. Initially funded by the Chinese Six Companies, the dispensary was a charity institution that employed Western-trained physicians and Chinese herbalists.

In 1908 the University of California's medical school graduated its first Chinese physician. Over the next two decades, a cadre of Chinese Western-trained physicians emerged. Then, in 1925, through the organizational efforts of these Chinese physicians, Chinese Hospital was established. This marked a turning point in health care delivery for the community. Chinatown now had its own hospital. No longer would the Chinese need to battle racism while seeking health care outside the enclave.

To the disappointment of the pioneering physicians, the community did not share their enthusiasm over the completion of Chinese Hospital. Residents were generally disinterested. They had come to associate Western-style care with rejection of Chinese, strange medication, and a language barrier

(Chinn, Lai, and Choy, 1969). Despite the presence of a Western-based institution (Chinese Hospital) and the accessibility of Chinese Western-trained physicians, residents resisted Western medicine. According to Dr. Henry Cheu:

People didn't think they needed a hospital because they believed in herbs. Even though the cost was only four dollars a day, there were vacancies all the time. The Chinatown people regarded the hospital as a place of doom. The popular notion was "if you go there, you die." But they waited until the last minute when they were almost dead before they went to the hospital. Naturally, they died there. (personal communication, 1982)

Dr. Collin Dong conveyed the dilemma: "We competed with at least fifty acupuncturists and herbalists. It was not easy to introduce Western medical concepts to our Chinese patients. They were eclectic, taking our pills sometimes, and other times, they reverted to herbs and acupuncture" (Dong, 1979).

Time of Transition

Into the 1950s, outsiders still considered Chinatown a crowded place "of squalor and filth" that, once occupied by a Chinese, was destined to "remain a pest hole or be torn down" (McLeod, 1948, pp. 128–129). At a hearing before the Special Committee to Investigate Chinese Immigration, B. S. Brooks had testified that blame for this condition lay on city authorities, who made no attempt to clean the Quarter's streets (in Dillon, 1962, p. 165). Public amazement at how the whole Chinese population was not carried off by some epidemic disease persisted, leading some outsiders to query whether it was Chinese herbs that "cure[d] the Chinaman of his ills" (McLeod, 1948, p. 143).

The U.S. Chinese were not wiped out by an epidemic. But neither were they as healthy as outsiders assumed. In 1940 the death rate for Chinese in the United States was higher than for Americans overall. In the 1950s, the tuberculosis (TB) rate for Chinese in the United States was three to four times that of the nation (Kung, 1962). Figures from 1953 revealed that 92% of all the TB cases in San Francisco occurred in the Chinatown census tracts, with the highest prevalence being among the low-income workers and the "domestically" employed, that is, the cooks, restaurant helpers, laundry workers, waiters, and other semi-skilled and unskilled laborers (Lee, 1960).

In this second period of Chinatown's health history, we begin to see a slow and limited increase in health service provision to the community coupled with attitude changes toward Western medicine among the residency. By 1905, advances in medical science caused an end to medical scapegoating of the Chinese. Nevertheless, the failure of the San Francisco city and county to provide health services to Chinatown had a long-term effect (Trauner, 1978). Changes came undramatically. From the 1920s through the 1950s, the city showed some willingness to provide services to Chinatown. However, these services were minimal in scope and phlegmatic in coming. In 1928, San Francisco's health department placed a one-room, well-baby clinic in Chinese Hospital. Four years later, the health department opened a storefront on Powell Street that offered well-baby care, tuberculosis control and follow-up, immunizations, and limited dental care. In 1952, when the storefront moved to Pacific Street, the city increased its nursing services. Although enlarged, city services were still grossly inadequate. Major transformations would not occur until the 1970s.

Normally, change requires some breakthrough in health care delivery. Yet even after Chinese Hospital was established, its services were unused. Attitudes toward Western medicine had to change if residents were to use the new health delivery system. For example, resistance to Western treatment had caused needless suffering and death from tuberculosis, a disease prevalent in Chinatown due to crowded housing and grueling working conditions.

By chance, events of the 1940s and 1950s gave rise to such change. The Japanese invasion of China in World War II curtailed the importation of herbs and other goods from China. Scarcity of herbs forced a wider acceptance of Western medicine in Chinatown. The alliance of China and the United States during the war, a waning of discrimination against the Chinese, and a loosening of legal and economic restrictions on Chinese Americans lessened Chinese suspiciousness of Western medicine. By the war's end, the community fully accepted the Chinese Hospital.

The 1949 embargo of imports from the People's Republic of China again limited the supply of herbs, making them accessible only through Hong Kong. This restriction, which did not end until normalization of relations in 1979, essentially ensured residents' dependence on Western medicine.

Crisis and Major Expansion

The mid-1960s and 1970s were a pivotal period in Chinatown's history. Changes in the immigration laws resulted in a substantial increase in the number of immigrants and refugees entering the community. Housing and social service needs hit a crisis level. In 1969 the San Francisco Chinese Community Citizen's Survey and Fact Finding Committee Report depicted a myriad of Chinatown ills from severely overcrowded housing to inadequate dental care. Its writers urged the city to staff health care services with bilingual personnel because no health facility, outside of Chinese Hospital, offered bilingual services.

At both national and local levels, major developments quelled the crisis. The first major reform came in 1966 with the implementation of Medicare and Medicaid programs.[1] Such federally subsidized medical care for the elderly and the poor substantially reduced the economic barrier to proper health care. Throughout the nation, health service use by low-income and elderly populations steadily increased due to partial federal assumption of health costs (Anderson and Anderson, 1979). Chinatown was no exception. According to Dan Richardi, former administrator of Chinese Hospital, Medicare and MediCal together accounted for 85% of all patient days at Chinese Hospital in 1979 and 1980 (personal communication, 1982).

While national legislation broke the barrier to health care costs, funding from city, state, and federal sources created vital additions to health care services in the late 1970s. In 1979 the Northeast Medical Services (NEMS), a federally funded neighborhood clinic, was established. NEMS offered comprehensive health care and four specialty areas (dermatology, acupuncture, podiatry, and allergy). By contracting a large number of doctors, the NEMS plan allowed low-income residents to see private physicians in addition to NEMS medical staff. Dr. Paul Gee, former medical director of NEMS, reported that while most NEMS patients qualified for MediCal, the NEMS sliding fee scale allowed those who did not qualify to reduce their medical care costs (personal communication, 1982).

In the same year that NEMS was created, Northeast Health Center No. 4, a city-funded facility that provided free or low-cost preventative health care to the Chinatown populace, expanded. Bilingual staff provided the following services: well-baby clinic, prenatal classes, family planning, nutrition education, free blood pressure screening, and screening for eye, lung, and other organic functioning. The center developed and distributed bilingual health education materials where none had previously existed.

By the early 1980s, Chinatown's populace had a wider choice of medical services. Previously restricted to the Tung Wah Dispensary, health service choices now included NEMS, District Health Center #4, San Francisco General Hospital, Telegraph Hill, Chinatown/North Beach Family Planning, Kaiser Hospital, and Chinese Hospital.

During the 1970s, the number of professional and paraprofessional health practitioners in the community mushroomed. Paraprofessionals who had grown up during the 1960s brought their sociopolitical and ethnic consciousness to bear on problems of poverty and racial discrimination. In 1970 they opened a free health clinic. Three years later, they organized the Chinatown Health Fair, which has since become an annual tradition.

Since 1970, this nation has seen a greater representation of ethnic minority physicians and larger enrollment figures of minorities in medical schools, signaling the larger role that minorities are playing in delivering medical care services (National Center of Health Statistics, 1980). Chinatown saw the gains of this national change. In an 18-month period prior to 1981, Chinatown added 17 new doctors, eight of whom were in primary care when usually there were only two or three. Dr. Rolland Lowe observed: "Those who wanted to serve the community—many of whom were bilingual—have now finished medical school. Where previously, Chinese doctors practiced in Chinatown because it was the only place they could work due to racial discrimination, many of today's Chinese doctors *choose* to work in the community because of a social and ethnic commitment" (personal communication, 1982).

Increasing numbers of Chinese physicians made it largely unnecessary for residents to leave the community to obtain medical care; their presence also had the effect of lowering the private costs of health care. This critical mass also led to the establishment of the first National Chinese American Health Conference in 1981, the evolution of the Bay Area Health Alliance (comprised of Asian American physicians, administrators, and health care paraprofessionals), and the creation of a new Chinese Hospital building with expanded services, which was completed in 1982.

Proudly remarking on the community's successes in the health field, Dr. Rolland Lowe pointed to the existence of the Mental Health Unit of NEMS (now in its own building) and the On Lok Senior Health Services (a medical-social service for frail elderly). Reflecting back, he remarked: "We worked very hard and made measurable strides. We have extracted every federal dollar there was to extract for health and brought it into the community" (personal communication, 1982).

Indeed, health care programs at On Lok and NEMS have been cited as model programs. Many health professionals from other areas come to San Francisco to learn from these agencies (Springer, 1988).

Nevertheless, health conditions were poor. As of 1976, San Francisco had one of the highest rates of tuberculosis in the country (San Francisco Health Department Report, 1977). The Chinese were one of two ethnic groups with the highest TB rate in the city. While Western medicine can arrest this disease, it cannot prevent its contraction. Poverty, substandard housing, poor ventilation, crowding, and stress make contagious diseases inevitable. The provision of health care services can not by itself solve the problem.

CONTEMPORARY HEALTH CONDITIONS

Health Status

The health status of Chinatown adults was found to be very low, far lower than for Americans overall (see Table 7.1). Using age-adjusted national data, 40% of the American adults reported their health as "excellent" compared to only 10% of the Chinatown residents. Nationally, 80% of the Americans rated their health as "excellent" or "good" compared to only 43% of the Chinatown residents. Nationally, 19% said their health was "fair" or "poor" compared to 57% of the Chinatown sample. In fact, the percentage of those in "fair" or "poor" health in Chinatown was higher than for any other

Table 7.1
Self-Reported Health Status: Chinatown and the United States[1]

"Would you say your health in general is excellent, good, fair, or poor?"

	Excellent	Good	Fair	Poor
Chinatown	10%	33%	43%	14%
United States	40%	40%	14%	5%

[1]The U.S. figures are age-adjusted to reflect the age distribution of the Chinatown sample. For one age category, the national survey used ages 15-44 years while the Chinatown sample used ages 18-44 years. All other age categories were the same. Without the age-adjustment, 49% of the nation said their health was "excellent," 30% "good," 10% "fair," and 3% "poor" (U.S. Department of Health, Education, and Welfare, Sept. 1977, Health of the Disadvantaged: Chart Book, also Division of Health Interview Statistics, National Center for Health Statistics).

socioeconomic or racial group analyzed in the 1970s by the National Center of Health Statistics.

Predictors of Health Status

Analyses of the predictors of health status have direct implications for the design of interventions. Eight variables were analyzed with regard to their predictive power to explain health status: social support, live alone or with others, age, income, gender, English-speaking ability,[2] quality of heating in one's dwelling (a proxy for substandard housing), and core/noncore area (a proxy for commercial-residential mix and population density).

A multiple regression analysis makes it possible to study the effects of social support on health status while controlling for other variables. It also makes it possible to analyze for the effects of age on health status while controlling for other variables. Increased illness vulnerability with age is understood, and numerous studies have shown that social support is linked to psychological and physical health or well-being (Cohen and Syme, 1985; cf. Cohen and Wills, 1985; House, 1981; Kessler and McLeod, 1985; Turner, 1983; Wallston, Alagna, DeVellis, and DeVellis, 1983). This analysis permits us to examine social support and age simultaneously, while also controlling for environmental variables (heating and density); a cohabitation variable (live alone or with others); and demographic variables (age, income, gender, and English-speaking ability). Within an immigrant population, we would expect that non-English speaking ability would be a deterrent to social support if there were few other persons speaking the person's mother tongue or few health service providers who speak the persons's mother tongue, but this does not appear to be the case in Chinatown, where Chinese-speaking physicians are available and three-quarters of the population are Chinese-speaking.

While the mechanisms through which social support is related to physical illness remain to be clarified, Cohen and Wills (1985) have posited that a lack of positive social relationships leads to negative psychological states such as anxiety or depression. These, in turn, may influence physical health through a direct effect on physiological processes that affect susceptibility to disease or through behavioral patterns that increase risk for disease and mortality. This is what Cohen and Wills have referred to as the Support as Main Effect model. In this model social support serves a generalized beneficial effect by providing regular positive experiences and a set of stable, socially rewarded roles in the community that would be expected to provide positive affect, stability, and recognition of self-worth. Cohen and Wills (1985) alternatively considered the Social Support as Stress Buffer model, wherein support may intervene between the stressful event or expectation of that event and a stress reaction by attenuating or preventing a stress appraisal response. The perception that others can and will provide necessary resources may redefine the potential for harm posed by a situation and, hence, may prevent a situation from being appraised as highly stressful. Alternatively, support may intervene by reducing or eliminating the stress reaction or by influencing the physiological processes (as in providing a solution to the problem; reducing the perceived importance of the problem; tranquilizing the neuroendocrine system, thereby lowering reactivity to perceived stress; or facilitating healthful behaviors). Social support can provide the following functions: emotional support, informational support, social companionship, or instrumental aid. In reviewing the literature, Cohen and Wills (1985) concluded that there is evidence for both the buffering and main effect models.

Because structural measures of support assess only the existence or number of relationships and do not provide measures of the functions actually provided by those relationships (Cohen and Wills, 1985), the measure of social support used in the Chinatown survey included both structural and functional elements: "Now I want you to think about any friends or relatives you feel free to talk with about your worries and problems or can count on for advice or help. . . . Would you say you have many, some, a few, or no such friends or relatives?" This measure specifically defines social support as the general quantity of persons who provide emotional support ("free to talk with about worries and problems"), informational support ("can count on for advice"), and instrumental aid ("can count on for help"). Because it combines several functional indices, this measure can be considered a global functional measure.

In another study of health status among San Francisco Chinatown residents, Carp and Kataoka (1976) found that social support, income, ability to

Table 7.2
Analyses for Health Status

"Would you say your health in general is excellent, good, fair, or poor?"
(1 = excellent, 5 = poor)

Independent Variable	Standardized Beta Coeffecient	F-value	r
Social support (1 = many, 5 = none)	0.2560	6.382**	.25
Age	0.2333	4.103*	.31
English-Speaking (1 = Eng spk, 0 = non)	-0.2090	3.248	-.37
Core/Noncore (1 = core, 0 = noncore)	0.0879	0.792	.13
Live Alone (1 = live alone, 0 = not)	-0.0698	0.481	.05
Income	-0.0611	0.295	-.21
Dwelling Heat (B15) (1 = v. gd, 5 = not gd)	-0.0340	0.106	-.15
Gender (1 = male, 0 = female)	-0.0293	0.001	-.15

$$R^2 = 0.243$$
$$\text{Adjusted } R^2 = 0.171$$
$$F = 3.338**$$
$$df = 8, 83$$

*$p < .05$.   **$p < .01$.   ***$p < .001$

Note: Weighted data: Social support and dwelling heating were significant
predictors of health status. Those without social support and those with poor
dwelling heating reported poorer health.

use English, and better housing were significantly related to health status.
However, since their study was on elderly only, it was important to determine
the predictors of health status for the general adult Chinatown population.

Results of the multiple regression analysis were statistically significant (see
Table 7.2). The combined effect of the eight variables accounted for one-
fourth of the variance. In terms of individual variables, social support and
age were significant predictors of health status. Non-English speaking ability
was also correlated with poorer health status but did not reach statistical
significance because of its simultaneous correlation with other variables.

Social Support. Social support was the most powerful predictor of health
status when controlling for age, English-speaking ability, population density
of neighborhood of residency, cohabitation, income, adequacy of dwelling
heat, and gender. Persons with more friends or relatives that they felt free to
talk with about worries and problems or could count on for advice or help
reported better health status, all other factors being held constant. The perceived presence of persons who provided emotional support, informational
support, and/or instrumental aid was significantly related to perceived
health status. Because the measure for social support combined structural
and functional aspects, additional research is needed to determine exactly
which of these functions is most important and how these functions interre-

late. As Cohen and Wills (1985) have stated: "More research is needed before we can understand how the support processes are related to physical health" (p. 352)—although researchers have theorized that social support could affect exposure to disease agents, influence susceptibility to infection, affect self-care or medical help seeking once disease has been contracted, or modify the severity of the disease course (cf. Jemmott and Locke, 1984; Kasl, Evans, and Neiderman, 1979).

It is certainly the case that once a person becomes ill, supportive others in this community can provide instrumental support by providing transportation to physicians' offices, securing medication, and providing health-related Chinese herb soups or foods. It is also the case that once a person becomes ill, supportive friends or relatives can provide emotional support by visits that provide encouragement and caring and that contribute to mood elevation, which may facilitate healing or well-being. In a community composed primarily of immigrants, informational support can be especially facilitative in securing advice on where to seek proper and affordable medical care. At the preventative end (or main effects model), given the multiple stresses imposed by immigration, cultural dislocation, language barriers, low-income status, long work hours, and occupational constraints, it might be particularly the case that social support plays a vital preventative role in not lowering resistance to contracting disease in this crowding community.

In summary, our finding lends support to the existing body of findings that indicate a positive association between social support and well-being, specifically in the physical health domain. The finding also extends Carp and Kataoka's finding of a relationship between social support and health status for Chinatown elderly to that of adults overall. The implications are that those without social support are at high risk in terms of ill health. Since health status has already been determined to be extremely low in this community, one cannot overstate the importance of designing interventions that provide greater social support for persons in this community. This is particularly the case given the extent to which residents feel they have social support. The majority (52%) reported having "few" friends or relatives they could talk to about worries and problems or count on for advice or help; 25% reported having "some" such persons; 12% reported having "many" such persons in their life; and 11% reported having "none."

Age. Age was also a significant predictor of health status. When all other variables were held constant, older persons were in poorer health than younger adults. This finding probably reflects increased illness vulnerability with age. Health services are especially needed for elderly populations who are at high risk for ill health.

Dental Health Care

Chinatown residents were aware of appropriate dental care practices. Of those interviewed, 72% said they thought that dental check-ups and biannual teeth cleaning were necessary to keep healthy. At the same time, practices did not follow beliefs. Only 29% said they obtained dental check-ups and had their teeth cleaned biannually. Because dental services are least apt to be covered by health plans, dental care is widely neglected among the poor.

This unmet dental need parallels that of other low-income minority communities. Nationally, dental care was the area in which the greatest inequities in use by family income and race persisted. Nonwhites, those with lower incomes, less education, and older adults saw a dentist in much lower proportion than the general population (Anderson, 1979).

Smoking, Alcohol, and Drug Use

Many of the health problems of Chinatown's residents are externally inflicted rather than self-inflicted. The prevalence of self-inflicted precipitants of ill health, such as smoking and alcohol or drug use, was low.

The percentage of smokers in Chinatown (20%) was close to half that of the national population (38%).[3] Among the Chinatown respondents, 80% were nonsmokers, of whom 16% were ex-smokers, leaving at least two-thirds who had never succumbed to the habit. Nationally, 62% of all Americans were nonsmokers, of whom 29% were ex-smokers, leaving a third who had not been smokers.

The percentage of Chinatown residents who had two or more drinks of alcohol per day was 7%; all of these persons said that neither they nor anyone else thought they had a drinking problem. As for drugs, only 1% of the Chinatown sample reported having a drug problem, and they appeared to be referring to prescription drugs.

Health Services Use

Health conditions are affected not just by health status but by the extent to which the population uses health services. Poor health status in this community was not due to low use of services, for the rate of medical service use was similar to the nation overall (National Center of Health Statistics, 1981, pp. 157–160). Eighty-two percent of the Chinatown residents had seen a doctor in the previous year, compared to 75% of Americans overall. Furthermore, of the 18% who had not seen a doctor in the previous year, all said they would seek medical care if they had an illness that needed treatment.

The average number of physician visits over the previous year was 3.32 for the Chinatown sample, compared to 3.62 for the age-adjusted national data (National Center of Health Statistics, 1981). Chinese residents showed little or no resistance to seeking medical care.

Most residents sought treatment from physicians in the community. Sixty-three percent saw a Chinese doctor, 20% saw a Caucasian doctor, and 17% saw both Caucasian and Chinese doctors. The higher rate of visits to Chinese physicians compared to Caucasian physicians is probably due to geographic convenience, language and cultural familiarity, and the lower office visit fees of Chinatown physicians.

Western versus Eastern Forms of Treatment

Of interest to any health study of a Chinese American community is the extent to which residents use Chinese or Western medicine. In Boston's Chinatown, Hessler, Notan, Ogbru, and New (1975) found that the majority of residents used both Western and Chinese medical care systems. Relatively few residents exclusively used Chinese forms of treatment.

In San Francisco's Chinatown, there is widespread acceptance of Western medicine to the point that it dominates over Chinese methods of treatment. In the previous year, 28% of the residents had gone to a Chinese herbalist and only 9% had gone to an acupuncturist. These rates pale against the 82% who sought treatment from a Western-trained physician.

I surmise that the dominance of Western medicine is largely due to economics and attitudes. MediCal and Medicare do not cover acupuncturists and herbalists. Thus, on a per-visit basis, Western medical services are less costly than Chinese forms of treatment. In addition, health attitudes have changed owing to the effectiveness of the Western-based health delivery system in the community and to the increased presence of Western medicine in Asian cities from which these immigrants come.

Acceptance of Chinese forms of treatment was broader than its actual use. Of those who had not seen a Chinese herbalist, 50% said they would if they had needed to. Of those who had not seen an acupuncturist, 33% said they would if they had an ailment that acupuncture could treat. In total, 62% of the respondents either did or were willing to seek treatment from a Chinese herbalist, and 37% of the respondents did or were willing to see an acupuncturist. Dramatic evidence of the Westernization of medical attitudes among Chinatowners was seen in the fact that only about one-third of the residents expressed willingness to use acupuncture, a treatment modality that originated in China.

Chinatown residents have an eclectic attitude toward health care. They commonly seek Western medical care but also take Chinese herbs and home remedies. While Western-trained physicians are commonly sought for serious health problems, Chinese herbs were most often used for health maintenance or minor health ailments. Asked how often they drink soups made with Chinese herbs, 20% said "once a week or more often," 33% said "once a month," 42% said "less often than once a month," and 6% said "never." Asked how often they use Chinese home remedies like Po Chai Yuen or Chinese herb teas like Hop Chai Cha, 63% said "a few times a year," 8% said "once a month or more often," and 30% said "not at all." Chinese herb remedies are most often used for ailments such as the flu, gastrointestinal ailments, or a cold. Many of today's health care professionals accept this eclecticism. According to Dr. Rolland Lowe: "Today, there is a bridging of the two factions. We can accept both [Western and Chinese medicine] rather than pit one against the other. It's healthy for Chinatown. In this new atmosphere, the Western doctor in Chinatown no longer downplays herbs, some are even trained in both Western and Eastern medicine" (personal communication, 1982).

Predictors of Health Service Use

What variables predicted health service use in Chinatown? The following variables were tested for their power in explaining the number of times a resident saw a doctor in the previous year: health status, age, income, sex, English-speaking ability, social support, live alone/with others, dwelling heating, and population density (core/noncore). Results of the multiple regression analysis were statistically significant (see Table 7.3). Together, these variables explained one-third of the variance.

The individual variables that significantly predicted health service use were health status and age. When all other variables were held constant, persons in poorer health were more likely to seek medical services than those in better health. Not surprisingly, this finding demonstrates that need is

Table 7.3
Analyses for Number of Times Seen a Doctor in the Past Year

"In the past 12 months, how many times have you been to a doctor?"

Independent Variable	Standardized Beta Coeffecient	F-value	r
Health Status (1 = excellent, 5 = poor)	0.328	10.025**	.41
Age	0.288	6.708**	.41
Core/Noncore (1 = core, 0 = noncore)	0.175	3.504	.28
Income	-0.171	2.584	-.27
Social Support (1 = many, 5 = none)	-0.101	1.036	-.09
Gender (1 = male, 0 = female)	-0.074	0.521	-.05
English-Speaking (1 = Eng. spk, 0 = non)	0.092	0.688	-.21
Live Alone (1 = live alone)	0.019	0.041	.07
Dwelling Heating (1 = v. gd, 5 = not gd at all)	0.005	0.000	-.11

$$R^2 = 0.336$$
$$\text{Adjusted } R^2 = 0.263$$
$$F = 4.60***$$
$$df = 9,82$$

*$p < .05$.   **$p < .01$.   ***$p < .001$

Note: Weighted data: Health status and social support predicted number of times one had seen a doctor. Those who reported poor health and less social support had seen a doctor more often.

related to service use. Also, older persons were more likely to seek medical services, all other variables being constant. Core residency and income were also correlated with health service use (core residents and the poor saw a doctor more often than noncore or higher income residents), but the correlation of these variables with other variables meant they did not reach statistical significance in the regression analysis.

Health Education

Health education is often obtained through health practitioners. If health service use was high, we expected that residents would be well educated in health matters. Dr. Rolland Lowe confirmed this, saying that "Chinatown residents today are better health-educated than one would expect" (personal communication, 1982).

Indeed, the survey findings revealed that Chinatowners were fairly well educated with respect to nutrition, general areas of health care, and knowledge of basic service provision. Asked if each of the following were necessary to keep healthy, the following proportions said "yes": 99% to "enough sleep to feel rested the next day," 98% to "a daily diet that includes protein," 97% to "a daily diet that includes fruits and vegetables," 93% to "drinking at least three glasses of nonalcoholic liquids daily," and 90% to "a daily diet that includes rice, noodles, or bread daily." A majority said that to keep healthy, one must have daily exercise (88%), dental check-ups and biannual teeth cleaning (72%), be aware of changes in how you feel or look (65%), get a tetanus shot every 10 years (46%), and take multiple vitamins daily (36%). Discrepancies between healthy beliefs and practices revealed that exercise, dental care, and tetanus shots were areas of greatest neglect.

Residents also showed appropriate differentiation between those ailments best handled by a physician and those best handled by a health center. Residents preferred a private physician over a health center for specialized or serious problems (such as dental care, diabetes, high blood pressure, urinary problems, chest pain, and back pain). The preference for a private physician over a health center was less pronounced for health maintenance needs (such as prenatal care or a checkup for one's job, school, or child).

A majority said they would seek professional help for a urinary problem, back pain, chest pain, high blood pressure, diabetes, insomnia of one month's duration, a check-up, check-up for a child, a sore tooth, teeth that need cleaning, and a burn that blistered. For a cold, 57% would take care of it themselves, 42% would seek professional help, and 1% "didn't know." For a sore throat, 41% would take care of it themselves, 57% would seek professional help, and 1% "didn't know." For constant tiredness, 42% would take care of it themselves, 51% would seek professional help, and 8% "didn't know."

SUMMARY

This chapter documents changes in the health attitudes of Chinese Americans and transformations in the health delivery system available to them. Eighty years ago, the city's sole means of correcting Chinatown's health problems was condemnation and isolation. Fifty years ago, Chinatown still lacked adequate health care. The Chinese were suspicious of Western medicine. There were no Western-trained Chinese physicians.

Changes in health attitudes and health delivery services occurred as a result of several factors: (1) the efforts of local organizations that led to the first medical facility (Tung Wah Dispensary); (2) Western-trained Chinese American physicians, whose efforts led to the establishment of Chinese Hospital and other health facilities within the community; (3) the decline of anti-Chinese discrimination in the United States; (4) the limitation of herb imports to this country during and after World War II; (5) the institution of federally subsidized medical care for the poor and elderly; and (6) public attention to Chinatown's ills. In total, Chinatown has been a sterling example of what community leadership, collective action, and government-funded health programs can accomplish.

Today, ignorance of Western medicine and fear of hospitals are ghosts of the past. The city has shown increased responsiveness to the community's needs. Chinatown residents have a high rate of health service use; 82% of those interviewed had seen a doctor in the previous year. The average number of physician visits per person over the past year was 3.3, which is similar to the nation as a whole. It can be assumed that residents' increased use of health services has been due to changes in health attitudes, reductions in economic barriers to health care, and reforms in the health delivery system.

But pride in past accomplishments should not lull us into complacency. Nor should the finding of comparable service use to other Americans distract us from the major problem raised by this research—the low health status of Chinatown's residents. Despite the use of health care services, the battle of securing good health for all members of this ethnic community is far from over. The self-reported health status of Chinatown residents is very low—and especially so when compared to national statistics. Only 43% of the Chinatown sample rated their health as "excellent" or "good," compared to 80% of the age-adjusted national sample. The average Chinatowner reported his or her health status as "fair," while the average American reported his or her health somewhere between "excellent" and "good."

There was a strong predictive relationship between social support and reported health status, which builds on an already existing literature on the positive relationship between social support and well-being. Having few or no friends or relatives who can provide emotional, informational, or instrumental aid was related to poorer health. With regard to the implications of these findings, there is a clear need for programs and interventions that reduce social and emotional isolation. In addition, greater efforts need to be forged to improve the health condition of Chinatown's elderly, since age was also a predictor of health status. The problem is not that residents are unaware of existing services or that they do not use them. Health status (along with age) was a significant predictor of health service use, indicating that need and use were highly correlated.

The problem is that health needs in low-income, immigrant communities do not disappear. Despite improvements in health service use, greater efforts must be made. Recent budget cuts have curtailed service delivery in a community that requires more services, bilingual staff, and financial support. Health service demand is high, and health needs remain. Checking the pulse of Chinatown revealed that the poorer health status of its residents is a serious problem despite increased services. As Chinatown is likely to remain a refuge for the aged and socially isolated, Dr. Rolland Lowe soberly stated that "this job will be forever (personal communication, 1982).

NOTES

1. Medicare assistance is based on age; it serves people aged 65 and over. MediCal (or Medicaid) assistance is based on income; it serves those below a certain income level relative to family size.

2. English-speaking ability was defined as reflecting people who either: (1) chose to be interviewed in English or (2) chose to be interviewed in Chinese but said they could carry on a conversation in English "very well" or "pretty well."

3. National data were obtained from the National Center of Health Statistics (1981).

Crowding in Chinatown is a within-dwelling phenomenon as well as a neighborhood index of persons per acre. This occupant of a residential hotel lives in a room comparable in size to a wealthy San Franciscan's walk-in closet. All available space is utilized. This is a residence of constraints, not of choice. The harmful effects of crowding are evident to nearly all residents. 1984. (Photograph by Crystal K. D. Huie.) Reprinted by permission.

Lost Almost Everything

This respondent and her two children lived in a one-bedroom apartment in a large, bright, clean building in the heart of Chinatown. This woman of some 30 years was neatly attired, wearing light make-up and expensive jewelry. Well-traveled and well-educated, she looked like she came from an upper-class background. Indeed, this woman was born in Vietnam of a wealthy family. She was receptive and responsive. She graciously but repeatedly asked me if I would like some tea. Even though the interview was conducted in sam yup, she replied in English once in a while. She confided how irritated she gets when people think she's uneducated or can't speak English.

In her early teens, her father sent her to Hong Kong for schooling. There she married a man whom she believed later died in the Vietnam war. Sadly, she reflected: "I lost my husband and my country." Now she's widowed with a teenaged son and young daughter.

Three years ago, with the expectation of starting a new life, she immigrated to the United States to join a boyfriend. The relationship did not work out. After breaking up with this man, she moved from another Bay Area city to Chinatown.

This woman was currently unemployed and looking for work. Ever since her relationship ended, she hadn't been able to concentrate: "It's not that I can't find a job. I can speak several languages. The problem is that I can't concentrate on anything. I've lost my country, my husband, my boyfriend, and my job. I feel very lonely."

For most of the questions, she stopped for several minutes, stared at me, and then answered. At first I thought I hadn't read the questions clearly or perhaps she had a hearing problem. So I repeated the questions. But she replied: "I understand the question. I just want to think it over before I give you an answer. Oftentimes, I can't concentrate when I think. For the last few minutes, my mind was somewhere else, so please excuse me for my slow reaction."

This respondent was very depressed. Within a short period of time, she felt she had lost almost everything.

8

"Too Bloated with Misery to Eat a Salted Bean": Mental Health Status and Attitudes

Statistical data on the mental disorders of Asian Americans are scanty (Kung, 1962). There has been little direct study of their mental health needs or problem-solving strategies. With so few empirical studies on Asian Americans, particularly on non-college student populations, mental health planners and service providers have had to rely on personal experiences, historical observation, demographic material, or limited available data. As a consequence, planning for the delivery of social services has often been made on the basis of the "best guess" approach (Kim, 1978).

Disagreements exist over the status of well-being of Asian Americans (Sue, Sue, and Sue, 1975). Kung (1962) and Bourne (1973) have proposed that the Chinese have few psychological problems. Kung characterized the Chinese as less vulnerable to mental suffering than other racial groups, more accepting of life as it is, and less tense in facing problems. Bourne described the Chinese as relatively free of mental illness. However, notions that Asian Americans are without mental health problems have been discredited (Brown, Stein, Huang, and Harris 1973; Sue and Kitano, 1973; Sue and McKinney, 1975; Sue and Sue, 1974; Tsai, Teng, and Sue, 1980). The suicide rate for U.S. Chinese from 1950 to 1958, which was two and one-half times the national rate (Kung, 1962), made real the fact that Chinese Americans suffer from mental health disorders.

Mental health surveys of Asian Americans—particularly non-college student, non-patient populations—are needed. As noted by Veroff, Kulka, and

Douvan (1981), studies of treated groups usually fall short of a complete picture of help-seeking. Moreover, research on non-patient populations provides a more valid indicator of emotional disturbance in the larger population (Berk and Hirata, 1973; Sue and Morishima, 1982).

To test whether the mental health movement had been nationally effective, Veroff, Kulka, and Douvan (1981) conducted a 20-year national follow-up survey of Gurin, Veroff, and Feld's (1960) earlier survey. Veroff and colleagues found that Americans increased their service use of mental health professionals over time. Only 3% of the Americans sampled in 1957 had sought mental health services. By 1976, the percentage had risen to 12%. The researchers concluded that the community mental health movement had been nationally effective. However, a major aim of the community mental health movement was to make mental health services more accessible and relevant to poor and ethnic minority populations. Existing data suggested that members of Chinatown's community have not seen the gains intended by this movement. From July 1965 to June 1966, the San Francisco Chinese constituted 27% of the population but their use rate of mental health facilities amounted to only 7% (Report of the San Francisco Chinese Community Citizens Survey and Fact Finding Committee, 1969). Lacking survey data, we have no comprehensive knowledge of whether Asian American communities have seen the gains promised by the community mental health movement. One purpose of our survey was to assess service use, which was ascertained by asking: "Have you ever gone to a mental health center or seen a mental health professional for any problem you've had?"

If mental health service use in Chinatown is found to be low, as has been found for Asian Americans overall (Leong, 1986), our objective was to investigate why. Hypotheses offered for low service use among ethnic minorities that were not tested in our survey included lack of cultural, ethnic, and linguistic sensitivity or competence on the part of service providers or lack of cultural appropriateness of intervention strategies. Hypotheses proposed for low service use among Chinese Americans that were tested in our survey included: (1) lack of knowledge of available services, (2) reluctance to admit to psychological symptoms, (3) tendency to suffer in silence, (4) use of alternative cultural sources of help, (5) different methods of coping with personal problems, (6) beliefs that discourage use of mental health services, or (7) low priority attached to seeking professional treatment for mental health problems. Severe psychopathologies more typically found among hospitalized patients were not studied because the community sample consisted of functioning adults.

This chapter begins with a literature review of each of the aforementioned factors that have been proposed by others to contribute to low use of mental health services by Chinese Americans. Section two consists of the findings on mental health—specifically, rate of service use, knowledge of services, psychological systems, use of alternative forms of help, predisposition to seeking help or self help, coping strategies, beliefs about mental disorders, and priority given to seeking professional help for mental disorders.

POSSIBLE CONTRIBUTORS TO LOW SERVICE USE

Knowledge of Services

Kim (1978) found that 26% of the Chicago Chinese interviewed did not know where to go for help with mental health problems. In the present survey, knowledge of services was assessed by asking: "Do you know of medical clinics or mental health centers that counsel people with mental or emotional problems?"

Stigma and Silent Suffering

Brown, Stein, Huang, and Harris (1973) and Sue and McKinney (1975) proposed that low use of mental health services by Asian Americans originated from a reluctance to admit to psychological disorders and/or access to alternative sources of mental health care. Many had assumed that Chinese Americans were reluctant to admit to psychological disorders because of the stigma and shame attached to mental illness and the tendency to suffer in silence (Duff and Arthur, 1967; Kim, 1978; Kitano, 1969; Kleinman, 1977; Lin and Lin, 1981; Marsella, Kinzie, and Gordon, 1973; Sue and Morishima, 1982). Stigmatization and a tendency to suffer in silence were thought to be responsible for Chinese somatization of psychiatric disorders, particularly depression and other neurotic symptoms (Duff and Arthur, 1967; Kim, 1978; Kitano, 1969; Kleinman, 1977; Lin and Lin, 1981; Marsella, Kinzie, and Gordon, 1973; Sue and Morishima, 1982). Kleinman and Mechanic (1981) and Lin and Lin (1981) claimed a long history of stigmatization of mental illness in China, which they maintained has continued in present day Taiwan, Hong Kong, and overseas Chinese communities.

Despite a literature suggesting that Asian Americans suffer in silence, there has been contradictory evidence. Lin, Tazuma, and Masuda's (1979) study of Vietnamese refugees showed no reticence to psychological symptom expression. I suggest two possible explanations for this finding. First, the multiple, vivid life stress events encountered by immigrants and refugees may make them more willing to report problems, lessening their fear of social stigma. Second, Asian Americans may be reluctant to initiate self-disclosure about psychological problems (i.e., seek professional services) but not unwilling to admit to specific symptoms in response to inquiry about them. One aim of this Chinatown survey was to test these hypotheses.

To examine whether Chinese Americans suffer in silence, we investigated the extent to which Chinatowners sought informal help for personal problems. If Chinese Americans suffered in silence, one might expect them to show greater reluctance to seeking help from others than was found for Americans overall; that is, one might expect greater self-help among Chinese Americans. Among a national sample of Americans, from 65% to 86% sought informal help when worried, and 50% sought help when unhappy (Veroff, Douvan, and Kulka, 1981). In this Chinatown survey, help-seeking was assessed by the following questions: (1) "If something's bothering you and you don't know what to do about it, what do you usually do?" (If R does not mention talking to someone, ask, "Would you talk to anyone about it?"); (2) "Have you ever had a personal problem where you sought advice or help from someone?" (If "no," ask, "Is there any problem you can think of where you'd seek advice or help from someone?"); and (3) "I'd like to know what you usually do or say when you're having frustrations or problems in your life."

One way to test the validity of the "suffer in silence" and "reluctance to admit" hypotheses was to assess the mental health status of the residents. If urbanization and migration were related to higher prevalence of neurosis and psychophysiological reactions, as was found among Taiwanese Chinese (Lin, Kleinman, and Lin, 1981), we would expect the incidence of psychological disorders in Chinatown to be high because the location is urban and the population largely immigrant. If residents do not report disorders, we could either assume that stigma or silent suffering could be inhibiting factors to symptom admission or that incidence of psychological symptoms is low. If residents do report disorders, the finding would argue for willingness to report upon inquiry. In our survey, mental well-being was measured by the Langner scale (Srole, Langner, Michael, Opler, and Rennie, 1962) and by items designed for this survey. Although the Langner scale has been criticized on grounds that symptoms of physical illness are potentially confounded with those of mental illness (Crandall and Dohrenwend, 1967; Dohrenwend and Dohrenwend, 1969), because Chinese Americans have been thought to somatize many of their psychological problems, we felt that the scale would not be problematic as long as it is acknowledged that psychological and/or physiological disorders were being measured. Prior administration of the Langner scale to samples in Hong Kong (Lo, 1976), Midtown Manhattan (Srole, Langner, Michael, Opler, and Rennie, 1962), and the midwestern town of Hennepin (Summers, Seiler, and Hough, 1971) made the administration of the Langner scale useful for comparative purposes. Other items intended to assess mental health status and stress included: "Do you find there are many things that have been making you angry?" "Do you find there are many things that have been making you upset at work or at home?" "Do you feel that people annoy or irritate you?" "Do you get depressed? . . . would you say often, sometimes, rarely, or never?" "Have you ever had a 'sinking down feeling' (like being depressed)?"[1] Effects for age, gender, income, and nativity were analyzed for each symptom variable.

Alternative Sources of Help

Lin, Tardiff, Donetz, and Kenny (1978) found that many Chinese in Vancouver assisted others with their personal problems. Tsai, Teng, and Sue (1980) proposed that Asian Americans relied on cultural forms of mental health assistance as an alternative to professional mental health care: "the kinship system of the Chinese encourages a mutual dependence which forms the basis of psychological security. . . . shopkeepers, respected leaders, acupuncturists, herbalists, and benevolent association members may be called upon to help a distressed person" (p. 305). However, Kim's (1978) findings contradicted Tsai, Teng, and Sue's proposition—Chicago Chinese were found to seek public resources such as hospitals, doctors, and police rather than private ones such as family, friends, or relatives.

One aim of this Chinatown survey was to test the extent to which Chinese Americans have alternative forms of mental health assistance, that is, social support that may or may not be cultural in nature. The assumption being tested here is that one contributing cause for low use of mental health services by Asian Americans may be heavy use of alternative forms of support or help. The question "Are there any community agencies you've gone to for problems you've had?" was intended to be a measure of cultural forms of help, since most community agencies are bilingual-bicultural service agencies. The next item was intended to measure use of cultural forms of assistance (acupuncturists, herbalists, Chinese temple), use of professional forms of mental health care (social worker, psychologist, psychiatrist, counselor) or other professionals (doctor, nurse, Chinese doctor), use of religious professionals (reverend, priest, or pastor), use of non-scientific practitioners (astrologist or spiritual reader), or use of friends or family: "Thinking about the last time you had a problem where you sought advice or help from someone . . . here's a list of people you might have talked to about your problem. Did you talk to any of these people about your problem? Which ones: [spouse, son, daughter, mother, father, co-worker, social worker, psychologist, psychiatrist, counselor, doctor/nurse, Chinese doctor, herbalist, acupuncturist, Chinese temple, reverend, priest or pastor, astrologist or spiritual reader, other?]"

An additional measure was used to assess social support, that is, the general availability of persons who provide emotional support, informational support, and/or instrumental aid to the individual: "Now I want you to think about any friends or relatives you feel free to talk with about your worries and problems [emotional support] or can count on for advice [informational support] or help [instrumental aid]. . . . would you say you have many, some, a few, or no such friends or relatives?" There has been consistent evidence of a positive association between social support and well-being, and the evidence indicates that this may be due to either a direct effect of social support or to a buffering effect of social support in response to stressful events (Cohen and Wills, 1985).

Another measure—"Do you ever wish there was someone you could really talk to?"—was a confidant measure (availability of or desire for a relationship that probably provides emotional and informational support). Research evidence provides consistent evidence of buffering effects of confidant relationships to well-being (cf. Cohen and Wills, 1985). The measure can also be interpreted as an indicator of loneliness or social isolation. If many persons indicate a desire for a confidant, such findings would contradict the hypothesis that Chinese Americans have alternative sources of help for their personal problems.

Coping Strategies

Veroff, Douvan, and Kulka (1981) found that among Americans, the poor had styles of coping that reflected considerable resignation; also, the poor tended to pray in times of need, while the affluent talked to others. Do these styles reflect those of Chinese Americans? With regard to Chinese, Kleinman and Mechanic (1981) found a vital sense of determination and purpose among the Chinese in China. Kung (1962) remarked that religion did not seem to hold much significance for Chinese Americans. Presumably, Chinese Americans may not use mental health services because of a coping strategy of determination, and they may not rely on prayer to the extent that other Americans do. These hypotheses needed to be tested.

Mental Health Beliefs

Low use of mental health services by Chinese Americans has been attributed to beliefs that discourage use of mental health services (Tsai, Tent, and Sue, 1980). Sue and Sue (1971) proposed that Asian Americans equate psychological problems with shameful and disgraceful behaviors, personal weakness, or "bad blood." Sue, Wagner, Ja, Margullis, and Lew (1976) suggested that the Chinese are reluctant to seek mental health services because they believe in organic causes of mental disorders and believe that mental disorders can be prevented through the avoidance of morbid thoughts. This Chinatown survey sought to test the aforementioned notions. In this survey, mental health beliefs were assessed by asking: "What do you think causes mental problems or mental illness?" "Do you think there are any things that can be done to prevent mental problems or mental illness?" "What do you think can be done to cure mental problems or mental illness?"

Seeking Professional Help

Finally, with regard to the priority given to seeking professional help, the literature suggests that Asian Americans who use services are more disturbed than non-Asians who use services (Brown, Stein, Huang, and Harris, 1973;

Sue and McKinney, 1975; Sue and Sue, 1974). The implication is that Asian Americans with mild problems avoid seeking professional help. To test this assumption, respondents in this survey were asked what they would do if they had a "depression that won't go away."

CONTEMPORARY MENTAL HEALTH CONDITIONS

Rate of Use

Chinatown has not seen the gains promised by the community mental health movement. Only 5% of the Chinatown sample had sought mental health services, a proportion close to the national sample of Americans who sought mental health care three decades earlier! There appears to have been no improvement in mental health service use in Chinatown from the 1960s through the 1970s. The crucial question is "Why?"

Lack of Knowledge about Services

In Chinatown, low use rates could be partly due to lack of knowledge about existing mental health services. Three-quarters of the sample (74%) said they did not know of any medical clinics or mental health centers that counsel people with mental or emotional problems. The proportion of Chinatowners who lacked information about available mental health services was substantially higher than the proportion of uninformed Chicago Chinese.

Psychological Problems

Emotional Tension. Admission to symptoms of emotional tension was prevalent, with over one-third of the Chinatown sample reporting one or more symptoms. Forty-one percent of the respondents said there had been many things that had been making them upset at work or at home; 30% said there were many things that had been making them angry; and 44% felt annoyed or irritated by others. As one respondent stated, "I can't handle everyday pressures when my son gets irritated and mad and talks back. I can't do much. I just feel like socking him in the head."

Analyzing for effects of age, gender, income, and nativity on symptoms of anger, upset, and annoyed/irritable revealed no significant effects when the variables were analyzed together. When analyzed individually, there was a significant effect for age on feeling upset.[2] Feeling upset was more prevalent among younger adults and less common among the elderly.

Depression. Although most of the literature suggests that Asian Americans do not admit to symptoms of depression, up to 44% of the Chinatown respondents reported having had feelings of depression. Close to half of the respondents said they get depressed sometimes or often (5% "often," 39% "sometimes," 42% "rarely," 13% "never," and 2% "didn't know"). Four out of ten (39%) said they have had a sinking down feeling like being depressed. One-fifth (21%) admitted to feeling like nothing ever turns out the way they want it to. One-fourth of the residents admitted having periods of days, weeks, or months when they couldn't take care of things because they couldn't get going, and 17% said they were in low or very low spirits most of the time. The intercorrelations of these items were statistically significant, with only one exception.[3]

There were no significant effects for age, gender, income, and nativity on depression when these variables were considered together, but when analyzed individually, there was a significant effect for nativity on depression.[4] Immigrants reported more depression than native-born Chinese. Lincoln Lin, a mental health worker at Northeast Mental Health Services, was not surprised by this finding: "There's a lot of pressure on residents, especially immigrants. Chinese employers are not always fair. . . . employees work long hours and get minimum pay. Workers worry about money, their job, and they can't get out of Chinatown because of language" (personal communication, 1982).

Tseng and Hsu (1969) proposed a linguistic explanation for low rates of reported depression, claiming that low reported rates were due to a dearth of colloquial expressions for depression in the Chinese language. Connie Young Yu, conducting research for the present study, found Tseng and Hsu's claim without merit. Yu found a variety of colloquial expressions for depression among the San Francisco Chinese. These phases translated to: "not happy," "gloomy," "emotionally I'm low," "I don't want to do anything," "I feel frustrated," "my spirits are weak," "the heart hurts and the head is numb," "disgusted with life," "a sinking feeling in my stomach," "I feel like I'm eating bitterness," "I'm dying," "I feel like I want to die," "the feeling of falling down into a well," and "I feel too bloated with misery to eat a salted bean."

Psychological/Physiological Impairment. Langner and Michael (1963) interpreted a score of four or more symptoms on the Langner scale as an indicator of psychiatric impairment, while Seiler (1973) used a score of seven or more. The proportion of Chinatowners who reported four or more symptoms (35%) was higher than that found in Hong Kong (32%), Midtown Manhattan (31%), or Hennepin (17%). The proportion of the Chinatown sample who reported seven or more symptoms (20%) was higher than that found in Hong Kong (12%), Midtown Manhattan (11%), or Hennepin (6%). Table 8.1 contains the prevalence of each scale item for the Chinatown and Midtown Manhattan samples respectively. Mental health problems in Chinatown are apparently substantial and more prevalent than in two other crowded, urban areas and one rural area.

In Chinatown, the two symptoms of highest frequency on the Langner scale were "a memory that's not alright" (40%) and "worrying a lot" (42%). The prevalence of memory loss may be due to the high proportion of elderly in this community, since dementia becomes more prevalent among the aged. The prevalence of extensive worrying may be due to disadvantage, low income, immigrant status, and age. In response to the question, "What kinds of things do you worry about most?" health (28%), finances and job (23%), and family (22%) were most often mentioned. Comments conveyed this: "I worry about my own and my husband's health." "Financial situation is my biggest worry." "I worry about my son and his family in Hong Kong." "I worry about my insomnia, being unable to find a job, having difficulty trying to survive."

Income, nativity, age, and gender did not correlate with scores on the Langner scale.[5] Curious as to the effects of a psychological variable on psychological-physiological health, we added personal effectiveness to the analysis. The items designed to measure personal effectiveness were roughly similar to those used by Douvan and Walker (1956) in their survey. These items were: (E7) "Do you think it's better to plan your life a good ways ahead or would you say life is too much a matter of luck to plan ahead very far?" (E8) "When you do make plans ahead, do you usually get to carry out things the way you expected, or do things usually come up to make you change your plans?" (E9) "Have you usually felt pretty sure your life would work out the way you want it to, or have there been times when you haven't been sure about it?"[6] Personal effectiveness significantly predicted psychological and physiological health. Persons who felt a greater sense of effectiveness and control over their lives reported fewer psychological or physiological disorders.[7]

Use of Alternative Forms of Help

There was some use of community-based agencies in Chinatown. For help with personal problems, slightly over one-fourth of the residents (26%) had gone to a community agency, such as Self Help for the Elderly, Chinese Newcomers Service Center, and Chinese for Affirmative Action. However, use of culturally based forms of help was minimal. Few Chinatown residents (less than 1%) sought help from herbalists and acupuncturists for help with personal problems. Only 1% of the sample went to a Chinese temple the last time they sought help. Tsai, Teng, and Sue's hypothesis about reliance on cultural alternatives to mental health care was not found valid for these Chinese Americans.

A majority of individuals in the sample (52%) reported having "a few" friends or relatives with whom they felt free to talk to about worries and problems or whom they could count on for advice or help. One-fourth reportedly had "some" individuals who provided such social support, 12% had "many," and 11% had "none." Apparently, this is not sufficient social sup-

Table 8.1

Langner 22-Item Screening Test Distributions for Chinatown and Midtown Manhattan Surveys

Item			Chinatown	Midtown Manhattan
1. Does your memory seem to be right?		Yes	58%	93%
	*	No	40%	6%
		DK	2%	0%
2. Have you ever been bothered by nervousness (irritable, fidgety, tense)? Would you say often, sometimes, or never?	*	Often	3%	18%
		Sometimes	41%	56%
		Never	57%	26%
3. Have you ever had any fainting spells? Would you say never, a few times, or more than a few times?		Never	58%	82%
		A few times	33%	16%
	*	More than a few times	8%	2%
		DK	1%	0%
				0%
4. Would you say your appetite is poor, fair, good, or too good?	*	Poor	4%	5%
		Fair	52%	16%
		Good	36%	58%
		Too Good	8%	21%
5. Do you ever have any trouble getting to sleep or staying asleep?	*	Often	8%	15%
		Sometimes	57%	30%
		Never	35%	55%
6. Do you feel weak all over much of the time?	*	Yes	20%	9%
		No	78%	91%
		DK	2%	0%
7. Are you ever troubled with headaches or pains in the head? Would you say often, sometimes, or never?	*	Often	10%	11%
		Sometimes	47%	55%
		Never	43%	34%
8. Have you had periods of days, weeks, or months when you couldn't take care of things because you couldn't get going?	*	Yes	25%	16%
		No	74%	83%
		DK	1%	0%
9. In general, would you say that most of the time you are in high (very good) spirits, good spirits, low spirits, or very low spirits?		High	14%	10%
		Good	69%	81%
	*	Low	15%	6%
	*	Very Low	2%	1%
		DK	0%	1%
10. Do you feel like nothing ever turns out for you the way you want it to?	*	Yes	21%	11%
		No	72%	87%
		DK	7%	1%

Table 8.1 (*Continued*)

Item			Chinatown	Midtown Manhattan
11. Do you have periods of such great restlessness that you cannot sit long in a chair?	*	Yes	22%	19%
		No	76%	87%
		DK	2%	0%
12. Do you worry a lot?	*	Yes	42%	47%
		No	58%	52%
13. Have you ever been bothered by shortness of breath when you were not exercising or working hard? Would you say often, sometimes, or never?	*	Often	2%	4%
		Sometimes	25%	15%
		Never	73%	80%
14. Are you bothered by acid or sour stomach several times a week?	*	Yes	10%	10%
		No	86%	89%
		DK	4%	0%
15. Do you ever so often suddenly feel hot all over?	*	Yes	17%	16%
		No	83%	83%
16. Have you ever been bothered by your heart beating hard?	*	Often	4%	4%
		Sometimes	30%	28%
		Never	66%	68%
17. Have you ever been bothered by "cold sweats"? or unusual sweating? Would you say often, sometimes, or never?	*	Often	1%	2%
		Sometimes	11%	15%
		Never	86%	82%
		DK	2%	1%
18. Do your hands ever tremble enough to bother you? Would you say often, sometimes, or never?	*	Often	0%	2%
		Sometimes	16%	11%
		Never	83%	87%
		DK	1%	0%
19. Does there seem to be a clogging in your head or nose much of the time?	*	Yes	22%	14%
		No	78%	85%
20. Do you have personal worries that get you down physically?	*	Yes	28%	20%
		No	71%	79%
		DK	1%	0%
21. Do you feel alone even among friends?	*	Yes	20%	18%
		No	78%	80%
		DK	2%	1%
22. Do you sometimes wonder if anything is worthwhile anymore?	*	Yes	25%	27%
		No	69%	71%
		DK	6%	1%

* Indicates those scored in the direction of physiological or psychiatric impairment.

port for a majority of Chinese Americans interviewed. The need for a confidant was prevalent, with nearly two-thirds (65%) of the sample reportedly wishing that there was someone they could really talk to. This finding indicates a fairly commonly expressed need among Chinese Americans for social support, particularly of an emotional and informational nature. Regression analyses for age, gender, income, and nativity revealed no significant effects when all variables were considered together, but when variables were analyzed separately, age was a significant predictor of need for a confidant. The need for a confidant declined with age, indicating that younger Chinese American adults were in greater need of emotional and informational social support than the more elderly.[8]

In summary, the evidence does not support the notion that Chinese Americans use culturally relevant alternative forms of mental health care as a substitute for professional mental health services, nor does it appear that most needs for social support are being met by informal others.

Seek Help or Self Help?

Between 26% and 41% of the residents were self-help oriented, depending on the question asked. When bothered about something without knowing what to do, roughly one-fourth of the residents were self-help oriented. Specifically, 26% chose self-help, 50% would talk to others, 9% would use self-help along with seeking help, 9% would do nothing, and 1% did not know what they would do (see Table 8.2).

In terms of past behavior, one-third of those interviewed had never sought advice or help from anyone and could not conceive of doing so. The other

Table 8.2
Ways of Coping with Problems

"If something's bothering you and you don't know what to do about it, what do you usually do? [If R doesn't mention talking to others, ask "Would you talk to anyone about it?]

	Percent
Seek Help ("talk to others")	49.8%
Talk to Others along with Self Help	8.9%
Self Help	(26.3%)
A. Think/solve problem by self	10.9%
B. Avoidance ("Don't think about it," Forget it")	6.3%
C. Distractions or do things to relax	6.1%
D. Other ("Tell myself not to worry," "worry some more," removal from source of problem)	3.0%
Do Nothing or Accept Fate ("Let it be")	9.1%
"Don't know"	1.3%
Inappropriate Responses	4.6%
Total	100%

Table 8.3
Ways of Handling Frustrations or Problems in Life

"Now I'd like to think more generally about some of the ways in which you deal with frustrations or problems. I'd like to know what you do or say when you're having frustrations or problems in your life?"

I.	Single Method[a]		
	Seek Help ("talk to others")		20.8%
	Self Help		
	Think/solve by self	19.7%	
	Exercise/walk/distractions	7.3%	
	Rest/sleep/quiet	5.4%	40.5%
	Avoidance	3.2%	
	Emotion ("I'll cry")	2.7%	
	Other	2.2%	
	Do Nothing or Accept Fate		12.0%
II.	Multi-Method[b]		
	Solve by Self, Talk with Others		10.1%
	Talk with Others, Relax/Distractions		4.6%
	Talk with Others, Forget It		3.5%
	Solve by Self, Talk with Others, Forget It		3.0%
	Talk with Others, Emotion		0.6%
	Distractions, Forget It		0.6%
	Solve by Self, Forget It		0.6%
	Solve by Self, Relax/Distractions		0.3%
III.	Don't Know		3.3%
		Total	99.9%

[a] Sixty-one percent of the respondents gave single-method responses.
[b] Twenty-three percent of the respondents gave multi-method responses. All multi-method responses combined self-help and talk-with-others responses.

two-thirds had either sought help for a personal problem (53%) or could imagine seeking help (14%). Persons sought were largely "informal others": 63% spoke to family members, 28% talked to friends, 6% spoke to professionals such as health or mental health professionals or a reverend, and 4% spoke with "others." A small percentage had sought professional help.

With regard to everyday problems, 41% of the residents interviewed were entirely self-help oriented, 22% combined self-help with seeking help, 21% only sought help, 12% said they would "do nothing," and 3% did not know what they usually do (see Table 8.3). The most common forms of self-help included: (1) thinking about and solving the problem oneself; (2) avoiding the problem by not thinking about it or forgetting it; (3) distracting oneself with TV, music, or movies; and (4) rest or sleep.

Overall, the proportion who sought or were willing to seek help from others for personal problems ranged from 43% to 67%. This was somewhat less than the proportion in the nation overall, but differences could be due to sample size (Chinatown's sample being smaller than the national sample).

While one-fourth of those interviewed were self-help types, the remaining three-fourths were willing to share their personal problems with others. Chinese Americans may be unaccustomed to seeking a professional stranger's help for personal matters, but they are not silent about their problems. They talk with family and friends, although possibly to a lesser extent than Americans overall.

Testing for effects of gender, income, nativity, and age on past help-seeking behavior revealed a significant effect for the regression analysis of all variables combined. The combined effect of younger adults, higher income, American-born, and males tended to be more help-seeking. There was also a significant effect for age alone. Elderly were more self-help oriented, while younger adults were more likely to seek help.[9]

Coping Strategies

Veroff, Douvan, and Kulka (1981) found that poor Americans tended to cope in ways that reflected resignation and that they tended to resort to prayer. Chinatown residents did not respond to problems in the same way. Chinatown residents tended not to pray. Only one resident mentioned "church" or "prayer" as a way of handling problems. A few Chinatown residents said they accepted fate, which can be interpreted as a form of resignation: "Fate can't be changed. Whatever happens to me, I would take as the way it's supposed to be." However, among Chinese Americans overall, determination was a more prevalent means of coping than resignation. The former was voiced as follows: "Be logical." "Try to improve the situation." "Think about the problem." "I'll keep looking for those who know how to deal with the problem until the problem is resolved." "I'll try to find out the reasons for the failure and learn a lesson from it. Hopefully, I can succeed next time. I'd try to get advice and suggestions from friends."

What we do not know is whether the determination of Chinatown residents is related to culture or to immigrant characteristics. The latter causal factor is what Chiswick (1978) called self-selection in migration (the hypothesis that immigrants are more motivated and able than native born) or what Galton (1908) referred to as considerable force of character ascribed to those who immigrate. Additional research is needed to answer this question.

One out of every four residents reported using multi-method forms of coping that were sequential or conditional upon the nature of the problem or consequences of the first-attempted solution (see Table 8.3). Self-help was sometimes followed by seeking help, and seeking help was sometimes followed by avoidance: "Whenever I have problems, I would tell myself to be strong and calm. I would try to solve it unless it was too big for me, then I would get help from people." "I take a walk and think at the same time. If I can't solve it, I'll consult with someone. Some particular problems I choose to ignore." "I try my best to face and solve them, and I get advice from friends. If it's too hard to solve, I try to forget it." "I think about why I have this problem. Then I talk to someone about it. Then let time take care of the problem but do not lose self-control and try to put daily tension aside while I have a problem." In all, the approaches that Chinese Americans used to handle problems were varied and complex, indicating that Chinatowners were not as culturally homogeneous in their styles of coping as was previously assumed.

Beliefs about Mental Disorders

Causes of Mental Disorders. Of those interviewed, 29% did not know what caused mental problems or mental illness. Thirty percent believed that mental disorders were caused by pressures and problems, 20% believed they were caused by personality, 8% by neglect, 5% by some combination of the above, and 7% by genetics.

Responses that were coded as pressures and problems included: "the pressure of living," "overstress, overwork, pressure at work" "too much stress and strain in daily life," "too much pressure," "too many problems that a person couldn't handle or too many bad experiences," "frustrations in life," "problems greater than normal, everyday ones," "personal problems," "too many unhappy incidents happened," and "too many worries." As Rudy Kao, a psychiatric social worker with Northeast Mental Health Services, stated: "You can't separate mental illness from life problems. There's a whole variety of environmental stressors from overcrowdedness to unemployment to housing problems" (*East West*, 1987, p. 10).

Causes of mental illness that were coded as personality included: "think too much," "worry too much," "too sensitive," "too emotionally involved with their problems that they cannot understand or reason to calm their emotions," "psychologically too weak to handle problems," "neurotic problems," "inability to cope with the stress of life," "unable to deal with reality," "have pressure inside they don't let out. They don't talk to people." Causes of mental disorders that were coded as neglect included: "neglect," "lack of understanding," "abnormal family life," "lack of love," and "isolation."

The data did not support the hypothesis posed by Sue, Wagner, Ja, Margullis, and Lew (1976) that low rate of service use was due to a belief that mental illness is caused by organic factors. Only 7% of the Chinatown sample mentioned genetic or organic causes of mental disorders.

The notion that avoidance of morbid thoughts enhances mental health, proposed by Sue and his researchers, was also not supported by the data. In terms of coping strategies, only 6% to 8% of the respondents mentioned avoidance, which was often expressed as "forget it" (see Table 8.2). In summary, among the two-thirds who offered some cause for mental disorders, beliefs were progressive and varied.

Prevention. Nearly half of the respondents (44%) believed that mental disorders could be prevented. Preventative methods were coded as: self-help (65%), seek help (15%), help others (13%), other (5%), and don't know (2%). Self-help means of prevention included relaxation, self-awareness, self-esteem, positive attitudes and emotions, and clarity of thinking. Responses included: "Relax, try not to be too nervous." "Don't worry too much, go do more relaxed activities." "Don't take things so seriously." "Take it easy." "Understand your situation." "Persons should have self-awareness all the time that they need help." "Develop self-esteem." "The person must have a clear mind to be able to analyze his or her problem." "Keep yourself happy." "Be satisfied with what you have. Don't expect too much from life." "Take a positive attitude."

Seeking help responses included: "Go to a doctor." "See a psychiatrist." "Get counseling." "Be able to talk to someone." Comments that were coded as help others were perceptive: "Show concern and love to a person." "Try to understand and relate to where the person's coming from." "Don't let someone become isolated." "Give everyone a break in life." and "Comfort them whenever problems arise."

While many residents held sophisticated beliefs about the causes and preventions of mental illness, half the respondents (51%) did not believe that mental disorders could be prevented, and 5% "did not know."

Treatment. Over half of the residents interviewed (60%) believed that mental disorders could be treated. One-third (32%) did not know. Very few (5%) did not believe that mental disorders could be treated. Of those who believed disorders could be treated, 29% cited professional help, 25% cited self-help, and 14% recommended the presence of caring people or family. The remainder suggested rest or exercise (3%), church (2%), or "other" strategies (1%). The fact that a majority of Chinatown residents considered mental disorders treatable is an optimistic sign for service deliverers. Also, many of those who "did not know" whether mental disorders could be treated cited their uneducated status as reason for their lack of knowledge. Commenting on these findings, Dr. Allen Seid, a psychiatrist in northern California, attributed low use of services among California Chinese to a lack of mental health education: "Many Chinese have negative feelings about seeing a shrink, which comes from a lack of awareness of what they do" (personal communication, 1982).

To Seek Professional Help: What Priority?

Nearly half (45%) of the residents said they would seek professional help for "a depression that won't go away." Findings indicated that for about one-third of the sample, depression was not considered a problem serious enough

Table 8.4
Ways of Handling Symptoms

Seek Symptoms[a]	Seek Professional Help[b]	Take Care of It Themselves	Didn't Know
A cold	42%	57%	1%
Sore throat	57%	41%	1%
Constant tiredness	51%	42%	8%
Depression	45%	35%	17%

[a]See Appendix B for total list of symptoms (Item GB24). For purposes of this chapter, only four symptoms are mentioned.

[b]"Professional help" included: acupuncturist, herbalist, Health Center #4, Northeast Mental Health Clinic, Northeast Medical Services, private doctor, Telegraph Hill Medical Clinic, and other agency or service.

to warrant seeking professional help. In terms of the proportion who would seek professional help, residents treated prolonged depression as they would a sore throat, constant tiredness, or a cold, but they relied on self-help more often for a cold, sore throat, or tiredness than they did for depression. A sizeable number were mystified over what they would do to treat depression; nearly a fifth (17%) didn't know that they would do (see Table 8.4). There are no over-the-counter medications for depression. A long snooze cannot correct the blues like it can treat fatigue. Indeed, insomnia is one of the symptoms of depression.

SUMMARY

This chapter has examined the issue of underutilization of services by assessing the rate of mental health service use among Chinatown residents and possible reasons for underutilization. Use of mental health services was found to be extremely low. Only 5% of the respondents sought mental health services. This proportion is roughly comparable to the proportion of Americans overall who sought services 30 years ago, and it is one-fourth the proportion of Americans who sought services in 1976. Chinatown has not yet seen the gains promised by the community mental health movement.

Survey data suggest that underutilization may be due to several factors: (1) lack of knowledge on the part of three-fourths of the residents about existing mental health services; (2) the belief held by roughly half the sample that mental disorders cannot be prevented; (3) the belief held by one-third of the sample that problems should be handled by oneself; (4) lack of knowledge on the part of one-third of the residents regarding how psychological problems can be treated; (5) reluctance to seek help for depression or uncertainty about what to do, reported by half the residents; and (6) a slightly greater tendency toward self-help means of dealing with problems than was found in the nation overall.

Underutilization is not due to unwillingness to admit to symptoms of psychological distress. A sizeable proportion of respondents admitted to symptoms of emotional tension, depression, loneliness, and psychological-physiological troubles. Four out of every ten respondents felt many things had been making them upset, three out of every ten residents found that many things had been making them angry, four out of ten sometimes got depressed, and a majority expressed need for a confidant. Immigrants comprised a high-risk group for depression. Emotional tension was more prevalently reported by younger adults than by the elderly, and younger adults were also in greater need of someone they could really talk to. Between one-fifth and one-third of the sample were psychologically and/or physiologically impaired, a proportion that exceeded those found in Hong Kong, Midtown Manhattan, and Hennepin. In addition, four out of every ten residents worried a lot (mostly about health, finances, job, and family), some to a physically debilitating degree.

What accounts for this admission to symptoms of psychological disturbance? We can speculate about the causes. Unlike college students, Chinatowners are primarily low-income immigrants with limited education. Most live in substandard housing and work at low-paying, low occupational prestige jobs. As Veroff, Douvan, and Kulka reported, persons of less education have fewer resources available for help. Other researchers have cited how persons of low income are more vulnerable to psychological problems (Cochrane, 1977; Dohrenwend and Dohrenwend, 1969; Hollingshead and Redlich, 1954; Maltzberg, 1935; Reid, 1975; Srole, Langner, Michael, Opler, and Rennie, 1962; and Stoller, 1966). For immigrants burdened with poverty and a foreign culture, it may not be considered shameful to report life stresses. Problems that are due to poverty, aging, or immigration difficulties may be differentiated from "being crazy." Thus, stigmatization may apply to severe pathologies but not to affective disorders or life pressures. A second possible reason for admission to psychological problems is that Chinese Americans may be reluctant to initiate self-disclosure about psychological problems (and seek professional care) but they are not unwilling to admit to specific symptoms in response to others' inquiry about them.

Several Chinatown residents used multiple methods of coping with personal problems. There was more determination evidenced than resignation, and there was little use of prayer. These results suggests that Chinatown residents do not cope in quite the same ways as other low-income Americans and that determination as a coping mechanism may either be cultural in nature or due to immigrant/refugee self-selection.

Mental health beliefs held by Chinatowners were more Westernized than previously believed. This may be due to the fact that many residents were not recent immigrants. Forty percent of the foreign-born interviewed had lived in the United States for over 10 years. Thirty percent had lived in this country for over 20 years.

Many assumptions posed in the literature were not found to be valid. Chinatown residents apparently do not somatize all of their psychological complaints. Moreover, underutilization of mental health services in Chinatown was not due to "silent suffering," since many residents were willing to talk to informal others (particularly family and friends) about their personal problems.

Underutilization was also not due to use of alternative forms of treatment. Residents did not frequently seek treatment from herbalists and acupuncturists, and they did not commonly visit a Chinese temple. There was some use of community-based agencies, but these were not mental health agencies. And a majority felt the need for emotional and informational social support (a confidant), a need that was negatively associated with age. Research findings that do not support many of the prevailing hypotheses about Asian American mental health demonstrate the importance of empirically testing existing assumptions.

With regard to the implications of these findings, we need to closely examine where the delivery of mental health care has failed and what intervention strategies are required. Where only 5% of a sample of ethnic minorities have sought mental health services among a population in which mental and/or psychophysiological disorders are prevalent, something is amiss. Where three-quarters of a population in need are unaware of existing services, the community mental health movement has not moved into these communities.

Substantial efforts in outreach and public education are needed. Residents need to know where mental health services exist. They need to know how mental disorders can be prevented and treated. They need to know, for example, what to do about depression, debilitating worries, emotional stresses; in total, they need to know how mental health services can serve them. Linda Wang, acting director of the Northeast Mental Health Services, reacted to our survey findings with this statement: "We need to do more public education, more media announcements. It's necessary to broaden our means of informing the public" (personal communication, 1982).

In addition to mental health education, we need to institute forms of service delivery that take into account the specific life conditions that affect persons' ability or willingness to seek existing services even when they know where services exist. Most of Chinatown's workers are employed at jobs that require long hours and provide minimum pay. Many may not feel that they can afford to leave work to tend to mental health needs. Thus, interventions are needed that address residents' reluctance to take off time from work to seek professional care. One such strategy was implemented as an outcome of this study's findings. A 24-hour mental health telephone hot line, in Chinese, was instituted. In communities where a majority of residents are non-English speaking, bilingual hot lines can be very helpful, particularly if they serve crisis as well as educational purposes. Another strategy would be to provide mental health education through the Chinese newspapers, another intervention that does not require an employee to take time off from work.

The demystification of psychotherapy seems particularly important for low-income, ethnic communities. In this community, for example, a link could be made between the role of the psychotherapist and the expressed need on behalf of two-thirds of the persons interviewed for someone they could really talk to. In addition, in a community where a majority report having only "a few" friends or relatives with whom they felt free to discuss problems and secure advice, residents could be made aware of how a psychotherapist can serve such a function. The role of the mental health professional as a confidant should be emphasized.

A second approach to the demystification of psychotherapy is to relate mental disorders to life stresses. After all, 30% of the respondents did attribute the cause of mental disorders to pressures and problems. Interventions can be built upon the perceptions of the residents themselves. If residents think that mental disorders are caused by overstress, overwork, pressures at work, frustrations, and too many problems that a person can't handle, how can the field of mental health address and relieve these causal factors? The marketing of mental health services needs to match services with needs and consumer perceptions.

Mental health services also need to address the specific areas of worry—health, finances/job, and family. Respondents said they worried about their health, financial situation, family members in Hong Kong, insomnia, finding a job, and basic survival. But here we confront a challenge that is generalizable to other low-income, elderly, or immigrant populations. Mental health issues cannot be isolated from poverty, ill health, aging, immigration restrictions, occupational segregation, and labor exploitation. Hunger cannot be solved by eating one salted bean. Neither can a 50-minute session solve poverty, language liability, immigration policies, and occupational discrimination. The psychotherapist must be able to work for larger changes while also helping these individuals (in both functional and emotional ways) cope with problems and conditions. Traditional forms of psychotherapy need to be expanded to meet the needs of populations such as these.

Finally, the mental health delivery system could make use of existing informal help-giving networks and provide paraprofessional training to the community at large. The self-help movement nationally needs to be made useful to those who are marginal to the mainstream. Help-giving skills—such as active listening, reflection, clarifying and information-gathering probes, emotional support, informational support, instrumental aid, cognitive restructuring, behavioral therapy concepts, and self-monitoring—can be taught. In conclusion, comprehensive mental health delivery in communities like Chinatown require action on many fronts. The problems challenge the discipline to expand its strategies and perspectives in order to serve the underserved.

NOTES

1. This item is a translation of a Chinese phrase that refers to depression.

2. Feeling upset (H57): $R^2 = 0.075$, Adjusted $R^2 = 0.037$, Standard Deviation = 0.485, F = 1.98, ns, df = 4, 98; Standardized Beta Coefficients and F Values for Age, Gender, Income, and Nativity (U.S. born = 1) were: -0.220, 4.781, $p < .05$; -0.124, 1.381; 0.109, 0.943; and 0.040 and 0.147, respectively.

3. Item H55 was selected as the measure of depression here because of its face validity and its significant correlation to other depression items. Intercorrelations among the depression items are shown in the following table. All but one correlation was significant.

		H55	GB8	G23	G5
H55	Freq. of Depression				
GB8	Sinking down	.32***-			
G23	Nothing turns out	.20*	.28***		
G5	Couldn't get going	.28**	.27**	.19**	
G6	Spirits high/low	-.43***	-.32***	-.04	.36***

*$p < .05$ **$p < .01$ ***$p < .001$

4. Depression (H55): "Do you get depressed? Would you say often, sometimes, rarely, or never?" (1 = often, 4 = never) $R^2 = 0.051$, Adjusted $R^2 = 0.012$, Standard Deviation = 0.812, F = 1.29, ns, df = 4, 97; Standardized Beta Coefficients and F Values for Nativity (U.S. born = 1), Income, Gender (1 = male), and Age were: -0.231, 4.635, $p < .05$; 0.099, 0.746; 0.043, 0.161; 0.002, 0.000.

5. Langner scale: $R^2 = 0.051$, Adjusted $R^2 = -0.011$, Standard Deviation = 3.283, F = 1.293, df = 4, 97. Standardized Beta Coefficients and F Values for Income, Nativity (U.S. born = 1), Age, and Gender were: -0.205, 3.070; 0.108, 0.995; -0.064, 0.393; -0.066, 0.378.

6. These three items comprise three of the four items used by Campbell, Converse, and Rodgers (1976) to measure personal competence. Intercorrelations and item-total correlations were:

	E7	E8	E9	Total
E7		.04	.21***	.63***
E8			.20*	.59***
E9				.75***

* $p < .05$ **$p < .01$ ***$p < .001$

Although E7 is not correlated with E8, the item-total correlations are high.

7. Personal Effectiveness: $R^2 = 0.125$, Adjusted $R^2 = 0.079$, Standard Deviation = 3.182, F = 2.748, p < .01, df = 5, 96. Standardized Beta Coefficients and F Values for Personal Effectiveness, Income, Gender, Age, and Nativity were: −0.281, 8.196, p < 01; −0.151, 1.738; −0.070, 0.448, −0.058, 0.343; 0.045, 0.174, respectively. Personal Effectiveness was significantly correlated with scores on the Langner scale (r = −.33, p < .001) and personal income (r = 16, p < .05). Personal effectiveness was not correlated with age (r = .02), gender (r = .11), or nativity (r = −.10).

8. Confidant (H58): $R^2 = 0.068$, Adjusted $R^2 = 0.029$, Standard Deviation = 0.475, F = 1.781, df = 4, 98. Standardized Beta Coefficients and F Values for Age, Income, Nativity, and Gender were: −0.222, 4.829, p < .05; −0.180, 2.546; −0.043, 0.167; 0.030, 0.081.

9. Seeking Help (H68) where 1 = seek help, 0 = not seek help. $R^2 = 0.186$; Adjusted $R^2 = 0.152$, Standard Deviation = 0.457, F = 5.578, p < .001, df = 4, 98. Standardized Beta Coefficients and F Values for Age, Income, Nativity (U.S. born = 1), and Gender (1 = male) were: −0.201, 4.532, p < .05; 0.181, 2.924; 0.146, 2.177; 0.131, 1.765, respectively.

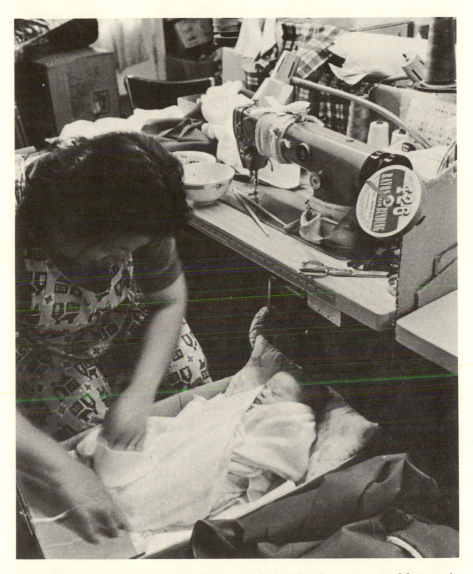

This photograph speaks to the life of the working-class immigrant woman. Many working-class households cannot survive without two income earners in the family. Poverty precludes paid day care. Raised in a sweatshop, these infants grow up to the sounds of zooming sewing machines, not to the hum of a lullaby or the educational animation of Sesame Street. They play in spools of cloth, not with Fisher-Price toys. The merger of workplace and nursery does not make this a safe environment in which to raise children, as the precarious position of the scissors above the baby's face indicates. With chopsticks and rice bowl to the left of her sewing machine, infant to the right, the woman experiences no physical or temporal separation of work, meals, or parenting. The children grow up amidst clutter and noise, tended by mothers who do not have the luxury of providing their children with much undivided attention. 1979. (Photograph by Peter Man.) Reprinted by permission.

To Be a Man in My Next Life

The address was on the top floor of a three-story apartment building on a main street in core Chinatown. The apartment was small. The kitchen occupied one-third of the total space. The living room was untidy. Paper bags and other dried food stuff lined the floor. Blankets and pillows covered the couch, which served as a child's bed.

The respondent, a woman in her 40s, appeared depressed and tired. Having immigrated from Hong Kong just a few years ago, she had been lonely in this country. She had no friends and no time to make friends since she held two part-time jobs as a housekeeper and home health aide. This woman had no one to turn to when she was frustrated or depressed. She felt handicapped due to the language barrier.

Her life as a woman had been hard. Speaking of her past, she was tearful. At age three, her father deserted her and her mother. At age 10, she was sold as a "daughter-in-law-to-be," working as a slave girl for her future husband's family. This was the tradition in the village in which she was raised. Later, after marrying, she worked as a domestic servant for European families in Hong Kong. Her mother had held the same type of job.

Some years after she married, her husband had an affair with another woman. She left him and went to Hong Kong with her son. There she met her present husband, who told her he had never married. Later, she discovered that he had a son in China, one year older than her own son. Having supported this man for some time, she felt cheated and angry at his deception. Her second husband was initially not too kind to her son, who once had to be placed in an orphanage because of her working situation.

Fortunately, things changed for the better. She was now grateful to her husband for bringing her son to this country. Content that he took care of the family, she was happy that her children were obedient and hard-working and did well in school.

This woman grew up with a mother who was prejudiced against women and showed her no respect or understanding. She felt she had suffered a great deal as a woman. If she had her life to live over, she expressed her desire to be a man—to gain a higher social status and not be cheated on in marriage. This woman felt "pretty dissatisfied" with her life as a whole and "very dissatisfied" with the amount of education she had attained.

This woman believed in hard work and believed that those who worked hard got rewarded. She looked forward with hope to a better and happier life as her children grow up in this country.

9

Slaying Demons with a Sewing Needle: Gender Differences and Women's Status

An analysis of the hierarchical structure of society cannot be complete without an examination of gender differences, for non-English speaking, ethnic immigrant women fall at the bottom of the wage and occupational prestige scale, behind both ethnic men and white men and women. The purpose of this chapter is to examine the extent and nature of disadvantage faced by Chinatown's women along multiple domains of analyses. Differences in conditions and status between men and women of the same ethnicity as well as differences between ethnic women and Americans in general reveal the disadvantaged position faced by ethnic minority women in this society. While normally these differences are described in economic and occupational terms, it is the purpose of this chapter to examine psychological differences as well, specifically differences in psychological attitudes, satisfaction, and well-being. Conditions facing ethnic immigrant women in this community are very similar to conditions facing ethnic immigrant women in general.

To provide a cultural backdrop for the contemporary period, the first section of this chapter reviews the position of women in traditional China. The second section contains data on the general characteristics of Chinatown's women, which include their employment condition and job perceptions, perceptions of life satisfaction, well-being, and marital satisfaction as compared to men. The third section addresses psychological attitudes of women as compared to men, specifically the topics of personal effectiveness, assertiveness-accommodation, self-esteem, individual-system blame, and intergroup comfort and social distance.

THE POSITION OF WOMEN IN TRADITIONAL CHINA

As in many other societies, social role expectations in traditional China placed women in a subordinate position to men. This subordination originated in ancient Chinese cosmological beliefs that date back to the first millennium B.C. In essence, the universe was said to be composed of two interacting elements, yin (female) and yang (male). Yin represented what was dark, weak, and passive, while yang represented what was bright, strong, and active. Men were believed to be endowed with the "firm nature of heaven," while women were the "yielding nature of earth" (Croll, 1978). Although originally conceived of as complementary forces, these elements were soon arranged hierarchically so that in time, women symbolized what was inferior and men what was superior. These beliefs were incorporated into the teachings of Confucius, which became the ruling ideology starting in the second century B.C. The primary purpose of the Confucian filial tradition was the maintenance of social order through principles that governed the rigidly defined relationship of women to men, children to parents or elders, and commoners to gentry. The result was a feudal system in which legal codes strengthened patriarchal authority (Stacey, 1983). Proverbs further reinforced this ideology (Croll, 1978). Rules of correct conduct for women involved submission, obedience, reticence, respectfulness, domesticity, chastity, cleanliness of person, and unselfishness (as dictated in the Book of Rites, the Precepts for Women, and the Classics for Girls). The word for women literally meant "inside person" (Croll, 1978, p. 16), emphasizing the seclusion of women to the domestic sphere. In a similar way, the character for "peace" combined the characters for "a woman" and "under a roof," and the character for "good" combined the character for "a female" and "with a male child." A respectable Chinese woman was not to be seen or heard. She was expected never to be freed from male domination, as her duty was to obey her father at home, her husband after marriage, and her eldest son when widowed. Proverbs warned against women being entrusted with tasks or interests outside the home for fear that it would cause national disorder or shame. Men were counseled against listening to women for fear that disaster would result (Bloodworth, 1966; Van Gulik, 1974). The exercise of willfulness and ambition, considered heroic in a man, was considered wicked and depraved in a woman (Yung, 1986). Thus, women were essentially segregated and rendered invisible and powerless. While common people sacrificed to educate their sons, girls were discouraged from receiving much education. As a uterine pawn in a male system, a woman's real value was in producing sons, thereby perpetuating the lineage of her husband's family (Wolf, 1974). Confucius's statement that "Women and villains are the only people that are hard to deal with" is indicative of his contemptuous attitude toward women (Croll, 1978, p. 86). Girls were of lesser value since, by custom, they could neither carry on their father's lineage nor be of economic value—hence the proverb "Eight model daughters are not equal to a boy with a limp" (Smith, 1902, p. 302).

Footbinding was perhaps the most perverse form of female subjugation. Begun in 960 by neo-Confucian philosophers who reemphasized women's segregation and seclusion, the practice involved wrapping girls' feet so tightly as to break the arches and permanently bend the toes beneath the foot. Small bowed feet were considered a sign of gentility and the resultant swaying gait was considered sensually tantalizing to men (Lin, in Croll, 1978). Because the custom was first practiced among the upper class, its association with wealth and status led aspiring mothers from all but the poorest families (and certain groups) to subject their daughters to this crippling process.[1] Describing the agony, one woman recalled how her "feet felt on fire" and she couldn't sleep; another recalled how her feet hurt so much for two years that she was forced to crawl on her hands and knees (Levy and Pruitt, both in Croll, 1978). Nearly ten centuries later, the practice was put to an end in 1902 by the Empress Dowager when she decreed that gentry should abstain from the custom.

Women were denied participation in government or local community institutions and were prevented by law from inheriting property (Croll, 1978). Except for the poor, women were prevented from acquiring any independent source of income. Women in traditional China were said to live the life of "a frog in a well" (Smith, in Croll, 1978), a metaphor for their constrained status. Female suicide was often considered the single recourse to brutality available to a Chinese woman because it brought public disgrace upon the husband's family (Stacey, 1983, p. 43).

Several persons contributed to the changing position of China's women—reformists within China and missionaries who served in China. In the late 1800s, women missionaries opened schools for girls. The revolutionary nationalist movement, which sought to topple the Manchu dynasty and establish social reforms, had a major role in altering the women's place. Several exceptional women played very nontraditional roles in this movement, an all-women battalion being but one example (Croll, 1978). In 1911, when the Republic was established, women struggled for the right to vote, although many suffragette activities were crushed and women's political activities were repressed by conservative forces of the new nationalist republic (Croll, 1978). During Mao Zedong's Cultural Revolution, the "Women's Question" was a central issue, as the Confucian ideology and practices of concubinage, footbinding, seclusion of women, arranged marriages, and the double standard of morality were criticized as hindering China's modernization. Anti-footbinding and anti–arranged marriage associations were founded. From 1958 to 1960, with the Great Leap Forward, women anticipated a new age of emancipation. Contemporary films produced in China, such as *The Good Woman* and *The Wild Mountains*, convey the more liberated position of women—the acceptance of a woman's request for divorce and the depiction of an assertive, nonsubmissive wife as heroine.

In reference to Chinese American women, three factors need to be kept in mind. First, many of the Chinese immigrants to America were from the peasant class. While the classical Confucian traditions affected all Chinese, they were primarily followed by the upper class. The peasant tradition was a more eclectic one. Second, although Chinese American women were influenced by both the Confucian tradition and the new ideology of the People's Republic, they were at the same time distanced from both due to their increased exposure to American customs. In the former case, immigrating to the United States, these women faced survival needs that necessarily dictated certain deviations from Confucian traditions. In the latter case, until 1972 the United States refused to recognize the People's Republic. The communist hysteria of the McCarthy era made any perceived association with China dangerous. Many Chinese Americans supported Nationalist China (Taiwan) to escape possible charges of being communist sympathizers. Nevertheless, certain cultural, class, and urban traditions have filtered down to today's Chinese American women.

GENERAL CHARACTERISTICS
OF CHINATOWN'S WOMEN

The life of the typical Chinatown woman is that of an immigrant woman. Among the women sampled, 85% were immigrants. Three-quarters of these immigrants entered the United States after 1964. Discriminatory legislation dictated this unbalanced immigration pattern. Due to the Chinese Exclusion Act and economic constraints, Chinese immigration during the first half of this century was largely a chain of sons following fathers to the United States in search of work. Their wives stayed at home to raise children and serve in-laws. After World War II, the number of women entering this country increased. But only since the 1965 revision of the immigration laws have large numbers of women been able to immigrate to the United States. Most of the newcomers came with their immediate families. They were of working age and entered the labor market as partners in dual-wage earner families. Some were elderly women who had been separated from their spouses for decades. For them, the opportunity came too late. Their husbands had passed away. Only their adult offspring remained. For other women, reunion with their spouses lasted only a few years before their husbands died.

Women represented slightly over half (53%) of Chinatown's population, signaling a change from the once predominantly bachelor society. Today, women are highly visible. They are found resting on red benches in Portsmouth Square; fingering the freshest produce; gingerly selecting fish, *lap cheong*, and whole chickens; or pushing their way onto Stockton Street buses.

Married persons comprised only a slight majority in this community, as the proportions of married and nonmarried did not differ greatly. Of the women sampled, 59% were married, 26% widowed, 10% never married, 5% divorced, and 0% separated. Of the men sampled, 58% were married, 2% widowed, 34% never married, 6% divorced, and 0% separated. Demographic points of interest included the occurrence of divorce in a culture that discourages divorce, and the high proportion of widows that roughly approximated the proportion of bachelor men. Widows and bachelors combined comprised over half the community population. Many widowed women had no family remaining. Some had been rejected from their children's home: "I used to live with my son and his family, but they didn't want me, so they asked me to leave their house and found me this place in Chinatown."

Compared with Chinatown's men, who averaged 46 years of age, the mean age for Chinatown's women was 52 years. Of those interviewed, 12% were between 18 and 19 years of age, 22% were between 30 and 44 years of age, 38% were between 45 and 64 years, and 28% were 65 years or older. A majority of Chinatown's women were middle-aged or elderly.

The median level of education for a Chinatown woman was a sixth-grade education. By contrast, the median level of education for men in the community was 14 years. Women's lack of parity with the average Chinatown man (who is a high school graduate) was pronounced. The differential reflects traditional Chinese customs that accorded women fewer opportunities and a lower status then men. As for their English-speaking ability, 26% of the women could speak English, 74% could not. Among the men, 50% could speak English, 50% could not. Here again, women were more disadvantaged.

Employment: Job Perceptions and Job Satisfaction

The majority of women were in the paid labor force. Among all women interviewed, 60% were in the labor market (92% of these had a job; the remainder were unemployed but looking for work). Another 16% of the women were retired. Nineteen percent were full-time housewives; many were out of the labor market only temporarily to care for young children. Five percent of the women were on welfare, which is a small percentage given Chinatown's poverty level. Of the female residents between the working ages of 18 and 65, 68% were working.

Because 32% of the respondents' mothers had been employed, the prevalence of working women is roughly double that of their mothers' generation. Economic necessity dictated this change in the women's role: "My husband had to retire so there's no income from *him*. The children still go to school so there's no income from *them*. So *I* have to be responsible and support the whole family."

Eight out of ten families with multiple wage earners in Chinatown said they would "barely get by" if there were but one breadwinner in the family. Although sons and daughters occasionally provide additional income, the burden of being the second breadwinner falls on the wives. Holding down a job is nothing new for most of these women. Two-thirds of the recent immigrants who were of working age prior to entering the United States had worked while overseas.

Chinatown's women are highly segregated into low prestige occupations. Nearly half (47%) of the working women were employed as sewing machine operators in the apparel industry, primarily for small sweatshops located within the enclave. One-fifth (22%) worked in services (janitoring, dishwashing, waitressing, or doing health service work). Another fifth (19%) had jobs in clerical or sales positions. Six percent were professionals, and another 6% were private household workers (cooks or maids).

The distribution of occupations held by women substantially differed from that of men.[2] Women are heavily represented in the operative, clerical, and private household occupations, while men were in the service, professional, managerial, and craft trade jobs. Pay was low. At times, pay fell below the minimum wage—especially in garment shops, which pay by piecework wages. In 1979 the median for those paid by hourly wages was $3.25.

Perceived occupational prestige was assessed by asking respondents: "Do you feel proud of the kind of work you do?" and "Would you want your children to be doing the same kind of work?" The majority of women working in this community were not proud of the jobs they held, a percentage far greater than was found for men.[3] Of the working women, 74% were not proud of their job, over twice the percentage of working men who were not proud of their job (32%). Only 26% of the working women (compared to 68% of the working men) were proud of their occupation.

The majority of employed men and women did not want their children to be doing the same kind of work they did: 93% of the working women compared to 77% of the working men did not want their children employed in the same type of work as they.[4] There are two possible explanations for these findings and they are not mutually exclusive. First, these findings could suggest that parents have higher occupational aspirations for their children than for themselves. Many immigrants may not have high hopes for themselves but, rather, live through the anticipated success of their children. Second, these findings suggest that most women and many men considered their jobs undesirable. Overall, women and men in this community attributed very little status to their occupations, but among women, this phenomenon was more widespread.

Being in the labor force did not relieve most women of housework duties. In response to the question "Does anyone help you with the household chores?" 79% of the working mothers reported having to carry sole responsibility for all household chores. Most husbands apparently did not share responsibility for household work despite the fact that their wives helped support the family. Overall, Chinatown's women have not left the home for the labor market. They have always been in the labor market while at the same time never being relieved from home responsibilities.

In many ways, Chinatown's women have work experiences similar to those of other lower-class women. Participation in the labor force is governed by economic necessity. They entered the labor force to augment the household income and withdrew temporarily until their children were old enough to be cared for by older children, relatives, or day care centers. Job opportunities were confined to what have been traditionally considered "women's" jobs. There is the continuing double burden of work in the marketplace and work at home.

Although Chinatown's women shared many work experiences with other lower-class women, the world of working women is uniquely structured by the ethnic labor market, which is isolated from the larger labor market. Employment in Chinatown offers few good jobs, minimal rewards, and very limited opportunities for upward mobility. Because some of Chinatown's working men suffer the same constraints on their employment opportunities as women, the ethnic labor market forges a common bond between men and women in this community.

The majority of working women in this community did not feel that their jobs allowed them to use their abilities and skills well (69%). They felt that their jobs did not (1) provide opportunities for promotions or raises (66%), (2) teach them new skills (61%), or (3) provide them with meaningful work (57%). Physical conditions at the workplace were not perceived as bad, yet nearly half said their workplace was noisy and the work physically exhausting. Problems with their boss, coworkers, and receiving their paycheck were not common. However, this was small compensation for nonactualizing, meaningless, low occupational prestige, dead-end jobs (see Table 9.1).

Low proficiency with the English language is a major factor perpetuating the ethnic labor market. Only 27% of all working women interviewed stated that they could converse in English "very well" or "pretty well." In response to the question "If you could speak English well, would you feel qualified for a better job than the one you have now?" 85% said "yes." Language was seen as a major barrier to a better job. A full 96% of the women who had problems with the English language said they would want to leave their present job if they "knew English well."

Chinatown's women want to learn English for they believe it might lead to better jobs outside the ethnic labor market. However, their work schedules and home responsibilities make it difficult to take ESL (English as a Second Language) classes. While only half of the working women worked 40 hours or more, nearly all (97%) worked five days or more. The typical woman not

Table 9.1
Women's Perceptions of Attributes of Their Jobs

	Yes	No
Problems with your boss	7%*	93%
Problems with persons you work with	7%*	93%
Physical conditions of work place not good	10%*	90%
Problems getting paycheck	6%*	94%
Opinions taken seriously by boss	63%	37%*
Risk of getting laid off or fired	29%*	71%
Allow you to use your abilities/skills well	31%	69%*
Job boring	26%*	74%
Job meaningless	57%*	43%
Provide opportunities for promotions/raises	34%	66%*
Emotionally stressful	16%*	84%
Under time pressures/deadlines	22%*	78%
Teach you any new skills	39%	61%*
Receive benefits on your job	59%	41%*
Feel proud of the kind of work you do	26%	74%*
Want children to do same kind of work	7%	93%*
Have to compete with others at job	19%*	81%
Work too demanding	19%*	81%
Work physically exhausting	45%*	55%
Have friends at your job	59%	41%*
Work place noisy	41%*	59%

*Indicates those scored in the direction of problems on the job

only puts in six to eight hours at work during work days, she must also do the daily housework, run errands, and entertain family and relatives on weekends.

In terms of English language skills, Chinatown's women were more disadvantaged than men. Twice as many working men than women could speak English "very well" or "somewhat well" (54% compared to 27%). A higher proportion of immigrant men than women could converse in English (67% compared to 50%) and understand spoken English (72% compared to 54%).

We might expect Chinatown's women to be dissatisfied with their jobs, given their lack of job pride and the negative attributes they attach to their job. At the other extreme, immigrant women might be satisfied with less because their evaluation of current conditions is relative to what they imagine life might have been had they remained in China. Tong (1971) described a Chinese American sensibility of being "satisfied-with-little," which he purported to have originated as a means of survival and then solidified into an actual identity. If the "satisfied with less" model has validity, we would expect these women to report satisfaction with their jobs or not to report dissatisfaction. To test these alternative hypotheses, two job satisfaction questions were asked: one, a 7-point scale, and the other, a 4-point scale. The 7-point scale had been used in national surveys. It read: "How satisfied or dissatisfied are you with your job . . . very satisfied, pretty satisfied, slightly satisfied, neutral, slightly dissatisfied, pretty dissatisfied, or very dissatisfied?" The 4-point scale asked: "Taking all things into consideration, how do you feel about your job? Are you very satisfied, somewhat satisfied, not too satisfied, or not satisfied at all?"

When given the option of "neutral" on the 7-point scale, the average Chinatown working woman felt "neutral" about her job. Yet when forced to pick between "somewhat satisfied" and "not too satisfied" on the 4-point scale, the average Chinatown woman reported feeling "somewhat satisfied" with her job.[5] This suggests that women may not be satisfied with their jobs but were reluctant to say they were dissatisfied. If we assume that the 7-point scale afforded more valid responses due to the greater differentiation of the scale, erroneous conclusions could be drawn that women were satisfied with their jobs if only the 4-point satisfaction scale were administered.

The "somewhat satisfied" finding on the 4-point scale might also be attributed to different phrasing; the phrase "Taking all things into consideration" may have caused respondents to evaluate their jobs as satisfying because they "took into consideration" their immigrant status, limited education, and non-English speaking constraints. In other words, these findings may illustrate how level of satisfaction is influenced by expectations. These women may have felt that they could not expect much better, given their limitations; thus, they should not be dissatisfied.

The finding that Chinatown's women felt "neutral" about their jobs may reflect an attitude of accommodation or endurance with less-than-desirable conditions. Chinese use the metaphor of being like a bamboo: "We bend but don't break," that is, there is pride in enduring hard times. The "satisfied with little" hypotheses need further study.

Men on average reported feeling "slightly dissatisfied" with their jobs on the 7-point scale and "somewhat satisfied" on the 4-point scale. Here again, we suspect that the deletion of the "neutral" alternative and insertion of "taking all things in consideration" on the 4-point scale biased responses in the satisfied direction. Without consideration for factors such as immigrant status, ethnicity, and education, Chinatown's men were dissatisfied with their jobs. In summary, job satisfaction was lower for men than for women.[6] Men's higher level of education may cause higher expectations—which, when not met, resulted in lowered levels of satisfaction, that is, in feeling dissatisfied.

Life Satisfaction

Two items were used to measure life satisfaction: Cantril's (1965) self-anchoring scale and an item designed for this survey that asked residents to compare their life to that of white Americans. Cantril's item read: "Here is a picture of a ladder. At the bottom of the ladder is the worst life you might expect to have. A person who is here would be very dissatisfied with his or her life. At the top of the ladder is the best life you might expect to have. A person who is here would be very satisfied with his or her life. Where would you put yourself on the ladder to show where your life is now?" [9-point scale, 9 = "best life" and 1 = "worst life"]

The following item was designed to assess life quality relative to a standard point of reference: "Think about how your life compares with the life of white Americans. Do you think your life is much better than white Americans, somewhat better than white Americans, about the same as white Americans, somewhat worse than white Americans, or much worse than white Americans?"

On the ladder of life quality scale, Chinatown's women felt less satisfied with their lives than Chinatown's men did. On the comparative with whites scale, Chinatown's women compared their lives to white Americans less favorably than Chinatown's men did.[7] While Chinatown's men felt their lives were "about the same" as white Americans, Chinatown's women described their lives as "somewhat worse" than white Americans.

Marital Satisfaction

Asked what they would do if they had their life to live over again, some of the wives, but none of the husbands, conveyed dissatisfaction with their gender or their spouse. Wives remarked: "I don't want to be a woman . . . because it's too much responsibility to take care of the family and go out to work." "I would like to be a male and not be cheated on in marriage." "I wouldn't get married to the same guy that I married." "I wouldn't work. I'd look for another man." One woman summed it up this way: "Had I my life to live over again, I'd get more education, get a better job, and find a better husband."

Asked if their spouse was meeting their expectations and whether there were marital conflicts, members of both genders complained. Husbands said: "She didn't adapt to the American culture, always stuck to the old Chinese fashion and customs." "She considers her job more important than mine. She doesn't clean the house as well as I want. I could clean it better." "Money, job, differences. They're usually communication problems. I'm an engineer and I like precise answers. She gives me ones that are not precise." Wives said: "My first husband just didn't want me—he just wanted a slave in the restaurant." "He's not faithful to me. He fooled around with other girls. He didn't take good care of the family." "We have different ideas in dealing with things. My husband is not cooperative in educating our children." "Different interests and hobbies. He likes to gamble. I hate to gamble." "We don't communicate as well as we should."

Despite these complaints, the majority of married persons reported satisfaction with their marriage: 21% said they were "very satisfied," 51% said "pretty satisfied," and 14% said "slightly satisfied." Nationally, husbands have been found to be more satisfied with their marriages than wives (Veroff, Douvan, and Kulka, 1981). However, in Chinatown there was no statistically significant difference in marital satisfaction between men and women when the unweighted data were analyzed, but husbands were more satisfied with their marriages than wives when the weighted data were analyzed.[8]

The current findings did not reveal whether women's reported marital satisfaction was due to lower expectations or actual satisfaction. There are several perspectives on this. First, Confucian traditions of acceptance, lower levels of education for women, or less patriarchal gender relations today could explain why Chinatown's women did not in general express great marital dissatisfaction. Confucian traditions admonished women to accept their fate. As the proverb read, "When you marry a chicken, stick with a chicken; when you marry a dog, stick with a dog" (Chiu, in Croll, 1978). Only in the next life could one's fate be changed (Smith, 1900). Second, lower expectations for marital satisfaction on women's part could also be due to their lower level of education compared to men. Campbell, Converse, and Rodgers (1976) found that Americans with lower levels of education were more satisfied with their jobs and marriage than persons with higher levels of education. Thus, education has the effect of raising expectations. Third, wives may not express dissatisfaction in their marriages because spousal relations are less patriarchally oppressive today than they were in traditional Chinese society, and poverty, which forces the wife into the labor market, makes the sequestering of women impossible. Thus, their presence in the ethnic labor market alters the nature of the marital relationship, making for more equalitarianism.

Findings revealed that while more husbands reported receiving understanding, help, and respect from their wives than wives reported receiving from their husbands, the percentages were very close: 72% of the wives and 83% of the husbands reported having received "a lot" or "some" understanding from their spouse; 75% of the wives and 86% of the husbands reported receiving "a lot" or "some" help from their spouse; and 85% of the wives and 96% of the husbands reported having received "a lot" or "some" respect from their spouse. More wives than husbands reported receiving "very little" or "no" understanding, help, and/or respect from their spouse, but these differences were not statistically significant (12% compared to 3%, 15% compared to 4%, and 9% compared to 0%, respectively).[9]

PSYCHOLOGICAL ATTITUDES

In research on ethnic minority populations, one area often unexplored is whether psychological attitudes reflect disadvantage, as in feelings of helplessness, low self-esteem, or self-blame. Such research has been done on internal-external locus of control. Internal control referred to the perception of events as being a consequence of one's own actions and thereby under personal control, whereas external control referred to the perception of events as being unrelated to one's own behavior and therefore beyond personal control. In all reported ethnic studies, groups whose social position was one of minimal power either by race or class tended to score higher in the external direction (Rotter, 1966). Studies have found that blacks were more external than whites (Lefcourt and Ladwig, 1961; 1966; Zygoskee, Strickland, and Watson, 1971), American Indians more external than whites (Graves, 1961), and lower-class black children more external than lower-class white or middle-class black children (Battle and Rotter, 1963). In our survey, attitudes that were measured included personal effectiveness, assertiveness-accommodation, self-esteem, and individual-system blame.

Personal Effectiveness

Campbell, Converse, and Rodgers's (1976) items of perceived personal effectiveness were used. They included: (E7) "Do you think it's better to plan your life a good ways ahead or would you say life is too much a matter of luck to plan ahead very far?" (E8) When you do make plans ahead, do you usually get to carry out things the way you expected or do things usually come up to make you change your plans?" (E9) "Have you usually felt pretty sure your life would work out the way you want it to or have there been times when you haven't been sure about it?" (E10) "Some people feel they can run their lives pretty much the way they want to; others feel the problems of life are sometimes too big for them. Which one are you most like?" The intercorrelation of pairs of items were low although the item-total correlations were high, suggesting that the items tap a diffuse variable that has been sampled, but that there was no tightly scaled structure.[10]

Chinatown's men and women did not differ in their perceived sense of personal effectiveness.[11] Life was just as unpredictable for men as for women, with neither gender reporting much control over events in their lives. Among women, 79% felt that when they make plans, things usually come up to make them change their plans; 57% have had times when they haven't been sure life would work out the way they want; and 31% felt that life was too much a matter of luck to plan ahead very far. Among men, 75% felt that when they make plans, things usually come up to make them change their plans; 48% felt there have been times when they haven't been sure life would work out the way they want; and 24% felt that life was too much a matter of luck to plan ahead very far. The majority of men and women believed it was better to plan their life a good ways ahead but found they usually did not get to carry out plans as they expected.

While personal effectiveness was not related to age or nativity,[12] there was a slight but significant relationship between personal effectiveness and personal income.[13] The lower the personal income of the respondent, the lower was his or her reported perception of personal effectiveness.

Assertiveness-Accommodation

In order to assess tendencies of assertiveness versus accommodation that would have cultural relevance, items were designed for this study that would differentiate those prone toward passive, accepting means of coping (accommodating types) from those prone toward initiating, persisting, and taking action (assertive types). These items were: (E1a) "If you find that a grocer is overweighing your meat, would you tend not to do anything about it *or* would you try to do something about it?" (E1b) "If you've been waiting in a bus line for a long time and someone cuts in front of you, would you make the best of things *or* would you say or do something about it?" (E1c) "If you lived in a housing project and a resident had been robbed and injured because the security in the housing project was bad, would you join a rent strike to get better security *or* would you tend to just let the Housing Authority officials deal with it?" (E1d) "If someone's been giving you a hard time, would you tend to ignore it *or* try to get the person to stop?" (E1e) "If you don't have what you'd like, would you try to get what you want and/or get someone to help you *or* would you try to 'make do with what you've got'?" (E1f) "Do you think that if you've been faced with a lot of frustration that you should keep trying *or* that you should forget it because it's better not to be frustrated?" and (E1g) "If there were serious problems in your marriage, would you try to change things *or* make the best of things?" For all respondents combined, most intercorrelations of items were significant and all item-total correlations were statistically significant.[14]

Assertiveness was not a common coping style for Chinatown's women. The majority of women normally coped by accommodating at their own expense: 76% would make the best of things if someone cut in front of them in a bus line; 75% would not join a rent strike for better security in their housing project following a robbery there; 63% said they would not keep trying if faced with lots of frustration; 57% said they would make do with what they had rather than try to get what they needed; 57% said they would not try to change things if their marriage had serious problems; and 50% said they would do nothing to correct a grocer whom they knew was overweighing their meat. However, in one instance, a majority would assert themselves: 56% said they would try to get a person to stop giving them a hard time.

Taking the assertiveness-accommodation scale as a whole, there were no statistically significant differences between men and women when analyzing the unweighted data, but differences were significant when analyzing the weighted data, with men being more assertive than women.[15] There were statistically significant differences between men and women with regard to specific situations as well. Men were more assertive than women when a grocer was overweighing their meat: 73% of the men said they would do something about it compared to 49% of the women. Twice as many men (50%) would join a rent strike than women (25%). Men were more likely than women to get a person to stop giving them a hard time: 80% of the men would get the person to stop compared to 56% of the women. Men were more likely to try to get what they needed or get someone to help them: 70% of the men would assert themselves compared to only 43% of the women. Faced with frustration, men were more likely to keep trying, while women were more likely to give up: 58% of the men would keep trying compared to 37% of the women.[16] There were no statistically significant gender differences with regard to handling serious marital problems[17] or in handling persons who cut in line.

Self-Esteem

Low self-esteem was more common among women than men.[18] Asked "Do you feel as smart and as capable as most other people?" 65% of the women said "no" compared to only 28% of the men. Economic position reinforces the impact of sex-role socialization on low self-esteem. Garment operatives were the only occupational category in which more persons felt "less" smart and capable than felt "as" smart and capable as others. Eighty-two percent of the operatives felt less smart and capable as most other people. Low self-esteem was also associated with low income and foreign birth,[19] two characteristics that are common to most Chinatown women.

Individual-System Blame

In their endeavor to differentiate external locus of control orientation that refers to chance from more systematic constraining forces such as racial discrimination, Gurin, Gurin, Lao, and Beattie (1969) developed the concept of individual-system blame and tested it in reference to blacks. Individual blame put the burden for social or economic failure on blacks for their lack of skill, ability, training, effort, or proper behavior. System blame put the responsibility for their failure on the social system because of its lack of opportunities and racial discrimination. Personal control and individual-system blame were found to be independent variables. Personal control did not correlate with civil rights activities, while system blame correlated with both civil rights activities and racial militancy. Those who blamed the system tended to favor group action rather than individual action in dealing with discrimination and had participated in more civil rights activities. Thus, individual-system blame tapped a political dimension; as such, it was important in our investigation of the propensity of Chinatown's women to engage in social-political movements.

Modeled after the items developed by Gurin and her colleagues, the following items were used to measure individual-system blame for Chinese Americans. "IB" refers to choices scored as individual blame, "SB" refers to choices scored as system blame. "Now I'm going to read you different opinions that people have. Please tell me which statement describes your opinion:" (E5a) "Many qualified Chinese can't get a good job because they're Chinese. White people with the same skills wouldn't have any trouble getting that job" (SB) *or* "Many Chinese can't get a job because they lack skill and abilities. If they had the skill and ability, they'd have as good a chance to get a job as a white person" (IB); (E5b) "Many Chinese don't do well in life because they haven't prepared themselves to make use of the opportunities that come their way" (IB) *or* "Many Chinese have good training but they don't do well in life because they don't get as many opportunities as whites" (SB); (E6a) "The problem for many Chinese in America is that white society discriminates against them even when Chinese do what's proper and adapt to white American customs" (SB) *or* "The problem for many Chinese is that they refuse to adapt to white American customs. If they did adapt, they'd be accepted and would get ahead" (IB). There were significant intercorrelations among all items for each gender and for all respondents.[20]

Chinatown's women were more likely than men to be individual-blaming than system-blaming.[21] Table 9.2 presents the analysis for each item by gender. The majority of women blamed their own race for lacking skills and abilities, for not having prepared themselves to make use of opportunities, and for not adapting to white American customs. By contrast, the majority of men blamed the system for not providing Chinese with as many opportunities as are provided to whites. Half of the men blamed the system for discriminating against Chinese Americans, while only 29% of the women acknowledged any effect of anti-Chinese discrimination. Women held far more self-blaming attributions than men.

Table 9.2
Chi-Square Analyses of Individual-System Blame Items by Gender

	System-Blame	Individual-Blame	
E5a "Can't get a good job"			
women:	28%	72%	$X^2 = 1.71$, df = 1, ns
men:	42%	58%	
E5b "Don't do well in life"			
women:	41%	59%	$X^2 = 5.62$, df = 1, p < .05
men:	66%	34%	
E6a "Problems facing Chinese Americans"			
women:	29%	71%	$X^2 = 3.72$, df = 1, p < .05
men:	50%	50%	

X^2 = Chi-Square

The greater tendency for Chinatown's women to blame themselves or their own race rather than the system may be related to education. Without the educational advantages that lead one to understand how racism functions in this society, individuals may be more prone to self-blame. Self-blame may then serve to lower women's self-esteem, making them feel more psychologically and politically powerless and, therefore, less likely to engage in collective efforts aimed at eliminating racial, gender, or class injustice.

In summary, both men and women in this community experienced low levels of personal effectiveness, but women evidenced less assertiveness, lower self-esteem, and more self-blame. Most of these women blamed themselves or their ethnicity for problems facing them. This psychological profile makes involvement in political action very difficult.

Intergroup Comfort and Social Distance

Undoubtedly, the potential for gains that can be achieved through collective socio-political action is great. However, in addition to psychological barriers, interethnic barriers keep these ethnic women from engaging in collective action. First, many of Chinatown's women (and men) do not relate comfortably with persons outside their own ethnic subgroup. Asked how comfortable or uncomfortable they felt associating with different ethnic and racial groups, 70% of the respondents said they felt uncomfortable with blacks and Filipinos, 63% uncomfortable with Chicanos, 48% uncomfortable with Japanese Americans, and 45% uncomfortable with whites. Even more surprising is the finding that discomfort exists within their own race: 37% of the Chinese immigrant women felt uncomfortable with American-born Chinese.[22] Second, these women appear to be socially isolated: 62% said they would like to have more friends, but 90% did not belong to any clubs, organizations, or associations of which they regularly attended functions.[23] Thus, social distance and isolation are major deterrents from participation in political movements of persons of color despite the need for greater assistance.

SUMMARY

In contemporary Chinatown, women constitute slightly more than half of the population. Unlike the bachelor society of times past, women today form a highly visible part of the community. In terms of their demographic characteristics, over three-quarters were immigrant. Slightly over half were married, one-quarter widowed. Their mean age was 52 years. By contrast, men in this community were younger (their mean age being 46 years), and bachelors (who form one-third of the male population) were second in proportion to those who were married.

Women were not only visible, they were visibly disadvantaged relative to men of their own ethnicity. In their perception, they were disadvantaged relative to Americans overall. Women in this community were less educated than men: their median level of education was at the sixth grade level compared to a high school graduate level for men. Fewer of the women were English-speaking: three-quarters could not speak English compared to half of the men. A majority of the women were in the paid labor force. Of those married, most worked out of economic necessity since the vast majority of families with multiple wage earners reported that they would barely get by if there were but one wage earner. Women were concentrated in the low prestige occupations—primarily the operative, clerical, and private household occupations—while men primarily occupied the service, professional, managerial, and craft trade jobs. Nearly half of the working women were employed as sweatshop workers in Chinatown for the apparel industry.

Most working women expressed no pride in the jobs they held; this perceived low occupational prestige was substantially more prevalent among women than among men. Three-quarters of the working women were not proud of the kind of work they did, and nearly all did not want their children to be doing the same type of work. We suspect that many immigrant women have little hope for anything better for themselves but have occupational aspirations for their children and vicariously live through their children's actual or anticipated success. While three-quarters of the men did not want their children to be doing the same type of work as they, only a third were not proud of their current form of employment. Thus, men also had higher aspirations for their children than for themselves, but they did not express such a wholesale lack of pride in their type of work.

The jobs held by the working women of this community were perceived as nonactualizing jobs with little to no job mobility or training benefits. Their pay was often below the minimum wage. Nearly all of the non-English speaking felt that their low proficiency with the English language was a major barrier to a better job; but their long work schedules, the double burden of working in the marketplace and at home, their age, a long ESL waiting list, and jobs that provide no English language training make it nearly impossible for them to acquire English language skills.

Most working women felt "neutral" about their jobs; they reported feeling neither satisfied nor dissatisfied. By contrast, men felt "slightly dissatisfied" with their jobs. I suspect that women's awareness of the disadvantages of their immigrant status, limited education, non-English language skills, and their expectation of worse conditions for their family had they remained in China caused them to report less dissatisfaction with their jobs than the actual, objectively considered conditions of their job would dictate. We might wonder if their level of job satisfaction would decline if they were to become better educated. Additional research on the relationship between subjective reports of job satisfaction and objective data or reports of specific job attributes is needed, given the discrepancy between actual job conditions for men and women, discrepancies in job pride, and their reported levels of job satisfaction.

These Chinese American women reported less satisfaction with their lives than Chinese American men did. These ethnic women also compared their lives to white Americans less favorably than Chinese American men did. Chinatown's men and women did not differ in their perceived sense of personal effectiveness: both felt that life was unpredictable and that they often could not carry out their plans as expected. Income was associated with personal effectiveness. The lower the personal income of the individual, the lower his or her perceived personal effectiveness. This finding demonstrates the relationship between psychological attitudes and economic conditions.

On several individual items on the assertiveness-accommodation scale, women were less assertive than men; they tended to accommodate to conditions that were to their disadvantage. Moreover, the majority of women did not feel as capable or smart as most other people, a proportion that was significantly higher than men. We assume this was related to women's lower levels of education, lower wages, and their immigrant status. In addition, Chinatown's women were more likely to be individual-blaming than system-blaming than men when it came to making attributions of blame for problems facing Chinese Americans. Additional research is needed to examine the relationship between self-blame cognition and mental health status and attitudes.

A majority of Chinese American women reported discomfort with persons outside their own ethnic group, while also expressing a desire for greater social integration. From a political point of view, the disadvantaged condition of these women could be bettered through mass movements like the feminist movement. The goals of the women's movement—which include quality day care, equal pay, fair employment practices, impartiality in the granting of credit, decent treatment for AFDC (Aid to Families with Dependent Children) families, the right to choose, and the recognition of the value and dignity of housework—benefit all women regardless of race (Almquist, 1975). But integration of these women, despite the potential for gains, is difficult. On one hand, feminist women of color have attributed their exclusion from the movement to racism and the movement's middle- and upper-class, white, college-educated focus (Davenport, 1981; Hooks, 1984; Yamada, 1981). On the other hand, many women in Chinatown did not feel comfortable with persons of other ethnic groups and races and did not feel any more comfortable with other persons of color than with whites. Such alienation would make it difficult for Chinatown's women to easily unite with persons of other ethnic minority groups.

The disadvantaged status of these ethnic women spans multiple life domains and conditions. Interventions must address these multiple fronts, for any action that addresses just one domain to the exclusion of others might have as much effect as slaying demons with a sewing needle. Low-income, ethnic women need greater opportunities for education, for this impacts not just occupation and salary but also psychological attitudes of job pride, personal effectiveness, self-worth, attributions of blame, and well-being. Furthermore, it lessens the educational inequities of gender.

Low-income, ethnic immigrant women need greater opportunities for English language training. Federal, state, and county funding for ESL classes should be made available to all non-English speaking immigrants in this country as part of this nation's commitment to newcomers and to their future contributions to our society. Moreover, if ethnic immigrant women are going to be afforded any opportunity for job mobility and integration into the American mainstream, their places of employment need to be less concerned with economic exploitation and more concerned with providing language training on the job, opportunities for promotions and raises, improved working conditions, decent wages and wage equity, and child care. A breakdown of inequities and restrictions along class, culture, and gender lines is needed to better the conditions of Chinatown's women. While we cannot determine here whether changes at the systemic level cause psychological attitudes or vice versa, it is certain that changes at both levels are needed. Efforts to eliminate sex-role inequities or traditions that lower the opportunities afforded to women relative to men, or minorities relative to whites, are essential.

NOTES

1. There were certain groups among whom the practice of footbinding was not common (i.e., the Manchu, Hakka, and Boat people of Canton).

2. $X^2 = 25.59$, df = 7, p < .001.

3. $X^2 = 8.86$, df = 1, p < .01.

4. There were no significant gender differences for "children do same work" using unweighted data. However, using weighted data, gender differences were significant ($X^2 = 3.93$, df = 1, p < .05); 8% of the women and 30% of the men wanted their children to be doing the same work they do.

5. Their mean score was 3.7 on the 7-point scale (1 = very satisfied, 7 = very dissatisfied) and 2.2 on the 4-point scale (1 = very satisfied, 4 = not satisfied at all).

6. Gender differences were not statistically significant using unweighted data but were significant using weighted data. Men's mean scores were 3.1 and 2.4 using unweighted data for the 7-point and 4-point scales, respectively (t = 1.44, df = 67; t = 1.24, df = 59). For weighted data (t = 2.56, df = 67, p < .01, X men = 2.4, X women = 2.0 for the 4-point scale; t = −2.77, df = 74, p < .01, X men = 2.7, X women = 3.8 on the 7-point scale). On both scales, men were less satisfied. Note that scales were scored in reverse direction from each other.

7. Self-anchoring scale: t = 2.32, df = 106, p < .05; X men = 5.4, X women = 4.8 where 1 is lowest rung of life, 9 is highest. Compared to white Americans scale: t = −2.53, df = 86, p < .01; X men = 3.0, X women = 3.5 where 1 = much better, 5 = much worse.

8. Unweighted data means for men and women were 2.2 and 2.3, respectively, where 1 = very satisfied, 7 = very dissatisfied. Weighted data means for men and women were 1.8 and 2.5, respectively (t = −.20, df = 68, p < .05).

9. Weighted data: gender differences were found for respect from spouse (X^2 = 14.23, df = 4, p < .01); the majority of wives reported that their husbands showed them "a lot" of respect, while the majority of husbands said their wives showed them "some" respect.

10. An analysis of the items suggested that E10 added very little to E7, E8, and E9 totaled; E7–E10 totaled correlated with E7–E9 at r = .996. Item-total correlations between the two varied no more than .02. Therefore, E10 was eliminated from the analysis. Item-item and item-total correlations for personal effectiveness:

All Rs

	E7	E8	E9	Total
E7	--	.04	.21**	.63***
E8		--	.20*	.59***
E9			--	.75***

Women

	E7	E8	E9	Total
E7	--	-.12	.13	.55***
E8		--	.33**	.58***
E9			--	.78***

Men

	E7	E8	E9	Total
E7	--	.21	.30*	.75***
E8		--	.06	.59***
E9			--	.71***

* p < .05   **p < .01   ***p < .001

11. r = .11, no differences on any of the individual items either.

12. r = .02, r = .10, respectively, using unweighted data. Relationships were significant using weighted data: the relationship between personal effectiveness and age was r = .16, p < .05; older people had a greater sense of personal effectiveness. The relationship between nativity and personal effectiveness was r = −.17, p < .05; foreign-born had a stronger sense of personal effectiveness than American-born.

13. r = .16, p < .05.

14. Item-item and item-total correlations for assertiveness-accomodation:

All Rs:

	E1a	E1b	E1c	E1d	E1e	E1f	E1g	Total
E1a	--	.32***	.28**	.34***	.27**	.30***	.17	.62***
E1b		--	.27**	.27**	.25**	.21*	.19	.57***
E1c			--	.36***	.29**	.33***	.35****	.66***
E1d				--	.29**	.26**	.21*	.61***
E1e					--	.49***	.32***	.66***
E1f						--	.35***	.67***
E1g								.59***

Women:

	E1a	E1b	E1c	E1d	E1e	E1f	E1g	Total
E1a	--	.34**	.25	.25	.23	.45***	.13	.67***
E1b		--	.24	.23	.08	.07*	.17*	.50***
E1c			--	.32*	.26	.12	.31*	.61***
E1d				--	.25	.25	.23*	.61***
E1e					--	.50***	.09	.58***
E1f						--	.36**	.69***
E1g								.54***

Men

	E1a	E1b	E1c	E1d	E1e	E1f	E1g	Total
E1a	--	.26	.21	.38**	.20	.03	.15	.50***
E1b		--	.25	.27	.40**	.30*	.19	.63***
E1c			--	.30*	.22	.45***	.33*	.64***
E1d				--	.22	.18	.10	.54***
E1e					--	.42**	.53***	.69***
E1f						--	.30*	.63***
E1g								.61***

* $p < .05$ **$p < .01$ ***$p < .001$

15. Unweighted data: $t = -1.23$, df = 100, ns; X = 3.4 and 3.1. Weighted data: $t = -3.35$, df = 104, $p < .001$, X women = 2.9, X men = 3.7 (highest score is most assertive).

16. $X^2 = 5.19$, df = 1, p < .05; $X^2 = 6.38$, df = 1, p < .01; $X^2 = 5.85$, df = 1, p < .05; $X^2 = 6.81$, df = 1, p < .01; $X^2 = 3.98$, df = 1, p < .05, respectively.

17. Gender differences were significant when weighted data were analyzed: 60% of the men would try to change things compared to 43% of the women. $X^2 = 7.77$, df = 1, p < .01; 72% of the men would try to change things compared to 43% of the women.

18. $X^2 = 10.962$, df = 1, p < .001.

19. $X^2 = 11.91$, p < .001; $X^2 = 4.24$, p < .05, respectively.

20. The intercorrelations between pairs of items and the item-total correlations were sufficiently high to comprise a scale. Item-item and item-total correlations for individual-system blame:

All Rs:

	E5a	E5b	E6a	Total
E5a	--	.57***	.46***	.82***
E5b	--	--	.57***	.85***
E6a				.80***

Women

	E5a	E5b	E6a	Total
E5a	--	.60***	.37**	.81***
E5b		--	.55***	.89***
E6a			--	.78***

Men

	E5a	E5b	E6a	Total
E5a	--	.53***	.49***	.82***
E5b	--	--	.42**	.78***
E6a			--	.80**

* p < .05   ** p < .01   *** p < .001

21. $X^2 = 8.74$, df = 3, p < .05.

22. For men, 36% of the immigrants felt uncomfortable with American-born Chinese. Gender differences for comfort using unweighted data were not significant but were significant using weighted data ($X^2 = 11.05$, df = 3, p < .01); 40% of the immigrant women felt uncomfortable with American-born Chinese compared to 27% of the immigrant men.

23. Of the men, 78% did not belong to any clubs, organizations, or associations; 22% did. Gender differences were not significant for unweighted data but were significant for weighted data ($X^2 = 4.21$, df = 1, p < .05); 7% of women and 23% of the men belonged to some club or organization.

They wait in line. Their faces speak of hard times. 1986. (Photograph by **Deanne** Fitzmaurice, courtesy of the *San Francisco Chronicle*.) Reprinted by permission.

My Fate to Be Unmarried

It was raining. I walked briskly to the assigned address with hope and enthusiasm because it was my first interview. Walking along Grant Avenue, I found the address in an old three-story building. In clothes soaked with rain, I rang the doorbell, then waited.

This was a man in his 40s, wearing pajamas. He lived in a one-room unit on the third floor of a run-down building. The room was small and filled with lots of furniture. When I introduced myself and the study, he said he was too old to be interviewed. After I explained that we didn't just interview young people, he politely let me enter. Leaning on his pillow while lying on his bed, he lit a cigarette and told me to start.

He reported that his life was "slightly interesting" yet he felt that his life was also "slightly empty," "slightly discouraging," "slightly disappointing," and "slightly unhappy." Although his income was high, he chose to live in a one-room unit in Chinatown because the rent was cheap. Many Chinese prefer to save as much money as possible for future needs or unexpected emergencies. This respondent worked as a pharmacist at a drugstore outside of Chinatown. Although his work schedule was regular and his salary high, he was not satisfied with his job. He regretted having chosen this profession, for he felt it didn't make good use of his abilities and skills.

Finally, this man sighed and said it was due to fate that he wasn't married. He hadn't found a mate. In Chinese tradition, marriage is strongly urged by parents and childbearing is important. If children don't get married and have a couple of kids, especially boys, they're considered nonfilial to parents and ancestors.

He appeared to be a lonely person even though he has many brothers and sisters and lots of friends.

10

"Fook, Look, Sow": Quality of Life

Chalsa M. Loo and Don Mar

In 1932, Herbert Hoover's presidential promise to the American people was "a car in every garage and a chicken in every pot." This was hailed the American dream. Postwar affluence raised American expectations for the good life. By 1970, this prosperity was reflected in the form of increasing rates of home ownership, possession of consumer durables, investment in individual savings, and expenditures in travel, health, and education (Campbell, Converse, and Rodgers, 1976). The American dream now included less tangible goals—a sense of achievement in one's work, fulfillment of one's potential, and an appreciation of beauty in nature and the arts: "The experience of life must be stimulating, rewarding, and secure. The revolution of rising expectations was not simply a desire for a larger house and a second car but a growing demand for the fulfillment of needs. . . . for a larger and more satisfying life experience" (Campbell, Converse, and Rodgers 1976, p. 2).

Previous chapters of this text have examined residents' perceptions of specific domains of their life. In this chapter we focus on perceptions of life as a whole. Specifically, we evaluate the well-being of Chinatown residents, the nature of their life goals, the extent to which these goals are met, and how this compares to Americans overall. We evaluate the material domains of life expectations by determining whether Chinatowners have been party to the revolution of rising expectations, that is, whether their desires have risen beyond a car in every garage or a chicken in every pot. In so doing, we evaluate the less tangible goals of life, a field of inquiry in which data on ethnic minorities have been lacking. There has been a "growing realization among social scientists of the need for social indicators on the life of American minorities [but] there have been far too few surveys of any type with ample populations of blacks, let alone the smaller numbered minorities" (Bracy, 1976, pp. 443).

Survey results also provide the empirical data needed to partially test the validity of the "successful" stereotype of Asian Americans. Sue and Kitano (1973) stated: "Asians have made enormous strides in society, but the notion that they are satisfied and successful is questionable" (p. 9). To this date, no research on life satisfaction among Asian Americans has been conducted to answer this question.

Research on life satisfaction and nature of everyday concerns is also valuable to clinicians who need to globally assess a patient's functioning on Axis V of the *Diagnostic and Statistical Manual of Mental Disorders* (American Psychiatric Association, 1987). In evaluating ethnic minorities, this assessment is most valid when the clinician has norms of satisfaction and life problems for the patient's subcultural group against which to make valid comparisons.

There is also a need to assess the determinants of well-being among various cultures because the structure of subjective well-being for one cultural group may not necessarily hold for another (Andrews and Inglehard, 1979). For example, in Chinese culture, *Fook, Look, Sow*—happiness, prosperity, and long life—reflect the three principles of the good life. In this chapter we investigate whether such life goals reflect those of these Chinese Americans and how their life goals compare to Americans overall.

This chapter is also devoted to an evaluation of the cultural validity of scales of well-being. Quality of life scales that were developed for a national population provide comparative norms. However, when such scales are applied to ethnic minorities, validity issues are raised; this is because scales can be culture- and class-bound and can have different meanings across cultural groups and classes. Even without the cultural variable, other variables such as education, age, and number of children have been found to affect levels of satisfaction. Persons with lower levels of education felt more satisfied with their jobs, community, housing, marriage, and friends than persons with higher levels of education; in addition, persons with lower levels of education felt less satisfied with their health (Campbell, Converse, and Rodgers, 1976). Increasing age was related to increased satisfaction and declining aspirations. Among married individuals, satisfaction in marriage was inversely correlated with number of children. Campbell, Converse, and Rodgers (1976) concluded that aspirations were a function of past experiences and referent groups and that satisfaction on any domain reflected the gap between the individual's current situation and his or her aspirations. Given these results and the concern for cultural validity, multiple measures were used in our Chinatown survey to assess well-being.

The first section of this chapter describes the multiple measures used to assess well-being and quality of life in this community. Section two, the most substantial part of the chapter, contains the findings on quality of life.

MULTIPLE MEASURES

"Satisfaction" is defined as an evaluation based upon a comparison between one's expectations and one's perception of objective conditions. Satisfaction is assumed to be subjective. Since expectations and perceptions of objective conditions can be affected by age, education, number of children, ethnicity, and class, individuals may differ in their reported levels of satisfaction even when faced with the same objective conditions. Because satisfaction is a problematic indicator and is prone to a positive response set, multiple measures were used to assess well-being. These measures included: (1) the 7-point satisfaction scale, (2) Cantril's (1965) self-anchoring ladder scale, (3) the Index of General Affect, which captures different descriptions of life quality and is less subject to response bias (Campbell, Converse, and Rodgers, 1976), (4) a 7-point and a 3-point happiness scale, (5) measures of life quality comparisons, and (6) open-ended questions.

The 7-point satisfaction scale was used to measure overall quality of life as well as satisfaction in specific life domains (e.g., income, job, education). Three measures of the ladder scale were used to assess long-term change on global well-being: "Where was your life five years ago?" "Where was your life most of the time during the past year?" and "Where do you expect your life to be five years from now?" Andrews and Withey (1976) found that for Americans overall, estimates of life five years in the future were all optimistic, all better than the present, and (except for persons over 64 years of age) judged to be better than five years ago. Andrews and Withey also found that the amount of expected life improvement declined with age. Analyzing for class effects, they also found that perceptions of well-being five years earlier were virtually the same for most of the different socioeconomic groups. All socioeconomic groups, except the lowest, thought their life had improved over the past five years. People near the top of the scale saw the greatest improvements, while those at the bottom felt their life had worsened. Analyzing for ethnic differences, Andrews and Withey (1976) found that blacks had higher expectations than whites; both expected about the same levels of well-being five years in the future, but blacks reported lower levels of well-being five years earlier and in the present.

Global measures of past, present, and future well-being were used to ascertain whether Chinatown residents felt that their lives had improved, stayed the same, or deteriorated. The measures were also used to indicate how these ethnic Americans saw their prospects for the future and how these perceptions of long-term change differed from mainstream America.

The Index of General Affect provides descriptive specificity about the nature of a resident's life. Its items capture the less tangible value of life quality, that is, the extent to which an individual evaluates his or her life as rewarding, stimulating, fulfilling, or challenging. A sample item read: "How boring or interesting is your life right now? Is it very boring, pretty boring, slightly boring, neutral, slightly interesting, pretty interesting, or very interesting?" The other dichotomous items included: "easy–hard," "miserable–enjoyable," "empty–full," "discouraging–hopeful," "tied down–free," "disappointing–rewarding," and "have not been given a chance–have had a lot of opportunities." Previous research on blacks revealed that their scores on the Index of General Affect were slightly less positive than scores for whites. Previous research showed the general affect scale items to be highly intercorrelated,[1] with the exception of "easy–hard" and "tied down–free." The latter finding suggested that these two items were peculiar and probably could not be treated as reliable or valid indicators of general life affect (Campbell, Converse, and Rodgers, 1976). "Easy–hard" was more predictive of overall life satisfaction for women than for men and was more predictive for persons with family incomes under $5,000 than for those with family incomes over $12,000.

Happiness was studied because it has not been found to be identical to satisfaction, although some overlap exists (Bradburn and Caplovitz, 1965).[2] Happiness has connotations involving short-term moods of gaiety and elation, while satisfaction ranges from perceptions of fulfillment to deprivation. The opposite of happiness is sadness or depression, while the opposite of satisfaction includes a strong flavor of frustration. Satisfaction implies a judgmental or cognitive experience, while happiness suggests a feeling. Some persons reported happiness along with dissatisfaction and the converse (Campbell, Converse, and Rodgers, 1976). Although the 3-point happiness scale is used nationally, a 7-point happiness scale was also used in this study in order to provide range equivalence to the 7-point satisfaction scale.

Measures of comparisons are life quality items that use a relative perspective, such as: "Is your life much worse, somewhat worse, about the same, somewhat better, or much better than other people?" Andrews and Withey (1976) did not find such measures to be predictive in national surveys. However, we believed that measures of comparison could be particularly useful when studying ethnic minorities because there are at least two different referents (whites and one's own ethnic group). The importance of referent specificity can be seen in problematic past attempts to compare blacks with whites where specificity of the term "people" by race was not made. For example, Katz, Gutek, Kahn, and Barton (1975), in studying attitudes toward violence among white and black men, found that blacks were less trusting of others than whites were. However, because there was no racial referent to the term "people," we cannot determine whether blacks were more distrustful of whites, of whites and blacks, or of blacks alone. In other words, we cannot determine whether there were any differences in trust perceptions as a function of the race of persons mentioned.

In the Chinatown survey, measures of comparison were used to assess how respondents perceived their lives relative to both white Americans and to other Chinatown residents: "Think about how your life compares with the life of white Americans. Do you think your life is much better than white Americans, somewhat better, about the same, somewhat worse, or much worse than white Americans?" and "Now which one of these statements best describes how you think your life compares to the Chinese who live in San Francisco's Chinatown? My life is much better than the average Chinatown resident, somewhat better, about the same, somewhat worse, or much worse than the average Chinatown resident."

Open-ended questions have the advantage of allowing individuals to discuss anything they deem important about content that cannot be easily gathered through closed-ended questions. The following open-ended questions were used to gather data on global life goals: "Now I'd like us to talk about your life as a whole and some of your feelings about it. . . . First, people strive for different things in life. Are there things in your life that you're striving for?" [If yes, "What might these be?"] "As you think about the best life you'd want for yourself, what would that be?" "Now I'd like you to think about your life as it is now. What things in your life are most satisfying for you now . . . things that make you feel very happy or very good or very contented?" "Now try to think about what things in your life you are least satisfied with . . . things you're not very happy about, things that could be a lot better. What would they be?"

QUALITY OF LIFE

This section discusses the results for general measures of well-being, comparison measures of well-being, results from open-ended questions regarding life aspirations and goals, findings on satisfaction for specific life domains, predictors of life quality, and demographic differences in well-being.

General Measures

On the tangible domains of life, Chinatowners have hardly been party to the revolution of rising expectations where desires have ascended beyond a car in every garage. Only one-third of these ethnic Americans owned a car and a mere 6% of the sample had a garage in which to put a car. As for home ownership, only 13% of the residents owned a home. In short, the vast majority of these ethnic Americans have no car and no garage and cannot afford to buy a house.

On the life satisfaction scale, Chinatowners, black Americans, and Americans as a whole were satisfied with their lives, but Chinatowners were much less satisfied with their lives than Americans overall (see Table 10.1). The average Chinatown resident was "slightly satisfied" with his or her life, while

Table 10.1
Life Satisfaction: Comparisons between Chinatown Residents, Blacks, and the United States

"Overall, how satisfied or dissatisfied are you with your life as a whole?"
(1 = "very dissatisfied" to 7 = "very satisfied")

	Dissatisfied				Satisfied			Mean
	1	2	3	4	5	6	7	
Nation[a]	1	2	3	11	20	41	22	5.6
Chinatown	1	4	7	3	39	40	6	5.2[b]
Blacks[c]	0	4	7	16	22	33	18	5.3

[a] Campbell, Converse, and Rodgers (1976), 1971 data, p. 449.
[b] t = 3.48, p < .01 for the difference between the means for Chinatown and the Campbell, Converse, and Rodgers national survey. There was no statistically significant difference between Blacks and Chinatown residents.
[c] Campbell, Converse, and Rodgers (1976), p. 449.
Note: For purposes of comparison, coding for Chinatown survey (1 = very satisfied, 7 = very dissatisfied) was reversed for comparable coding direction with national survey (1 = very dissatisfied, 7 = very satisfied).

the average American was "pretty satisfied." At the positive end of the scale, over one-fifth of the nation was "very satisfied" as compared to only 6% of the Chinatown sample. At the negative end of the scale, nearly twice as many Chinatowners were dissatisfied with their life (12%) as compared to the nation overall (6%). Relating these findings to national findings, both Chinatown residents and black Americans showed lower levels of life satisfaction than white Americans. These Asian Americans clearly did not see themselves as a successful minority, for they evaluated their life quality very much as black Americans evaluated theirs.

On Cantril's ladder of life scale, Chinatown residents evaluated their life as less satisfying than other Americans did on all three time dimensions—life five years ago, life now, and life five years hence (see Table 10.2 and Figure 10.1). Figure 10.1 contains a comparison of 1979 Chinatown data to 1973 U.S. data (Andrews and Withey, 1976). We have no reason to believe that life quality should have declined over that six-year period, therefore we presume that differences were not due to different time periods. The average Chinatowner judged his or her life to be on the middle ladder rung, midway between the worst and best life he or she could expect to have. Life was judged to be neither satisfying nor unsatisfying. By contrast, other Americans, on average, placed their life within the satisfied range. Close to half of the American sample placed their life today among the top three rungs as compared to less than one-fifth of the Chinatown sample. The great majority of Chinatown residents (73%) placed themselves among the middle three

Table 10.2
Cantril's Self-Anchoring Scale for Chinatown and the United States[1]

Cantril's Scale	Rung	Life Five Years Ago U.S.	Chinatown	Life Now U.S.	Chinatown	Life Five Years Hence U.S.	Chinatown
Best life I could	9	9%	4%	7%	3%	24%	10%
expect to have	8	14	4	11	3	25	7
	7	18	6	23	11	23	12
	6	17	19	23	15	11	16
	5	17	28	23	39	9	29
	4	9	22	7	19	4	18
Worst life I could	3	6	9	3	6	2	4
expect to have	2	4	5	2	3	1	2
	1	6	5	1	3	1	2
	D.K.	0	0	0	0	0	1
	Mean =	5.8	4.8[2]	6.1	5.0[3]	7.1	5.7[4]
Rungs in Thirds:							
Top 3 Rungs:		41%	14%	41%	17%	72%	29%
Middle 3 Rungs:		43	69	53	73	24	51
Bottom 3 Rungs:		16	19	6	12	4	8

[1] The national data are taken from Andrews and Withey's (1976) survey, p. 314. Although we are not comparing identical years, life satisfaction norms for the nation have not been found to change much over time (Andrews, personal communication).

[2] t-test coefficients for differences between Chinatown and United States: $t = 5.92$, $p < .001$.

[3] $t = 7.38$, $p < .001$.

[4] $t = 7.91$, $p < .001$.

rungs of life. Twice as many Chinatowners placed themselves among the bottom three rungs as compared to the national sample. Comparing results on the ladder scale with those on the 7-point satisfaction scale, respondents evaluated their life less favorably on the ladder scale than on the 7-point scale; the average respondent was "neutral" on the ladder scale and "slightly" satisfied on the 7-point scale.

For Chinatowners and other Americans, life has improved over the past five years, but for Americans overall, the degree of improvement was slightly greater. Both Chinatowners and Americans as a whole expected their life to be better five years hence. However, the horizon of that dream was much higher for Americans overall. Nearly three-fourths of the nation anticipated that in five years their life would be within the top three rungs, while the majority of Chinatowners anticipated their life would be within the middle

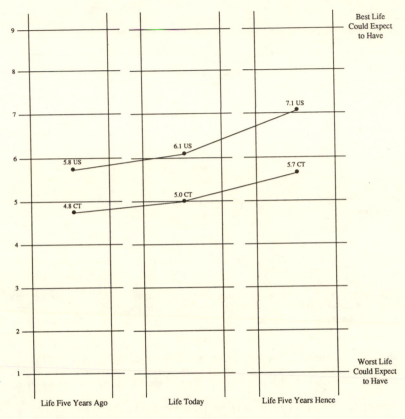

Source: Andrews and Withey (1976). From 1973 U.S. data.

Figure 10.1
Mean Scores for Chinatown and the United States for Cantril's Ladder of Life Satisfaction

three rungs. In other words, anticipations of life improvement among Chinatowners were constrained by a ceiling much lower than that of Americans overall. For these ethnic Americans, there were no great expectations. The revolution of rising expectations has bypassed this community.

Blacks expected the same level of well-being five years from now as did whites, which meant that blacks had higher expectations in terms of rate of improvement because they judged their current life to be lower than whites did (Andrews and Withey, 1976). For Chinatown residents, expectations for the future were lower in terms of the anticipated rate of improvement—less than whites and less than blacks.

In terms of the general affect variables, the intercorrelations had a greater range (.02 to .66) than has been found for the nation overall. While most correlations were significant, "tied down–free" did not correlate with five of the seven other variables.[3]

To what extent is life stimulating, rewarding, and enjoyable for these ethnic Americans and how does this compare to Americans as a whole? Compared to evaluations made by Americans overall, these Asian Americans evaluated their life as less interesting, less enjoyable, less full, less hopeful, less rewarding, and affording fewer opportunities (see Table 10.3). On six of the eight scales, the mean rating for Chinatown was significantly lower than the national mean rating.

Chinatown may be interesting, but the lives of its residents are not. Of the Chinatowners interviewed, 35% placed their lives at the "boring" end of the scale as compared to only 10% of the national sample. On the other end of the scale, 46% of the Chinatowners viewed their lives as "interesting" as compared to 74% of the nation. Only 4% of these ethnic Americans called their life "very interesting" as compared to over one-third of the nation. Compared to Americans overall, fewer Chinatown residents felt their life afforded much opportunity. A majority of Chinatown residents placed themselves midway between the advantaged and disadvantaged ends. On the negative side, 24% of the Chinatowners reported that life had not given them a chance, twice the proportion of the national sample who viewed their lives in this negative light. At the positive end, 67% of the national sample said that "life brought out the best in them" as compared to only 24% of the Chinatown sample.[4]

Far more Chinatowners described their lives as "empty" (26%) than Americans overall (7%). Fewer Chinatowners (56%) saw their lives as "full" than Americans overall (81%). A higher proportion of Chinatown residents (14%) saw their lives as "miserable" as compared to the national sample (6%). Alternatively, a smaller proportion of the Chinatown sample (66%) described their lives as "enjoyable" as compared to the national sample (81%).

A much higher proportion of Chinatown residents saw their lives as "disappointing" (20%) as compared to the national sample (9%). Conversely, a smaller proportion of the residents (56%) viewed their lives as "rewarding" as compared to the nation overall (78%). A higher proportion of Chinatowners were "discouraged" with their lives (17%) than was the case for Americans as a whole (8%). Correspondingly, fewer Chinatown residents felt "hopeful" about their lives (64%) than was the case for the nation overall (81%).

There were no statistically significant differences between Chinatown residents and Americans as a whole on the "easy-hard" and "tied down–free" variables. Nearly one-third of the Chinatowners described their life as "hard," citing these reasons: "Not enough income to support the family." "I don't have a job and I'm expecting a baby." "I've been unemployed and I feel lonely." "To start a new life in a new country, low income, poor housing."

Table 10.3

Comparison of Distributions for General Affect: Chinatown and the United States[1]

Measure	Distribution of Responses							Mean	t-coefficient
	1	2	3	4	5	6	7		
	BORING				INTERESTING				
Nation	2%	2%	6%	16%	17%	21%	36%	5.5	9.03***
Chinatown	8	7	20	18	23	19	4	4.1	
	MISERABLE				ENJOYABLE				
Nation	1	1	4	13	16	27	38	5.7	8.93***
Chinatown	3	2	9	20	43	22	1	4.7	
	HARD				EASY				
Nation	8	7	11	29	15	13	17	4.4	0.00
Chinatown	3	6	20	17	31	21	3	4.4	
	EMPTY				FULL				
Nation	1	2	4	12	15	22	44	5.8	9.22***
Chinatown	1	6	16	18	27	25	4	4.8	
	DISCOURAGED				HOPEFUL				
Nation	3	2	3	11	13	23	45	5.8	7.81***
Chinatown	3	1	13	19	32	25	7	4.8	
	TIED-DOWN				FREE				
Nation	5	4	6	17	12	20	36	5.3	0.63
Chinatown	3	5	16	5	15	35	22	5.2	
	DISAPPOINTING				REWARDING				
Nation	3	2	4	13	16	25	37	5.6	9.48***
Chinatown	2	4	14	24	37	17	2	4.5	
	HAVEN'T BEEN GIVEN A CHANCE				LOTS OF OPPORTUNITIES				
Nation	3	3	6	21	18	23	26	5.2	9.45***
Chinatown	6	6	12	52	12	7	5	4.0	

[1]National data (Campbell, Converse, and Rodgers, 1976, p. 38).

Note: Certain items were reversed in both interview schedules (same items) to minimize the effect of any tendency simply to check boxes down a column, ignoring distinctions among adjective pairs. When calculating means, reversed items were reassigned values so that 1 designated the least favorable response, 7 the most desirable.

*** $p < .001$

"I have a health problem so I can't work. There's not enough money to support my living." "No money. I'm poor." "Insomnia. I'm unable to find a job. My husband divorced me, and I don't get enough alimony." "My business has gone downhill. I'm afraid that it will get worse." "I'm too old. I can't go out to shop for what I need. It's very inconvenient. Also, I can't speak English. When I make phone calls to some agencies, I can't communicate with them."

Chinatown residents had lower income, less adequate housing, more limited language skills, more cultural dislocation, more health problems, and fewer job options than Americans overall. Their life should be harder, but surprisingly these ethnic Americans did not judge their life to be harder than other Americans judged their lives. Why would this be? One explanation is that Chinatowners may not have evaluated their lives as being very hard because their life expectations were lower on the ladder scale than was the case for other Americans. A second explanation is that most immigrants and refugees immigrated to this country for a better life, thus their judgment of current life is probably relative to how hard they imagined their life would be if they were still abroad.

Not only were there no differences between Chinese Americans and Americans overall with regard to "tied down–free," but, like the national sample, this item did not correlate well with some of the other general affect items. This suggests, as had been found for Americans overall, that the item is invalid as an indicator of life quality. One possible cause for the problematic validity of this item for ethnic immigrants is that "tied down–free" confounds political freedom (from oppression) with personal freedom (from being tied down by children).

On nearly all affective dimensions, there was far more enthusiasm expressed by the national sample than the Chinatown sample. Over one-third of the nation described their life as "very interesting," "very enjoyable," "very full," "very hopeful," and "very rewarding." The proportion of Chinese Americans who used such positive terms ranged from a meager 1 to 7%. Residents did not describe their life as exciting. A meager 1% of the Chinatown residents called their life "very enjoyable," a mere 2% described their life as "very rewarding," and only 3% called their life "very easy." A cultural argument that Chinese emotional inexpressiveness may account for such findings is unsupported by the fact that 22% of the Chinatown residents reported their life to be "very free"—an evidence of some enthusiasm.

Findings comparing happiness with satisfaction were similar to what had been found nationally; that is, while the two variables were significantly correlated, there was not complete overlap. The prevalence of unhappiness was greater than that of dissatisfaction; 23% of the Chinatowners felt their life was unhappy, while half this proportion judged their life to be unsatisfying (see Table 10.4). Also, the proportion of residents who felt happy about their life was smaller than the proportion of residents who felt satisfied with their

Table 10.4
Life Happiness and Life Satisfaction: Chinatown and the United States

H16: "How happy or unhappy do you feel about your life..."

Very Happy	Pretty Happy	Slightly Happy	Neutral	Slightly Unhappy	Pretty Unhappy	Very Unhappy
2%	35%	34%	6%	15%	4%	4%

H34: "How satisfied or dissatisfied are you with your life as a whole?"

Very Satisfied	Pretty Satisfied	Slightly Satisfied	Neutral	Slightly Dissatisfied	Pretty Dissatisfied	Very Dissatisfied
6%	40%	39%	3%	7%	4%	1%

U.S. "Taking all things together, how would you say things are these days..."[a]

	Very Happy	Pretty Happy	Not Too Happy
U.S. Overall	22%	68%	10%
Blacks[b]	12%	67%	21%

[a]Campbell, Converse, and Rodgers, (1976) p. 26.
[b]Campbell, Converse, and Rodgers, (1976) p. 447.

life. *Fook* has yet to grace nearly one-third of the community. Since general affect was depressed among these ethnic Americans, it is not surprising that their feelings about life lack the elation of extreme happiness.

Chinese Americans in Chinatown were far less happy than Americans overall. Thirty-seven percent of these Chinese Americans were "very happy" or "pretty happy" as compared to a full 90% of the nation (scales were not of equal range; Chinatown's sample was given a 7-point scale, the United States a 3-point scale). Only 2% of the Chinatowners said they were "very happy" as compared to ten times that proportion nationally; 35% of the Chinatown sample were "pretty happy" as compared to nearly twice that proportion nationally.

Methodologically, the 7-point happiness scale was judged to be a more valid measure than the 3-point happiness scale because of its finer differentiation and conceptual equivalence to the Chinese *fook*.

Comparison Measures

Nearly half of the Chinatown sample (46%) thought their life was "about the same" as white Americans. A quarter felt their life was "worse" than white Americans, and a few (10%) judged their life to be "better." The remaining 19% "did not know," citing "Nobody told me how white people live. I've not been in the United States too long."

Those who judged their life to be worse than white Americans cited less income, fewer material possessions, less education, fewer opportunities, and lower occupational status: "My income is less than whites, and I must work harder." "We have to start everything all over, a new adjustment. We don't know their language or culture." "[White] Americans are physically healthier than Chinese." "Work, play, language—all are not as good as for white Americans." "Living, working. I have to work six days a week, sometimes 10 hours. Americans don't. They work five days a week." "They don't have to worry about being discriminated against. I feel a little inferior compared to them." "Being a Chinese immigrant with language problems in the United States, I can't go anywhere. I have to stay in Chinatown for my whole life." "My life is worse than white Americans because of lower education, lower income, lousy English, and lower position."

Although very few Chinese Americans thought their life was better than whites, the reasons given by those who did feel this way were interesting. Some cited cultural advantages: "I feel that the upbringing of Orientals is more strict than whites and thus Orientals are brought up better." "We have a dual culture. If I have any problem, I can go to either philosophy or side." The most provocative reasons were offered by those who evaluated their lives as better because they had less. Assets normally considered desirable by American standards (such as home ownership, leveraging money, and material goods) were deemed liabilities: "They [whites] have kids and a home, which is a burden." "The way of life. I enjoy a simpler life. White Americans make life too complicated." "I'm not into the craze of being in debt [taking out bank loans]. White people are after personal gain. Their ends are unattainable. Being poor where I came from, I can appreciate what I attain."

The majority felt that the quality of their life was about the same as the average Chinatown resident (64%), some felt their life was better (26%), and a few thought their life was worse (7%). The remaining (3%) "did not know." Those who felt their life was better than the average Chinatown resident were primarily those who lived in the noncore area; their reasons pertained to education, income, job, housing, and breadth: "My life is more diversified. In Chinatown, they are more secluded and closed in." "I have a promising job, and my housing is far better than those in Chinatown." "I live in a less crowded place than they live in." "I have a home, good health, and enough money to live on." "We are going to have a home of our own. Money is not a problem. My husband is open to my suggestions." "I've attained a high level of education. Achieving what society expects of me. In the eyes of the Chinese, they would view me as a success." "My income is better. I have freedom of choice. A lot of the other residents don't. I live here because I want to. Most Chinese live here because they have to." "The language barrier and income force them to live in Chinatown. I don't have the economic burden that a lot of Chinese here have." "Their lives are pretty much isolated and tied down to Chinatown. I actually know some of them never cross over the Stockton tunnel; it's almost like a hell's gate to them." "I know how to enjoy life better than the typical Chinese. Chinese are penny-savers—they have no entertainment." "Some residents in Chinatown can't even afford to live comfortably. Some have to starve themselves to get by. They eat the same kind of diet every day to get by." "I have some education, a chance to experience white society and their white superiority feelings toward minorities whom they consider inferior."

Those who felt their life was worse than the average Chinatown resident cited income and health reasons: "My health is poorer. I'm unable to support myself. I don't have enough money to live." "My husband and I don't have a good education. We come from poor backgrounds so we don't make as much money as others." "I'm not as well off as many of them. I don't have as much money. I have to work hard." Overall, while there was a tendency for some to feel better off than the average Chinatowner, the majority felt representative of the community.

Aspirations and Goals

So far, we have seen that on nearly all measures (satisfaction, happiness, ladder of life quality, and the majority of general affect measures), the quality of life of these Chinese Americans was lower than that reported by Americans as a whole. This was not due to higher levels of life expectations among Chinatowners, for the ladder of life findings revealed that these ethnic Americans had lower levels of life expectations. Therefore, we must assume that lower levels of well-being were due to objectively worse conditions such as substandard housing, crowding, low income, low occupational status, few job options, ill health, mental health stresses, limited education, and language and cultural barriers. Details of these conditions have been discussed in previous chapters of this book.

Three questions remain unanswered: (1) What constitutes the best life for these Americans? (2) What are their levels of satisfaction for specific life domains? and (3) Why would nearly half of the sample think their life was "about the same" as white Americans when their subjective life quality was consistently less? Were Chinatowners unaware of white Americans' living conditions because of their limited contact with outsiders, which made them blind to the discrepancy between themselves and middle America? Responses to open-ended questions helped us explore the aforementioned questions. These questions included the components of the best life, goals in life, components of satisfaction, and components of dissatisfaction. Each of the following sections covers the findings for each of these topics.

Components of the Best Life. Thinking about the best life they would want for themselves, these residents most often mentioned family, health, housing, and a worry-free life. Job, leisure activities, happiness, self-actualization, and friends were also mentioned but with much less frequency. In their words, the best life included: "enough clothing, good food, a nice place to live, good transportation, a stable life," "money and a house," "job security, being married, having a couple of kids," "no worries, a peaceful life, no trouble, good health," "to live happily with my son and his family," "no arguments, have a happy life, be secure, confident, and healthy," "have a good job, good pay, own an apartment and a car, own my own business. Be free of worries, no problems in life, good health, and good friends," and "a better paying job for my husband and a house with three bedrooms in the Richmond or the Sunset, good children and all of us holding good jobs."

Some residents had grand dreams, such as: "living in the nicest place, travel, have everything I want . . . health, wealth, and a long life," "play *maj jong,* buy jewelry, go on tours and enjoy life," "have a lot of money, a big house, a big car," and "live in the suburbs, a humongous house, a good decent job, healthy life, that's about it." But most residents' desires were strikingly modest. Very basic needs of food and survival were often mentioned: "I would want to have enough to support myself, enough money to spend and be able to eat." "I'd want sufficient food and clothing so I don't have to worry about my daily life." "I'd like to have enough food to eat and a place to live close to Chinatown." "To not worry about money." "I'd want to be wealthy but I don't have to be too wealthy, just so I don't have to live in a little room." "As long as I get enough money to live on, I'm satisfied. The best life that I want is a very simple and peaceful life."

Job-related desires of job security, job satisfaction, having a steady job, or just a decent job were unpretentious. Dreams of "working five days a week, traveling once a year for two weeks, going to movies, shows, and listening to music" were humble, considering how the best life for this man represents what is normal for most Americans. Other expressions of humble wants included: "Being satisfied with what I have is the best life for me" and "I don't have any choice in life. I spend my days at work. That is my life."

Goals in Life. Money (*look,* or prosperity) was the most often mentioned goal for residents: "Nothing except money. I feel that money can make a lot of things work out." "Money is the main thing I'm striving for." In small Chinatown rooms, the deity of prosperity hangs on the wall, a reflection of this life dream. Many residents were also striving for a better job, a good job, or a better paying job. Several were striving for good health. Many wanted to be able to buy a home. Some were striving for family-related goals such as becoming a good parent, taking care of the family, keeping the family together, or having respectful children: "I hope my son and daughter can have a better life than I." "See to it that my parents have everything they need." A few were striving for career or educational goals. "[I'm striving for] a college education, a good job, a good roof over my head, good health . . . you know, the three Chinese characters . . . 'Fook, Look, Sow'." Here again, the theme of unassuming goals was repeated: "To have food to eat every day. To have the energy to walk around." "I'm too old to strive for anything. I'm settled and satisfied with what I have." "I'm not asking for much, just two meals a day."

Components of Satisfaction. Sources of satisfaction most often mentioned were: children and family (n = 48); job (n = 15); enough money to live on (n = 12); and health (n = 11). Friends, leisure activities, and school or education were also mentioned, but less frequently.

Children were the greatest source of satisfaction, particularly children's educational achievements ("doing well in school," "studying hard," "my children have good educational opportunities at UC Berkeley"), attainment of adulthood ("having children who are grown and married"), and companionship ("having the companionship of my children"). Of those with children, a large majority felt satisfied with how their children turned out (26% were "very satisfied," 59% were "pretty satisfied," 7% were "slightly satisfied," and only 8% were "neutral" or "slightly dissatisfied"). Grandchildren were also mentioned as a source of satisfaction. Other family-related sources of satisfaction included one's spouse ("my wife takes good care of me," "being with my wife," "I have a good husband") and family ("having a nice family," "my family life is very happy").

Sources of satisfaction related to one's job included: "I'm very satisfied with my job," "I've got a good job," and "I have a job." Notable was how the basic need of having a job was most satisfying. The mention of personal fulfillment in one's career was rather absent.

Sources of satisfaction related to finances included: "not having to worry about making a living," "having enough to live on," and "being self-supporting." For one resident, "to eat chicken, salted fish, and vegetables every day," her notion of the most satisfying life, read like a culturally specific echo of Herbert Hoover's promise of a chicken in every pot.

Not all Chinatowners found satisfaction in their lives; nearly one-fifth of the residents said "nothing" was satisfying: "Right now, I don't have any satisfaction." "Nothing. I feel my life is pretty simple and nothing really makes me feel satisfied or dissatisfied." "Nothing at all. I am not happy." "There's nothing that I'm satisfied with right now. I have nothing, no job and no husband." "I am not happy, not satisfied at all. I am unemployed, divorced by my husband, suffer from insomnia, and been hurt physically by my son."

More people reported dissatisfaction in answer to an open-ended question about satisfaction than in any of the life quality scale measures, an astounding finding that suggests less willingness to report dissatisfaction on scaled items than on open-ended questions. There is apparently a more positive response set to scales of well-being, a finding of methodological import for researchers of ethnic persons.

Components of Dissatisfaction. Domains of dissatisfaction included family (n = 31), "nothing" (n = 30), job (n = 18), finances (n = 18), health or aging (n = 15), housing (n = 8) and social life (n = 8). One Chinese American summed it up this way: "My personal life could be better, working conditions could be better, and living conditions could be better."

The description of the Chinese family as tenaciously indestructible has been called a misnomer (Lee, 1960), and the finding that family was the source of greatest dissatisfaction documents Lee's point. The family in Chinatown is not so indelibly ideal. Sources of dissatisfaction included family conflicts, separated or broken family, widowhood, problems with spouse or children, or having no children: "Broken family, being divorced." "Not living with my son's family." "Family friction and conflict." "My husband gambles a lot." "I still have one daughter in China." "I get very upset when I think of my son and daughter-in-law." "We've been a broken family ever since coming to the United States. Also, there are poor relations with relatives." "I don't have any relatives in the United States. I hope all my family members in Hong Kong can come over here." Immigrants and refugees face a particular problem in coping with nonunited families. Parenting was another type of family problem; 40% of the parents interviewed reported difficulties, most commonly disciplinary ones: "My kids won't listen to me." "My son causes a lot of trouble."

Job dissatisfactions were voiced as follows: "I don't like my job." "I can't find a job." "I can't find a better job." "I don't like working as a busboy." "I should be getting a promotion but I can't convince my boss that I should get one." Financial sources of dissatisfaction included: "It's so hard to make a living." "The bank won't loan me money to start a business." "I don't have enough money." "I don't have enough luxuries that other kids have outside of Chinatown, like a cat or good clothes. When I was a kid, I had only one pair of shoes."

Dissatisfactions with health were expressed as follows: "Getting old, can't go out and walk around Chinatown anymore." "My wife's health, she can't walk." "Poor physical health." Sometimes specific organic ailments were mentioned. Expressions of dissatisfaction with housing included: "My living place is no good." "The landlord plans to raise the rent again." "I don't have my own place to live."

Social discontent focused on loneliness: "I have no good friend to 'talk heart' with, to share my frustrations." "Almost all my best friends are living in Hong Kong. My living here is rather lonely." "I am an old man now and I feel lonely all the time. I can't find anyone to talk with." "I'm too lonely. I live all by myself in this apartment. My children hardly come here to see me. I have a feeling they don't want me."

Dissatisfaction with some aspect of life was not universal. Nearly one-third of the respondents (n = 30) said they were dissatisfied with nothing.

Satisfaction on Specific Life Domains

Chinatowners were less satisfied than Americans overall with regard to their education, job, health, success,[5] family life, marriage, friendships,[6] and leisure[7] (see Table 10.5). Half of the Chinatown residents interewieved were dissatisfied with the amount of education they had received, which compared to only 28% of the national sample. A greater proportion of Chinatown residents were dissatisfied with their job (23%), dissatisfied with their health (23%), and dissatisfied with their life accomplishments (30%) as compared to Americans as a whole (8%, 10%, and 15%, respectively).

The lower level of satisfaction with attained education was consistent with objective data of low levels of education for persons in this community. Hopes lie in aspirations for their children. Fathers tell sons: "Don't end up like me—a busboy in a Chinese restaurant. Go to college. Study hard. Get a good job." The lower level of job satisfaction is consistent with the low occupational prestige, nonactualizing nature of the jobs held by Chinatown residents. Moreover, the lower level of perceived success among Chinatown residents is related to lower job satisfaction and less education.

The lower level of health satisfaction among Chinatowners corresponded to their poorer health status and the higher proportion of elderly in the population. Nearly half of all Americans sampled were very satisfied with their health as compared to only 16% of the Chinatown sample. The proportion of the national sample that was very satisfied with their friendships/ companionships was three times that found in Chinatown.

Survey findings revealed that the family was not a wellspring of social support, as the literature would suggest (Hsu, 1971). The family is both a source of satisfaction and dissatisfaction, with affect ranging from happiness to frustration. The proportion of the national sample that was very satisfied with their marriage (58%) was over twice that found in the Chinatown sample. The proportion of the national sample that was very satisfied with their family life (44%) was over twice that found in Chinatown. Family satisfaction among these ethnic Americans was far less than for Americans overall. While causes for greater marital and family satisfaction in this enclave were unknown, possible factors include the loss of family or spouse as a result of age, fragmentation of families due to immigration restrictions or exclusionary laws, cultural expectations of family cohesiveness and filial piety that are at variance with white American norms, irregular working hours that leave little family time, and a work obsession that diverts energy from activities that enhance marital and familial enjoyment. The latter explanation is supported by data showing that the proportion of the national sample that was very satisfied with the way they spend their spare time was three times

Table 10.5

Comparison of U.S. and Chinatown Distributions for Satisfaction in Domains of Life

Domain		Dissatisfied 1	2	3	Percent 4	5	Satisfied 6	7	Mean	t coefficient differences between Chinatown & nation
Marriage	U.S.[a]	0%	1%	2%	7%	7%	25%	58%	6.3	3.85**
	CT	3	0	3	5	14	53	22	5.7	
Family Life	U.S.[a]	1	2	3	7	13	30	44	5.9	2.19*
	CT	1	1	6	7	17	49	18	5.6	
Health	U.S.[a]	3	3	4	9	9	27	45	5.8	4.73**
	CT	3	9	8	3	24	34	16	5.0	
Friendships/ Companionship	U.S.[a]	1	1	4	12	15	30	37	5.7	2.75**
	CT	1	1	0	22	15	48	12	5.4	
Job	U.S.[a]	2	2	4	13	13	30	36	5.7	5.36**
	CT	10	3	10	13	28	29	7	4.6	
Amount of Education	U.S.[a]	11	8	9	16	14	15	27	4.7	5.06**
	CT	13	15	22	8	15	22	5	3.8	
Success/ Accomplished	U.S.[b]	2	4	9	21	35	22	7	4.8	4.29**
	CT	6	9	15	22	29	17	3	4.2	
Income	U.S.[b]	5	5	14	14	36	23	3	4.5	0.59[1]
	CT	4	7	14	17	34	21	1	4.4	
Spare time/ Leisure	U.S.[a]	2	2	5	13	17	27	34	5.6	4.29***
	CT	3	3	14	9	25	37	9	5.0	
Housing	U.S.	3	2	5	13	15	26	36	5.6	
Neighborhood	U.S.	3	2	4	11	13	21	46	5.8	

		not satisfied at all 1	not too satisfied 2	somewhat satisfied 3	very satisfied 4	
Dwelling	CT	3%	19%	67%	11%	2.9
Neighborhood	CT	1	26	59	14	2.9

[a] Data from Campbell, Converse, and Rodgers, (1976), p. 63.
[b] Data from Andrews and Withey (1976). Scales range from terrible to delighted, p. 267 and p. 254.

[1]Weighted data: t = 2.35, p < .05.
Note: Coding for Chinatown survey (1 = very satisfied, 7 = very dissatisfied) was reversed for comparability to national norms where coding was 1 = very dissatisfied, 7 = very satisfied.

* p < .05.   ** p < .01.   *** p < .001.

greater than the proportion in Chinatown that was very satisfied with the amount of time they have for leisure activities.

With regard to environmental concerns, the percentage of Americans who were very satisfied with their housing (36%) was over three times that of Chinatown residents. The proportion of the national sample who were very satisfied with their neighborhood (46%) was also over three times the proportion in Chinatown.[8] Lower levels of satisfaction with both neighborhood and housing in this enclave reflect the data reported in earlier chapters.

Chinatown residents did not differ from Americans overall with regard to satisfaction with their income, a surprising finding considering the lower wages made by Chinatown's labor force. This may be due to lower expectations based on limited education and lack of English language skill. In a comparison of income satisfaction with national findings for "pay and fringe benefits you get and job security"[9] (Andrews and Withey, 1976), Chinatowners were significantly less satisfied. And in a comparison of income satisfaction with national findings for "standard of living"[10] (Andrews and Withey, 1976), Chinatowners were again significantly less satisfied.

Predictors of Life Quality

Which life domains serve as the best predictors of overall life quality and how do these predictors compare to those of the nation as a whole? Campbell, Converse, and Rodgers (1976) found that family, marriage, and finances were the best predictors of overall life satisfaction (see Table 10.6). We used the life satisfaction scale and the ladder scale to ascertain whether differences existed in the predictors for these respective scales, and if so, what implications this had for scale validity.

Health ranked second in importance in explaining well-being on both the life satisfaction and ladder measures in Chinatown, but for the nation as a whole, health ranked eighth. Thus, health was a more salient concern for residents of this low-income community than it was for Americans overall—which was probably due to residents' lower health status and higher mean age.

Marital satisfaction was the most powerful predictor of overall well-being in Chinatown on both measures, a finding similar to the nation overall (where marital satisfaction ranked second). Comparing the Cantril ladder and the satisfaction findings in Chinatown in terms of correspondence to rankings on the satisfaction scale for the nation overall, the ladder scale more closely approximated the rankings on the satisfaction scale used for the nation. Money earned (or finances) ranked third in predicting life quality for the nation; it ranked third for Chinatowners on the ladder scale and ninth on the satisfaction scale. Housing satisfaction ranked fourth in importance as a predictor of life quality for the nation. It also ranked fourth in Chinatown on the ladder scale, but it ranked seventh on the life satisfaction scale.

Table 10.6
Rank Order and Regression Coefficients for Variables by Sample and Measure in Predicting Life Satisfaction

Variable	U.S.[1]		Chinatown - Sat.[2]		Chinatown-Cantril[3]	
	Rank	Beta Coefficient	Rank	Beta Coefficient	Rank	Beta Coefficient
Family	1	0.408	3	0.379 ***	5	0.226 *
Marriage	2	0.364	1	0.504 ***	1	0.381 **
Finances	3	0.333				
Money Earned			9	0.136	3	0.270 *
Housing	4	0.303	7	0.272 **	4	0.267 **
Job	5	0.274	4	0.301 **	6	0.219
Friendship	6	0.256				
Companionship			6	0.284 **	8	0.084
Community	7	0.253				
Neighborhood			8	0.205 *	9	0.057
Health	8	0.219	2	0.404 ***	2	0.313 ***
Nonwork Activities	9	0.213				
Leisure Time			5	0.297 **	7	0.150

[1]National data from Campbell, Converse, and Rodgers, 1976, p. 85. Statistical significance of correlations not indicated.

[2]7-point life satisfaction scale used in Chinatown sample. Statistical significance calculated for correlation of proportion of variance accounted for by individual variables to life satisfaction variable.

[3]Cantril's self-anchoring scale for Chinatown sample. Statistical significance was calculated for correlation of proportion of variance for individual variables to ladder of life quality variable.

$*p < .05.$ $**p < .01.$ $***p < .001.$

We suspect that differences in rankings between the ladder and satisfaction scales reflect a difference in what each scale measures. Although Campbell and his fellow researchers conceived of satisfaction as a cognitive judgment, it is our feeling that the satisfaction scale taps residents' short-term assessment of their life, while the ladder scale taps a long-term evaluation. Since measures on the satisfaction scale and the happiness scale were correlated more closely than the ladder scale and happiness,[11] the satisfaction scale may tap more of an emotional state than the ladder scale. Thus, satisfaction with money earned may not be as important to a sense of well-being on a short-term affective basis but may be far more important to the well-being of Chinatown residents in a long-term perspective.

Demographic Differences in Well-Being

Analyses of subgroup differences on Cantril's self-anchoring scale were found for gender and nativity.

Men's evaluation of their well-being was significantly higher than women's.[12] Moreover, Chinatown women's evaluation of their life quality was lower than the nation's evaluations of its life quality. Women's lesser sense of well-being is hypothesized to be due to poorer educational and occupational status; heavier burdens of responsibility as parent, spouse, and housekeeper coupled with wage earner responsibilities; and social conditioning of less privilege, power, assertiveness, and self-esteem.

American-born Chinese evaluated their lives in better terms than did the foreign-born.[13] Chinese immigrants face greater loneliness, cultural dislocation and differences, language barriers, and constrained job opportunities than American-born Chinese. Chinese who were born on American soil judged their life quality similarly to the way Americans in general judged theirs.

SUMMARY

A major research question addressed in this study was the quality of life experienced by Asian Americans and how these evaluations compared with Americans overall. A multi-measures approach was used. Chinatown residents have not been party to the revolution of rising expectations. Only 13% owned a home and only one-third of the residents owned a car. Herbert Hoover's 1932 presidential promise of a car in every garage is still not a reality for the vast majority of these ethnic Americans. Furthermore, subjective evaluations of life quality are consistent with the objective indicators. While on average, Americans—white, black, or Chinese American—are satisfied with their lives, Chinatown residents were less satisfied with their life than Americans overall, and these differences were statistically significant. Chinatown residents evaluated their life satisfaction at a level similar to the level that blacks used to describe theirs.

Chinese Americans in this community felt their life had improved over the last five years but only very slightly. On all three time dimensions—five years ago, today, and five years hence—Chinatown residents rated their life lower on the ladder of life quality than the national sample rated theirs. These ethnic Americans anticipated a better life five years hence, but their expectations were lower than those of Americans overall. For these Americans, prospects for the future were dimmer. Life quality horizons were considerably lower than the nation overall, lower than whites, and lower than blacks.

On the less tangible indicators of life quality—those dealing with the experience of life as stimulating, rewarding, enjoyable—the Asian Americans who were interviewed evaluated their life quality far lower than Americans overall. Compared to how Americans perceive their life, Chinatown residents evaluated their life as less interesting, less enjoyable, less full, less hopeful, less rewarding, and affording fewer opportunities. Less enthusiasm was expressed on all general affect items in this ethnic community than was found for the nation overall.

The average Chinese American rated his or her life on the midpoint between boring and interesting and on the midpoint between "haven't been given a chance" and having had "lots of opportunities." The average Chinese American rated his or her life only slightly above the midpoint on the "miserable–enjoyable," "empty–full," "disappointing–rewarding," and "discouraged–hopeful" scales.

Less happiness was felt than satisfaction (71% as compared to 85%), and most of those who reportedly felt happy were "pretty happy" or "slightly happy." Nearly one-fourth felt unhappy with their life, which was similar to the proportion reported by blacks and two and a half times more than was reported by whites in the nation.

With regard to the "successful" stereotype of Asian Americans, empirical findings indicate that these Asian Americans do not fit the stereotype either by objective or subjective indices. Their level of life satisfaction and well-being was less than has been found for Americans overall, a factor that clinicians need to bear in mind when making assessments. We assume that lower levels of life quality were not due to higher levels of expectations because respondents reported lower levels of expectations for the future. It can be assumed instead that lower levels of well-being were due to objectively worse conditions, that is, the reasons provided by those who said their life was worse than white Americans and those reported throughout this text.

On specific life domains, Chinatown residents felt significantly less satisfied than Americans did with regard to levels of education, job, health, success in life, marriage, family life, friendships, and leisure time. Predictors of life satisfaction were marriage, health, family, and job, while predictors of life quality were marriage, health, money, and housing. Family was a major component of both life satisfaction and life dissatisfaction, revealing its overall salience to emotional contentment.

Chinatown residents felt that family, health, housing, and a worry-free life comprised the best life they could imagine, but their goals in life centered around money, job, and health. *Fook* (happiness) is an intangible goal that takes a back seat to tangible goals of basic survival—money, job, and health.

A hierarchy by gender and nativity was found for well-being. Men's evaluation of their life was significantly higher than women's evaluation of their life. American-born Chinese reported their quality of life in better terms than immigrant Chinese. The American-born conceived of their well-being in similar ways to how Americans overall reportedly felt about their well-being.

It was also our purpose to evaluate the cultural usefulness of various measures and scales. Comparison measures were found to be useful for this ethnic population if they were followed by an open-ended probe question to ascertain the factors that account for these cognitions. With regard to a comparison with white Americans, for example, the quarter who rated their life as "worse" cited objective indicators—fewer material possessions, less education, less income, lower occupational status, less leisure time, cultural and language adjustment, and discrimination. However, among the 10% who judged their life to be "better" than white Americans, reasons had nothing to do with objective indicators. Rather, they involved cultural value preferences, or a "less is more" cognitive set—an attribution of gain to losses, as in being better able to appreciate attainments because of having had a poorer upbringing or not being "burdened" by capital accumulation. The relationship between this cognitive set and mental health deserves additional research. Unfortunately, we are unable to assess why close to half of the sample perceived their life to be "about the same" as white Americans, since no probe was made to that response. What is important is that a determination of person's cognitive set apparently directly relates to attitudes, perceptions, and sense of well-being, suggesting that the cognitive paradigm has much to offer in understanding human experience.

Asking respondents to compare themselves to the average Chinatown resident was also useful. It revealed a perceived distinction between those who lived in the noncore area and those who lived in the core area. The former perceived themselves to have better life conditions and portrayed a view of the fearful, constricting life of the less-advantaged immigrant that comes from being just outside of that life condition. The comparison question also provided a validity check for the sampling procedure; the sample overall saw itself as representative of the population of interest.

With regard to culturally relevant issues applicable to scale construction, this study revealed that open-ended questions yielded greater disclosures about life dissatisfactions than scaled items did. Also, the ladder scale appeared to be a more objective and global evaluation of life status than the satisfaction scale. Two general affect items did not reveal significant differences between the sample studied and the general population. This suggests that with regard to ethnic and immigrant populations, the "easy–hard" item is problematic because it tends to be evaluated on the basis of how immigrants imagine their life might have been in their home country. Thus, a confounding variable is involved. In addition, "tied down–free" is suspected to confound political freedom with personal freedom, thereby making it invalid for use among immigrant populations.

This study reinforced the importance of using multiple measures or a multi-scaled approach to an assessment of well-being and to evaluating these measures in terms of their cultural relevance for ethnic and immigrant populations. Multiple measures revealed a consistent theme—that Chinatown residents have not yet seen the success that the media has associated with Asian Americans.

NOTES

1. The general affect scale items were highly correlated, ranging from .40 to .61. The eight items combined correlated .55 with the 7-point satisfaction measure and explained 33% of the variance in life satisfaction.

2. Happiness and satisfaction were correlated at .50 in Campbell, Converse, and Rodgers's (1976) survey.

3. Intercorrelations of the general affect variables:

	H9	H10	H11	H12	H13	H14	H15
H8	-.52***	-.45***	-.54***	.47***	.06	.50***	-.32***
H9		.57***	.66***	-.45***	.02	-.45***	.34***
H10			.50***	-.42***	-.29***	-.44***	.27**
H11				-.48***	-.05	-.51***	.36***
H12					.20*	.47***	-.36***
H13						.13	-.06
H14							-.44***

* $p < .05$ ** $p < .01$ *** $p < .001$

Note:

H8: Boring - Interesting

H9: Enjoyable - Miserable

H10: Easy - Hard

H11: Full - Empty

H12: Discouraging - Hopeful

H13: Tied down - Free

H14: Disappointing - Rewarding

H15: Opportunities - No Chance

4. On the dimension used in the national survey "haven't been given a chance–life brings out the best in me," the latter phrase could not be translated into Chinese. The closest linguistically equivalent translation was "have had a lot of opportunities."

5. The English term "success" was translated to "what you've accomplished in life" in Chinese.

6. The term "friendships" in English was translated to "companionship" in Chinese.

7. The phrase "leisure activities" was translated to "spare time" in Chinese. These differences were due to closest linguistic equivalency.

8. The 4-point scale item was not identical to the 7-point scale used nationally, but both included "very satisfied" in their scales.

9. Andrews and Withey, 1976, p. 154, mean of 5.0.

10. Campbell, Converse, and Rodgers, 1976, p. 63, mean of 5.3.

11. In the Chinatown survey, satisfaction and happiness had a correlation of .62, p < .001, which is higher than it was for the nation overall. Happiness and the ladder scales were correlated at .39. Life satisfaction and the ladder scale were correlated at .34.

12. The mean level of well-being for males was 5.4 compared to 4.8 for women (t = 2.32, p < .01).

13. The mean level of life quality for American-born was 6.3 compared to 4.8 for foreign-born (higher scores indicate higher sense of well-being).

Universal to all U.S. Chinatowns is biculturalism. While watching a Chinese New Year's celebration parade, this man holds up a doll clothed in the American flag. 1970. (Photograph by Crystal K. D. Huie.) Reprinted by permission.

Very Bitter

My assigned address was in the North Beach area on Greenwich Street. Since most of my addresses in this area lacked eligible respondents, I expected the same this time. Instead, a young Chinese lady exited the door I sought. My fears of "another ineligible" were gone as I made an appointment with her for the following week.

On the prearranged day I returned, only to find an apologetic brother who said his sister couldn't make it. He agreed to take her place. I was led through a long hallway (common for this type of San Francisco apartment) to a living room.

At age 21, this man was kicked out of the house by his father for not finishing high school and not doing anything productive with his life. When his father passed away, he was asked to return. As the oldest son he was now bearer of the family responsibilities. If he could live his life over again, he would have followed his father's advice and stayed in school eventually to become a doctor or lawyer. He was bitter about not "being allowed" to graduate from high school "because of a dean who hated Chinese." The dean's facial scar was a reminder of an attack from Chinese students.

An 80-hour work week at his job put a strain on his family life. His wife complained that he didn't even know his own daughter. Despite a high salary, this man felt bitter toward his union for trying to exclude him because he was Chinese. He felt "tested" more than the usual number of times.

11

Conclusion

IMPLICATIONS OF HISTORY AND ETHNICITY

Chinatown is one of the longest-standing ethnic minority communities in the United States. As such, it provides a testing ground for sociological theories of community demise and preservation and demonstrates how larger social, political, and economic forces have impacted a group of ethnic Americans over time. Several points gleaned from an analysis of this history have implications for legislative policies on ethnic minorities and ethnic immigrants today.

Chinatown's 140-year-old history is a reminder of how this nation excluded and discriminated against one group of Americans and the effects this had. Our text began with an historical analysis of the generally unknown saga of the nation's persecution of the Chinese in American amidst their struggle to work and survive. Called the indispensable enemy, the Chinese were vital to the development of California. Their contributions in labor gave the state a decided place in the twentieth century. The Chinese built the western portion of the transcontinental railroad, transformed California swampland into the nation's premier agricultural state, and established light manufacturing industries in San Francisco. Yet from the mid-1800s into the twentieth century, a crescendo of labor exploitation, racist taxation, and discriminatory legislation descended upon the Chinese, crippling their ability to thrive. Continual attempts were made to eliminate the Chinese from fair competition. The anti-

Chinese movement—which began most noticeably with the Foreign Miners Tax, then was fueled by a multitude of ordinances, demonstrations, and laws—ultimately escalated to the 1882 Chinese Exclusion Act, which was the first national law that restricted immigration to this country on the basis of race. For Chinese already in this country, other restrictive laws curtailed their chances of success. The 1913 Alien Land Law, for example, prevented the Chinese from buying or leasing property. Land represented power and wealth, and persons of color were denied both. Soon after, the 1924 Immigration Act set the quota of Chinese persons permitted to emigrate into this country at zero. The Chinese laborer was locked out. It was not until China and the United States were allies in World War II that the United States repealed the Chinese Exclusion Act. In 1943 the Chinese became eligible for immigration and naturalization, and an amendment to the 1924 Immigration Act raised the quota for Chinese to 105 per year. In 1947 the restrictive covenant on real estate was lifted. One year following this, anti-miscegenation laws were nullified.

What implications does this history have for policies and legislation today? First, immigration legislation and discriminatory legislation had dramatic effects on the size, nature, and condition of the Chinese American population and on the Chinatown community, its social character, and the civic consciousness of its people. A shrinkage of the Chinese population resulted from restrictive immigration legislation, which left this group segregated and neglected. Families could not develop. The community and population could not thrive. The Chinese were forced to retreat into the Chinese Quarter, an enclave that became a crowded, isolated ghetto, a refuge from racist hostility. However, in 1943 when the Chinese became eligible for naturalization, persons previously designated as "aliens" could finally become citizens. With changing legislation that led to the legal entry of women, the social character of the population changed from a bachelor society to an emerging family society. There was an emerging presence of American-born Chinese. Civic consciousness, enhanced by naturalization, led to long-term community planning. In the case of Chinatown, this form of advocacy led to federal funding for low-cost public housing and to the establishment of a variety of programs and nonprofit organizations in the areas of health, employment, mental health, and the law. The presence of these new programs was vital: with the liberalized Immigration Act of 1965, the needs of thousands of new immigrants and refugees pressed the community's resources to crisis proportions.

Second, racist legislation affected the population density of the community. While it is true that traditional Chinese value "five generations under one roof," Chinatown's crowding was not caused by cultural predilection, as many have claimed. Instead, crowding was the undesired consequence of poverty and racism. When conditions changed as a result of normalization and immigration reform during World War II, Chinese Americans were permitted to move out of the crowded enclave to secure homes elsewhere. Those who could afford to move did so, and the population density was consequently reduced.

Current restrictions in immigration policies that affect Mexicans are causing a similar misperception among government officials. Undocumented workers live in highly crowded conditions dictated by poverty and their illegal status. In the 1980s an assistant to the director of Housing and Urban Development stated that Hispanics did not need public assistance in housing because they had a cultural predilection for crowding. Members of the Hispanic Caucus in Congress protested this myth. Again, behaviors that result from poverty and labor exploitation have been erroneously attributed to cultural factors.

Third, racism affected the occupational segregation of this population and still has an effect today. For over 90 years Chinese laborers were forced into the lowest-paying, least desirable jobs. As racism against Chinese declined during World War II and jobs became available in the war industries, educated Chinese Americans acquired employment in government and business, which expanded their occupational distribution. Yet even today, Chinese in America are still more occupationally segregated than white Americans. The occupational distribution for Chinese Americans is much more restricted than it is for white males, and the condition for women is much worse. In 1976, at least 61% of Chinese American males and at least 80% of Chinese American females would have had to change occupations in order to have an occupational distribution identical to the majority males (U.S. Commission on Civil Rights, 1978).

Fourth, racist attitudes affected the services provided to Chinese Americans. From the mid-1800s into the 1920s and 1930s, despite their disproportionate share of tax contributions to the city, counties, and state, the Chinese received few benefits. The Chinese in San Francisco were generally denied health care, police protection, and sanitary services to their community. Today, we need to evaluate the extent to which services are adequately allocated according to needs in housing, health, mental health, education, and training for Native Americans, Asian Americans, Pacific Islanders, Hispanics, and African Americans—particularly those most isolated by income, language, culture, and a history of dispossession and disadvantage.

Fifth, discriminatory immigration legislation led to efforts on the part of some Chinese to survive through unofficial means, which in turn had some undesirable costs. After the San Francisco earthquake and fires eliminated official records, the Chinese took advantage of a legal loophole and thousands entered as "paper sons." While this action helped to prevent the elimination of the Chinese presence in the United States, it led to harassment of entering Chinese and did not help newcomers acculturate into the mainstream. Visibility was not sought by those who immigrated under unauthorized entry. Understandably, their civic and sociopolitical participation in the American society was marginal.

Finally, the history of Chinese in this nation depicts the contradictory treatment that the United States has often meted out to persons of color. Ethnic minorities have been prevented from assimilating, then have been criticized and rejected for not assimilating. Statutes that prevented the Chinese from testifying for or against a white person in court, anti-miscegenation laws, restricted covenants regarding residential occupancy, denied privileges of naturalization, and labor agitation to restrict Chinese labor in desirable economic niches were distinctive measures aimed at preventing the Chinese from assimilating.

Today, English-Only advocates accuse Asian and Hispanic immigrants of not wanting to assimilate or learn the English language. If their objective is for new immigrants to acquire the English language, their solution is punitive rather than facilitative. Rather than (1) advocate for provision of English language training to all non-English speaking immigrants, (2) require employers to provide English language training on the job, or (3) press for legislation that will increase opportunities for job mobility and pay equity for ethnic immigrants, these English-Only advocates seem intent to further isolate and exclude those they accuse. Non-English speaking immigrants are locked into a secondary labor market that provides them with no opportunity to learn English. What opportunities are there for a Hispanic farm worker or a Chinatown sweatshop worker beyond these dead-end jobs? America needs to analyze how labor exploitation under capitalistic profit making makes acculturation difficult for its non-English speaking newcomers.

Moreover, the difficulties facing immigrant Asian Americans affect a sizably greater number in the 1980s than in the previous decade. In 1970, the proportions of Chinese in America that were native born (53%) versus foreign born (47%) were roughly balanced. In 1980, however, the proportion of foreign-born Chinese in the United States has risen to 63%, while the proportion of American-born Chinese has dropped to 37%. There were over half a million immigrant Chinese in the United States in 1980, more than twice the numbers ten years earlier.

In summary, the saga of Chinese American history has larger implications. Legislation that impacts ethnic minorities in either a negative or positive way has far-reaching consequences. Immigration policies have a major impact on nearly all areas of life for many ethnic minorities. The effects of racially discriminatory legislation and racist attitudes extend to nearly all niches of an immigrant's life. These need to be considered thoroughly when policy makers consider legislation that will either facilitate or deny opportunities to Americans of color. Unfortunately, our nation under the past two presidencies has not passed legislation that could help to reduce occupational segregation and discrimination, two major problems facing ethnic minorities and women today. The 1990 Civil Rights Act, for example, which would have helped women and minorities in cases of discrimination on the job, was vetoed by President Bush.

RESEARCH ON ASIAN AMERICANS

Dispelling Stereotypes and Myths

While this author intended to portray contemporary conditions within a historical context and to present thematic implications of the history, the major thrust of the text was to examine the condition, perceptions, and cognitions of a sample of Asian Americans. Data were collected on the quality of life of this American ethnic population in order to contribute to the body of empirical knowledge on ethnic minorities in the social sciences. Findings of this study dispelled stereotypes and myths about Asian Americans.

First, the study documented that Chinatown residents are not part of the "success story" that the media has attributed to Asian Americans. The quality of life reported by Chinatown residents was far lower than that reported by Americans overall; their levels of satisfaction and status of well-being were far less. Most Chinese Americans in this enclave are disadvantaged, and results from multiple measures confirmed this. These ethnic Americans live without what most Americans consider basic. The majority of Chinatown residents had no car and could not afford to buy a home. The average male had a high school degree, the average woman had a sixth-grade level of education.

Chinatown residents who were interviewed were less satisfied with their life than Americans overall. The average Chinatown resident felt "neutral" or "slightly satisfied" with his or her life, while the average American was "pretty satisfied" with his or hers. The disparities of life quality between Americans as a whole and these Asian Americans held true for three points in time—five years ago, now, and five years hence. Compared to Americans' ratings of their life, Chinatown residents rated the quality of their life lower on all three time dimensions. The ceiling of future life expectations for Chinatown respondents was lower than the expectations held by the average white or black American.

Residents in this Asian American community described their life as less interesting, less enjoyable, less full, less hopeful, less rewarding, less happy, and offering fewer opportunities than Americans overall described their life. On specific domains, Chinatown residents were less satisfied with their level of education, job, health, housing, family life, marriage, friendships, and leisure as compared to ratings made by Americans overall.

Neighborhood, housing, job, language, health, and mental health were major problem areas for these ethnic Americans. Chinatown residents' level of neighborhood satisfaction was significantly lower than it was for Americans overall. On average, white Americans felt "pretty satisfied" with their neighborhood, while average Chinatown residents felt "neutral" about theirs. Only 42% of the Chinatown sample were satisfied with their neighborhood as compared to 80% of Americans as a whole. Crowding, filth, and noise were the most disliked aspects of the Chinatown neighborhood.

Occupational segregation was another problem for ethnic minorities, particularly immigrants. Most residents, particularly women, worked at jobs that were nonactualizing, lacking in occupational prestige, and lacking in opportunities for training or job mobility. Nearly half of the working women were employed as sweatshop workers and one-fifth were service workers. The majority of working women reported no job pride, and both men and women did not want their children to be employed in the same occupations. The language barrier was another problem. Nearly two-thirds of the residents were monolingual Chinese or spoke English poorly. Half of the men spoke English; only one-quarter of the women spoke English.

Health was a major area of concern for these Asian Americans. In rankings of life domains as predictors of quality of life, health was ranked second by Chinatown respondents. This was higher than for Americans overall, signifying the importance of health to the well-being of Chinatown residents. The salience of health to Chinatown residents' overall well-being was probably related to two other findings: first, compared to other Americans, Chinatown residents were significantly less satisfied with their health, and second, their reported health status was substantially lower than it was for Americans overall. Only 10% of the Chinatown respondents reported their health as "excellent" as compared to 40% of the American adults. While most Americans rated their health as "excellent" or "good," the largest percentage of Chinatown respondents rated their health as "fair."

Need for mental health services was high, as evidenced by the high proportions admitting to symptoms of psychological and/or physiological disorders, higher than has been found in other large urban areas. Reported prevalence of depression, worry, and emotional tension was also very high. Marital satisfaction ranked first as the most powerful predictor of well-being, yet the proportion of the Chinatown sample who reported feeling very satisfied with their marriage was half that found among Americans overall. Family well-being was another predictor of life satisfaction for Chinatown residents. Here again the level of satisfaction in Chinatown was less than for Americans overall. The proportion of the Chinatown sample who were very satisfied with their family life was less than half the proportion of the nation who reported being this satisfied.

Chinese Americans nationally have a rather unique bimodal distribution, heavily occupying both the highest and lowest strata of the education and occupation distribution. In 1970 the illiteracy rate for U.S. Chinese (11%) was higher than for whites (1%), blacks (3%), or Japanese (2%).[1] Asian Americans are a highly diverse population but the American media has neglected the less advantaged, the heavy concentration of Chinese Americans at the lowest end of the occupation and education distribution. While some Asian Americans have attained levels of income, education, occupational prestige, and satisfaction on a variety of life domains equivalent to whites, Chinatown residents are constrained by low levels of education, low occupational prestige, low income, and residency in one of the most crowded neighborhoods in America.

In addition to dispelling the myth of the successful Asian American, the findings of this study dispelled the myth that Chinese like crowding, do not value space, and do not suffer ill effects from crowding. Chinese Americans who were interviewed disliked crowding, valued space, and reported a multitude of harmful effects from this environmental stressor. These effects included environmental and health problems, psychological problems, and social problems. The survey findings supported Wirth's (1938) theory that crowding is related to social conflicts and psychological stress. Moreover, more responses were volunteered in response to the question on crowding effects than for any other question of the three-hour interview. This revealed the direct impact that crowding has on these residents and their clear awareness of its impact. Also, nearly half of the residents interviewed wanted to move out of the community, and crowding was the reason most often given for wanting to move.

With regard to attitudes about crowding, findings from this study also disproved the theory of environmental adaptation with greater exposure. Rather than adapting to crowding, residents who grew up in crowded conditions appeared to have an intensified dislike of crowded conditions with increased exposure to this stressor. Crowding perceptions were found to be affected by cultural frame of reference; the more acculturated these Chinese became, the more likely they were to perceive of Chinatown as very crowded.

This study also dispelled assumptions that have been advanced by advocates of the English as the Official Language movement. Those who advocate elimination of the biliterate provisions of the Voting Rights Act maintain that non-English speaking immigrants not only resist acculturation but are unaware that English language speaking ability is essential for social mobility. They further maintain that second language acquisition of English should not be difficult for Asian immigrants and they question why certain non-English speaking language groups should be afforded biliterate ballot assistance and not others. This study did not find empirical support for these assumptions. Most Chinese foreign-born believed that immigrants should make cultural changes; they evaluated the Chinese and white American cultures in terms of the respective assets and drawbacks of both; and nearly all believed that English facility would qualify them for a better job, ease their life functioning, and eliminate their dependence on an ethnic enclave. Nearly all of the employed respondents who had difficulty with the English language believed that they would qualify for a better job if they could speak English well, and the vast majority wanted a better job. However, second language acquisition requires the opportunity for such learning. Segregation into an ethnic labor market that is labor exploitative, offers no language training, and provides wages sufficient for mere survival alone does not provide immigrants with opportunities to learn English and thereby participate in the larger society.

In addition, several other factors make English language acquisition difficult for certain minority language groups. For Asians, orthographic differences between one's primary language and the language being acquired create an additional barrier; Asian languages do not use an Arabic written base, which all languages in the Indo-European family do. Other factors that make for greater difficulty in second language acquisition include the size and proportion of the minority group that are recent immigrants, age at time of immigration, the geographical concentration of the minority population, and the structure of the labor market that segregates non-English speaking immigrants into a secondary, ethnic labor market. American ethnocentrism with regard to English-only language use not only discourages the sociopolitical participation of immigrants whose mother tongue is not English, but it is contrary to the goals of a culturally pluralistic society. American language ethnocentrism also puts Americans at a disadvantage in the arena of international trade. Ironically, many Americans have found the acquisition of Asian languages extremely difficult, yet public attacks of Asian language groups have often centered on how Asians should not find learning the English language difficult at all.

Asian Americans have been stereotyped as reluctant to report mental health problems. Hypothesized explanations for low use of mental health services have included stigma and shame of admitting to mental disorders, belief that mental disorders are due to genetics, and alternative uses of culturally relevant care (such as acupuncturists or herbalists). Little validation was found for these stereotypes. Although few sought services of mental health professionals, many Chinatown respondents were not reluctant to admit to mental health problems in response to direct inquiry. Few believed that mental disorders were due to genetics; instead, most maintained that mental disorders were due to life stresses and problems. Use of alternative sources of care that were culturally relevant was low. While some respondents tended to be self-help oriented, many were willing to talk to others (especially informal others) about their problems. Lack of awareness of the availability of centers for mental health service delivery appeared to be one major factor affecting low use of services. Mental health awareness of how professional treatment and prevention could be effective was also limited.

Finally, the endurance of this Chinatown community revealed certain limitations of Park's (1923, 1936) theory of assimilation. As Park's theory predicted, ethnic neighborhoods serve as first settlement areas to ease new immigrants' way into the mainstream society. Chinatown San Francisco serves this purpose for some residents, and the finding that nearly half would like to move out of the community supports this theory. The community serves as way station for the low-income, non-English speaking immigrant whose choices are minimal and who would leave the area as soon as it becomes economically feasible to do so. But over time Chinatown has not disappeared, as Park might have predicted. Chinatown's existence has been sustained by a flow of new low-income immigrants who need to live among other Chinese-speaking residents and who need affordable housing. What Park and other early urban sociologists did not predict was that: (1) many immigrants cannot escape the ethnic settlement, poverty, or ethnic labor market (all of which are related); (2) some Chinese prefer to reside among others of the same ethnic group (regardless of their socioeconomic status); (3) communities like Chinatown provide an important home for many elderly because of the cultural comfort and conveniences provided; and (4) certain ethnic communities like Chinatown persist because they function as capital city for all Chinese in America and stand as an historic landmark of their legacy.

Implications for Service Delivery and Policy Planning

In addition to dispelling stereotypes and myths regarding Asian Americans, the findings of this study offer valuable data for the planning of services and policies that affect ethnic minorities in America. The structure of the labor market, exploitative labor practices, poverty, occupational discrimination, and America's inattention to the language needs of its newcomers need to be on the American agenda for change. As already recommended, this nation should provide English language training to all non-English speaking immigrants. Federal funding should be made available for ESL classes, particularly in areas where there is a heavy concentration of non-English speaking. Long waiting lists for ESL classes indicate that this nation is inadequately addressing the need. English language training should be provided as part of the passage of right to newcomers to the United States. Freedom cannot be obtained if this country fails to provide the means by which its immigrants can participate meaningfully in society. Language, occupational opportunities, equitable wages, and nondiscrimination in the labor force are essentials, and legislation to create and assure these goals is needed.

Mental health problems were prevalent in this community, yet only 5% of the sample had used mental health services. Depression, worries, emotional tension, loneliness, and psychophysiological disorders were but a few of the many symptoms reported by these Chinese Americans. Social support appeared to be lacking among this population. The proportion of the sample that was very satisfied with their friendships was three times less than the proportion of the nation as a whole. Two-thirds of the Chinatown respondents expressed a need for a confidant—someone they could really talk to—which incidently is precisely one function served by a trained psychotherapist, psychiatrist, or social worker. The proportion of the Chinatown sample that were very satisfied with their marriage was half that found among Americans overall, implying that interventions are needed for couples as well as for individuals. Community training in providing emotional and instrumental support and in interpersonal communication could be helpful.

Moreover, there were gender and nativity differences with regard to disadvantage and need. Immigrant Chinese reported significantly more depression than native-born Chinese. Women reported lower levels of life quality, lower self-esteem, lower occupational pride, and lower level of life satisfaction than men. Women's level of education, English-speaking skill, and occupational prestige were all lower than for men, and their tendency to be more self-blaming and less assertive is not psychologically helpful.

Residents in this community were generally uninformed about existing mental health services. Three-quarters did not know where to go for help with mental health problems. Awareness of mental health treatment and prevention were also lacking. Many did not know what to do with a depression that would not go away. As already mentioned extensive programs in mental health education are needed, creative methods of providing mental health prevention and treatment need to be developed for individuals who feel they cannot afford to take time off from work, and specific interventions for women and foreign-born are particularly essential. Mental health service delivery in low-income, ethnic minority communities needs to be very comprehensive, for problems and stresses are very much tied in with external causes—low-paying, nonactualizing jobs; separation from family; health problems; language difficulties; low levels of education; and housing problems, to name a few. As findings indicated that sense of personal efficacy was related to psychophysiological disorders, interventions that provide persons with a greater sense of control and personal efficacy need to be considered. Again, what is implied is a relationship between psychological cognition and external variables.

Health status in this community was low, but poor health status was not due to nonuse of services. Residents were generally aware of available health services. Eight out of every ten respondents reported that she or he had seen a doctor in the past year, a rate similar to Americans overall. In addition, the average number of physician visits over the previous year was similar to that found in national surveys. The record of health care services in Chinatown has been a sterling example of what other communities can accomplish. Yet the effort must be continually sustained and expanded. The two significant predictors of health status—social support and age—offer implications for intervention. Those without social support and those who are elderly constituted the high risk groups for health problems.

Survey findings supported an urban anonymity hypothesis of neighborhood safety. Improving residents' confidence in police protection, which findings indicated is much lower than it is for Americans overall, would positively affect residents' perceptions of safety. The police department's efforts of increased recruitment of bilingual Chinese Americans and procedures by which residents can more easily gain police protection are positive strategies, but more needs to be done. Perceptions of neighborhood safety were also found to be related to number of units in one's building. The effort to increase housing by building large multi-unit structures must be weighed against the decreased sense of residents' safety that will most likely result. Under these conditions, careful attention to building designs is important.

Survey findings supported the urban scale, life stage, and local neighborhood conditions hypotheses. Population density/commercial intrusions were related to lower levels of neighborhood satisfaction, as were age and perceived neighborhood crowding. Younger adults were less satisfied with their neighborhood than older adults, which speaks to the functions served by the neighborhood and the aspirations and/or constraints of the subgroup. Both objective and subjective indicators of crowding were related to lower neighborhood satisfaction. Given the fact that Chinatown residents are substantially less satisfied with their neighborhoods than Americans overall, increased crowding can be expected to lower residents' level of neighborhood satisfaction even farther. Efforts to reduce the filth, crowding, and noise while retaining the location, convenience, and ethnic quality of the neighborhood represent residents' desires for the ideal neighborhood. Ethnic communities like Chinatown can only survive if there are concerted planning efforts on the part of the city, community, and residency that are aimed at preserving Chinatown's distinctive urban character, cultural heritage, supply of low- to moderate-priced housing, and mutually supportive functions as residential neighborhood and capital city. The Master Plan is a model that can be used by other neighborhoods, for specifying the larger objectives and policies for implementing these goals is needed. Otherwise, single decisions on development will be made and the neighborhood will be ultimately altered or destroyed. All economic, political, and cultural sectors must collaborate if ethnic-serving neighborhoods such as Chinatown are to endure.

Survey findings revealed that the proportion of residents who wanted to move out was no less and no more than for any other American neighborhood. The diversity represented among the residents there was of interest. Survey findings revealed that communities such as Chinatown serve a needed function for specific groups of persons. Class, race, and life stage variables predicted the desire to move. The neighborhood was most desired by the lower-income persons, those wanting or needing to be among other Chinese, the elderly, and those without children. Housing units with moderate rents are an irreplaceable resource upon which the aforementioned persons depend. One way to preserve this resource is to pass zoning controls that insure that low-cost housing removed by new development must be replaced on a unit-for-unit basis by other low-cost housing. Controls on development are vital. This study has suggested that there is little margin for planning error if those with little choice in housing are to retain their community.

Perceptions are affected by one's experiences. The survey findings suggested that as immigrants become more white acculturated and obtain jobs in the larger labor market, some of their perceptions will change. High population density will appear more crowded to them and they can be expected to perceive more racial discrimination against the Chinese. More research in these areas is needed.

For those in the human service, educational, or policy planning professions, these are the realities that define the agenda for change. For those who are training to work with ethnic minority populations, this text has tried to spell out the domains of need. Scholars have emphasized that cross-cultural training must involve a knowledge of ethnic minority groups, the history of their treatment in this country, the impact of the sociopolitical system upon them, and the institutional barriers that prevent them from using services. This book has tried to address the conditions and context for them. Problems in housing, health, mental health, employment, language, and discrimination are all interrelated for populations like those in Chinatown.

In conclusion, studies on the status of America's ethnic minorities or low-income persons present a challenge of what our society must accomplish in order to eliminate the problems that face its less advantaged members—those for whom life is "most time, hard time." The American agenda must include concrete strategies to better the quality of life for those who have not yet seen the opportunities promised by our nation. This book offers a beginning in that process.

NOTE

1. U.S. Bureau of the Census (1970), *Subject Reports:* Publication Nos. PC(1) C1; PC(2) 1B; PC(2) 1G (Washington, DC: U.S. Government Printing Office).

Appendix A

The Interview Schedule

Now before we start I want to tell you that the information you give me must be very accurate in order to be useful. This means that I'll do my best to ask my questions clearly and that you'll do your best to give me honest and complete answers. I'd like to mention that no names will be used. All interviews and all opinions are confidential.

SECTION A: GENERAL RESIDENCE BACKGROUND AND NEIGHBORHOOD

First, I'd like to ask you some questions about where you've lived in the past.

A1. Where were you born?

| CITY | STATE (OR PROVINCE) | COUNTRY (IF NOT U.S.) |

> A1a. IF NON-U.S.-BORN, ASK, "How long have you lived in the United States?" IF LESS THAN ONE YEAR, GET NUMBER OF MONTHS.
>
> _____YEARS   _____MONTHS

A2. Where did you grow up? IF MORE THAN ONE PLACE, ASK, "Where did you spend the most time when you were growing up?" (GROWING UP = 12 YEARS OR YOUNGER)

| CITY | STATE (OR PROVINCE) | COUNTRY (IF NOT U.S.) |

A3. The place you grew up in, would you consider it a rural area or village, a town, a small city, a suburb near a large city, or a large city?

| 1.RURAL AREA OR VILLAGE | 2.TOWN | 3.SMALL CITY | 4.SUBURB | 5.LARGE CITY |

A4. How many other cities, besides San Francisco, have you lived in? (INCLUDING OUTSIDE U.S.)

| 0 | 1 | 2 | 3 | 4 | 5 | 6 | 7 | 8 | 9 | 10+ |

A5. Have you ever lived in a mostly White neighborhood?

| 1. YES | | 5. NO |

A6. Have you ever lived in a neighborhood where the people were much richer or much poorer than your present neighbors?

| 1. YES | | 5. NO | -- GO TO Q. A7

> A6a. Was it a richer or poorer neighborhood?
>
> | 1. RICHER | 3. POORER | 5. HAS LIVED IN BOTH RICHER AND POORER |

A7. The place you grew up in, was it a house, a flat, an apartment, a room, or what?

1. HOUSE	2. FLAT	3. APARTMENT	4. ROOM	5. _____

OTHER

A8. How crowded was the (room/apartment/flat/house) you grew up in? Was it very crowded, somewhat crowded, a little crowded, or not crowded?

1.VERY CROWDED	2.SOMEWHAT CROWDED	3.A LITTLE CROWDED	4.NOT CROWDED

A9. [SHOW CARD] Was the home you grew up in much more crowded, somewhat more crowded, about the same, somewhat less crowded, or much less crowded than the home you live in now?

1.MUCH MORE CROWDED	2.SOMEWHAT MORE CROWDED	3.ABOUT THE SAME	4.SOMEWHAT LESS CROWDED	5.MUCH LESS CROWDED

A10. Now think about the place you lived in before moving here. Is that place the same place you grew up in as a child?

1. YES	-- GO TO Q. A11	5. NO

A10a. [SHOW CARD] Now I want you to think about the home you lived in before moving here and whether that home was more or less crowded than the home you're living in now. Looking at the card, please tell me whether your last home was much more crowded, somewhat more crowded, about the same, somewhat less crowded, or much less crowded than you present home.

1.MUCH MORE CROWDED	2.SOMEWHAT MORE CROWDED	3.ABOUT THE SAME	4.SOMEWHAT LESS CROWDED	5. MUCH LESS CROWDED

A11. Now I'd like to ask you about your neighborhood and what you like or don't like about your neighborhood.

First, how long have you lived at this address? (IF LESS THAN ONE YEAR, GET NUMBER OF MONTHS.)

_____ YEAR(S)   _____ MONTH(S)

A12. And how long have you lived in this neighborhood?

_____ YEAR(S)   _____ MONTH(S)

A13. What neighborhood do you consider yourself to be living in?

1.CHINATOWN OR AROUND CHINATOWN OR JUST OUTSIDE CHINATOWN	2.RUSSIAN HILL	3.TELEGRAPH HILL	4.NOB HILL	5.NORTH BEACH
	6.POLK GULCH	7.FINANCIAL DISTRICT OR EMBARCADERO		8.DON'T KNOW

OTHER_____

A13a. Have you ever lived in any other neighborhood in San Francisco

1.YES	5.NO

A13b. Have you ever lived in San Francisco Chinatown?

1.YES	5.NO	--GO TO Q.A14

A13c. Why did you move out of Chinatown?

A14. We're interested in the reasons why people live where they live. Could you tell me why you originally decided to live in this neighborhood?

A15. What do you like about your neighborhood?

A16. And what do you dislike about your neighborhood?

A17. Thinking about what an ideal neighborhood would be like for you, please tell me what things about it would make an ideal neighborhood?

A18. [SHOW CARD] For elderly people, how would you rate this neighborhood as a place to live? Would you say it's very good, good, O.K., not so good, or poor?

| 1.VERY GOOD | 2.GOOD | 3.O.K. | 4.NOT SO GOOD | 5.POOR | 8.DON'T KNOW |

└─ GO TO Q.A19

    A18a. Why's that?_____

A19. For teenagers, how would you rate this neighborhood as a place to live? Would you say it's very good, good, O.K., not so good, or poor?

| 1.VERY GOOD | 2.GOOD | 3.O.K. | 4.NOT SO GOOD | 5.POOR | 8.DON'T KNOW |

└─ GO TO Q.A20

    A19a. Why's that?_____

A20. As a place to raise children under twelve, how would you rate this neighborhood? Would you say it's very good, good, O.K., not so good, or poor?

| 1.VERY GOOD | 2.GOOD | 3.O.K. | 4.NOT SO GOOD | 5.POOR | 8.DON'T KNOW |

└─ GO TO Q.A21

    A20. Why's that?_____

A21. When the children in your neighborhood play, how often do thay play in the alleys and streets...always, most of the time, sometimes, rarely, or never?

| 1.ALWAYS | 2.MOST OF THE TIME | 3.SOMETIMES | 4.RARELY | 5.NEVER |

A22. If you could choose the kind of neighbors you'd most want, what kind of neighbors would you want?

A23. Is this neighborhood mostly Chinese, about half Chinese and half non-Chinese, or mostly non-Chinese?

| 1. MOSTLY CHINESE | 2. HALF & HALF | 3. MOSTLY NON-CHINESE | 8. DON'T KNOW |

A23a. What's the race or ethnicity of the non-Chinese?

| 1. WHITE | 2. BLACK | 3. OTHER (specify)_____ |

A24. How many of your neighbors are about the <u>same age</u> as you? Most, some, a few, or none of them?

| 1. MOST | 2. SOME | 3. A FEW | 4. NONE | 8. DON'T KNOW |

A25. [SHOW CARD] Overall, how well do you know your neighbors? Would you say you know them very well, know them pretty well, know them a little, not know them very well, or not know them at all?

| 1. VERY WELL | 2. KNOW PRETTY WELL | 3. A LITTLE | 4. NOT KNOW WELL | 5. NOT KNOW AT ALL | 8. DON'T KNOW |

A26. [SHOW CARD] In general, how friendly, or unfriendly are your neighbors? Are they very friendly, somewhat friendly, neutral, somewhat unfriendly, or very unfriendly?

| 1.VERY FRIENDLY | 2.SOMEWHAT FRIENDLY | 3.NEUTRAL | 4.SOMEWHAT UNFRIENDLY | 5.VERY UNFRIENDLY | 8.DON'T KNOW |

A27. How important is it for you to have other Chinese Americans in your neighborhood? Is it very important, somewhat important, not too important, or not important at all?

| 1.VERY IMPORTANT | 2.SOMEWHAT IMPORTANT | 3.NOT TOO IMPORTANT | 4.NOT IMPORTANT AT ALL | 8.DON'T KNOW |

A28. Would you prefer to have neighbors who are around your own age, neighbors of all different ages, or does it matter?

| 1. OWN AGE | 2. DIFFERENT | 3. DOESN'T MATTER |

A29. What do you think of when you think of a safe neighborhood?

A30. How safe do you think your neighborhood is? Is it completely safe, usually safe, not too safe, or not safe at all?

| 1. COMPLETELY SAFE | 2. USUALLY SAFE | 3. NOT TOO SAFE | 4. NOT SAFE AT ALL | 8. DON'T KNOW |

A31. If you were in trouble, how likely would it be that a neighbor would come and help you or go and get help? Would it be very likely, somewhat likely, somewhat unlikely, or very unlikely?

| 1. VERY LIKELY | 2. SOMEWHAT LIKELY | 3. SOMEWHAT UNLIKELY | 4. VERY UNLIKELY | 8. DON'T KNOW |

A32. How is police protection in your neighborhood? Would you say it's very good, fairly good, neither good nor bad, not very good, or not good at all?

| 1. VERY GOOD | 2. FAIRLY GOOD | 3.NEUTRAL | 4.NOT VERY GOOD | 5.NOT GOOD AT ALL | 8. DON'T KNOW |

A33. Which of these words best describes housing in your neighborhood? Is there a lot of space for everyone, enough space for everyone, or is it a little crowded, or very crowded?

| 1. LOTS OF SPACE | 2. ENOUGH SPACE | 3. LITTLE CROWDED | 4. VERY CROWDED | 8. DON'T KNOW |

A34. Would you ever want to move out of _____ (R'S NEIGHBORHOOD - SEE Q.A13)

| 1. YES | 5. NO OR NEVER THOUGHT ABOUT IT | 8. DON'T KNOW |

└-SKIP TO Q.A35

A34a. Why? (IF NECESSARY, ASK "Could you be more specific?")

A34b. Where would you want to move to?

A34c. Why?

A34d. Why is it that you haven't already moved out of this neighborhood?

A35. Are there any conditions under which you would want to move out of your neighborhood?

| 1. YES | 5. NO | -- GO TO Q.A36 |

A35a. What are they?

A36. How do you feel about your neighborhood? Do you feel very satisfied, somewhat satisfied, not too satisfied, or not satisfied at all?

| 1. VERY SATISFIED | 2. SOMEWHAT SATISFIED | 3. NOT TOO SATISFIED | 4. NOT SATISFIED AT ALL |

A37. Would you consider yourself to be living in a particular community?

| 1. YES | 5. NO |-- GO TO Q. A38 |

A37a. What community do you consider yourself to be living in?

| 1. CHINATOWN | 2. OTHER _____ | 8. DON'T KNOW |

└-------------------------SKIP TO Q.A38

A37a1. Nowadays, how often would you say you leave Chinatown for any reason at all. For example, to go to work, to go shopping, to visit friends, or for any other reason. Would you say you leave Chinatown daily, about once a week, every other month or so, a few times a year, or never?

| 1.DAILY | 2.ONCE A WEEK | 3.EVERY OTHER MONTH OR SO | 4.FEW TIMES A YEAR | 5.NEVER |

A38. Which of these words best describes Chinatown in terms of how crowded or not crowded it is? Is there a lot of space for everyone, enough space for everyone, or is it a little crowded, or very crowded?

| 1. LOT OF SPACE | 2. ENOUGH SPACE | 3. LITTLE CROWDED | 4.VERY CROWDED | 8. DON'T KNOW |

A39. Now I'd like to ask you a few questions about yourself.

Do you have any children?

| 1. YES | 5. NO -- GO TO Q.A40 |

A39a. How many sons and how many daughters do you have?

_____ SONS   _____ DAUGHTERS   -- GO TO Q.A39b

A39b. Where are they living now?

A40. Are you married, widowed, divorced, separated, or have you never been married?

| 1.NOW MARRIED (INCLUDING COMMON-LAW MARRIAGES) | 2.WIDOWED | 3.DIVORCED | 4.SEPARATED | 5.NEVER MARRIED (INCLUDING ANNULMENTS) |

A41. How old are you?
_____ YEARS

A42. What's the month and year of your birth?
_____ MONTH   _____ YEAR

SECTION B: BUILDING, DWELLING, AND CROWDING ATTITUDES

(IN SINGLE HOME DWELLING, SKIP TO Q.B9)

B1. Next I'd like to ask some questions about the (building/housing project) you live
     in. By (building/housing project) I'm not referring to your (apt/flat/room/house).
     I'll ask you questions about that later on--for now, I want your comments about the
     structure, condition, or feelings you have about this building, O.K.? First, was
     there anything about this (building/housing project) that made you originally want
     to live here?

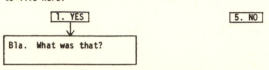

(IF R LIVES IN DUPLEX, SKIP TO Q.B9)

B2. What do you like about living in this (building/housing project)?

B3. And what do you dislike about living in this (building/housing project)?

B4. What kinds of changes would need to be made in your (building/housing project)
     to make it a better place to live in?

B5. Which words best describe the living conditions in your (building/housing project)?
     Is there a lot of space for the residents, enough space for the residents, or is
     it a little crowded, or very crowded?

1. LOT OF SPACE	2. ENOUGH SPACE	3. LITTLE CROWDED	4. VERY CROWDED	8. DON'T KNOW

B6. How kept up or run down is your (building/housing project)? Is it very well kept
     up, somewhat kept up, a little run down, or very run down?

1. VERY WELL KEPT UP	2. SOMEWHAT KEPT UP	3. A LITTLE RUN DOWN	4. VERY RUN DOWN	8. DON'T KNOW

B7. How safe or unsafe do you feel in the public areas of your (building/housing
     project)--places like the elevator, stairwell, hallways, or laundry room.
     Do you feel very safe, somewhat safe, not too safe, or very unsafe?

1.VERY SAFE	2.SOMEWHAT SAFE	3.NOT TOO SAFE	4.VERY UNSAFE	8.DON'T KNOW

B8. How do you feel about your (building/housing project)? Do you feel very
     satisfied, somewhat satisfied, not too satisfied, or not satisfied at all?

1. VERY SATISFIED	2. SOMEWHAT SATISFIED	3. NOT TOO SATISFIED	4. NOT SATISFIED AT ALL

B9. Now I'd like to ask you some questions about your (room/apartment/flat/house).
     (IF R HAS A ROOM IN A FLAT, LIVING WITH ROOMMATES, USE THE TERM FLAT.)

     What do you like about your (room/apartment/flat/house)?

B10. And what don't you like about your (room/apartment/flat/house)?

B11. What kinds of changes would make your (room/apartment/flat/house) a better place for you to live in?

B11a. Can you think of anything else?

B12. Do you rent or own this (room/apartment/flat/house)?

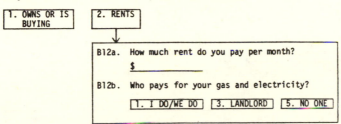

| 1. OWNS OR IS BUYING | 2. RENTS |

B12a. How much rent do you pay per month?

$ _____

B12b. Who pays for your gas and electricity?

| 1. I DO/WE DO | 3. LANDLORD | 5. NO ONE |

B13. When you're in your (room/apartment/flat/house), how often do you hear voices or sounds of your neighbors...a lot of the time, some of the time, rarely, or never?

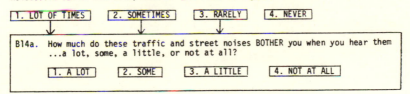

| 1. LOT OF TIMES | 2. SOMETIMES | 3. RARELY | 4. NEVER |

B13a. How much do these sounds BOTHER you...a lot, some, a little, or not at all?

| 1. A LOT | 2. SOME | 3. A LITTLE | 4. NOT AT ALL |

B14. From your (room/apartment/flat/house), how often do you hear traffic and street noises...a lot of the time, some of the time, rarely, or never?

| 1. LOT OF TIMES | 2. SOMETIMES | 3. RARELY | 4. NEVER |

B14a. How much do these traffic and street noises BOTHER you when you hear them ...a lot, some, a little, or not at all?

| 1. A LOT | 2. SOME | 3. A LITTLE | 4. NOT AT ALL |

B15. How good is the heating in your (room/apartment/flat/house) when the weather's cold? Is it very good, fairly good, O.K., not too good, or not good at all?

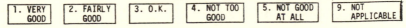

| 1. VERY GOOD | 2. FAIRLY GOOD | 3. O.K. | 4. NOT TOO GOOD | 5. NOT GOOD AT ALL | 9. NOT APPLICABLE |

B16. How good are the facilities provided in your (room/apartment/flat/house)... such as the kitchen and bathroom facilities? Are they very good, fairly good, O.K., not too good, or not good at all?

| 1. VERY GOOD | 2. FAIRLY GOOD | 3. O.K. | 4. NOT TOO GOOD | 5. NOT GOOD AT ALL |

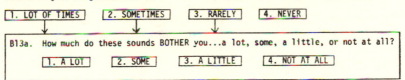

B17. What about the living conditions in your (room/apartment/flat/house)? Is there a lot of space, enough space, or is it a little crowded, or very crowded?

| 1. LOT OF SPACE | 2. ENOUGH SPACE | 3. LITTLE CROWDED | 4. VERY CROWDED | 8. DON'T KNOW |

B17a. What makes it crowded?

B18. I'd like you to pretend that you could have twice as much space or twice as many rooms in your home and you could either use the extra space for yourself (and your family) or rent it out. If you had this choice, would you rather use the extra space for you (and your family) or rent it out?

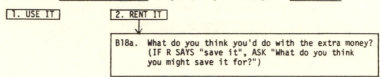

| 1. USE IT | 2. RENT IT |

B18a. What do you think you'd do with the extra money? (IF R SAYS "save it", ASK "What do you think you might save it for?")

B19. Do you feel you need more space in the place you're now living?

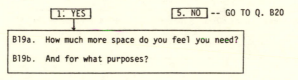

| 1. YES | 5. NO | -- GO TO Q. B20

B19a. How much more space do you feel you need?

B19b. And for what purposes?

B20. How safe or unsafe do you feel in your (room/apartment/flat/house)? Do you feel very safe, somewhat safe, not too safe, or very unsafe?

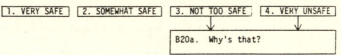

| 1. VERY SAFE | 2. SOMEWHAT SAFE | 3. NOT TOO SAFE | 4. VERY UNSAFE |

B20a. Why's that?

B21. How conveniently located is your home to places you want to get to? Is it very convenient, somewhat convenient, somewhat inconvenient, or very inconvenient?

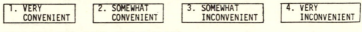

| 1. VERY CONVENIENT | 2. SOMEWHAT CONVENIENT | 3. SOMEWHAT INCONVENIENT | 4. VERY INCONVENIENT |

(IF R OWNS HOME--Q.B12--SKIP TO Q.B25)

B22. Since living here have you ever had problems with rats, mice, fleas, or cockroaches?

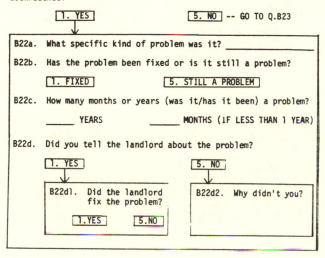

| 1. YES | 5. NO -- GO TO Q.B23 |

B22a. What specific kind of problem was it? _____

B22b. Has the problem been fixed or is it still a problem?

| 1. FIXED | 5. STILL A PROBLEM |

B22c. How many months or years (was it/has it been) a problem?

_____ YEARS _____ MONTHS (IF LESS THAN 1 YEAR)

B22d. Did you tell the landlord about the problem?

| 1. YES | 5. NO |

B22d1. Did the landlord fix the problem?

| 1.YES | 5.NO |

B22d2. Why didn't you?

B23. Have you had any problems with something broken, like the electricity, plumbing, heat, window, stairs, or mailbox?

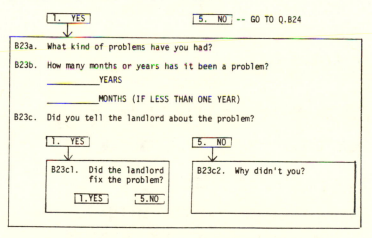

| 1. YES | 5. NO -- GO TO Q.B24 |

B23a. What kind of problems have you had?

B23b. How many months or years has it been a problem?

_____YEARS

_____MONTHS (IF LESS THAN ONE YEAR)

B23c. Did you tell the landlord about the problem?

| 1. YES | 5. NO |

B23c1. Did the landlord fix the problem?

| 1.YES | 5.NO |

B23c2. Why didn't you?

B24. If you had a problem with unsafe or unhealthy living conditions or housing repairs and you told the landlord about it but he didn't fix it, do you know of any city department or agencies that could help you get the landlord to fix the problem?

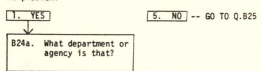

| 1. YES | 5. NO -- GO TO Q.B25 |

B24a. What department or agency is that?

B25. How many people live here in this (room/apartment /flat/house)?

[1] --GO TO   [2] [3] [4] [5] [6] [7] [8] [9] [10] [11] [12+]
Q.B26

B25a. Could you tell me who these people are that live with you, in terms
of their relationship to you...like your son, mother, (husband/wife),
roommate, boarder, or whatever? And their age?

HOUSEHOLD ENUMERATION

	Relationship to Respondent	Sex	Age at Last Birthday		Relationship to Respondent	Sex	Age
1		1.MALE 2.FEMALE		5		1.MALE 2.FEMALE	
2		1.MALE 2.FEMALE		6		1.MALE 2.FEMALE	
3		1.MALE 2.FEMALE		7		1.MALE 2.FEMALE	
4		1.MALE 2.FEMALE		8		1.MALE 2.FEMALE	

(ADDITIONAL PEOPLE SHOULD BE LISTED ACCORDINGLY ON BACK SIDE OF THIS PAGE)

B26. Now I need to know about the rooms in your dwelling unit.

Do you have a bathroom included in your (room/apartment/flat/house) or do
you share a bathroom with other tenants of other units?

| 1. INCLUDEDS BATHROOM | | 5. SHARED BATHROOM |

B25a. How many?

[1] [2] [3]

B27. And do you have your own kitchen or do you share a kitchen with tenants
of other units?

| 1. PRIVATE KITCHEN | | 5. SHARED KITCHEN |

B28. And how many <u>rooms</u> do you have in your (room/apartment/flat/house) <u>not</u>
including any bathroom or kitchen or closets or hallways?

[1] [2] [3] [4] [5] [6] [7] [8] [9] [10] [11] [12] _____

B28a. How do you use these rooms? (ENUMERATE NUMBER AND TYPE OF EACH
TYPE OF ROOM. BE SURE R ACCOUNTS FOR ALL ROOMS.)

NUMBER   TYPE   _____

B29. How many people sleep in each bedroom?

B29a. BEDROOM #1 _____

B29b. BEDROOM #2 _____

B29c. BEDROOM #3 _____

B29d. BEDROOM #4 _____

B30. Do you have _____

    B30a.   the use of a basement?

           1. YES   5. NO

    B30b.   a backyard?

           1. YES   5. NO

    B30c.   a garage?

           1. YES   5. NO

    B30d.   a telephone?

           1. YES   5. NO

    B30e. Do you own an automobile?

           1. YES   5. NO

B31. [SHOW CARD] Looking at the card, can you tell me how you feel about the (room/apartment/flat/house) you live in...Is it the ideal place for you, close to the ideal for you, the best you were able to find but it's not your ideal place, a tolerable place, an unsatisfactory place in several ways, or an unsatisfactory place in many ways?

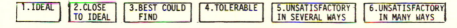

1.IDEAL	2.CLOSE TO IDEAL	3.BEST COULD FIND	4.TOLERABLE	5.UNSATISFACTORY IN SEVERAL WAYS	6.UNSATISFACTORY IN MANY WAYS

B32. How much choice do you feel you have in terms of your housing? A lot, some, a little, or none?

1. A LOT	2. SOME	3. A LITTLE	4. NONE

B33. If you had a chance, would you like to move out of your present home into another place in your neighborhood?

1. YES	5. NO	7. NOT POSSIBLE; NONE IN REALITY

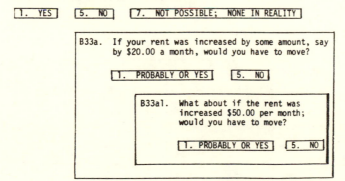

    B33a. If your rent was increased by some amount, say by $20.00 a month, would you have to move?

         1. PROBABLY OR YES   5. NO

        B33a1. What about if the rent was increased $50.00 per month; would you have to move?

             1. PROBABLY OR YES   5. NO

B34. How likely is it that you will move out of your present home in the next year or two? Is it very likely, somewhat likely, or not likely?

1. VERY LIKELY	2.SOMEWHAT LIKELY	3. NOT LIKELY	8. DON'T KNOW

B35. Where do you usually find it easier to relax...at home or someplace away from home?

1. AT HOME		5. SOMEPLACE AWAY FROM HOME		8. DON'T KNOW

B36. [SHOW CARD] Oftentimes people feel the need to get away from the house. How often do you wish you could get away from the house? Would you say it's always, much of the time, sometimes, rarely, or never?

1. ALWAYS	2. MUCH OF THE TIME	3. SOMETIMES	4. RARELY	5. NEVER	8. DON'T KNOW

B36a. And how often do you actually get away from the house?

1. ALWAYS	2. MUCH OF THE TIME	3. SOMETIMES	4. RARELY	5. NEVER	8. DON'T KNOW

(IF R LIVES ALONE--Q.B25--SKIP TO Q.B38)

B37. How often do you wish you could be alone and undisturbed when you're at home? Would you say you feel this way always, much of the time, sometimes, rarely, or never?

1. ALWAYS	2. MUCH OF THE TIME	3. SOMETIMES	4. RARELY	5. NEVER	8. DON'T KNOW	9. NOT APPLIC

B37a. And how often do you actually get to be alone and undisturbed at home?

1. ALWAYS	2. MUCH OF THE TIME	3. SOMETIMES	4. RARELY	5. NEVER	8. DON'T KNOW	9. NOT APPLIC

B38. Overall, how satisfied or dissatisfied do you feel about your (room/apartment/ flat/house)? Do you feel very satisfied, somewhat satisfied, not too satisfied, or not satisfied at all?

1. VERY SATISFIED	2. SOMEWHAT SATISFIED	3. NOT TOO SATISFIED	4. NOT SATISFIED AT ALL	8. DON'T KNOW NEUTRAL

B39. We've talked about your present living conditions. Now I'd like to ask you about experiences you might have had looking for housing in the past. Have you ever felt in any way discriminated against in finding housing because you're Chinese?

1. YES		5. NO	-- GO TO Q.B40

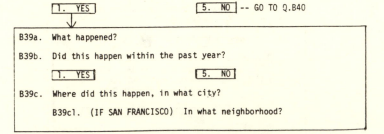

B39a. What happened?

B39b. Did this happen within the past year?

1. YES		5. NO

B39c. Where did this happen, in what city?

B39c1. (IF SAN FRANCISCO) In what neighborhood?

B40. What about your age? Have you ever felt in any way discriminated against in obtaining housing because of your age?

1. YES		5. NO	-- GO TO Q.B41

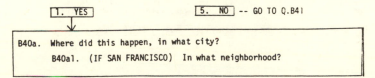

B40a. Where did this happen, in what city?

B40a1. (IF SAN FRANCISCO) In what neighborhood?

(IF R DOES NOT HAVE (CHILD/CHILDREN), SKIP TO Q.B42)

B41. Have you ever felt in any way discriminated against in obtaining housing because you had children?

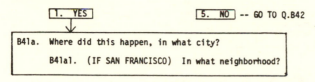

```
[ 1. YES ]                    [ 5. NO ] -- GO TO Q.B42
       |
       v
+-----------------------------------------------------------+
| B41a.  Where did this happen, in what city?               |
|                                                           |
|        B41a1. (IF SAN FRANCISCO) In what neighborhood?    |
+-----------------------------------------------------------+
```

B42. Do you know of any agency that helps people in cases of housing discrimination?

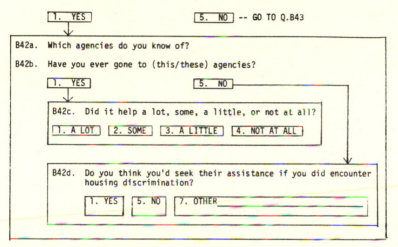

```
[ 1. YES ]                    [ 5. NO ] -- GO TO Q.B43
       |
       v
+---------------------------------------------------------------------+
| B42a.  Which agencies do you know of?                               |
|                                                                     |
| B42b.  Have you ever gone to (this/these) agencies?                 |
|                                                                     |
|    [ 1. YES ]                    [ 5. NO ]                          |
|         |                                                           |
|         v                                                           |
|    +---------------------------------------------------------+     |
|    | B42c.  Did it help a lot, some, a little, or not at all? |     |
|    | [1. A LOT] [2. SOME] [3. A LITTLE] [4. NOT AT ALL]      |     |
|    +---------------------------------------------------------+     |
|                                                                     |
|    +---------------------------------------------------------+     |
|    | B42d.  Do you think you'd seek their assistance if you   |     |
|    |        did encounter housing discrimination?            |     |
|    |    [1. YES] [5. NO] [7. OTHER _____ ]     |     |
|    +---------------------------------------------------------+     |
+---------------------------------------------------------------------+
```

B43. Now, I'd like to end the Housing Section with some questions about crowding.

Some people don't like crowding; some people like crowding. First, how do you feel about a crowded neighborhood. Would you say a crowded neighborhood is very good, somewhat good, neutral, somewhat bad, or very bad?

1. VERY GOOD	2. SOMEWHAT GOOD	3. NEUTRAL	4. SOMEWHAT BAD	5. VERY BAD

B44. Now what about a crowded building or housing project? Would you say a crowded building is very good, somewhat good, neutral, somewhat bad, or very bad?

1. VERY GOOD	2. SOMEWHAT GOOD	3. NEUTRAL	4. SOMEWHAT BAD	5. VERY BAD

B45. Now what about a crowded room or apartment? Would you say a crowded room is very good, somewhat good, neutral, somewhat bad, or very bad?

1. VERY GOOD	2. SOMEWHAT GOOD	3. NEUTRAL	4. SOMEWHAT BAD	5. VERY BAD

B46. Do you think that crowding causes any problems?

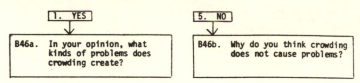

```
   ┌─────────┐                      ┌─────────┐
   │ 1. YES  │                      │ 5. NO   │
   └─────────┘                      └─────────┘
        ↓
```

┌────────────────────────────────┐   ┌────────────────────────────────┐
│ B46a. In your opinion, what   │   │ B46b. Why do you think crowding│
│   kinds of problems does │   │   does not cause problems? │
│   crowding create?   │   │   │
└────────────────────────────────┘   └────────────────────────────────┘

B47. Now I want you to think about what effects crowding has on <u>you</u>. What
     effects does crowding have on how you feel and what you do?

B48. Do you know of any families in Chinatown that are so crowded they have to
     sleep in shifts?

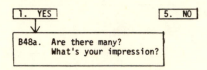

```
   ┌─────────┐                      ┌─────────┐
   │ 1. YES  │                      │ 5. NO   │
   └─────────┘                      └─────────┘
        ↓
```

┌──────────────────────────────────┐
│ B48a. Are there many?   │
│   What's your impression?   │
└──────────────────────────────────┘

B49. We've now finished the sections of housing and neighborhood. Is there
     anything important that I neglected to ask you about?

```
   ┌─────────┐                      ┌─────────┐
   │ 1. YES  │                      │ 5. NO   │
   └─────────┘                      └─────────┘
        ↓
```

SECTION C: IMMIGRANTS

(IF R IS U.S. BORN--Q.A1--SKIP TO SECTION D, Q.D1)

C1. How old were you when you moved to the U.S.? _____ YEARS OLD

C2. What year was it that you came to the U.S.? _____

C3. Did you come with family, or relatives, or did you come alone?

| 1. FAMILY | 2. RELATIVES | 3. ALONE | 4. OTHER_____ |

C4. Did you have family or relatives who were already in the U.S. when you arrived?

| 1. YES | 5. NO |

C5. Why did you (or your family) move to the U.S.? (IF VAGUE, PROBE FOR ELABORATION)

C6. Lots of people have expectations about how life will be in the United
     States. Then after they've been here awhile they find their expectations
     were or were not met.

     [SHOW CARD] Which description best describes how you feel? Life for me in
     the United States has been much better than I expected, somewhat better than
     I expected, about what I expected, not as good as I expected, or much worse
     than I expected? (IF R INDICATES BEING TOO YOUNG TO HAVE EXPECTATION, CODE 6
     AND GO TO Q.C7)

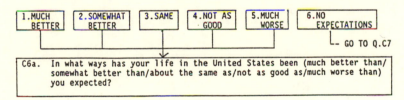

| 1.MUCH BETTER | 2.SOMEWHAT BETTER | 3.SAME | 4.NOT AS GOOD | 5.MUCH WORSE | 6.NO EXPECTATIONS |

└─ GO TO Q.C7

C6a. In what ways has your life in the United States been (much better than/
      somewhat better than/about the same as/not as good as/much worse than)
      you expected?

C7. Have you ever thought of returning to your country ?

| 1. YES | 5. NO | -- GO TO Q.C8 |

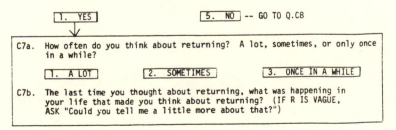

C7a. How often do you think about returning? A lot, sometimes, or only once
      in a while?

| 1. A LOT | 2. SOMETIMES | 3. ONCE IN A WHILE |

C7b. The last time you thought about returning, what was happening in
      your life that made you think about returning? (IF R IS VAGUE,
      ASK "Could you tell me a little more about that?")

C8. Have you ever felt disillusioned or disappointed about the way things are in the United States or about the way things aren't working out for you?

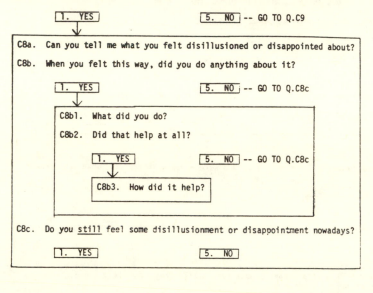

| 1. YES | | 5. NO | -- GO TO Q.C9 |

C8a. Can you tell me what you felt disillusioned or disappointed about?

C8b. When you felt this way, did you do anything about it?

| 1. YES | | 5. NO | -- GO TO Q.C8c |

C8b1. What did you do?

C8b2. Did that help at all?

| 1. YES | | 5. NO | -- GO TO Q.C8c |

C8b3. How did it help?

C8c. Do you still feel some disillusionment or disappointment nowadays?

| 1. YES | | 5. NO |

C9. What are the most major ways in which this country differs from your country of origin? (IF R INDICATES WAS TOO YOUNG WHEN IMMIGRATED, CODE 9)

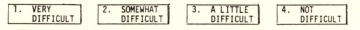

_____ | 9. NA |

C10. Coming from another country and culture often makes it difficult to adjust to living in the United States. What kinds of adjustment difficulties, if any, have you had?

_____ | 5. NONE | | 9. NA |

C11. Overall, how difficult has it been for you to adjust to living in the United States? Would you say it's been very difficult, somewhat difficult, a little difficult, or not difficult at all?

| 1. VERY DIFFICULT | 2. SOMEWHAT DIFFICULT | 3. A LITTLE DIFFICULT | 4. NOT DIFFICULT |

C12. Since coming to the United States, have you changed some of your old customs and ways to American customs and ways? Have you chaged a lot, some, a little, or not at all?

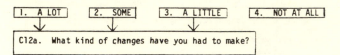

| 1. A LOT | 2. SOME | 3. A LITTLE | 4. NOT AT ALL |

C12a. What kind of changes have you had to make?

C13. Do you think that an immigrant needs to take on American customs in order to get along in this country or do you think an immigrant can get along alright without changing old ways and customs?

    C13a. What __American__ ways should be taken and what ways should be rejected?

    C13b. And what __Chinese__ ways should be retained and what ways should be rejected?

C14. Do you think that Chinese immigrants to the United States experience quite a bit of loneliness or not?

    | 1. YES | | 5. NO |

    C14a. Has any member of your family experienced loneliness because of being an immigrant?

    | 1. YES | | 5. NO |

    C14b. And what about you?

    | 1. YES | | 5. NO |

    Comments:

C15. Are you a U.S. citizen, a permanent resident, on student visa, or what?

    | 1. CITIZEN | | 2. PERMANENT RESIDENT | | 3. STUDENT VISA | | 4. OTHER_____ |

C16. [SHOW CARD] All things considered, how do you feel about life in the United States? Do you feel completely satisfied, somewhat satisfied, slightly satisfied, neutral, slightly dissatisfied, somewhat dissatified, or completely dissatisfied?

| 1.COMPLETELY SATISFIED | 2.SOMEWHAT SATISFIED | 3.SLIGHTLY SATISFIED | 4.NEUTRAL | 5.SLIGHTLY DISSATISFIED | 6.SOMEWHAT DISSATISFIED |

                                                          | 7.COMPLETELY DISSATISFIED |

C17. Now we've finished the section about your experience as an immigrant. Is there anything important about that experience that I forgot to ask that you'd like to tell me?

    | 1. YES | | 5. NO |
       ↓

SECTION D: JOB

D1. Now I'd like to ask you about work. Are you working now for pay, looking
for work, retired, going to school, keeping house, or what?

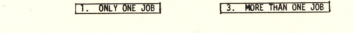

| 1.WORKING NOW | 2. TEMPORARILY LAID OFF | 3.LOOKING FOR WORK, UNEMPLOYED | 4.RETIRED | 5.PERMANENTLY DISABLED |

└─ SKIP TO Q.D44 ─┘   └─SKIP TO Q.D53 └─SKIP TO Q.E1

| 6.KEEPING HOUSE, F/T NONSALARIED | 7.STUDENT | 8.ON WELFARE | 9.OTHER_____ (SPECIFY) |

└─SKIP TO Q.D60   └─SKIP TO Q.E1 ─┘

D2. Are you working at one job or do you have more than one job?

| 1. ONLY ONE JOB | | 3. MORE THAN ONE JOB |

D3. What kind of work do you do...that is, what's your main occupation called?

D3a. (IF NECESSARY ASK, "What kind of business or industry is that in?"
and/or "What do they do or make at the place where you work?")

D4. Do you work for somebody else or for yourself?

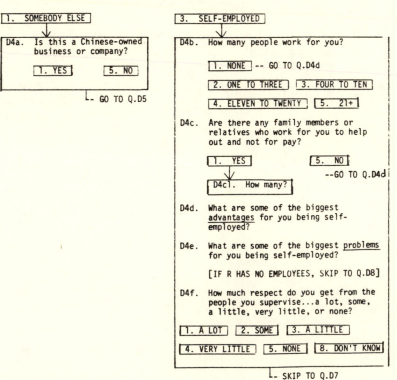

| 1. SOMEBODY ELSE | | 3. SELF-EMPLOYED |

D4a. Is this a Chinese-owned business or company?

| 1. YES | | 5. NO |

L─ GO TO Q.D5

D4b. How many people work for you?

| 1. NONE | -- GO TO Q.D4d

| 2. ONE TO THREE | | 3. FOUR TO TEN |

| 4. ELEVEN TO TWENTY | | 5. 21+ |

D4c. Are there any family members or relatives who work for you to help out and not for pay?

| 1. YES | | 5. NO |

--GO TO Q.D4d

| D4c1. How many? |

D4d. What are some of the biggest advantages for you being self-employed?

D4e. What are some of the biggest problems for you being self-employed?

[IF R HAS NO EMPLOYEES, SKIP TO Q.D8]

D4f. How much respect do you get from the people you supervise...a lot, some, a little, very little, or none?

| 1. A LOT | | 2. SOME | | 3. A LITTLE |

| 4. VERY LITTLE | | 5. NONE | | 8. DON'T KNOW |

L─ SKIP TO Q.D7

D5. Is your immediate supervisor or boss Chinese or non-Chinese?

| 1. CHINESE | | 5. NON-CHINESE |

D6. About how many people are employed at your place of work?

| 1. 1-9 | 2. 10-49 | 3. 50-99 | 4. 100-499 | 5. 500-999 | 6. 1000+ |

D7. Are the people at your work place all Chinese, mostly Chinese, mostly White, all White except for you, or something else?

| 1. ALL CHINESE | 2. MOSTLY CHINESE | 3. MOSTLY WHITE | 4. ALL WHITE | 5. OTHER_____ SPECIFY |

D8. How long have you been employed at your present place of work?

_____YEARS   _____MONTHS [IF LESS THAN 1 YEAR]

D9. And how long have you been doing this kind of work?

_____YEARS   _____MONTHS [IF LESS THAN 1 YEAR]

D10. Is your work place inside of or outside of Chinatown?

| 1. INSIDE | 5. OUTSIDE | 7. OTHER_____ |

D11. How many days a week do you usually work? [IF R WORKS AT 2 OR MORE JOBS, CHECK TOTAL DAYS OF ALL WORK COMBINED.]

| 0 | 1 | 2 | 3 | 4 | 5 | 6 | 7 |

D12. What time do you usually begin work?

TIME_____ ☐ AM
                     ☐ PM

D13. And what time do you usually end work?

TIME_____ ☐ AM
                     ☐ PM

D14. How many hours a week do you work, including any time spent on the weekends or at nights?

_____HOURS PER WEEK

D15. Is there anything about your job that you particualrly like?

| 1. YES | | 5. NO | -- GO TO Q.D16 |

| D15a. What things do you particualrly like about your job? |

D16. Is there anything about your job that you particularly don't like?

| 1. YES | | 5. NO | -- GO TO Q.D17 |

| D16a. What are these things? |

D17. How good would you say you are at doing this kind of work...very good, a little better than average, just average, or not very good?

| 1. VERY GOOD | 2. BETTER THAN AVERAGE | 3. JUST AVERAGE | 4. NOT VERY GOOD |

D18. Now I'd like to ask you a few questions about your education and language as they apply to your job.

Did you receive your education abroad or in the United States or both?

| 1. ALL ABROAD | 3. ALL IN U.S. | 5. ABROAD: FROM____ TO____ GRADE____ U.S. : FROM____ TO____ GRADE____ |

D19. What was the highest grade of school or level of education you completed?

_____YEARS

[NOW CODE, AND CLARIFY IF NEEDED]

☐ 00 NONE

☐ 10 GRADES 1-7 (SOME GRADE SCHOOL)

☐ 20 GRADE 8 (COMPLETION OF GRADE SCHOOL)

☐ 30 GRADES 9-11 (SOME HIGH SCHOOL)

☐ 40 GRADE 12 (HIGH SCHOOL DIPLOMA, GED, OR ANY HIGH SCHOOL EQUIVALENT)

☐ 50 SOME COLLEGE WITHOUT DEGREE

☐ 60 GRADE 16 (COLLEGE DEGREE)

☐ 70 GRADUATE OR PROFESSIONAL EDUCATION IN EXCESS OF COLLEGE DEGREE

D20. Have you ever gone to a trade or vocational training school?

| 1. YES | 5. NO |

| D20a. How many months or years of trade school or vocational training did you complete? _____YEARS _____MONTHS [IF LESS THAN 1 MONTH] |

D21a. [FOR CHINESE SPEAKING RESPONDENTS]   D21b. [FOR ENGLISH SPEAKING RESPONDENTS]

Do you have difficulty with English?

| 1. YES | | 5. NO |→ Do you feel that you are qualified for
                                    a better job than the one you have
                                    now? (by job training, education or
                                    experience)

D21a1. If you could speak English
        well, would you feel
        qualified for a better job
        than the one you have now?

| 1. YES | | 5. NO |

| 1. YES | | 2. NO |
        └─ GO TO Q.D22 ─┘

D22c.   If you could speak English
        well, would you want
        another job or would you
        stay at your present job?

| 1. ANOTHER | | 5. STAY |
     JOB

D22. On your (main) job, how are you paid? Are you salaried, paid by the hour,
      by the piece, or some other way?

| 1. SALARIED | | 5. PAID BY HOUR | | 7. OTHER |

D22a. What is your hourly
       wage rate for your
       regular work time?
       $_____ PER HOUR

D22b. How are you paid?

D22c. (IF R WORKS FOR SOMEONE ELSE, ASK, "Are you paid for overtime?"

| 1. YES | | 5. NO |

D23. Do you feel that your rate is higher than it should be, about what it should
      be, or lower than it should be?

| 1. PAY TOO HIGH | | 5. PAY ABOUT RIGHT | | 7. PAY TOO LOW |

D23a. Why do you think it's
       lower than it should be?

D24. What kinds of satisfactions, if any, do you get from working?

[ ] NONE

D25. What kinds of problems, if any, result from your working?

[ ] NONE

D26. Now I'm going to read you a list if different kinds of feelings people have
      about their jobs. I'd like you to tell me if any of these is a problem that
      you have. [IF R SAYS "Sometimes" CODE YES]

a. Do you have problems with your boss or | 1. YES | | 5. NO | | 9. NA |
    supervisor?

b. Do you have problems with any of the | 1. YES | | 5. NO | | 9. NA |
    people you work with?

c. Are the physical conditions of your work | 1. YES | | 5. NO | | 9. NA |
    place in anyway not good--like poor
    lighting, dirty, unhealthy, or unsafe?
    Too crowded, bad ventilation, bad
    heating?

d. Have you had problems getting your pay check or your due amount of pay? [1. YES] [5. NO] [9. NA]

e. Are your opinions valued or taken seriously by your boss or supervisor? [1. YES] [5. NO] [9. NA]

f. Is there a risk that you will get laid off or fired on your job? [1. YES] [5. NO] [9. NA]

g. Does your job allow you to use your abilities and skills well? [1. YES] [5. NO] [9. NA]

h. Is your job boring? [1. YES] [5. NO] [9. NA]

i. Do you feel your job is rather meaningless? [1. YES] [5. NO] [9. NA]

j. Does your job provide opportunities for promotions or raises? [1. YES] [5. NO] [9. NA]

k. Is your work emotionally stressful to you? [1. YES] [5. NO] [9. NA]

l. Are you under constant time pressures or deadlines? [1. YES] [5. NO] [9. NA]

m. Does your job teach you any new skills? [1. YES] [5. NO] [9. NA]

n. Do you receive any benefits on your job, such as medical, profit-sharing, vacation time, sick leave, etc. [1. YES] [5. NO] [9. NA]

o. Do you feel proud of the kind of work you do? [1. YES] [5. NO] [9. NA]

p. Would you want your children to be doing the same kind of work? [1. YES] [5. NO] [9. NA]

q. Do you have to compete with other people at your job? [1. YES] [5. NO] [9. NA]

r. Is your work too demanding? [1. YES] [5. NO] [9. NA]

s. Is your work physically exhausting? [1. YES] [5. NO] [9. NA]

t. Do you have any friends at your job? [1. YES] [5. NO] [9. NA]

u. Is your work place noisy? [1. YES] [5. NO] [9. NA]

[IF R LIVES ALONE--Q.B25--SKIP TO Q.D28]

D27. Does your work or your work schedule affect your home life in any way?

[1. YES]   [5. NO]
   ↓
[D27a. How? [ENCOURAGE ELABORATION]]

[IF SELF-EMPLOYED OR BOSS--Q.D4--SKIP TO D29]

D28. [SHOW CARD] How much respect do you get from your boss...a lot, some, a little, very little, or none?

[1. A LOT] [2. SOME] [3. A LITTLE] [4. VERY LITTLE] [5. NONE] [8. DON'T KNOW] [9. NA]

D29. Taking all things into consideration, how do you feel about your job? Are you very satisfied, somewhat satisfied, not too satisfied, or not satisfied at all?

[1. VERY SATISFIED] [2. SOMEWHAT SATISFIED] [3. NOT TOO SATISFIED] [4. NOT SATISFIED AT ALL] [8. DK NEUTRAL]

D30. Now I'd like you to think about all the jobs you've held. Have you ever been treated worse or different on a job because you're Chinese?

[1. YES]   [5. NO] -- GO TO Q.D31

D30a. What happened? How were you treated differently?
CHECK AS MANY AS APPROPRIATE.

[ ] 1. DENIED PROMOTION
                                    (COMMENTS)
[ ] 3. RACIAL JOKES   _____

[ ] 5. RACIAL SLURS   _____

[ ] 7. DIFFERENTIAL PAY   _____

[ ] 9. OTHER   _____

D30b. How often have you been treated worse or different on a job because you're Chinese? Once, two or three times, or more than three times?

[1. ONCE]   [2. TWO-THREE TIMES]   [3. MORE THAN THREE TIMES]

D30c. People often have different feelings when things like this happen. Sometimes they feel angry, resentful, hurt, disappointed, disillusioned. Sometimes they don't feel anyways about it. Did you have any of these feelings about it?

D30d. What did you do to try to deal with it, the time or times you were treated worse?
                                                    [ ] NOTHING

D31. Have you ever suspected that you were denied a job because you're Chinese?

[1. YES]   [5. NO] -- GO TO Q.D32

D31a. Would you care to tell me something about that--when it was, what kind of job it was, what kind of company, business, or industry it was?

                                        [ ] I'D RATHER NOT

D31b. People often have different felings when things like this happen. Sometimes they feel angry, resentful, hurt, disappointed, disillusioned. Sometimes they don't feel anyways about it. Did you have any of these feelings about it?
                                        [ ] NOTHING

D32. Are you aware of any agency that helps Chinese in cases of employment discrimination?

[1. YES]   [5. NO] -- GO TO Q.D33

D32a. Which agency or agencies are you aware of?

D32b. Have you ever gone to (this/these) agencies?

[1. YES]   [5. NO]

D32b1. Did it help a lot, some, a little, or not at all?

[1. A LOT]   [2. SOME]

[3. A LITTLE]   [4. NOT AT ALL]

D32b2. Do you think you'd seek their assistance if you did encounter discrimination on a job?

[1. YES]   [5. NO]   [8. DON'T KNOW]

D33. Now I'd like to ask you some questions about what you think labor unions do.

Do you think that labor unions in this country

a. protect workers against unfair action by their employees? [1.YES] [3.SOMEWHAT SOMETIMES] [5.NO] [8.DK]

b. improve the job security of workers? [1.YES] [3.SOMEWHAT SOMETIMES] [5.NO] [8.DK]

c. are more powerful than employers? [1.YES] [3.SOMEWHAT SOMETIMES] [5.NO] [8.DK]

d. improve the wages and working conditions of workers? [1.YES] [3.SOMEWHAT SOMETIMES] [5.NO] [8.DK]

e. give members their money's worth for the dues they pay? [1.YES] [3.SOMEWHAT SOMETIMES] [5.NO] [8.DK]

f. require members to go along with decisions they don't like? [1.YES] [3.SOMEWHAT SOMETIMES] [5.NO] [8.DK]

D34. An Open Union Shop is a work place where workers can decide whether or not they want to join a union. A closed union shop is where all workers are required to be union members. Is your work place non-unionized, an open union shop, or a closed union shop?

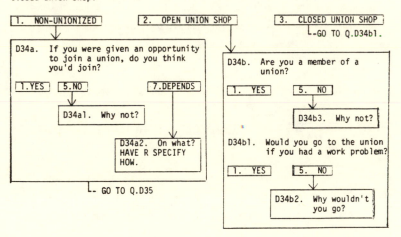

D35. Now a few questions on how you're managing to make ends meet or plan for your future. As we all know, some people do things to increase their income in order to make ends meet, to plan their future, or to live better. Some people work extra jobs, borrow money from the bank, from friends or from family members, have more than one member of the household work, have family members help them at their jobs, invest in real estate, stocks, bonds, or other things.

Do you do any of these or other things to make ends meet or to increase your earnings?

[1. YES] -- GO TO Q.D35a   [5. NO] -- GO TO Q.D36

What do you do?

D35a. work extra jobs?   [1. YES] [5. NO]

D35b. borrow money [ ] BANK [ ] FAMILY [ ] FRIENDS   [1. YES] [5. NO]

D35c. have more than one person in the household   [1. YES] [5. NO]
      working?

D35d. have family help?   [1. YES] [5. NO]

D35e. invest? [ ] REAL ESTATE [ ] STOCKS, BONDS   [1. YES] [5. NO]

      [ ] INTEREST IN BANK

      [ ] OTHER_____

D35f. Any other things?

[IF R LIVES ALONE--Q.B25--SKIP TO Q.D37]

D36. How many people in your family, including yourself, who live in your household,
     are working for pay?

[1] -- GO TO Q.D37   [2] [3] [4] [5] [6] [7+]

      D36a. If only one person brought in money, would you say that your
            household would make its expenses just as well, barely get
            by, or what?

            [1. MAKE IT JUST   [3. BARELY GET   [5. OTHER_____]
                AS WELL]   BY]

D37. As an adult have you ever been unemployed for longer than a month when you
     wanted work? Don't include any period of unemployment when you were a
     full-time student.

      [1. YES]   [5. NO]

      D37a. How many different times have you been unemployed as best as you
            can remember? Once or twice, 3-4 times, or 5 or more times?

            [1. ONCE OR TWICE] [3. 3-4 TIMES] [5. 5 OR MORE TIMES]

      D37b. What was the longest period of time that you were out of work
            and looking for a job?

            _____YEARS   _____MONTHS (IF LESS THAN 1 YEAR)

      D37c. The last time you were unemployed, was it within the last year?

            [1. YES]   [5. NO]

(IF R IS A MARRIED MAN--Q.A40--SKIP TO Q.D65)

(IF R IS AN UNMARRIED MAN--Q.A40--SKIP TO Q.D80)

(IF R IS A MARRIED WOMAN WITHOUT CHILDREN--Q.A39-40--SKIP TO Q.D65)

(IF R IS A MOTHER--Q.A39--CONTINUE WITH Q.D38)

(IF R IS AN UNMARRIED WOMAN--Q.A40--SKIP TO Q.D80)

IF R IS A WORKING MOTHER

D38. Why are you working?

D39. Does anyone help you with the household chores?

1. YES   5. NO

D40. Do you usually take any of your children to work with you?

1. YES   5. NO

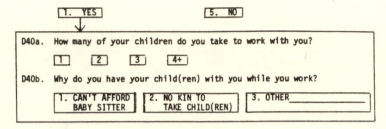

D40a. How many of your children do you take to work with you?

1   2   3   4+

D40b. Why do you have your child(ren) with you while you work?

1. CAN'T AFFORD BABY SITTER   2. NO KIN TO TAKE CHILD(REN)   3. OTHER_____

D41. (Is/are any of) your child(ren) looked after at a daycare center or nursery school on a regular basis?

1. YES   5. NO

D42. (Is/are any of) your child(ren) (also) looked after by someone else on a regular basis?

1. YES   5. NO -- GO TO Q.D43

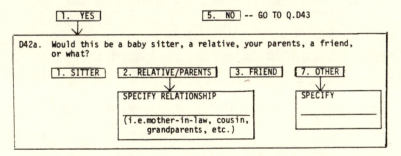

D42a. Would this be a baby sitter, a relative, your parents, a friend, or what?

1. SITTER   2. RELATIVE/PARENTS   3. FRIEND   7. OTHER

SPECIFY RELATIONSHIP

(i.e.mother-in-law, cousin, grandparents, etc.)

SPECIFY

D43. What kinds of problems does being a working mother create for you?

D43a. (PROBE AND ASK, "Any other?" OR "Could you say more about that?")

(IF R IS MARRIED--Q.A40--SKIP TO Q.D65)

(IF R IS UNMARRIED--Q.A40-- SKIP TO Q.D80)

IF R IS UNEMPLOYED OR LOOKING FOR A JOB

D44. What sort of work did you do on your last job? _____

D44a. Was it a full-time job, or a part-time job?

1. FULL-TIME   5. PART-TIME

IF R IS UNEMPLOYED OR LOOKING FOR A JOB

D44b. What kind of business or industry (is/was) that?

D44c. What happened to that job? Did the company go out of business, were you laid off, quit, went back to school, retired, or what?

☐ LAID OFF ☐ QUIT ☐ SCHOOL ☐ RETIRED ☐ FIRED ☐ OTHER

SPECIFY _____

D45. About how long has it been since you left this job?

| 1. LESS THAN 3 MONTHS | 2. 4 TO 8 MONTHS | 3. 9 TO 11 MONTHS | 4. 1 TO 2 YEARS | 5. OVER 2 YEARS |

D46. Sometimes being without a job can cause worries or problems. Would you say that being without a job caused a lot of worries or problems, some worries or problems, a few worries or problems, or no worries or problems?

| 1. A LOT | 2. SOME | 3. A FEW | 4. NONE | -- GO TO Q.D47

D46a. What kinds of problems or worries did it cause you?

D46b. Sometimes people who are without work do things to forget about their worries--they play M.J., have hobbies, drink, smoke, do Tai Chi, read, go to movies, watch T.V., entertain friends. Did you do anything to help you forget your worries?

| 1. YES | 5. NO |

D46b1. What did you do?

D47. In your most recent job, were you ever treated worse or different because you're Chinese?

| 1. YES | 5. NO | -- GO TO Q.D48

D47a. What happened? How were you treated differently? [CHECK AS MANY AS APPROPRIATE]

☐ 1. DENIED PROMOTION

☐ 3. RACIAL JOKES

(COMMENTS)

☐ 5. RACIAL SLURS

☐ 7. DIFFERENTIAL PAY

☐ 9. OTHER _____

D47b. How often have you been treated worse or different on a job because you're Chinese? Once, two or three times, or more than 3 times?

| 1. ONCE | 2. TWO-THREE TIMES | 3. MORE THAN 3 TIMES |

D47c. People often have different feelings when things like this happen. Sometimes they feel angry, resentful, hurt, disappointed, disillusioned, sometimes they don't feel anyways about it. Did you have any of these feelings about it?

[CONTINUE WITH D47d]

IF R IS UNEMPLOYED OR LOOKING FOR A JOB

D47d. What did you do to try to deal with it the time or times you were treated worse?

☐ NOTHING -- GO TO Q.D48

D47e. Did that help a lot, help some, help only a little, or not at all?

1. A LOT │ 2. SOME │ 3. A LITTLE │ 4. NOT HELP AT ALL

D48. Since you've been without a job, have there been any changes in your life-- say in your family life, your social life, your personal life, your moods or your activities...changes that have resulted because you no longer have a job? Changes that might be either good or bad?

1. YES   5. NO -- GO TO Q.D49

D48a. What have these changes been? [LIST UP TO FIVE IN THE ORDER MENTIONED]	D48b. Would you say this has been a good or bad change?
1. _____	1.GOOD 5.BAD 8.DK
2. _____	1.GOOD 5.BAD 8.DK
3. _____	1.GOOD 5.BAD 8.DK
4. _____	1.GOOD 5.BAD 8.DK
5. _____	1.GOOD 5.BAD 8.DK

D49. Are you looking for a job now?

1. YES   5. NO

D50. How do you feel about being unemployed...very satisfied, somewhat satisfied, not too satisfied, or not satisfied at all?

1. VERY SATISFIED │ 2. SOMEWHAT SATISFIED │ 3. NOT TOO SATISFIED │ 4. NOT SATISFIED AT ALL

D51. Now a few questions on how you're managing to make ends meet or planning for your future.

Are you getting along on your present income or savings fairly well, adequately, not so well, or not well at all?

1. FAIRLY WELL │ 2. ADEQUATELY │ 3. NOT SO WELL │ 4. NOT WELL AT ALL

D52. How many people in your family, including yourself, who live in this household, are working for pay?

0   1   2   3   4   5   6   7   8   9+

D52a. If only one person brought in money, would you say that your household would make its expenses just as well, barely get by, or what?

1. MAKE IT JUST AS WELL │ 3. BARELY GET BY │ 7. OTHER_____

(IF R IS <u>MARRIED</u> --Q.A40--ASK Q.D19, AND THEN SKIP TO Q.D65)

(IF R IS <u>UNMARRIED</u>--Q.A40--ASK Q.D19, AND THEN SKIP TO Q.D80)

| IF R IS RETIRED |

D53. In what year did you retire?   _____YEAR

D54. Why did you retire? (AND ASK "Are there any other reasons?")

    D54a. [IF REASON UNCLEAR] Did you have to retire or is this something that you wanted to do?

      | 1. HAD TO | | 5. WANTED TO |

D55. Are you glad you've retired or do you wish you were employed?

| 1. GLAD RETIRED | -- GO TO Q.D56 | 5. WISH TO BE EMPLOYED |

    D55a. Have you been looking for a job?

      | 1. YES | | 5. NO |

                                       | D55d. Why not? |

      D55d. How long have you been looking?

         _____YEARS   _____MONTHS (IF LESS THAN 1 YEAR)

      D55c. How much happier do you think you would be if you were employed again? Would you be much happier, somewhat happier, or a little happier?

      | 1. MUCH HAPPIER | | 2. SOMEWHAT HAPPIER | | 3. A LITTLE HAPPIER |

D56. What kinds of changes occurred in your life as a result of being retired?

D57. How do you feel about being retired? Do you feel very satisfied, somewhat satisfied, not very satisfied, or not satisfied at all?

| 1. VERY SATISFIED | | 2. SOMEWHAT SATISFIED | | 3. NOT VERY SATISFIED | | 4. NOT SATISFIED AT ALL |

D58. What are some of the problems, if any, that you're having as a retired person?

_____ | NONE |

(IF THE FOLLOWING ASPECTS WERE NOT MENTIONED BY R, ASK, "Do you...")

a. miss the people at your old job? | 1. YES | | 5. NO |

b. have trouble finding anything to do? | 1. YES | | 5. NO |

c. have trouble with your pension plan or social security? | 1. YES | | 5. NO |

d. worry about whether you and your family have enough money to live on? | 1. YES | | 5. NO |

e. feel useless? | 1. YES | | 5. NO |

f. Is there <u>anything else</u> that's a problem for you as a retired person? _____

IF R IS RETIRED

D59. As a retired person are you involved in any volunteered work or social activities or programs?

1. YES   5. NO

(IF R IS MARRIED--Q.A40--ASK Q.D19, AND THEN SKIP TO Q.D65)

(IF R IS UNMARRIED--Q.A40--SKIP TO Q.D80)

IF R IS KEEPING HOUSE, UNSALARIED, MALE OR FEMALE

D60. Some people take care of the house because they like this type of work over a paid job outside the house. Other people take care of the house because of necessity and not becuase they really like it. How do you feel about taking care of the house? Do you do it out of preference or out of necessity?

1. PREFERENCE -- GO TO Q.D61   3. NECESSITY

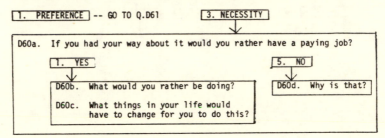

D60a. If you had your way about it would you rather have a paying job?

1. YES   5. NO

D60b. What would you rather be doing?   D60d. Why is that?

D60c. What things in your life would have to change for you to do this?

D61. What are some of the problems, if any, you're having as a (housewife/keeping house full-time)?

[ ] NONE

D62. Does your (husband/wife) want you to keep house full-time? Would you say (he/she) definitely does, probably does, probably doesn't, definitely doesn't, or doesn't care one way or the other?

1. DEFINITELY DOES | 2. PROBABLY DOES | 3. PROBABLY DOESN'T | 4. DEFINITELY DOESN'T | 5. DOESN'T CARE

(IF R DOES NOT HAVE CHILDREN UNDER 18, SKIP TO Q.D64)

D63. Does your child(ren) go to a day care center or school?

1. YES   5. NO -- GO TO Q.D64

D63a. How many hours a day do you spend taking care of your child, that is when (he's/she's/they're) not in school, not asleep? _____HOURS/DAY

D64. How do you feel about (being a housewife/taking care of the house) full-time? Do you feel very satisfied, somewhat satisfied, not too satisfied, or not satisfied at all?

1. VERY SATISFIED | 2. SOMEWHAT SATISFIED | 3. NOT TOO SATISFIED | 4. NOT SATISFIED AT ALL

(FIRST, HAVE R ANSWER Q.D19, THEN: IF R IS MARRIED --Q.A40--CONTINUE WITH Q.D65

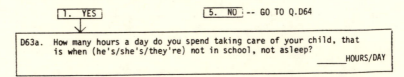

OR IF R IS UNMARRIED--Q.A40--SKIP TO Q.D80)

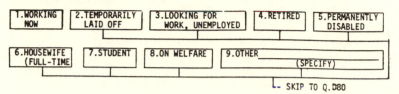

IF R IS MARRIED

D65. Is your (husband/wife) working now for pay, looking for work, retired, going to school, keeping house or what?

| 1.WORKING NOW | 2.TEMPORARILY LAID OFF | 3.LOOKING FOR WORK, UNEMPLOYED | 4.RETIRED | 5.PERMANENTLY DISABLED |

| 6.HOUSEWIFE (FULL-TIME | 7.STUDENT | 8.ON WELFARE | 9.OTHER_____ (SPECIFY) |

└─ SKIP TO Q.D80

D66. Is (he/she) working at one job or more than one job?

| 1. ONE | | 5. MORE THAN ONE |

D66a. What kind of work does (he/she) do?

D66b. What kind of business or industry is that?

D67. Does (he/she) work for (himself/herself) or for somebody else?

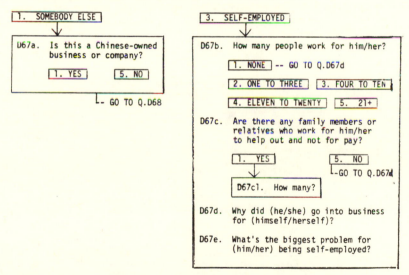

| 1. SOMEBODY ELSE |

D67a. Is this a Chinese-owned business or company?

| 1. YES | 5. NO |

└─ GO TO Q.D68

| 3. SELF-EMPLOYED |

D67b. How many people work for him/her?

| 1. NONE | -- GO TO Q.D67d

| 2. ONE TO THREE | 3. FOUR TO TEN |

| 4. ELEVEN TO TWENTY | 5. 21+ |

D67c. Are there any family members or relatives who work for him/her to help out and not for pay?

| 1. YES | 5. NO |
└─GO TO Q.D67d

D67c1. How many?

D67d. Why did (he/she) go into business for (himself/herself)?

D67e. What's the biggest problem for (him/her) being self-employed?

D68. What's the ethnic background of your (husband/wife)?

| 1. CHINESE | 3. WHITE | 5. OTHER_____ (SPECIFY) |

D69. Not counting your (husband/wife), are the people at your (husband's/wife's) work place all Chinese, mostly Chinese, mostly White, all White or something else?

| 1. ALL CHINESE | 2. MOSTLY CHINESE | 3. MOSTLY WHITE | 4. ALL WHITE | 5. SOMETHING ELSE _____ (SPECIFY) |

IF R IS MARRIED

D70. How long has (he/she) been at (his/her) present place of work?

_____YEARS _____MONTHS [IF LESS THAN 1 YEAR]

D71. Is (his/her) work place inside or outside of Chinatown?

| 1. INSIDE CHINATOWN | 5. OUTSIDE CHINATOWN |

D72. How many days a week does (he/she) usually work?

1 2 3 4 5 6 7

D73. What time does (he/she) usually begin work?

TIME_____ ☐ AM
                          ☐ PM

D74. And what time does (he/she) usually end work?

TIME_____ ☐ AM
                          ☐ PM

D75. Thinking about your working hours and your spouse's working hours, on the average, how many waking hours per week day do you see each other at home?

_____HOURS PER DAY

D76. What about on the weekends, Saturday or Sunday?

_____HOURS PER DAY

D77. Does your (husband/wife) ever bring (his/her) work frustrations home?

| 1. YES OR SOMETIMES | | 5. NO -- GO TO Q.D78 |

D77a. When this happens, does it cause alot of stress on your family, some stress, a little stress, or no stress?

| 1. LOT OF STRESS | 2. SOME STRESS | 3. A LITTLE STRESS | 4. NO STRESS |

D78. Is there anything about (his/her) work, like (his/her) salary, hours, travel, or the kind of work (he/she) does, that causes problems in your family life?

| 1. YES | | 5. NO -- GO TO Q.D79 |

D78a. What is it about (his/her) work that causes problems?

D78b. And what kinds of problems does it cause?

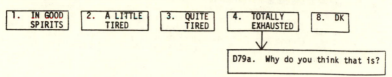

IF R IS MARRIED

D79. When your (husband/wife) returns home from work, does (he/she) usually appear in good spirits, a little tired, quite tired, or totally exhausted?

| 1. IN GOOD SPIRITS | 2. A LITTLE TIRED | 3. QUITE TIRED | 4. TOTALLY EXHAUSTED | 8. DK |

D79a. Why do you think that is?

D80. This ends the section on your job. Is there anything about your work or job that's important to talk about that I've neglected to ask you?

1. YES   5. NO

SECTION E: PSYCHOLOGICAL ATTITUDES

E1. People handle situations differently. I'm now going to ask you some questions about how you handle different situations. I'm going to read two sentences. I'd like you to choose which of the two best describes how you'd handle a situation. If you feel that you might do both, tell me which one is most like what you'd do. Choose the one that describes what you do and not what you should do. If you have any trouble understanding these sentences, just tell me to reread them.

a. If you find that a grocer is overweighing your meat, would you tend not to do anything about it or would you try to do something about it?

   | 0. NOT DO ANYTHING | | 1. DO SOMETHING |

b. If you've been waiting in a bus line for a long time and someone cuts in front of you, would you "make the best of things" or would you say or do something about it?

   | 0. MAKE THE BEST OF THINGS | | 1. DO SOMETHING |

c. If you lived in a housing project and a resident had been robbed and injured because the security in the housing project was bad, would you join a rent strike to get better security or would you tend to just let the Housing Authority officials deal with it?

   | 1. JOIN RENT STRIKE | | 0. LET HOUSING AUTHORITY DEAL |

d. If someone's been giving you a hard time, would you tend to ignore it or try to get the person to stop?

   | 0. IGNORE IT | | 1. GET PERSON TO STOP |

e. If you don't have what you'd like, would you try to get what you want or get someone to help you or would you try to "make do with what you've got"?

   | 1. GET IT OR GET HELP | | 0. MAKE DO |

f. Do you think that if you've been faced with a lot of frustration that you should keep trying or that you should forget it because it's better not to be frustrated?

   | 1. KEEP TRYING | | 0. FORGET IT |

g. If there were serious problems in your marriage, would you try to change things or "make the best of things"?

   | 1. CHANGE THINGS | | 0. MAKE THE BEST OF THINGS |

E2. [SHOW CARD] Now a few more pairs of sentences. Do you think...

   A. It's better to "look away" from situations that are unpleasant or painful or that...

   B. It's better to face reality and deal with situations even if they're unpleasant or painful.

   E2a.   1. [A]   2. [B]   8. DK

   E2b. OK, now which of these describes how your parents would think?

             1. [A]   2. [B]   8. DK

   E2c. [IF UNMARRIED, GO TO Q.E3] And which one best describes how your (husband/wife) would think?

             1. [A]   2. [B]   8. DK

E3. [SHOW CARD]

A. If things aren't going well for me, I'm usually determined to make things go better...or

B. If things aren't going well for me, I usually think "that's just the way things are."

E3a. Which one best describes how you think?

1. A   2. B   8. DK

E3b. And which one describes how your parents would think?

1. A   2. B   8. DK

E3c. [IF UNMARRIED, GO TO Q.E4) And what about your (husband/wife)?

1. A   2. B   8. DK

E4. [SHOW CARD] Now here you have three choices...

A. When White people don't think well of me, I try to prove myself to them.

B. When White people don't think well of me, I try to prove them wrong.

C. When White people don't well of me, it doesn't bother me.

E4a. Which one or ones best describes how you think?

1. A   2. B   3. C   8. DK

E4b. And your parents? Which one or ones describes how they think?

1. A   2. B   3. C   8. DK

E4c. [IF UNMARRIED, GO TO Q.E5) And what about your (husband/wife)?

1. A   2. B   3. C   8. DK

E5. [SHOW CARD] Now I'm going to read you different opinions people have. Please tell me which statement best describes your opinion.

a. 1. ☐ A. Many qualified Chinese can't get a good job because they're Chinese. White people with the same skills wouldn't have any trouble getting that job.

or

2. ☐ B. Many Chinese can't get a job because they lack skill and abilities. If they had the skill and ability, they'd have as good a chance to get a job as a White person.

Now this pair...

b. 1. ☐ A. Many Chinese don't do well in life because they haven't prepared themselves to make use of the opportunities that come their way.

or

2. ☐ B. Many Chinese have good training but they don't do well in life because they don't get as many opportunities as Whites.

E6. [SHOW CARD]

A. The problem for many Chinese in America is that White society discriminates against them even when Chinese do what's proper and adapt to White American customs.

B. The problem for many Chinese is that they refuse to adapt to White American customs. If they did adapt, they'd be accepted and would get ahead.

E6a. Which one is how you feel?

    1. ☐ A   2. ☐ B | 8. DK |

E6b. Which one is how your <u>parents</u> would feel?

    1. ☐ A   2. ☐ B | 8. DK |

E6c. [IF UNMARRIED, GO TO E7] What about your (<u>husband/wife</u>)?

    1. ☐ A   2. ☐ B | 8. DK |

E7. Do you think it's better to <u>plan your life a good ways ahead</u>, or would you say <u>life is to much a matter of luck to plan ahead</u> very far?

| 1. PLAN AHEAD | | 0. TOO MUCH LUCK TO PLAN |

E8. When you do make plans ahead, do you usually get to <u>carry out things the way you expected</u> or do <u>things usually come up</u> to make you change your plans?

| 1. CARRY OUT WAY EXPECTED | | 0. HAVE TO CHANGE PLANS |

E9. Have you usually felt <u>pretty sure</u> your life would work out the way you want it to, or have there been times when you <u>haven't been sure</u> about it?

| 1. PRETTY SURE | | 0. HAVEN'T BEEN SURE |

E10. Some people feel they can run their lives pretty much the way they want to; others feel the problems of life are sometimes too big for them. Which one are you most like?

| 1. CAN RUN OWN LIFE | | 0. PROBLEMS OF LIFE ARE TOO BIG |

E11. [SHOW CARD] Now I'm going to read you some statements. Please tell me if, in this society, you feel the statement is something you agree with or disagree with. Tell me if you <u>strongly agree</u>, <u>somewhat agree</u>, <u>somewhat disagree</u>, or <u>strongly disagree</u>.

    a. Endurance and trying hard will lead to success.

| 1. STRONGLY AGREE | 2. SOMEWHAT AGREE | 3. SOMEWHAT DISAGREE | 4. STRONGLY DISAGREE |

    b. Hardships in life are due to bad luck or bad fortune.

| 1. STRONGLY AGREE | 2. SOMEWHAT AGREE | 3. SOMEWHAT DISAGREE | 4. STRONGLY DISAGREE |

    c. Chinese must perform better than Whites to get ahead.

| 1. STRONGLY AGREE | 2. SOMEWHAT AGREE | 3. SOMEWHAT DISAGREE | 4. STRONGLY DISAGREE |

    d. Success is primarily due to good luck, good fortune, or chance.

| 1. STRONGLY AGREE | 2. SOMEWHAT AGREE | 3. SOMEWHAT DISAGREE | 4. STRONGLY DISAGREE |

    e. If people have hardships in life, it's because they bring it upon themselves.

| 1. STRONGLY AGREE | 2. SOMEWHAT AGREE | 3. SOMEWHAT DISAGREE | 4. STRONGLY DISAGREE |

f. People will get ahead in life if they are bright and capable and do a good job.

| 1. STRONGLY AGREE | 2. SOMEWHAT AGREE | 3. SOMEWHAT DISAGREE | 4. STRONGLY DISAGREE |

g. A great many people who work hard and make good decisions still don't get ahead in life.

| 1. STRONGLY AGREE | 2. SOMEWHAT AGREE | 3. SOMEWHAT DISAGREE | 4. STRONGLY DISAGREE |

h. Knowing the right people is important in deciding whether a person will get ahead.

| 1. STRONGLY AGREE | 2. SOMEWHAT AGREE | 3. SOMEWHAT DISAGREE | 4. STRONGLY DISAGREE |

i. There's really no connection between skill and ability and the rewards you get; many people who lack skill and ability reap the benefits of this society while many people who are skilled and have ability never get such rewards.

| 1. STRONGLY AGREE | 2. SOMEWHAT AGREE | 3. SOMEWHAT DISAGREE | 4. STRONGLY DISAGREE |

j. White people do not like Chinese Americans.

| 1. STRONGLY AGREE | 2. SOMEWHAT AGREE | 3. SOMEWHAT DISAGREE | 4. STRONGLY DISAGREE |

E12. [SHOW CARD] Now I'm going to read and show another group of paired statements. I want you to tell me which statement, A or B, best describes your own beliefs. Do you think that...

a. 1. ☐ A. success in this society is largely achieved by working hard and striving to better your position, or that

2. ☐ B. success doesn't largely depend upon working hard and striving to better your position?

Do you think that...

b. 1. ☐ A. who gets to be the boss depends upon who's got the best skill and ability, or

2. ☐ B. who gets to be boss doesn't usually depend upon who's got the best skill and ability?

Do you think that...

c. 1. ☐ A. getting a good job has nothing to do with chance or luck, or that

2. ☐ B. getting a good job has everything to do with chance or luck?

Do you think that...

d. 1. ☐ A. fate or fortune has little or nothing to do with how situations turn out, or that

2. ☐ B. fate or fortune have a great deal to do with how situations turn out?

Do you think that...

e. 1. ☐ A. many people are rewarded for doing nothing and many people who work hard don't get rewarded, or do you think

2. ☐ B. that those who work hard always get rewarded and those who don't work hard don't get rewarded?

E13. Do you feel that in the United States, Chinese are treated better than, worse than, or the same as Whites?

| 1. BETTER THAN | 3. WORSE THAN | 2. SAME AS |

E13a. What do you feel is the best way for Chinese Americans to cope with discrimination against them?

E13b. What do you feel is the best way for Chinese Americans to overcome obstacles to them in this society?

E14. Generally speaking, would you say that most people can be trusted or that you can't be too careful in dealing with them?

| 1. MOST CAN BE TRUSTED | 5. CAN'T BE TRUSTED |

E15. What about for Whites, would you say that most Whites can be trusted, or that you can't be too careful in dealing with them?

| 1. MOST WHITES CAN BE TRUSTED | 5. CAN'T BE TOO CAREFUL |

E16. Would you say that most of the time White people try to be helpful, or that they are mostly just looking out for themselves?

| 1. TRY TO BE HELPFUL | 5. JUST LOOKING OUT | 8. DK |

E17. Do you think most White people would take advantage of you if they had the chance, or would they try to be fair?

| 1. TRY TO TAKE ADVANTAGE | 5. TRY TO BE FAIR | 8. DK |

E18. What about for Chinese in America? Generally speaking, would you say that most Chinese Americans can be trusted, or that you can't be too careful in dealing with them?

| 1. MOST CHINESE CAN BE TRUSTED | 5. CAN'T BE TOO CAREFUL |

E19. Would you say that most of the time Chinese in America try to be helpful, or that they are mostly just looking out for themselves?

| 1. TRY TO BE HELPFUL | 5. JUST LOOKING OUT | 8. DK |

E20. Do you think most Chinese in America would try to take advantage of you if they had the chance, or would they try to be fair?

| 1. TRY TO TAKE ADVANTAGE | 5. TRY TO BE FAIR | 8. DK |

E21. [SHOW CARD] Sometimes people feel more or less comfortable with different groups of people. How comfortable or uncomfortable do you feel associating with _____; <u>very</u> comfortable, <u>somewhat</u> comfortable, a <u>little</u> <u>un</u>comfortable, or <u>pretty</u> <u>un</u>comfortable?

E21a. Chinese Immigrants

| 1. VERY COMFORTABLE | 2. SOMEWHAT COMFORTABLE | 3. LITTLE UNCOMFORTABLE | 4. PRETTY UNCOMFORTABLE |

E21b. American born Chinese

| 1. VERY COMFORTABLE | 2. SOMEWHAT COMFORTABLE | 3. LITTLE UNCOMFORTABLE | 4. PRETTY UNCOMFORTABLE |

E21c. Japanese Americans

| 1. VERY COMFORTABLE | 2. SOMEWHAT COMFORTABLE | 3. LITTLE UNCOMFORTABLE | 4. PRETTY UNCOMFORTABLE |

E21d. Filipino Americans

| 1. VERY COMFORTABLE | 2. SOMEWHAT COMFORTABLE | 3. LITTLE UNCOMFORTABLE | 4. PRETTY UNCOMFORTABLE |

E21e. Blacks

| 1. VERY COMFORTABLE | 2. SOMEWHAT COMFORTABLE | 3. LITTLE UNCOMFORTABLE | 4. PRETTY UNCOMFORTABLE |

E21f. Chicanos

| 1. VERY COMFORTABLE | 2. SOMEWHAT COMFORTABLE | 3. LITTLE UNCOMFORTABLE | 4. PRETTY UNCOMFORTABLE |

E21g. Whites

| 1. VERY COMFORTABLE | 2. SOMEWHAT COMFORTABLE | 3. LITTLE UNCOMFORTABLE | 4. PRETTY UNCOMFORTABLE |

We've completed about half of the interview at this point. We can stop now and schedule a second session. Would you want to do that? I don't want to interrupt too much of your day's schedule. Could we get together tomorrow or the next day? OK, thank you, I'll see you on _____

Here's a card to remind you. Bye   NEXT APP'T TIME

SECTION F: SOCIAL SUPPORT

F1. [SHOW CARD] Now I'd like to ask you some questions about your friends and relatives. First, about how often do you get together with friends or relatives, like going out together or visiting each other? <u>More than once a week</u>, <u>once a week</u>, <u>twice a month</u>, <u>less than once a month</u>, or never?

1. MORE THAN ONCE A WEEK	2. ONCE A WEEK	3. TWICE A MONTH	4. ONCE A MONTH	5. LESS THAN ONCE A MONTH	6. NEVER

F2. Now, I want you to think of any friends or relatives you feel free to talk with about your worries and problems or can count on for advice or help...would you say you have <u>many</u>, <u>some</u>, <u>a few</u>, or <u>no</u> such friends or relatives?

1. MANY	2. SOME	4. A FEW	5. NONE

F3. How often, if ever, have you talked with friends or relatives about your problems or asked them for advice or help...<u>often</u>, <u>sometimes</u>, <u>rarely</u>, or <u>never</u>?

1. OFTEN	2. SOMETIMES	3. RARELY	4. NEVER

F4. Do you feel you have as many friends as you want, or would you like to have more friends?

1. AS MANY FRIENDS AS WANTS	2. WOULD LIKE MORE FRIENDS

F5. Now I'm going to ask you about the amount of respect and help you've gotten from people. For some people, respect is a very important part of their culture and has meaning for how other people treat them. If someone respects you, they admire you, they trust your decisions, they listen to you and do as you say. If someone doesn't respect you, they don't listen to you, they do what they want and not what you want, they don't ask your opinion about things and they make you feel unimportant.

(IF R IS UNMARRIED WITH NO CHILDREN, SKIP TO Q.F7)

(IF R IS UNMARRIED WITH CHILDREN, SKIP TO Q.F6)

[SHOW CARD] Thinking about the amount of respect your (husband/wife) shows you, would you say you get a lot of respect, some respect, a little respect, <u>very</u> little respect, or no respect?

1. A LOT	2. SOME	3. A LITTLE	4. VERY LITTLE	5. NONE	8. DK

F6. IF R HAS CHILDREN ASK, "Now think about how much respect your children show you. Do they show you a lot of respect, some respect, a little respect, <u>very</u> little respect, or no respect?"

1. A LOT	2. SOME	3. A LITTLE	4. VERY LITTLE	5. NONE	8. DK

F7. How much respect do you think your friends show you? Do they show you a lot of respect, some respect, a little respect, <u>very</u> little respect, or no respect?

1. A LOT	2. SOME	3. A LITTLE	4. VERY LITTLE	5. NONE	8. DK

F8. IF R'S PARENT(S) STILL LIVING ASK, "Now think about your parents. Do your parents show you a lot of respect, some respect, a little respect, very little respect, or no respect?"

[1. A LOT] [2. SOME] [3. A LITTLE] [4. VERY LITTLE] [5. NONE] [8. DK]

(IF R IS UNMARRIED WITH NO CHILDREN, SKIP TO Q.F11)

(IF R IS UNMARRIED WITH CHILDREN, SKIP TP Q.F10)

F9. Some (husbands/wives) help their (wives/husbands). They do things that make things easier for their (wife/husband). Some (husbands/wives) aren't very helpful to their (wife/husband) for various reasons. How much help do you get from your (husband/wife)? Does (he/she) give you a lot of help, some help, a little help, very little help, or no help?

[1. A LOT] [2. SOME] [3. A LITTLE] [4. VERY LITTLE] [5. NO HELP] [8. DK]

F10. What about your children...how much help do they give you? Do they give you a lot of help, some, a little, very little, or no help?

[1. A LOT] [2. SOME] [3. A LITTLE] [4. VERY LITTLE] [5. NO HELP] [8.DK]

F11. How much help do you get from your friends...a lot, some, a little, very little, or none?

[1. A LOT] [2. SOME] [3. A LITTLE] [4. VERY LITTLE] [5. NONE] [8. DK]

F12. IF R'S PARENT(S) STILL LIVING ASK, "What about your parents...how much help do they give you? Do they give you a lot, some, a little, very little, or none?"

[1. A LOT] [2. SOME] [3. A LITTLE] [4. VERY LITTLE] [5. NONE] [8. DK]

F13. What about your relatives (and in-laws if R IS MARRIED)? How much help do they give you...a lot, some, a little, very little, or none?

[1. A LOT] [2. SOME] [3. A LITTLE] [4. VERY LITTLE] [5. NONE] [8. DK]

F14. Now I want you to think about how much understanding people give you when things aren't going well for you. A person who's understanding is someone you can confide in and trust. This person gives you emotional support and shows concern for your feelings and worries and sometimes gives you useful advice. A person who is not understanding is someone who's more concerned about themselves and is not sympathetic to your troubles.

(IF R IS UNMARRIED WITH NO CHILDREN, SKIP TO Q.F16)

(IF R IS UNMARRIED WITH CHILDREN, SKIP TO Q.F15)

How much understanding do you get from your (husband/wife) when things aren't going well for you? Do you get a lot of understanding, some, a little, very little, or none?

[1. A LOT] [2. SOME] [3. A LITTLE] [4. VERY LITTLE] [5. NONE] [8. DK]

F15. How much understanding do you get from your children when things aren't going well for you...a lot, some, a little, very little, or none?

[1. ALOT] [2. SOME] [3. A LITTLE] [4. VERY LITTLE] [5. NONE] [8. DK]

F16. How much understanding do you get from your friends when things aren't going well for you...a lot, some, a little, very little, or none?

| 1. A LOT | 2. SOME | 3. A LITTLE | 4. VERY LITTLE | 5. NONE | 8. DK |

F17. IF R'S PARENT(S) STILL LIVING ASK, "How much understanding do you get from your parents when things aren't going well for you...a lot, some, a little, very little, or none?

| 1. A LOT | 2. SOME | 3. A LITTLE | 4. VERY LITTLE | 5. NONE | 8. DK |

F18. Have you ever felt deserted or abandoned by someone whom you thought cared about you?

| 1. YES | | 5. NO | -- GO TO Q.F19

F18a. Can you tell me something about what happened?

F18b. Have there been any other times in which you've felt deserted or abandoned?

F18c. [IF APPROPRIATE] Have you ever felt this way in the past year?

| 1. YES | | 5. NO |

F19. Now a question about community agencies that help people. Are there any community agencies you've gone to for problems you've had?

| 1. YES | | 5. NO | -- GO TO Q.F20

F19a. Which agencies have you gone to? [NUMBER THEM IF MORE THAN ONE]

1. _____   3. _____

2. _____   4. _____

F19b. Now I'd like to know how much help you got from (this agency/these agencies). Did they help you a lot, some, a little, or not at all? (IF R NAMED MORE THAN ONE AGENCY, TAKE UP TO THE FIRST FOUR AGENCIES AND SAY, "Starting with _____, did they help you a lot, some, a little, or not at all?)

1. | 1. HELP A LOT | 2. SOME | 3. A LITTLE | 4. NOT AT ALL |

2. | 1. HELP A LOT | 2. SOME | 3. A LITTLE | 4. NOT AT ALL |

3. | 1. HELP A LOT | 2. SOME | 3. A LITTLE | 4. NOT AT ALL |

4. | 1. HELP A LOT | 2. SOME | 3. A LITTLE | 4. NOT AT ALL |

F19c. Which agency did you go to for the most important problem?

F19c1. What kind of problem was it?

F20. Do you belong to any clubs, organizations, or associations in which you attend functions or meetings pretty regularly?

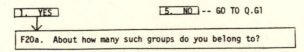

| 1. YES | | 5. NO | -- GO TO Q.G1

F20a. About how many such groups do you belong to?

SECTION G: HEALTH

G1. Now I'd like to ask you some questions about your health. Do you have any physical health problems?

| 1. YES | 5. NO | 8. DON'T KNOW |

— GO TO Q.G2 —

G1a. What kind of problems do you have?

G1b. Does it interfere with your work at all? (IF MORE THAN ONE PROBLEM, ASK, "Do any of these problems interfere with your work?")

| 1. YES | 5. NO |

G1c. Does it interfere with your personal or family life in any way? (IF MORE THAN ONE PROBLEM, ASK, "Do any of your health problems interfere with your personal or family life?")

| 1. YES | 5. NO |

G1d. Does it keep you from pursuing any activities that you'd like to do? (IF MORE THAN ONE PROBLEM, ASK, "Do any of your health problems keep you from pursuing any activities that you'd like to do?")

| 1. YES | 5. NO |

G1e. Have you done anything about (this/these) problem(s)?

| 1. YES | 5. NO |

G1e1. What have you done?

G2. In general, do you feel healthy enough to carry out the things you'd like to do?

| 1. YES | 5. NO | 8. DK | 9. NA |

G3. Do you worry about your health? Do you worry a lot, some, a little, or never?

| 1. A LOT | 2. SOME | 3. A LITTLE | 4. NEVER |

G4. Now I'd like to ask you more specific questions about your health?

Do you feel weak all over much of the time?

| 1. YES | 5. NO | 8. DK | 9. NA |

G5. Have you had periods of days, weeks, or months when you couldn't take care of things because you couldn't "get going?"

| 1. YES | 5. NO | 8. DK | 9. NA |

G6. In general, would you say that most of the time you are in high (very good) spirits, good spirits, low spirits, or very low spirits?

| 1. HIGH | 2. GOOD | 3. LOW | 4. VERY LOW | 8. DK | 9. NA |

G7. Do you every so often suddenly feel hot all over?

| 1. YES | 5. NO | 8. DK | 9. NA |

G8. Have you ever been bothered by your heart beating hard? Would you say often, sometimes, or never?

| 1. OFTEN | 2. SOMETIMES | 3. NEVER | 8. DK | 9. NA |

G9. Would you say your appetite is poor, fair, good, or too good?

| 1. POOR | 2. FAIR | 3. GOOD | 4. TOO GOOD | 8. DK | 9. NA |

G10. Do you have periods of such great restlessness that you cannot sit long in a chair (cannot sit still very long)?

| 1. YES | 5. NO | 8. DK | 9. NA |

G11. Do you worry a lot?

| 1. YES | 5. NO | 8. DK | 9. NA |

G12. Have you ever had any fainting spells? Would you say never, a few times, or more than a few times?

| 1. NEVER | 2. A FEW TIMES | 3. MORE THAN A FEW TIMES | 8. DK | 9. NA |

G13. Do you ever have trouble getting to sleep or staying asleep? Would you say often, sometimes, or never?

| 1. OFTEN | 2. SOMETIMES | 3. NEVER | 8. DK | 9. NA |

G14. Are you bothered by acid or a sour stomach several times a week?

| 1. YES | 5. NO | 8. DK | 9. NA |

G15. Have you ever been bothered by shortness of breath when you were not exercising or working hard? Would you say often, sometimes, or never?

| 1. OFTEN | 2. SOMETIMES | 3. NEVER | 8. DK | 9. NA |

G16. Have you ever been bothered by nervousness (irritable, fidgety, tense)? Would you say often, sometimes, or never?

| 1. OFTEN | 2. SOMETIMES | 3. NEVER | 8. DK | 9. NA |

G17. Does your memory seem all right?

[1. YES]   [5. NO]   [8. DK]   [9. NA]

G18. Have you ever been bothered by "cold sweats" or unusual sweating? Would you
      say often, sometimes, or never?

[1. OFTEN]   [2. SOMETIMES]   [3. NEVER]   [8. DK]   [9. NA]

G19. Do your hands ever tremble enough to bother you? Would you say often,
      sometimes, or never?

[1. OFTEN]   [2. SOMETIMES]   [3. NEVER]   [8. DK]   [9. NA]

G20. Does there seem to be a clogging in your head or nose much of the time?

[1. YES]   [5. NO]   [8. DK]   [9. NA]

G21. Do you have personal worries that get you down physically?

[1. YES]   [5. NO]   [8. DK]   [9. NA]

G22. Do you feel somewhat alone, even among friends?

[1. YES]   [5. NO]   [8. DK]   [9. NA]

G23. Do you feel like nothing ever turns out for you the way you want it to?

[1. YES]   [5. NO]   [8. DK]   [9. NA]

G24. Do you sometimes wonder if anything is worthwhile anymore?

[1. YES]   [5. NO]   [8. DK]   [9. NA]

G25. Are you ever troubled with headaches or pains in the head? Would you say
      often, sometimes, or never?

[1. OFTEN]   [2. SOMETIMES]   [3. NEVER]   [8. DK]   [9. NA]

SECTION G(B): OTHER HEALTH ITEMS

GB1. Are you ever bothered by pain or ailments in some other part of your body
      (other than your head)?

[1. YES]   [5. NO]   [8. DK]   [9. NA]

GB2. Do you find it difficult to get up in the morning? Often, sometimes, rarely,
      or never?

[1. OFTEN]   [2. SOMETIMES]   [3. HARDLY EVER]   [4. NEVER]

GB3. Have you ever had spells of dizziness? Many times, sometimes, hardly ever, or never?

| 1. MANY TIMES | | 2. SOMETIMES | | 3. HARDLY EVER | | 4. NEVER |

GB4. Do you ever have a bloated feeling?

| 1. YES | | 5. NO | | 8. DK | | 9. NA |

GB5. Do you ever feel numb in some part of your body?

| 1. YES | | 5. NO | | 8. DK | | 9. NA |

GB6. Do you suffer from severe itching?

| 1. YES | | 5. NO | | 8. DK | | 9. NA |

GB7. Does your mouth feel dry a lot?

| 1. YES | | 5. NO | | 8. DK | | 9. NA |

GB8. Have you ever had a "sinking down feeling" (like being depressed)?

| 1. YES | | 5. NO | | 8. DK | | 9. NA |

GB9. Do you have high blood pressure?

| 1. YES | | 5. NO | | 8. DK | | 9. NA |

GB10. Do you smoke cigarettes?

| 1. YES | | 5. NO |

GB10a. Do you smoke more or less than one pack a day?

| 1. MORE THAN ONE PACK | | 5. LESS THAN |

GB10b. Did you used to smoke?

| 1. YES | | 5. NO |

GB11. Do you have two or more drinks of alcohol per day?

| 1. YES | | 5. NO | -- GO TO Q.GB12

GB11a. Is it usually beer, wine, or liquor?

| 1. BEER | | 3. WINE | | 5. LIQUOR |

GB11b. Have you or has anyone else thought you had a drinking problem?

| 1. YES | | 5. NO |

GB12. Do you have any drug problem at all?

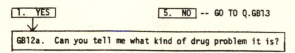

| 1. YES | | 5. NO | -- GO TO Q.GB13 |

| GB12a. Can you tell me what kind of drug problem it is? |

GB13. Some people think about their health a lot each day, while others almost
never think about it. What about you? How frequently do you think about
your health? Would you say you think about it often, sometimes, rarely,
or never?

| 1. OFTEN | 2. SOMETIMES | 4. RARELY | 5. NEVER |

GB14. Compared to other people your age, how often are you likely to get sick?
Would you say you get sick more often, just as often, or less often than
other people your age?

| 1. MORE OFTEN | 2. JUST AS OFTEN | 3. LESS OFTEN |

GB15. Would you say your health in general is excellent, good, fair, or poor?

| 1. EXCELLENT | 2. GOOD | 4. FAIR | 5. POOR |

GB16. Have you ever had a physical or health problem that you saw a doctor about
several times but you found no relief and the doctor couldn't find anything
wrong with you?

| 1. YES | 5. NO | 8. DK | 9. NA |

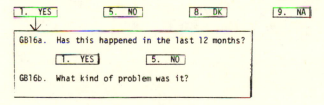

GB16a. Has this happened in the last 12 months?

| 1. YES | 5. NO |

GB16b. What kind of problem was it?

GB17. In the past 12 months, how many times have you gone to a doctor (M.D.) ?

| 0 | 1 | 2 | 3 | 4 | 5 | 6 | 7 | 8 | 9 | 10+ |

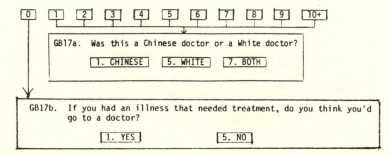

GB17a. Was this a Chinese doctor or a White doctor?

| 1. CHINESE | 5. WHITE | 7. BOTH |

GB17b. If you had an illness that needed treatment, do you think you'd
go to a doctor?

| 1. YES | 5. NO |

GB18. In the past 12 months , how many times have you gone to a Chinese Herbalist or had someone go for you?

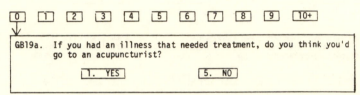

| 0 | 1 | 2 | 3 | 4 | 5 | 6 | 7 | 8 | 9 | 10+ |

GB18a. If you had an illness that needed treatment, do you think you'd go to an herbalist?

1. YES   5. NO

GB19. In the past 12 months, how many times have you gone to an acupuncturist?

| 0 | 1 | 2 | 3 | 4 | 5 | 6 | 7 | 8 | 9 | 10+ |

GB19a. If you had an illness that needed treatment, do you think you'd go to an acupuncturist?

1. YES   5. NO

GB20. Now I'd like to ask you some questions about medication or treatment. About how often do you use Chinese medicines like Po Chai Yuen or Chinese herb teas like Hop Chai Cha...once a week, once a month, a few times a year, or not at all?

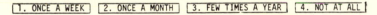

1. ONCE A WEEK   2. ONCE A MONTH   3. FEW TIMES A YEAR   4. NOT AT ALL

GB21. How often do you drink soups made with Chinese herbs...everyday, a few times a week, once a week, once a month, less often, or never?

| 1. EVERYDAY | 2. A FEW TIMES A WEEK | 3. LESS OFTEN | 4.NEVER |

GB22. Have you ever gone to a Chinese temple or to church to pray for health when you've been sick?

1. YES   5. NO

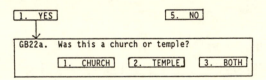

GB22a. Was this a church or temple?

1. CHURCH   2. TEMPLE   3. BOTH

GB23. Have you ever gone to a Chinese temple or to church to pray for a family member's health when they've been sick?

1. YES   5. NO

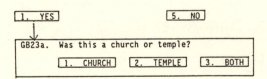

GB23a. Was this a church or temple?

1. CHURCH   2. TEMPLE   3. BOTH

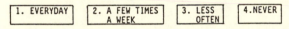

GB24. Different people do different things when they have a health condition. Some people go to a private doctor or to one of the community clinics or to an acupuncturist or an herbalist or else they take care of the problem themselves and don't seek help. I'm going to give you several cards, one at a time. Each card has a health condition typed on it. [SHOW CARD] On this page are listed different health care agencies or services--an acupuncturist, an herbalist, the Health Center #4, the Northeast Mental Health Clinic, NEMS or "that yellow card place", a private doctor or dentist, Telegraph Hill Medical Clinic, or any other agency or service. Also, there's a place for where you'd not seek outside help but take care of the health condition yourself. There's also a place for "don't know" if you don't know what you'd do. When I give you a card, please put it under the heading of the place you'd go or think you'd go if you had this health condition.

What would you do if you...	Acupuncturist	Herbalist	Health Center #4	Northeast Mental Health Clinic	NEMS - Yellow Card	Private Doctor or Dentist	Telegraph Hill Medical Clinic	Other Agency or Service	Take care of it myself	Don't know
a. had a cold										
b. had a urinary problem										
c. had a back pain										
d. had a chest pain										
e. had constant tireness										
f. had high blood pressure										
g. had diabetes										
h. had a burn that blistered										
i. couldn't sleep for 1 month										
j. needed a check-up for job or school										
[ASK WOMEN ONLY] k. needed prenatal care (for women going to have baby)										
l. wanted to make sure your child is healthy and stays healthy										
m. had a depression that won't go away										
n. had a sore thoat										
o. had a sore tooth										
p. had teeth that needed cleaning										

GB25. People get their information about health or illness from a variety of sources like T.V., the radio, newspaper articles, health programs in the community, pamphlets, family or friends, the doctor or dentist, from a clinic, or from some other source. Where do you get most of your information about health or illness?

GB26. What kinds of things do you think are necessary to do to keep healthy?

GB27. Do you do anything to keep yourself healthy?

| 1. YES | 5. NO |

GB27a. What do you do?

GB28. OK. Now I'd like you to tell me if you think any of the following things that I'll mention are necessary in order to keep healthy. Do you think it's necessary to _____ in order to be healthy?

a. exercise daily | 1. YES | 5. NO | 8. DK |

b. get dental check-ups and have your teeth cleaned twice a year | 1. YES | 5. NO | 8. DK |

c. get a tetanus (lockjaw) shot every 10 years | 1. YES | 5. NO | 8. DK |

d. drink three glasses of nonalcoholic liquids daily | 1. YES | 5. NO | 8. DK |

e. get enough sleep to feel rested the next day | 1. YES | 5. NO | 8. DK |

f. be aware of changes in how you feel or look | 1. YES | 5. NO | 8. DK |

g. take multiple vitamins daily | 1. YES | 5. NO | 8. DK |

h. eat fresh fruits and vegetables daily | 1. YES | 5. NO | 8. DK |

i. eat rice, noodles, or bread daily | 1. YES | 5. NO | 8. DK |

j. eat protein like meat, fish, or bean curd daily | 1. YES | 5. NO | 8. DK |

GB29. Even though we may feel we should eat or do certain things to be halthy, sometime we don't do these things for a variety of reasons. Can you tell me which of these things you actually do? Do you...

a. exercise daily | 1. YES | 5. NO | 8. DK |

b. get dental check-ups and have your teeth cleaned twice a year | 1. YES | 5. NO | 8. DK |

c. get a tetanus (lockjaw) shot every 10 years | 1. YES | 5. NO | 8. DK |

d. drink three glasses of nonalcoholic liquids daily | 1. YES | 5. NO | 8. DK |

e. get enough sleep to feel rested the next day | 1. YES | 5. NO | 8. DK |

f. be aware of changes in how you feel or look | 1. YES | 5. NO | 8. DK |

g. take multiple vitamins daily | 1. YES | 5. NO | 8. DK |

h. eat fresh fruits and vegetables daily | 1. YES | 5. NO | 8. DK |

i. eat rice, noodles, or bread daily | 1. YES | 5. NO | 8. DK |

j. eat protein like meat, fish, or bean curd daily | 1. YES | 5. NO | 8. DK |

GB30. In general, how do you feel about your health...very satisfied, somewhat satisfied, not too satisfied, or not satisfied at all?

| 1. VERY SATISFIED | 2. SOMEWHAT SATISFIED | 3. NOT TOO SATISFIED | 4. NOT SATISFIED AT ALL |

This ends the section on health. Is there anything else about your health that I forgot to ask that you'd like to tell me about?

| 1. YES | 5. NO |

SECTION H: LIFE SATISFACTION AND LIFE PROBLEMS

H1. We've talked about different aspects of your life--your housing, neighborhood, job, health, and opinions. Now I'd like us to talk about your life as a whole and some of your feelings about it. You might want to take a little time in thinking through these questions because they are broad questions and important questions about your life.

First, people strive for different things in life. Are there things in your life that you're striving for?

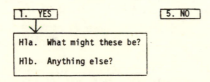

H2. As you think about the best life you'd want for yourself, what would that be? (IF VAGUE OR SHORT ANSWER GIVEN, ASK "Could you describe that more fully, what the best life for you would be?")

H3. Now I'd like you to think about your life as it is right now. What things in your life are most satisfying for you now...things that make you feel very happy, or very good, or very contented?

H3a. Are there any other things you're most satisfied with?

H4. Now try to think about what things in your life you are least satisfied with ...things you're not very happy about, things that could be a lot better. What would they be?

H4a. Are there any other things you're least satisfied with?

H5. (SHOW CARD)Here is a picture of a ladder. At the bottom of the ladder is the worst life you might expect to have. A person who is here would be very dissatisfied with (his/her) life. At the top of the ladder is the best life you might expect to have. A peson who is here would be very satisfied with (his/her) life. Where would you put yourself on the ladder to show where your life is now? (HAVE R TELL YOU WHAT RUNG NUMBER S/HE IS POINTING TO?)

| 1 | 2 | 3 | 4 | 5 | 6 | 7 | 8 | 9 |

H6. OK, now think about what your life was like five years ago? What place on the ladder represents where your life was five years ago?

| 1 | 2 | 3 | 4 | 5 | 6 | 7 | 8 | 9 |

H7. Now think about where you'd expect your life to be five years from now. Where exactly on the ladder do you expect your life to be five years from now?

| 1 | 2 | 3 | 4 | 5 | 6 | 7 | 8 | 9 |

H8. Now I'd like you to think about how you would describe your life now. For example I'd like you to think about how boring or interesting your life is right now. [SHOW CARD] Could you tell me if you think your life is <u>very boring</u>, <u>pretty boring</u>, <u>slightly boring</u>, <u>neutral</u>, <u>slightly interesting</u>, <u>pretty interesting</u>, or <u>very interesting</u>?

| 1.VERY BORING | 2.PRETTY BORING | 3.SLIGHTLY BORING | 4.NEUTRAL | 5.SLIGHTLY INTERESTING | 6.PRETTY INTERESTING | 7.VERY INTERESTING |

H9. [SHOW CARD] Now how would you describe your life in terms of how enjoyable or miserable it is? It is <u>very enjoyable</u>, <u>pretty enjoyable</u>, <u>slightly enjoyable</u>, <u>neutral</u>, <u>slightly miserable</u>, <u>pretty miserable</u>, or <u>very miserable</u>?

| 1.VERY ENJOYABLE | 2.PRETTY ENJOYABLE | 3.SLIGHTLY ENJOYABLE | 4.NEUTRAL | 5.SLIGHTLY MISERABLE | 6.PRETTY MISERABLE | 7.VERY MISERABLE |

H10. (SHOW CARD) How easy or hard is your life right now? Is it <u>very easy</u>, <u>pretty easy</u>, <u>slightly easy</u>, <u>neutral</u>, <u>slightly hard</u>, <u>pretty hard</u>, or <u>very hard</u>?

| 1. VERY EASY | 2. PRETTY EASY | 3. SLIGHTLY EASY | 4. NEUTRAL | 5. SLIGHTLY HARD | 6. PRETTY HARD | 7. VERY HARD |

H10a. What things make your life hard right now?

H11. [SHOW CARD] How full or empty do you feel your life is now? Is it <u>very full</u>, <u>pretty full</u>, <u>slightly full</u>, <u>neutral</u>, <u>slightly empty</u>, <u>pretty empty</u>, or <u>very empty</u>?

| 1.VERY FULL | 2.PRETTY FULL | 3.SLIGHTLY FULL | 4.NEUTRAL | 5.SLIGHTLY EMPTY | 6.PRETTY EMPTY | 7.VERY EMPTY |

H12. [SHOW CARD] How would you describe your life in terms of how discouraging or hopeful you feel about it? Is it <u>very discouraging</u>, <u>pretty discouraging</u>, <u>slightly discouraging</u>, <u>neutral</u>, <u>slightly hopeful</u>, <u>pretty hopeful</u>, or <u>very hopeful</u>?

| 1.VERY DISCOURAGING | 2.PRETTY DISCOURAGING | 3.SLIGHTLY DISCOURAGING | 4.NEUTRAL | 5.SLIGHTLY HOPEFUL | 6.PRETTY HOPEFUL | 7.VERY HOPEFUL |

H13. [SHOW CARD] How tied down or free do you feel your life is now? Is it <u>very tied down</u>, <u>pretty tied down</u>, <u>slightly tied down</u>, <u>neutral</u>, <u>slightly free</u>, <u>pretty free</u>, or <u>very free</u>?

| 1.VERY TIED DOWN | 2.PRETTY TIED DOWN | 3.SLIGHTLY TIED DOWN | 4.NEUTRAL | 5.SLIGHTLY FREE | 6.PRETTY FREE | 7.VERY FREE |

H14. How disappointing or rewarding do you feel your life is now? Is it <u>very disappointing</u>, <u>pretty disappointing</u>, <u>slightly disappointing</u>, <u>neutral</u>, <u>slightly rewarding</u>, <u>pretty rewarding</u>, or <u>very rewarding</u>?

| 1.VERY DISAPPOINTING | 2.PRETTY DISAPPOINTING | 3.SLIGHTLY DISAPPOINTING | 4.NEUTRAL | 5.SLIGHTLY REWARDING | 6.PRETTY REWARDING | 7.VERY REWARDING |

H15. [SHOW CARD] Some people feel that they've had a lot of opportunities in life, some feel they've had some opportunities in life, and some feel they haven't been given a chance. Where do you feel your life falls on this scale?

A LOT OF OPPORTUNITIES [1] [2] [3] [4] SOME [5] [6] [7] DOESN'T GIVE ME A CHANCE

H16. [SHOW CARD] How happy or unhappy do you feel about your life...very happy, pretty happy, slightly happy, neutral, slightly unhappy, pretty unhappy, or very unhappy?

1.VERY UNHAPPY	2.PRETTY HAPPY	3.SLIGHTLY HAPPY	4.NEUTRAL	5.SLIGHTLY UNHAPPY	6.PRETTY UNHAPPY	7.VERY UNHAPPY

H17. [SHOW CARD] Think about how your life compares with the life of White Americans. Do you think your life is much better than White Americans, somewhat better than White Americans, about the same as White Americans, somewhat worse than White Americans, or much worse than White Americans?

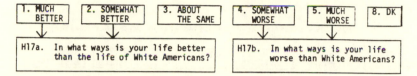

1. MUCH BETTER	2. SOMEWHAT BETTER	3. ABOUT THE SAME	4. SOMEWHAT WORSE	5. MUCH WORSE	8. DK

H17a. In what ways is your life better than the life of White Americans?	H17b. In what ways is your life worse than White Americans?

H18. [SHOW CARD] Now, which one of these statements best describes how you think your life compares to the Chinese who live in San Francisco Chinatown? My life is much better than the the average Chinatown resident, somewhat better than the average Chinatown resident, about the same as the average Chinatown resident, somewhat worse that the average Chinatown resident, or much worse than the average Chinatown resident.

1. MUCH BETTER	2. SOMEWHAT BETTER	3. ABOUT THE SAME	4. SOMEWHAT WORSE	5. MUCH WORSE	8. DON'T KNOW

H18a. In what ways is it better?	H18b. In what ways is it worse?

H19. Now I'd like to ask you about how satisfied or dissatisfied you are about a few things.

[SHOW CARD] How satisfied or dissatisfied are you with the community services available for Chinese Americans? Are you very satisfied, pretty satisfied, slightly satisfied, neutral, slightly dissatisfied, pretty dissatisfied, or very dissatisfied?

1.VERY SATISFIED	2.PRETTY SATISFIED	3.SLIGHTLY SATISFIED	4.NEUTRAL	5.SLIGHTLY DISSATISFIED	6.PRETTY DISSATISFIED	7.VERY DISSATISFIED

H20. How satisfied or dissatisfied are you with the overall living conditions in Chinatown?

1.VERY SATISFIED	2.PRETTY SATISFIED	3.SLIGHTLY SATISFIED	4.NEUTRAL	5.SLIGHTLY DISSATISFIED	6.PRETTY DISSATISFIED	7.VERY DISSATISFIED

H21. Now I'd like to ask you how satisfied you are with different things about yourself.

How satisfied or dissatisfied are you with the amount of education you've attained?

1.VERY SATISFIED	2.PRETTY SATISFIED	3.SLIGHTLY SATISFIED	4.NEUTRAL	5.SLIGHTLY DISSATISFIED	6.PRETTY DISSATISFIED	7.VERY DISSATISFIED

[IF R IS UNEMPLOYED--Q.D1--SKIP TO Q.H24]

H22. How satisfied or dissatisfied are you with your job?

| 1.VERY SATISFIED | 2.PRETTY SATISFIED | 3.SLIGHTLY SATISFIED | 4.NEUTRAL | 5.SLIGHTLY DISSATISFIED | 6.PRETTY DISSATISFIED | 7.VERY DISSATISFIED |

H23. How satisfied or dissatisfied are you with the amount of money you make?

| 1.VERY SATISFIED | 2.PRETTY SATISFIED | 3.SLIGHTLY SATISFIED | 4.NEUTRAL | 5.SLIGHTLY DISSATISFIED | 6.PRETTY DISSATISFIED | 7.VERY DISSATISFIED |

H24. How satisfied or dissatisfied are you with your health?

| 1.VERY SATISFIED | 2.PRETTY SATISFIED | 3.SLIGHTLY SATISFIED | 4.NEUTRAL | 5.SLIGHTLY DISSATISFIED | 6.PRETTY DISSATISFIED | 7.VERY DISSATISFIED |

H25. And how satisfied or dissatisfied are you with what you've accomplished in life?

| 1.VERY SATISFIED | 2.PRETTY SATISFIED | 3.SLIGHTLY SATISFIED | 4.NEUTRAL | 5.SLIGHTLY DISSATISFIED | 6.PRETTY DISSATISFIED | 7.VERY DISSATISFIED |

H26. How satisfied or dissatisfied are you with the amount of time you have for leisure activities?

| 1.VERY SATISFIED | 2.PRETTY SATISFIED | 3.SLIGHTLY SATISFIED | 4.NEUTRAL | 5.SLIGHTLY DISSATISFIED | 6.PRETTY DISSATISFIED | 7.VERY DISSATISFIED |

H27. How satisfied or dissatisfied are you with the companionship you have with others?

| 1.VERY SATISFIED | 2.PRETTY SATISFIED | 3.SLIGHTLY SATISFIED | 4.NEUTRAL | 5.SLIGHTLY DISSATISFIED | 6.PRETTY DISSATISFIED | 7.VERY DISSATISFIED |

[IF R DOESN'T LIVE WITH (HIS/HER) FAMILY--Q.B25--SKIP TO Q.H31]

H28. How satisfied or dissatisfied are you with your family life?

| 1.VERY SATISFIED | 2.PRETTY SATISFIED | 3.SLIGHTLY SATISFIED | 4.NEUTRAL | 5.SLIGHTLY DISSATISFIED | 6.PRETTY DISSATISFIED | 7.VERY DISSATISFIED |

[IF R IS UNMARRIED AND HAS NO CHILDREN--Q.A39-40--SKIP TO Q.H31]

[IF R IS UNMARRIED BUT HAS CHILDREN--Q.A39-40--SKIP TO Q.H30]

[IF R IS MARRIED--Q.A40--ASK Q.H29]

H29. How satisfied or dissatisfied are you with your marriage?

| 1.VERY SATISFIED | 2.PRETTY SATISFIED | 3.SLIGHTLY SATISFIED | 4.NEUTRAL | 5.SLIGHTLY DISSATISFIED | 6.PRETTY DISSATISFIED | 7.VERY DISSATISFIED |

H30. And how satisfied are you with the way your children have turned out?

| 1.VERY SATISFIED | 2.PRETTY SATISFIED | 3.SLIGHTLY SATISFIED | 4.NEUTRAL | 5.SLIGHTLY DISSATISFIED | 6.PRETTY DISSATISFIED | 7.VERY DISSATISFIED |

H31. How satisfied or dissatisfied are you with the way you handle problems?

| 1.VERY SATISFIED | 2.PRETTY SATISFIED | 3.SLIGHTLY SATISFIED | 4.NEUTRAL | 5.SLIGHTLY DISSATISFIED | 6.PRETTY DISSATISFIED | 7.VERY DISSATISFIED |

H32. How satisfied or dissatisfied are you with the way you handle responsibilities?

| 1.VERY SATISFIED | 2.PRETTY SATISFIED | 3.SLIGHTLY SATISFIED | 4.NEUTRAL | 5.SLIGHTLY DISSATISFIED | 6.PRETTY DISSATISFIED | 7.VERY DISSATISFIED |

H33. How satisfied or dissatisfied are you with the way you get along with people?

| 1.VERY SATISFIED | 2.PRETTY SATISFIED | 3.SLIGHTLY SATISFIED | 4.NEUTRAL | 5.SLIGHTLY DISSATISFIED | 6.PRETTY DISSATISFIED | 7.VERY DISSATISFIED |

H34. Now, overall, how satisfied or dissatisfied are you with your life as a whole?

| 1.VERY SATISFIED | 2.PRETTY SATISFIED | 3.SLIGHTLY SATISFIED | 4.NEUTRAL | 5.SLIGHTLY DISSATISFIED | 6.PRETTY DISSATISFIED | 7.VERY DISSATISFIED |

H35. Person A feels (s/he) has total control over (her/his) life, that (her/his) parents or family do not interfere with (her/his) life. Person B feels (s/he) has very little control over (her/his) life because the expectations or pressures of (her/his) parents or family determine what (s/he) does. Where do you fit between these two types of people? Is your life more like Person A or more like Person B or what?

| 1. LIKE PERSON A | 2. LIKE PERSON B | 7. OTHER_____ SPECIFY |

H36. What about expectations that your parents or relatives had for you? Are there any ways in which you feel you disappointed your parents?

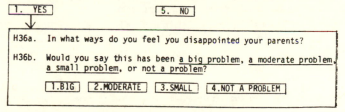

| 1. YES | 5. NO |

H36a. In what ways do you feel you disappointed your parents?

H36b. Would you say this has been a big problem, a moderate problem, a small problem, or not a problem?

| 1.BIG | 2.MODERATE | 3.SMALL | 4.NOT A PROBLEM |

[IF R IS UNMARRIED BUT HAS CHILDREN--Q.A39-40--SKIP TO Q.H41]

[IF R IS UNMARRIED AND HAS NO CHILDREN--Q.A39-40--SKIP TO Q.H43]

H37. When we think about expectations in our marriage, we think about what we'd like but are not getting in our marriage. Thinking about your marriage, do you ever feel that your (husband/wife) is not meeting your expectations?

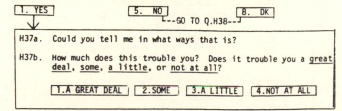

| 1. YES | 5. NO | 8. DK |
L--GO TO Q.H38--J

H37a. Could you tell me in what ways that is?

H37b. How much does this trouble you? Does it trouble you a great deal, some, a little, or not at all?

| 1.A GREAT DEAL | 2.SOME | 3.A LITTLE | 4.NOT AT ALL |

H38. Now looking at this in a different way, do you ever feel that you are not meeting your (husband's/wife's) expectations of you?

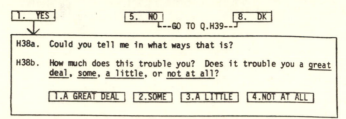

| 1. YES | 5. NO | 8. DK |

└--GO TO Q.H39--┘

H38a. Could you tell me in what ways that is?

H38b. How much does this trouble you? Does it trouble you a great deal, some, a little, or not at all?

| 1.A GREAT DEAL | 2.SOME | 3.A LITTLE | 4.NOT AT ALL |

H39. Even in the happiest marriages there are problems or conflicts. In your marriage, have you and your (husband/wife) ever had problems or conflicts with each other?

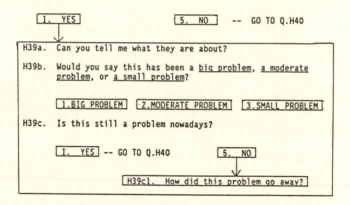

| 1. YES | 5. NO | -- GO TO Q.H40

H39a. Can you tell me what they are about?

H39b. Would you say this has been a big problem, a moderate problem, or a small problem?

| 1.BIG PROBLEM | 2.MODERATE PROBLEM | 3.SMALL PROBLEM |

H39c. Is this still a problem nowadays?

| I. YES | -- GO TO Q.H40 | 5. NO |

H39c1. How did this problem go away?

H40. Taking all things together, how would you describe your marriage? Would you say your marriage was very happy, a little happier than average, just about average, or not too happy?

| 1. VERY HAPPY | 2. LITTLE HAPPIER THAN AVERAGE | 3. JUST ABOUT AVERAGE· | 4. NOT TOO HAPPY |

[IF R IS NOT A PARENT--Q.A39--SKIP TO Q.H43]

H41. Most parents have had some problems in raising their children. What, if any, are the main problems you've had in raising your children?

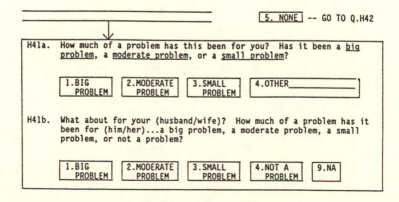

_____ | 5. NONE | -- GO TO Q.H42

H41a. How much of a problem has this been for you? Has it been a big problem, a moderate problem, or a small problem?

| 1.BIG PROBLEM | 2.MODERATE PROBLEM | 3.SMALL PROBLEM | 4.OTHER_____ |

H41b. What about for your (husband/wife)? How much of a problem has it been for (him/her)...a big problem, a moderate problem, a small problem, or not a problem?

| 1.BIG PROBLEM | 2.MODERATE PROBLEM | 3.SMALL PROBLEM | 4.NOT A PROBLEM | 9.NA |

H42. Some (men/women) feel they're not as good (fathers/mothers) as they'd like to be. Overall, would you say you're an <u>excellent</u> (father/mother), a <u>good</u> (father/mother), an <u>adequate</u> (father/mother), or <u>not a very good</u> (father/mother)?

| 1. EXCELLENT | 2. GOOD | 3. ADEQUATE | 4. NOT VERY GOOD |

H43. Everybody has some things he or she worries about. What kinds of things do you worry about the most?

_____

_____ | 5. NONE | -- GO TO Q.H44

> H43a. Do you worry about such things <u>all the time</u>, <u>a lot</u>, <u>sometimes</u>, <u>not very much</u>, or <u>never</u>?
>
> | 1. ALL THE TIME | 2. A LOT | 3. SOMETIMES | 4. NOT VERY MUCH | 5. NEVER |

H44. If something's bothering you, and you don't know what to do about it, what do you usually do?

(IF R DOES NOT MENTION TALKING IT OVER WITH SOMEONE, ASK "Would you talk to anyone about it?")

H44a. | 1. YES | | 5. NO |
                                    | H44a1. Why's that? |

H45. Have you ever felt like you just couldn't handle everyday pressures?

| 1. YES | | 5. NO |

> H45a. Think of a time when you felt that way very strongly. What was it about?
>
> H45b. How did you deal with it?
>
> H45c. Has this happened anytime in the last 12 months?
>
> | 1. YES | | 5. NO |

H46. Have you ever felt like some situation was driving you crazy?

| 1. YES | | 5. NO |

> H46a. Think of a time when you felt this way very strongly. What was it that was driving you crazy?
>
> H46b. When this (happened/happens), how do you deal with it?
>
> H46c. Has this happened anytime in the last 12 months?
>
> | 1. YES | | 5. NO |

H47. [SHOW CARD] Some people feel they can handle all their problems easily. Some feel they can't handle any problems easily. And some people feel somewhere in between. Do you think you can handle <u>all</u> problems easily, <u>most</u> problems easily, <u>some</u> problems easily, a <u>few</u> problems easily, or do you feel you <u>can't</u> handle any problems easily?

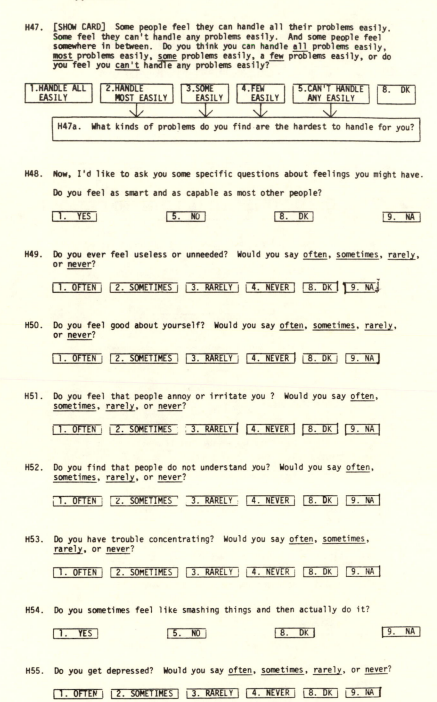

1.HANDLE ALL EASILY	2.HANDLE MOST EASILY	3.SOME EASILY	4.FEW EASILY	5.CAN'T HANDLE ANY EASILY	8. DK

H47a. What kinds of problems do you find are the hardest to handle for you?

H48. Now, I'd like to ask you some specific questions about feelings you might have.

Do you feel as smart and as capable as most other people?

1. YES	5. NO	8. DK	9. NA

H49. Do you ever feel useless or unneeded? Would you say <u>often</u>, <u>sometimes</u>, <u>rarely</u>, or <u>never</u>?

1. OFTEN	2. SOMETIMES	3. RARELY	4. NEVER	8. DK	9. NA

H50. Do you feel good about yourself? Would you say <u>often</u>, <u>sometimes</u>, <u>rarely</u>, or <u>never</u>?

1. OFTEN	2. SOMETIMES	3. RARELY	4. NEVER	8. DK	9. NA

H51. Do you feel that people annoy or irritate you ? Would you say <u>often</u>, sometimes, <u>rarely</u>, or <u>never</u>?

1. OFTEN	2. SOMETIMES	3. RARELY	4. NEVER	8. DK	9. NA

H52. Do you find that people do not understand you? Would you say <u>often</u>, sometimes, <u>rarely</u>, or <u>never</u>?

1. OFTEN	2. SOMETIMES	3. RARELY	4. NEVER	8. DK	9. NA

H53. Do you have trouble concentrating? Would you say <u>often</u>, <u>sometimes</u>, <u>rarely</u>, or <u>never</u>?

1. OFTEN	2. SOMETIMES	3. RARELY	4. NEVER	8. DK	9. NA

H54. Do you sometimes feel like smashing things and then actually do it?

1. YES	5. NO	8. DK	9. NA

H55. Do you get depressed? Would you say <u>often</u>, <u>sometimes</u>, <u>rarely</u>, or <u>never</u>?

1. OFTEN	2. SOMETIMES	3. RARELY	4. NEVER	8. DK	9. NA

H56. Do you find there are many things that have been making you angry?

| 1. YES | 5. NO | 8. DK | 9. NA |

H57. Do you find there are many things that have been making you upset at work or at home?

| 1. YES | 5. NO | 8. DK | 9. NA |

H58. Do you ever wish there was someone you could really talk to?

| 1. YES | 5. NO | 8. DK | 9. NA |

H59. Are you fearful of many things?

| 1. YES | 5. NO | 8. DK | 9. NA |

H60. Do you do many things that you later regret?

| 1. YES | 5. NO | 8. DK | 9. NA |

H61. At times do you have a strong urge to do something harmful or shocking?

| 1. YES | 5. NO | 8. DK | 9. NA |

H62. Do you find that frightening thoughts keep coming back in your mind?

| 1. YES | 5. NO | 8. DK | 9. NA |

H63. Do you worry about what people say?

| 1. YES | 5. NO | 8. DK | 9. NA |

H64. Does every little thing get on your nerves and wear you out?

| 1. YES | 5. NO | 8. DK | 9. NA |

H65. Do you sometime feel the need to apologize for no good reason?

| 1. YES | 5. NO | 8. DK | 9. NA |

H66. Do you often have trouble making decisions?

| 1. YES | 5. NO | 8. DK | 9. NA |

H67. If you had your life to live over again, would you do things very differently?

| 1. YES | 5. NO | 8. DK | 9. NA |

H67a. What would you differently? [PROBE FOR ELABORATION]

H68. Have you ever had a personal problem where you sought advice or help from someone?

| 1. YES | 5. NO |

H68a. Is there any problem you can think of where you'd seek advice or help from someone?

| 1. YES | 5. NO |

H68a1. What kind of problem might that be?

SKIP TO Q.H69c

H69. Thinking about the last time you had a problem where you sought advice or help from someone, what was the problem about? (IF R GIVES A VAGUE ANSWER, ASK "Can you tell me just a little more about that?") (IF R OBJECTS TO QUESTION AS TOO PERSONAL, SAY "You don't have to go into detail about the problem, I'd just like some general idea of what the problem was about.")

H69a. When was that? About how long ago did that happen?

_____ YEARS AGO   _____ MONTHS AGO   ☐ LESS THAN 1 MONTH AGO

H69b. [SHOW CARD] Here's a list of people you might have talked to about your problem. Did you talk to any of these people about your problem? Which ones?

☐ SPOUSE   ☐ NEIGHBOR

☐ SON   ☐ CO-WORKER

☐ DAUGHTER   ☐ SOCIAL WORKER, PSYCHOLOGIST, PSYCHIATRIST, COUNSELOR

☐ MOTHER
                            ☐ DOCTOR/NURSE
☐ FATHER
                            ☐ CHINESE DOCTOR, HERBALIST, OR ACUPUNCTURIST
☐ BROTHER

☐ SISTER   ☐ PERSON AT CHINESE TEMPLE

☐ OTHER RELATIVE   ☐ REVEREND, PRIEST, OR PASTOR

☐ GIRLFRIEND/BOYFRIEND   ☐ ASTROLOGIST OR SPIRITUAL READER

☐ FRIEND   ☐ OTHER

H69c. [SHOW CARD] I'm going to read you a list of things that happen when people have a personal problem. As I read each one, please tell me if you acted this way <u>a lot</u>, <u>a little</u>, or <u>not at all</u> when you had some very difficult problem.

		A LOT	A LITTLE	NOT AT ALL
a.	Were you depressed?	☐	☐	☐
b.	Were you nervous?	☐	☐	☐
c.	Did it affect your appetite or eating habits?	☐	☐	☐
d.	Did it affect your health?	☐	☐	☐
e.	Did you miss days at work?	☐	☐	☐
f.	Did you get angry or irritable more than usual?	☐	☐	☐
g.	Did you drink alcohol more than usual?	☐	☐	☐
h.	Did it cause problems in your family life?	☐	☐	☐
i.	Did you have trouble sleeping or have a restless sleep?	☐	☐	☐

j. Did it have any other effect on you?
   Like what? _____
   What else? _____

H70. Now I'd like you to think more generally about some of the ways in which you deal with your frustrations or problems. I'd like to know what you usually do or say when you're having frustrations or problems in your life.

_____

_____

H71. [SHOW CARD] I'm going to read some things people do to deal with a difficult personal problem. As I read them, please tell me if you do <u>any</u> of these things to help you bear your problems better or to forget your problems. Tell me if you do them <u>often</u>, <u>sometimes</u>, <u>rarely</u>, or <u>never</u> when you have a problem. When you have a problem, do you...

		OFTEN	SOMETIMES	RARELY	NEVER
a.	Reflect or analyze the problem?	☐	☐	☐	☐
b.	Drink liquor?	☐	☐	☐	☐
c.	Get high?	☐	☐	☐	☐
d.	Take Western pills or medicine?	☐	☐	☐	☐
e.	Take Chinese pills, herbs, or medicine?	☐	☐	☐	☐
f.	Keep busy by working?	☐	☐	☐	☐

H71. [CONTINUED]

When you have a problem, what do you do to deal with it or forget it, do you...

		OFTEN	SOMETIMES	RARELY	NEVER
g.	Go out and have a good time?	☐	☐	☐	☐
h.	Play Mah Jong or cards?	☐	☐	☐	☐
i.	Relax and try not to think about the problem?	☐	☐	☐	☐
j.	Watch T.V.?	☐	☐	☐	☐
k.	Listen to music?	☐	☐	☐	☐
l.	Do Tai-chi, exercise, or play sports?	☐	☐	☐	☐
m.	Meditate (like TM)?	☐	☐	☐	☐
n.	Seek advice from others?	☐	☐	☐	☐

H72. Have you ever gone to a mental health center or seen a mental health professional for any problem you've had?

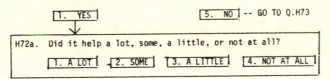

```
   1. YES                    5. NO  -- GO TO Q.H73
     |
     v
H72a.  Did it help a lot, some, a little, or not at all?
   1. A LOT   2. SOME   3. A LITTLE   4. NOT AT ALL
```

H73. Have you ever known anyone who was suffering from some kind of mental or emotional problem?

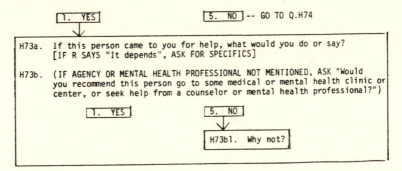

```
   1. YES                    5. NO  -- GO TO Q.H74
     |
     v
H73a.  If this person came to you for help, what would you do or say?
       [IF R SAYS "It depends", ASK FOR SPECIFICS]

H73b.  (IF AGENCY OR MENTAL HEALTH PROFESSIONAL NOT MENTIONED, ASK "Would
       you recommend this person go to some medical or mental health clinic or
       center, or seek help from a counselor or mental health professional?")

          1. YES              5. NO
                                |
                                v
                            H73b1.  Why not?
```

H74. Has any member of your family ever had a serious problem that caused him or her to act differently or feel differently than normal?

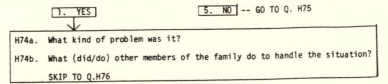

```
   1. YES                    5. NO  -- GO TO Q. H75
     |
     v
H74a.  What kind of problem was it?

H74b.  What (did/do) other members of the family do to handle the situation?

       SKIP TO Q.H76
```

H75. If such a situation were to happen, what would you do?

H76. Do you know of medical clinics or mental health centers that counsel people with mental or emotional problems?

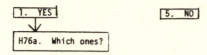

1. YES   5. NO

H76a. Which ones?

H77. What do you think causes mental problems or mental illness?

H78. Do you think there're any things that can be done to prevent mental problems or mental illness?

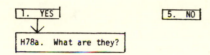

1. YES   5. NO

H78a. What are they?

H79. What do you think can be done to cure mental problems or mental illness?

SECTION I: PERSONAL DATA

I1. This is the last section of the interview. We just need to know a few things about your growing up.

On a regular basis, how many people lived in the dwelling unit (that is, the house, flat, or apartment) you grew up in? Including all family members, all relatives, and non-relatives?

☐1 ☐2 ☐3 ☐4 ☐5 ☐6 ☐7 ☐8 ☐9 ☐10 ☐11+

I2. How many of these people were immediate family members, which include your mother, father, brothers and sisters, and yourself?

☐1 ☐2 ☐3 ☐4 ☐5 ☐6 ☐7 ☐8 ☐9 ☐10 ☐11+

I3. Were there cousins, grandparents, aunts or uncles who also regularly lived in the household you grew up in?

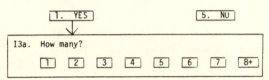

I4. Were there any people who lived with you on a regular basis when you grew up who were <u>not</u> related to you...such as boarders or friends?

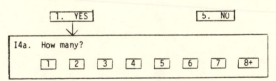

I5. Did anyone else who lived in your household sleep in the same room as you when you were a child (under the age of 12)?

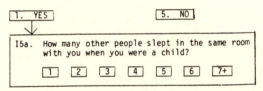

I6. Did anyone share the bed with you?

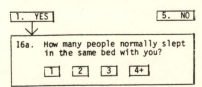

I7. How many older brothers and sisters do you have?

| 0 | | 1 | | 2 | | 3 | | 4 | | 5 | | 6 | | 7 | | 8 | | 9 | | 10+ |

I8. How many younger brothers and sisters do you have?

| 0 | | 1 | | 2 | | 3 | | 4 | | 5 | | 6 | | 7 | | 8 | | 9 | | 10+ |

I9. Was there any time in your growing up that either or both of your parents were absent from your home, say for any time longer than a couple of months, for any reason at all?

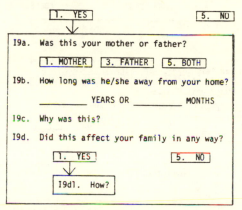

| 1. YES | 5. NO |

I9a. Was this your mother or father?

| 1. MOTHER | 3. FATHER | 5. BOTH |

I9b. How long was he/she away from your home?

_____ YEARS OR _____ MONTHS

I9c. Why was this?

I9d. Did this affect your family in any way?

| 1. YES | 5. NO |

I9d1. How?

[IF R IS NOT THE OLDEST CHILD--Q.I7--SKIP TO Q.I11]

I10. Did you feel that your parents had expectations of you as a first-born or as the oldest (son/daughter) that were different from their expectations of the other children?

| 1. YES | 5. NO |

I10a. What were these expectations?

I11. Did you feel that your parents treated you differently from your (brothers/ sisters/brothers and sisters) or did they treat all the children the same?

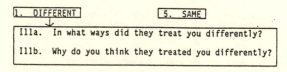

| 1. DIFFERENT | 5. SAME |

I11a. In what ways did they treat you differently?

I11b. Why do you think they treated you differently?

I12. Was your father born in the United States?

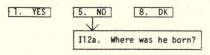

| 1. YES | 5. NO | 8. DK |

I12a. Where was he born?

I13. Was your mother born in the United States?

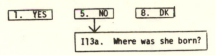

1. YES	5. NO	8. DK

↓

I13a. Where was she born?

I14. How many years of school did your father complete? [IF R IS UNSURE, OBTAIN BEST GUESS]

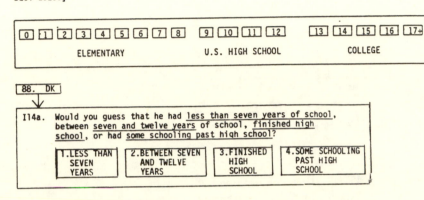

| 0 | 1 | 2 | 3 | 4 | 5 | 6 | 7 | 8 | | 9 | 10 | 11 | 12 | | 13 | 14 | 15 | 16 | 17+ |

ELEMENTARY   U.S. HIGH SCHOOL   COLLEGE

88. DK

↓

I14a. Would you guess that he had less than seven years of school, between seven and twelve years of school, finished high school, or had some schooling past high school?

1.LESS THAN SEVEN YEARS	2.BETWEEN SEVEN AND TWELVE YEARS	3.FINISHED HIGH SCHOOL	4.SOME SCHOOLING PAST HIGH SCHOOL

I15. How many years of school did your mother complete? [IF R IS UNSURE, OBTAIN BEST GUESS]

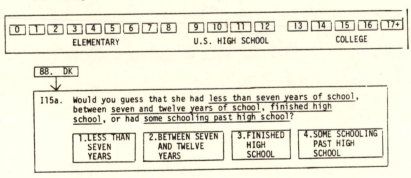

| 0 | 1 | 2 | 3 | 4 | 5 | 6 | 7 | 8 | | 9 | 10 | 11 | 12 | | 13 | 14 | 15 | 16 | 17+ |

ELEMENTARY   U.S. HIGH SCHOOL   COLLEGE

88. DK

↓

I15a. Would you guess that she had less than seven years of school, between seven and twelve years of school, finished high school, or had some schooling past high school?

1.LESS THAN SEVEN YEARS	2.BETWEEN SEVEN AND TWELVE YEARS	3.FINISHED HIGH SCHOOL	4.SOME SCHOOLING PAST HIGH SCHOOL

I16. What was your father's main occupation or job while you were growing up? [PROBE TO FIND OUT JOB TITLE AND SPECIFICS OF WHAT FATHER (DOES/DID) IN JOB]

I17. Did your mother ever work for pay while you were growing up?

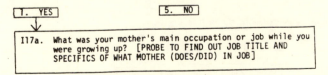

1. YES	5. NO

↓

I17a. What was your mother's main occupation or job while you were growing up? [PROBE TO FIND OUT JOB TITLE AND SPECIFICS OF WHAT MOTHER (DOES/DID) IN JOB]

I18. Do you think you come from a rich background, a poor background, or in between?

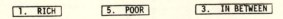

1. RICH	5. POOR	3. IN BETWEEN

I19. What about _now_...what class do you feel you belong to, upper class, upper-middle class, middle class, lower-middle class, or lower class?

| 1. UPPER | 2. UPPER-MIDDLE | 3. MIDDLE | 4. LOWER-MIDDLE | 5. LOWER |

[IF R IS _UNMARRIED_--Q.A40--SKIP TO Q.I21]

I20. [SHOW CARD] Would you please tell me the letter on this card which best represents your total _family_ income in 1978? This should include wages and salaries, net income from business, pensions, dividends, interest, rent from property, or any money you regularly get from family members. Just tell me the letter of the box on this page.

A. ☐	$000	I. ☐	$7,000 - $7,999
B. ☐	$001 - $999	J. ☐	$8,000 - $8,999
C. ☐	$1,000 - $1,999	K. ☐	$9,000 - $9,999
D. ☐	$2,000 - $2,999	L. ☐	$10,000 - $11,999
E. ☐	$3,000 - $3,999	M. ☐	$12,000 - $14,999
F. ☐	$4,000 - $4,999	N. ☐	$15,000 - $19,999
G. ☐	$5,000 - $5,999	O. ☐	$20,000 - $24,999
H. ☐	$6,000 - $6,999	P. ☐	$25,000 - $29,999
		Q. ☐	$30,000 OR MORE

I21. [SHOW CARD] What was your own _personal_ income in 1978? Again, please include wages, salaries, net income from business, pensions, dividends, interest, rent from property, or any money you regularly receive from family members or any other source. Just give the letter of the box on the page.

A. ☐	$000	I. ☐	$7,000 - $7,999
B. ☐	$001 - $999	J. ☐	$8,000 - $8,999
C. ☐	$1,000 - $1,999	K. ☐	$9,000 - $9,999
D. ☐	$2,000 - $2,999	L. ☐	$10,000 - $11,999
E. ☐	$3,000 - $3,999	M. ☐	$12,000 - $14,999
F. ☐	$4,000 - $4,999	N. ☐	$15,000 - $19,999
G. ☐	$5,000 - $5,999	O. ☐	$20,000 - $24,999
H. ☐	$6,000 - $6,999	P. ☐	$25,000 - $29,999
		Q. ☐	$30,000 OR MORE

I22. [SHOW CARD] What language do you speak at home now...only English, mostly English, both English and Chinese equally, mostly Chinese, only Chinese, or what?

| 1.ONLY ENGLISH | 2.MOSTLY ENGLISH | 3.BOTH ENGLISH AND CHINESE EQUALLY | 4.MOSTLY CHINESE | 5.ONLY CHINESE | 6.OTHER |

I22a. Which Chinese dialect is spoken?

| 1. SAAMYUP | 2. SEIYUP | 3. MANDARIN | 4.OTHER_____ |

[IF R HAS BEEN INTERVIEWED IN ENGLISH, SKIP TO Q.I31.]

I23. When you grew up as a child, what language was spoken in your home...only English, mostly English, both English and Chinese equally, mostly Chinese, only Chinese, or what?

| 1.ONLY ENGLISH | 2.MOSTLY ENGLISH | 3.BOTH ENGLISH AND CHINESE EQUALLY | 4.MOSTLY CHINESE | 5.ONLY CHINESE | 6.OTHER _____ |

I23a. Which Chinese dialect was spoken?

| 1. SAAMYUP | 2. SEIYUP | 3. MANDARIN | 4. OTHER_____ |

I24. When you grew up as a child, what language was spoken in your neighborhood... only English, mostly English, both English and Chinese equally, mostly Chinese, only Chinese, or what?

| 1.ONLY ENGLISH | 2.MOSTLY ENGLISH | 3.BOTH ENGLISH AND CHINESE EQUALLY | 4.MOSTLY CHINESE | 5.ONLY CHINESE | 6.OTHER _____ |

I24a. Which Chinese dialect was spoken?

| 1. SAAMYUP | 2. SEIYUP | 3. MANDARIN | 4. OTHER_____ |

I25. How important was it to your parents that you know the Chinese language... very important, somewhat important, somewhat unimportant, or not important at all, or it didn't matter?

| 1. VERY IMPORTANT | 2. SOMEWHAT IMPORTANT | 3. SOMEWHAT UNIMPORTANT | 4. NOT IMPORTANT AT ALL | 5. DIDN'T MATTER |

I26. Thinking about the friends you had as a child, would you say that they were all English-speaking, mostly English-speaking, half and half English and Chinese-speaking, mostly Chinese-speaking, all Chinese-speaking, or what?

| 1.ALL ENGLISH- SPEAKING | 2.MOSTLY ENGLISH- SPEAKING | 3.HALF & HALF ENGLISH & CHINESE | 4.MOSTLY CHINESE- SPEAKING | 5.ALL CHINESE SPEAKING | 6.OTHER _____ |

I27. Now, coming back to your present situation, what language is spoken in your neighborhood...mostly English, both English and Chinese equally, mostly Chinese, or what?

| 1. MOSTLY ENGLISH | 2. BOTH ENGLISH AND CHINESE EQUALLY | 3. MOSTLY CHINESE | 6. OTHER_____ |

I28. How important is it to you that your children know the Chinese language... very important, somewhat important, somewhat unimportant, not important at all, or it doesn't matter?

| 1.VERY IMPORTANT | 2.SOMEWHAT IMPORTANT | 3.SOMEWHAT UNIMPORTANT | 4.NOT IMPORTANT AT ALL | 5.DOESN'T MATTER |

I29. Thinking about the friends you have now, would you say that they are <u>all</u> English-speaking, <u>mostly</u> English-speaking, half and half English and Chinese-speaking, <u>mostly</u> Chinese speaking, <u>all</u> Chinese-speaking, or what?

1.ALL ENGLISH-SPEAKING	2.MOSTLY ENGLISH-SPEAKING	3.HALF & HALF ENGLISH & CHINESE	4.MOSTLY CHINESE-SPEAKING	5.ALL CHINESE-SPEAKING	6.OTHER _____

[IF R HAS BEEN INTERVIEWED IN ENGLISH, SKIP TO Q.I31]

I30. Now I am going to ask you some questions about whether or not you read, write, understand, and speak English. If you can't do any of these, don't be afraid to say so.

a. Can you read newspaper and books in English?

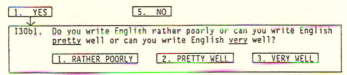

```
┌──────────┐              ┌──────────┐
│ 1.  YES  │              │ 5.  NO   │
└────┬─────┘              └──────────┘
     ↓
┌─────────────────────────────────────────────────────────────┐
│ I30a1.  Do you read English rather poorly or can you read English │
│         pretty well or can you read English very well?          │
│                                                                 │
│   ┌──────────────────┐  ┌─────────────────┐  ┌───────────────┐ │
│   │ 1. RATHER POORLY │  │ 2. PRETTY WELL  │  │ 3. VERY WELL  │ │
│   └──────────────────┘  └─────────────────┘  └───────────────┘ │
└─────────────────────────────────────────────────────────────┘
```

b. Can you write letters in English?

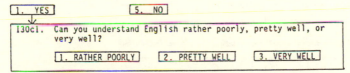

```
┌──────────┐              ┌──────────┐
│ 1.  YES  │              │ 5.  NO   │
└────┬─────┘              └──────────┘
     ↓
┌─────────────────────────────────────────────────────────────┐
│ I30b1.  Do you write English rather poorly or can you write English │
│         pretty well or can you write English very well?         │
│                                                                 │
│   ┌──────────────────┐  ┌─────────────────┐  ┌───────────────┐ │
│   │ 1. RATHER POORLY │  │ 2. PRETTY WELL  │  │ 3. VERY WELL  │ │
│   └──────────────────┘  └─────────────────┘  └───────────────┘ │
└─────────────────────────────────────────────────────────────┘
```

c. Can you understand a conversation in English?

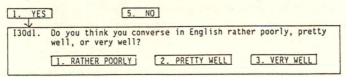

```
┌──────────┐              ┌──────────┐
│ 1.  YES  │              │ 5.  NO   │
└────┬─────┘              └──────────┘
     ↓
┌─────────────────────────────────────────────────────────────┐
│ I30c1.  Can you understand English rather poorly, pretty well, or │
│         very well?                                              │
│                                                                 │
│   ┌──────────────────┐  ┌─────────────────┐  ┌───────────────┐ │
│   │ 1. RATHER POORLY │  │ 2. PRETTY WELL  │  │ 3. VERY WELL  │ │
│   └──────────────────┘  └─────────────────┘  └───────────────┘ │
└─────────────────────────────────────────────────────────────┘
```

d. Can you carry on a conversation in English?

```
┌──────────┐              ┌──────────┐
│ 1.  YES  │              │ 5.  NO   │
└────┬─────┘              └──────────┘
     ↓
┌─────────────────────────────────────────────────────────────┐
│ I30d1.  Do you think you converse in English rather poorly, pretty │
│         well, or very well?                                     │
│                                                                 │
│   ┌──────────────────┐  ┌─────────────────┐  ┌───────────────┐ │
│   │ 1. RATHER POORLY │  │ 2. PRETTY WELL  │  │ 3. VERY WELL  │ │
│   └──────────────────┘  └─────────────────┘  └───────────────┘ │
└─────────────────────────────────────────────────────────────┘
```

[IF R ANSWERED "NO" TO Q.I30a, b, c, <u>or</u> d, ASK QI30e OTHERWISE GO TO Q.I31]

e. What problems have you because you don't know English well?

f. (IF R ANSWERED "NO" TO I30a, b, <u>and</u> d, ASK "Do you plan to learn English?")

```
┌──────────┐              ┌──────────┐
│ 1.  YES  │              │ 5.  NO   │
└──────────┘              └──────────┘
```

This is the end of our interview. I want to thank you for your cooperation
I know you have many things to do so I'm most appreciative of your taking
time out for this. Here's the resource booklet that's yours as a token of
our thanks. If you'd like, I can show you how to use the book.

[IF R WANTS DEMONSTRATION, BRIEFLY EXPLAIN CONTENTS OF HOW TO USE RESOURCE BOOK]
Here's the section you want, the first half of the book's in English, the
second half's in Chinese, now if you were interested in information on _____
you'd go to page _____ where you'd find questions commonly asked, followed by
information on the agencies, programs, or procedures that answer these related
questions. OK? I think the Resource Booklet can be very useful for you, your
family, or friends. So thank you again.

[IF R CANNOT READ, YOU CAN OFFER R THE CHOICE OF THE RESOURCE BOOKLET OR $5.00.
IF S/HE CHOOSES THE MONEY, WRITE AN I.O.U., TAKE DOWN HIS/HER NAME, SAY THAT
THE DIRECTOR WILL SEND YOU A CHECK, AND BE SURE TO INFORM THE DIRECTOR.]

[TO BE FILLED OUT AFTER THE INTERVIEW IS COMPLETED]

SECTION J: INTERVIEWER'S OBSERVATIONS

J1. What is R's sex?

| 1. MALE | | 2. FEMALE |

J2. Floor level of dwelling unit is _____ floor.

J3. Number of units in the building are _____ units.

J4. Was R suspicious about the study before the interview?

| 1. YES, VERY | | 3. YES, A LITTLE | | 5. NO |

J5. What was R's attitude at the beginning of the interview?

| 1. VERY COOPERATIVE | 2. SOMEWHAT COOPERATIVE | 3. UNCERTAIN, A LITTLE SUSPICIOUS | 4. NOT COOPERATIVE |

J6. Was there any change in R's attitude at the end of the interview?

| 1. NO CHANGE | 2. BECAME MORE COOPERATIVE | 3. BECAME LESS COOPERATIVE |

J6a. When did this happen? What section? What external event?

J7. In terms of sections, how would you describe R's interest level?

	HIGH	MILD	LOW (SEEMED BORED)	NA
a. Residence and Neighborhood				
b. Building, Dwelling, & Crowding				
c. Immigrant				
d. Job				
e. Psychological Attitudes				
f. Social Support				
g. Health				
h. Life Satisfaction & Problems				
i. Personal Data				

J8. In general, how would you describe R's interest level?

| 1. HIGH | | 2. MILD | | 3. LOW |

J9. Did R have any difficulty understanding the questions or format at any time?

| 1. YES | | 5. NO |

J9a. What sections? Which questions? Describe difficulties.

✓	QUESTION NO(S).	DESCRIBE DIFFICULTIES
a. Residence & Neighborhood		
b. Building, Dwelling, & Crowding		
c. Immigrant		
d. Job		
e. Psychological Attitudes		
f. Social Support		
g. Health		
h. Life Satisfaction & Problems		
i. Personal Data		

J9b. What did you do?

J10. Was R illiterate (couldn't read)?

| 1. YES | | 5. NO |

J11. How would you describe R's response to the Resource Booklet?

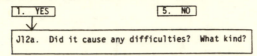

J12. Were there any other people present while you conducted the interview?

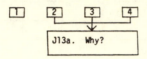

J13. How many sessions did you take to conduct the entire interview?

| 1 | | 2 | | 3 | | 4 |

J13a. Why?

J14. Any problems or suggestions?

J15. Write a descriptive sketch and impressions of R.

Appendix B

The Research Method and Sampling

Obtaining respondent participation in surveys of ethnic minority populations is difficult. In 1977, an entire issue of the *Journal of Social Issues* was devoted to the problems, prospects, and pitfalls of research among racial and cultural minorities. Myers (1977) noted that interviewing respondents of minority or low-income backgrounds had been problematic for decades and that criticisms of the survey method by spokespersons for racial and ethnic minorities underscored the need for innovative ways of carrying out survey tasks. In light of this literature, section one of Appendix B is devoted to the issue of research participation; the procedures that were used to optimize respondent participation are delineated. Section two covers the sample selection, sampling procedures, screening and eligibility procedures, and response rates. The final section describes the weighted and unweighted data procedures and comparisons.

RESEARCH PARTICIPATION

Many researchers have considered survey research to be a weak method in gaining the participation of America's poor because lower-class persons are more reluctant to engage in interviews (Clark, 1965; Josephson, 1970; Kelman, 1972; Liebow, 1967; Noblit and Burcart, 1975; Warwick and Lininger, 1975). With regard to San Francisco's Chinatown, See (1980) noted the obstacle of "uncooperativeness" among Chinatown residents and attributed it to their tendency "to be secretive and shy" (p. 124). While Nee and Nee (1972) succeeded in securing interviews with persons in Chinatown, these were persons selected through personal contacts. The task of gaining cooperation from a representative sample of Chinatown residents obtained through scientific means of sample selection was more difficult.

Tapping the pace and rhythm of Chinatown's heartbeat required residents' participation. Thus, the following procedures were implemented to optimize respondent participation: (1) providing remuneration for participation, (2) detailing the benefits of the study in an introductory letter, (3) careful selection and training of interviewers, and (4) designing the interview flow to minimize disinterest. This section concludes with a few sketches of the interview situation and feedback about the interview from the respondents, both of which relate to the research participation experience.

Remuneration for Participation

A Resource Book was given to each resident who completed an interview. The bilingual book of over 100 pages, compiled and designed by our staff, contained descriptions of 100 free or low-cost social service agencies in the area. It also contained information about tenant rights, procedures for handling housing problems, information on English language classes, and a map of agency locations. This author is not aware of any other survey that has provided such a form of remuneration. The decision to design this book was made after interviewers complained that carrying oranges or butter cookies was too cumbersome and after we found that some respondents were insulted when offered money to be interviewed (preferring instead to permit an interview based on graciousness).

The information contained in the Resource Book was obtained through three sources: (1) 24 San Francisco agency lists and directories; (2) completed questionnaires that had been sent to each agency in and near Chinatown; and (3) face-to-face or telephone interviews with agency directors. The book was user-friendly. Graphics delineated each section. Each agency was introduced with questions most often asked by laypersons in need of help (see Figures B.1, B.2, and B.3 for sample pages).

Responses to a post-interview evaluation form indicated that respondents found the book useful. Of those who returned the form, 71% rated it as "quite useful," 29% as "a little useful," and 0% as "not too useful." Comments included: "Informative. My friend borrowed it and has yet to return it. Please send me one more copy." "Having this book, there's less chance for me to meet with problems." "Thank you. I've already read the book. Because of it, I know the streets." "The booklet is designed very well." "The Resource Book is pretty practical."

Interviewer training involved the requirement that interviewers develop familiarity with the book's contents. If a respondent inquired about help for a problem, the interviewer was instructed to refer him or her to the relevant agency or procedure listed in the book at the close of the interview. For example, in response to the survey question "What kinds of problems do you find are the hardest for you to handle?" one respondent answered, "Finding a place to live in Chinatown. I've been applying for public housing for years. Now I'm forced to move by my landlord. Can you help me solve the problem?"

Introductory Letter

A bilingual letter was sent to each of the selected addresses. In part, the letter stated:

The Chinatown Housing and Health Research Project is conducting a comprehensive study that gathers the opinions and experiences of Chinese Americans on topics of their life, beliefs,

RESOURCE BOOKLET
of Services for Chinatown Residents

援助來源

華埠社區服務一般指南
資料手册

華埠住屋及健康研究中心

Chinatown Housing and Health Research Project

Figure B.1
Cover of Chinatown Resource Book

Index
目錄

Figure B.2
Index Page of Chinatown Resource Book

330

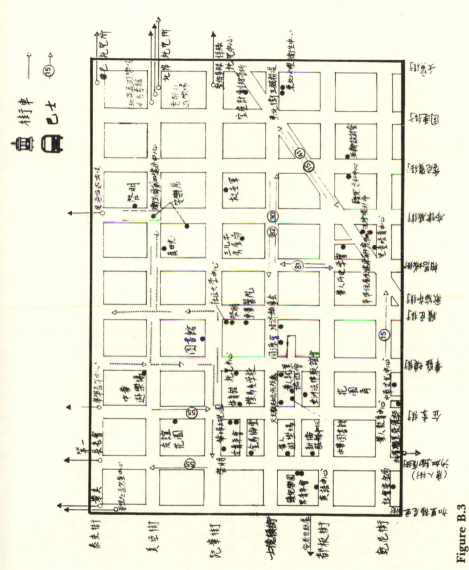

Figure B.3
Map from Chinatown Resource Book

331

problems, housing, neighborhood, health, and job. . . . It is the first comprehensive study on Chinese Americans. The information collected will assist community agencies in providing better services to Chinese Americans [and] help define community problems so that remedies can be sought. . . . Your household has been randomly selected to participate . . . no names will be used as all interviews will remain confidential. This study is being conducted by Chinese Americans concerned about the well-being of Chinese. The study is not affiliated with the Census Bureau. You or a member of your household will be representing many other Chinese Americans with similar experiences as your own, so your participation is needed. One of our project staff will be contacting you shortly to bring you your copy of the Resource Book as our expression of appreciation for your participation in this important study. . . . Some addresses may not have any Chinese Americans living there; if this applies to you, please accept our apologies. We appreciate your taking the time to welcome our staff member. Please accept our gratitude for your cooperation.

Selection and Training of Interviewers

Interviewers were selected who were Chinese and who behaved in a friendly, non-threatening but professional manner (this is in keeping with the literature that suggests that interviewers who are friendly but businesslike are most effective). Seven interviewers were fully bilingual. Two other interviewers, who were conversationally bilingual but stronger in English, conducted interviews with the English-dominant respondents. Many of the interviewers were familiar with the community. Five were female, four were men. Their ages ranged from the 20s into the 50s. Each had an identification card clipped to their person, showing photo, name, and affiliation with the project.

Interviewers were told that their competence and effort were critical to the study's success. Understanding the importance of a high response rate, they were trained to handle various types of reluctant responses. While being respectful of respondents' right to refuse, interviewers were taught to address respondents' reservations: "You should be able to sensitively and intuitively sense what these are and respond to them individually in ways that will alleviate their anxieties and fears, increase their involvement, show empathy and understanding for their conditions, and build their confidence about their importance."

To the remark, "I'm too old," interviewers were trained to say: "We want to interview people of *all* ages. Young people don't have the years of experience in life that you have." To the remark, "I'm not educated and I don't read," interviewers were instructed to say: "We don't want to talk only with people who had a lot of education. We want to know the opinions of people like yourself who have learned by day-to-day living. I will not be asking you anything about politics or current events— just your own views and experiences."

An interviewer's job involved making contact and screening for eligibility, turning in a screening form if there was no eligible member in the household, filling out a refusal form if all eligible persons in the household refused to be interviewed, handing in a call-back form if they were unsuccessful in making contact after four or five attempts at different times of the day, and conducting an interview with an eligible household member.

Interviewers were instructed to be warm and relaxed but to follow the interview schedules exactly. They were instructed to prevent invalid answers by speaking clearly and slowly and by seeking clarity in response to "don't know," vague, or general answers. They were warned to be unbiased in their responses, assure confidentiality, detect and handle waning interest, and respond promptly to coder questions.

Interviewer training involved video and audio recording of practice interviews. Role playing prepared interviewers, raised their confidence in handling difficult situations, and created a collaborative spirit. Weekly meetings were held to report on progress and to consult on problems.

Problems in the field added time and cost to the research endeavor. First, referrals were made to another interviewer when a resident spoke a dialect that differed from that of the assigned interviewer. Second, it was not always easy to find someone at home. There were a substantial number of single-person households. Many residents who worked at restaurants were not home in the evenings. Also, the high proportion of addresses in multi-unit buildings made it difficult to gain access to a front door. Locked front gates made doorbells inaccessible. To gain entry, interviewers were often forced to wait for a resident to enter or leave the building.

Interview Schedule and Flow

The topics of the interview were arranged from most impersonal (general residence background and perceptions of neighborhood) to the most personal (mental health attitudes, mental health status, and personal data such as income). If needed, the interviews were broken into more than one session. Over half of the interviews (57%) were conducted in one session, 39% in two sessions, and 4% in three sessions.

A mixture of open-ended and closed-ended questions relieved monotony but was also essential to the research objectives. Open-ended questions were used when the intent was exploratory, when spontaneous responses were sought, or when there was uncertainty regarding the categories into which responses would fall. Closed-ended questions were used when the intent was to gather factual data, when quantitative analyses were required, or when distinctions on a range of alternatives were sought. Closed-ended questions varied from dichotomous alternatives (i.e., "yes"/"no") to 7-point scales. With sensitivity to the educational and literacy limitations of members of this population, closed-ended items with complicated or multiple alternatives were accompanied by a visual display of the alternatives, indicated in the interview schedule as "show card." Show Cards were also used when item alternatives were thought to tax the concentration or memory of the respondent. More closed-ended questions than open-ended ones were used because a primary intent of this study was to measure social indicators and to test theories. Funnel questions (from general to specific) and inverted funnel questions (from specific to general) were used when data were needed for only those who had certain experiences.

The interview schedule included scales and items borrowed from other surveys as well as items specifically designed for this study. Items from other surveys were used when they were relevant to the research objectives and where norm comparisons were desired. For some variables, multiple indices were used to increase measurement validity.

Sketches of the Interview Situation

The following three sketches, written by different interviewers, provide a glimpse of the interview situation. "This respondent did not know that his household had been selected to be interviewed. He said his mother probably knew about the survey, but she was not home. So I interviewed this young man who was cooperative. Just as we finished the interview his mother returned. She was at first suspicious that I might be from a government agency. When I explained that I was not, she was more comfortable. Then she asked me where her son could get a job. I showed her the Resource Book and explained how to use it, and then she seemed very pleasant."

"Because she didn't want to be interviewed at home, this woman came to our office to participate in the study. She brought her daughter with her. The respondent was very responsive and cooperative. The interview was conducted in Sam Yup half the time and Sai Yup the other half since the respondent spoke both dialects. Whenever she talked about her daughter's mental problem, her eyes turned red. At the end of the interview, she pulled out an English letter from her pocket and asked me to translate it for her. It was a very short letter which took me only one or two minutes to translate."

"This respondent was very cooperative. She complained that her husband gambled a lot and had lost the money saved to buy a home. She didn't seem very satisfied with her marriage but she loved her children. At the end of the interview, she advised me to be careful when I choose a husband."

Respondents' Feedback

One-third of the respondents returned a feedback form; of these, all felt that the interviewer had explained the study well (69% said "very well," 31% "fairly well," and 0% "not very well"). With regard to how well the interview was conducted, 74% said "very well," 26% said "fairly well," and 0% said "not very well."

Ninety-seven percent said they were able to express their opinions fully and honestly. The majority found the interview "too long" but "interesting" (63% said the interview was "too long," 35% said "about right," and 3% said "too short"; as for interest, 29% said it was "very interesting," 57% said "fairly interesting," and 14% said it was "not interesting").

Forty-eight percent said the interview made them think about things they hadn't thought of before: "It made me think of my past and what I expect for the future." "It made me realize that the problems of my apartment are connected to the building and the building is part of the community." "Because of this interview, I feel someone cared and helped solve my problems." "In unity, there is power! Collecting a lot of people's opinions is to express and improve things. Let our area have improvement!"

SAMPLING

The sampling unit was defined as a room or group of rooms occupied by or intended for occupancy by a person or persons who normally live there as a separate living quarter and who normally eat apart from others in the building. Three sampling methods were used: the Polk City Directory, the Address Telephone Directory, and area sampling. The Polk City Directory is published yearly for San Francisco. Organized by street names, it includes residential and commercial addresses, names of occupants (with some phone numbers), and intersecting streets. The Address Telephone Directory, published by the telephone company, contains listings arranged alphabetically by streets and addresses rather than by last names, thereby permitting one to find individuals who have a telephone in their name within a particular geographical area. This directory is occasionally called the reverse phone directory. It is updated and published every three months by the phone company. Area sampling involves selecting the proper proportion of primary areas from different types (stratification), then selecting specific city blocks by probability methods, then listing the housing units (addresses) at selected chunks (or block faces) in order to estimate the number of housing units in the various parts of the chunk.

Area sampling is the preferred sampling scheme to use because it provides the most recent and greatest listing coverage. However, cost and time constraints required us to supplement area sampling with less expensive methods such as the Polk City Directory and the Address Telephone Directory. At the same time, the use of more than one sampling method provided a chance to evaluate the advantages and disadvantages of each method for future research.

Sample Selection

The sample selection and procedures were done in consultation with the Sampling Section of the University of Michigan's Survey Research Center. Figure 2.2 (in Chapter 2) and Table B.1 delineate the tract numbers and the estimated Chinese American population for each of the tracts and areas of Chinatown. In grand total, the proportion of Chinese Americans estimated to reside in greater Chinatown was 57%. The 1970 census was used for estimates of eligibility and sample selection because the 1980 census tract data for Asian Americans/Pacific Islanders was not available when the Chinatown sample was selected.

The sample was stratified by core and noncore areas. Based on 1970 census data, we estimated that 88% of the core residents and 50% of the noncore residents were Chinese. Based on these proportions, we anticipated an eligibility rate of 88% for the core area and 50% for the noncore area. The number of selections was based on an estimated acceptance rate of 70%, which provided a guideline as to how many listings to pull.

Constraints of time and cost led us to sample from 10 of the 13 census tracts. It was important that all three core tracts be represented in the sample because people commonly identify Chinatown as the core area. But it was also important to represent the noncore area in order to compare a highly dense area (core) with a less dense area (noncore). Included in the sample selection area were all three core area tracts, four of the five residential tracts, and four of the six expanded area census tracts. Census tract 15 was excluded because it had the smallest number of Chinese residing there of all Chinatown census tracts. Because all of the expanded area tracts had roughly the same proportion of Chinese, census tracts 103 and 112 were randomly selected for exclusion. In many people's minds, census tract 103 overlapped with Russian Hill or North Beach, and census tract 112 overlapped with Nob Hill.

The net acreage for each Chinatown area was 40 net acres, 184 net acres, and 204 net acres for the core, residential, and expanded areas, respectively. Both geographical dispersion plus the lowered proportion of Chinese living in the residential and expanded areas meant that much more time and money would be expended securing eligible respondents in the noncore area. Compared to the core area, the proportion of eligible respondents in the noncore area would be lower and the distance traveled to get from address to address would be longer. The high density and high concentration

Table B.1
Total Population and Asian/Pacific Islander Population for Chinatown Census Tracts, 1980

Census	1970 Total Population	1970 Asian & Pacific Islanders	1970 % Chinese[a]	1980 Total Population	1980 Asian & Pacific Islanders	1980 % Chinese[a]
Core Area						
113	3,831	3,090	81%	2,840	2,428	86%
114	3,697	3,549	96	3,084	3,025	98
118	1,596	1,434	90	1,515	1,376	91
Total	(9,124)	(8,073)	(88)	(7,439)	(6,829)	(92)
Residential						
106	4,411	2,842	64%	4,440	2,967	67%
107	5,598	4,201	75	5,349	4,566	85
108	6,103	4,085	66	5,511	3,614	67
110	5,306	3,376	67	5,247	3,509	64
115	1,011	666	66	842	709	84
Total	(22,429)	(15,170)	(68)	(21,389)	(15,365)	(62)
Expanded						
103	4,978	1,907	38%	4,508	1,976	44%
104	5,547	1,766	32	4,791	1,654	35
109	4,914	1,493	30	4,594	1,506	40
111	4,976	1,570	32	4,989	1,971	40
112	4,045	1,747	43	3,799	1,639	43
Total	(24,460)	(8,483)	(35)	(22,681)	(8,746)	(39)
Grand Total	(56,013)	(31,726)	(57)	(51,509)	(30,940)	(60)

[a]These percentages actually represent the percentage of Asian and Pacific Islanders and not Chinese; however since Chinese are generally known to represent most of the Asian and Pacific Islanders population in this area, we consider this a rough estimate of the percentage of Chinese in the area.

of Chinese in the core area (88%) meant that more eligible persons could be located in a shorter period of time. In order to work within the time and budgetary constraints, the core area was oversampled and the noncore area undersampled.

Of the sample, 66% (n = 71) were from the core area and 34% (n = 39) from the noncore area. Within the noncore area, 21% of the sample came from the residential area and 13% from the expanded area. The sampling ratios were 1:114 for the core area and 1:331 for the noncore area. Table B.2 displays the extent to which each census tract was represented in the sample and the percentage of greater Chinatown Chinese in each census tract according to the U.S. census.

Sampling Procedures

In the area sampling design, five city blocks were sampled from the core area and five from the noncore area. A two-stage probability sample selection procedure was used. In the first stage of selection, blocks were stratified by domain of study (core and noncore) and by percentage of Asian population (obtained from census block group

Table B.2
Chinatown Census Tracts: Percentage of Chinatown Population Represented in the Sample Compared to the Census (Unweighted Data)

Census Tract	Percent Represented in Sample		Percent of Greater Chinatown Chinese Population Represented in 1970 Census	Difference: Sample vs. Census
Core Area				
113	20%	(n=22)	10%	+10%
114	32	(n=35)	11	+21
118	13	(n=14)	5	+8
Total	(65)	n=71	(26)	(+39)
Residential				
106	4%	(n= 4)	9%	-5%
107	2	(n= 2)	13	-11
108	12	(n=13)	13	-1
110	4	(n= 4)	11	-7
115	0	(n= 0)	2	-2
Total	(22)	n=23	(48)	(-26)
Expanded				
103	0%	(n= 0)	6%	-6%
104	10	(n=11)	6	+4
109	2	(n= 2)	5	-3
111	1	(n= 1)	5	-4
112	0	(n= 0)	6	-6
Total	(13)	n=14	(28)	(-15)

data). We assumed all blocks within a block group to have the same percentage of Asians. Blocks were sampled with probabilities proportional to size (total housing units). The 10 selected blocks were listed for housing units. In the second stage of selection, housing units were obtained from a systematic sample taken from the listings of sampled blocks. Disproportionate sampling between core and noncore areas yielded a higher number of interviews from the core area.

A sampling frame of Chinatown listings was also constructed using the Polk City Directory. The advantages of the Polk listings as a sampling frame were its availability, low expense, and capability of providing a greater geographic "spread" of selected units throughout Chinatown than the area sampling of 10 blocks. Our analysis revealed that the Polk City Directory had fairly good coverage of households listed by the area sampling method. Comparing a listing of household units in 20 randomly selected block faces throughout greater Chinatown with listings of these same blocks in the Polk City Directory, we found that 89% of the total housing units, 97% of the total addresses, and 97% of the total commercial units were included in the Polk City Directory.

An equal probability sample was maintained in the selection from the Polk City Directory. Following the selection of addresses using area sampling procedures, we again ascertained the coverage of the Polk City Directory, this time by calculating the percentage of addresses from area sampling that were contained in the 1979 Polk City Directory. A full 100% of the addresses from area sampling were contained in the Polk City Directory.

We also found that the percentage of Chinese households in the core area determined by the Polk City Directory (85%) was very close to the percentage of Chinese in the total core population indicated in the 1970 census (88%). For the residential and expanded areas, the percentage of Chinese households indicated in the Polk City Directory was slightly less than the percentage of Chinese in the populations of those respective areas as indicated by the census (51% as compared to 68% for the residential area and 40% as compared to 35% for the expanded area). Differences may have been due to actual differences between counts of households (Polk) and counts of individuals (census) or to the Polk City Directory's non-count of those who live in boarding houses or residential hotels.

For listings taken from the Polk City Directory, all streets and alleys within the 13 census tracts were retrieved from the most recent Polk City Directory, then were separated into their respective census tracts. For each census tract, a count was made of the total number of households and the total number of Chinese-surnamed households, which permitted a calculation of the percentage of Chinese households in each census tract. The percentage of households in the core, residential, and expanded areas that had Chinese-surnamed residents was 84.8%, 51.2%, and 21.5%, respectively, with a total combined percentage for all three areas of 39.7%. These percentages were used to estimate the sampling fraction for the selection procedure used for the Polk City Directory. Listings were pulled using a random start number and a sampling interval for the core and noncore area separately.

Following stratification by core and noncore, we took a systematic sample of listings. The concept of a half-open interval was employed: given a selected listing, one includes all housing units up to but not including the next successive listing in the sample frame. Theoretically, this alleviates the noncoverage problems of using an imperfect listing; it allowed us to determine coverage of the Polk City Directory.

A listing was done for the multiple units and single units that were selected. For single-unit addresses, a staff member went to the selected unit and checked for unlisted units between this address and the next listed address on the same side of the street that appeared in the Polk City Directory. If any unlisted units were found, these were included into the sample if the unlisted unit was a single-unit address. If it was a multiple-unit structure, it was added to the multiple-unit listing. For multiple-unit addresses, a staff member went to the structure in which the selected units lay and listed all units in the structure whether or not they appeared in the Polk City Directory. If any missing unit was found between the structure and the next structure listed in the directory on the same side of the street, it was added to the next line of the listing sheet. For the selection of units in each multi-unit structure, if "n" = the number of listings for that structure from the Polk City Directory, a random number between 1 and "n" was selected ("x") and we took into the sample the unit with that line number, then "n" was added to that line number. If a unit was listed on line "n + x" on the corrected listing, then that unit was taken into the sample as well. This permitted addresses missed by the Polk City Directory to have some equal probability of being included in the sample.

The listings in the Address Telephone Directory included residential hotels and boarding houses, which the Polk City Directory listings did not. For example, 706 Jackson Street was listed only as "Mandarin Hotel" in the Polk City Directory, while the Address Telephone Directory listed 14 names and addresses of residents. While exclusive use of the Polk City Directory would exclude residents living in residential hotels from the sample and would constitute a less recent listing, the Address Telephone Directory listed fewer noncommercial names than the Polk City Directory. A comparison was made of the number of noncommercial names listed in the Address Telephone Directory and the number of noncommercial addresses listed in the Polk City Directory. One major street and one alley were randomly selected from each of the three areas of Chinatown (core, residential, and expanded), making a total of six streets and/or alleys that were enumerated. Results revealed that the Address Telephone Directory listed from 55% to 95% of the total number of listings of the Polk City Directory, with an average of 85%. Following this, an enumeration was made of Chinese-surnamed addresses for these same streets and alleys. The Address Telephone Directory listed an average of 82% of the listings of Chinese Americans listed in the Polk City Directory.

To compare the names listed in the Polk City Directory with those in the Address Telephone Directory, a major street from each of the three areas of Chinatown and one alley from the core area were randomly selected and enumerated; 56% of the residential names listed in the Polk City Directory were the same as those in the Address Telephone Directory, 12% were different, and 33% were not listed in the Address Telephone Directory. Thus, the Polk City Directory had an estimated 33% more listings than the Address Telephone Directory. Also, in the Address Telephone Directory it was more difficult to distinguish commercial units from residential units. Furthermore, use of the Address Telephone Directory excluded persons without a phone as well as persons with an unlisted number.

For the Address Telephone Directory listings, a two-stage selection procedure was used that would sample streets with equal probability for each area, stratified by size with respect to Chinese-surnamed listed units. For each area (core or noncore), streets were listed in increasing order on the basis of the number of Chinese-surnamed units.

A listing was created for each area by using a random start number and a sampling interval. An enumerator checked the listings in the field, as was done with the Polk City Directory listings to supplement missing addresses ("next door inclusions"). Then, as in the Polk listing, the sample was taken using a new sampling interval and random start number.

Of the interviews completed, 63% were from area sampling, 23% from the Polk City Directory, and 14% from the Address Telephone Directory. Of the interviews conducted, 66% were from the core area and 34% from the noncore area. Funding and time constraints dictated the sample size and combined use of three sampling methods. The principal investigator originally requested funding for two years to conduct survey research on crowding and stress. After consulting with community leaders, it became clear that a more comprehensive survey—including housing, health, mental health, and employment—was needed. However, the funding agency's review committee decided to fund only one year with reduced funds for a pilot study, recommending that the survey on crowding be scaled down. Financial support beyond the initial year was contingent on available funds and on the review committee's evaluation of work accomplished. Since there could be no guarantee of further funding, we decided to conduct a comprehensive survey in the event that additional funding would not be forthcoming. At the same time, there was pressure to conduct a study as quickly as possible to meet the renewal application deadline. In order not to sacrifice scope, we modified the sampling method; we decided to reduce the sample size in order to accommodate time and funding constraints. By the time we were informed that the renewal grant had been funded, the research intensity had exhausted the staff. We completed the interviews from the original screening and sampling methods and stopped interviewing when we had used up the sampling selections (108 interviews had been collected by then).

Screening and Eligibility

For purposes of sampling, Chinatown was defined as the 13 census tracts that the Department of City Planning had designated as greater Chinatown in 1970 (San Francisco Department of City Planning, 1972). Greater Chinatown consisted of the core and noncore areas, with the noncore area being comprised of residential and expanded Chinatown (see Figure 2.2 in Chapter 2).

Both residential and commercial screenings were conducted. In earlier years, many households served a dual function of work and residence. Since no data existed regarding the current prevalence of mixed commercial-residential units, commercial units were included in our listings and were screened for residential use in order to permit residents in mixed units to have an equal probability of selection as those who lived at residential addresses. Field researchers screened commercial units in the following ways: "In Chinatown, an address can sometimes be used for both a business and a residence. Is there any portion of this address that's used as a place to live by anyone who's 18 years of age or older? "(If answer is "yes," interviewers screened for eligibility using the same questions for residential screening: "Are you 18 years of age or older?" "Can you tell me if you are pure Chinese or have some percentage of another nationality?" "Are you a San Francisco resident who's lived in this neighborhood for more than one month?")

Results of the commercial screening for residential-commercial households revealed that among 15 Chinese commercial addresses screened in the core area and 14 in the noncore area, none were used simultaneously as residences. Further screening and listing of commercial units was deemed an inefficient use of time and money and, therefore, unnecessary.

A total of 259 residential addresses were screened. The eligibility rate was 58%, which represented 151 listings among 259 selected addresses. Due to the higher percentage of Chinese in the core area, the eligibility rate there was higher—71% in the core area, 45% in the noncore area. In the core area, 139 addresses were screened, of which 98 were eligible, 41 ineligible. There were 119 screened addresses in the noncore area, of which 53 were eligible, 66 ineligible.

The first eligible person contacted in a listing address who did not refuse to be interviewed became the respondent. We did not conduct equal probability sampling of eligible respondents within a household because of budgetary constraints and because the average household size was small. If, after five calls, no one was home, no substitution was made.

Response Rates

Of the 151 eligible listings, 108 interviews were completed, 36 were refusals, four were breakoffs (an interview started but not completed), and three persons could not be interviewed because of illness. The refusal rate for greater Chinatown was 24%; 36 eligible persons refused to be interviewed among the 151 eligible persons screened. The refusal rates for the core and noncore areas were comparable—23% and 25%, respectively. The rate of refusals from women (22%) did not differ greatly from men (28%). English-speaking persons refused more often than Chinese-speaking persons (37% and 19%). Older adults refused more often than younger adults (the proportions of those who refused by age groups were 30% of the 55-year-olds-and-over, 23% of the 35-to-54 year olds, and 16% of the 18-to-34 year olds). The most often mentioned reason for refusing was "too busy" or "no time." Other reasons included a family quarrel, spouse's illness, "too old," and lack of interest. Male interviewers were refused twice as often as female interviewers (34% and 16%), a phenomenon that is common to other surveys.

WEIGHTED AND UNWEIGHTED DATA

Because the sample overrepresented the core area and underrepresented the noncore area, our original intent was to weight the data so that the proportion of respondents in each of the three areas of Chinatown would represent the actual proportion of Chinese in greater Chinatown living there. This would permit the data to more closely represent the greater Chinatown population. However, since weighting the noncore data could distort reality due to the small noncore sample size, the decision of using weighted or unweighted data was based on which more closely reflected the 1980 census for Asian/Pacific Islanders. Interviews were conducted in 1979, but it was not until 1988 that the Census Bureau made the 1980 census data for Asian/Pacific Islanders available by census blocks.

The data were weighted in the following manner. First, the proportion of Asian/Pacific Islanders in greater Chinatown who reside in each of the areas of Chinatown was determined using figures from the 1980 U.S. census. Since the census does not break the Asian/Pacific Islander category into finer ethnic distinctions, it was assumed that in Chinatown, these were Chinese. There were 30,940 Chinese

Table B.3

Comparison of Respondent Characteristics of the Chinatown Sample (Unweighted and Weighted Data) with the 1980 U.S. Census

	Chinatown Sample		1980 Census[1]	
	Unweighted Data	Weighted Data		
Gender				
Women	53%	52%	51%	
Men	47	48	49	
Age				
0-14	--	--	--[3]	16%
18-24 (20-24)[2]	9%	10%	20%	17
25-34	19	25	17	15
35-44	10	0	11	9
45-54	21	21	15	13
55-64	15	18	15	12
65+	25	17	22	19
Mean Age	49 yrs	46 yrs		
Men	46	42		
Women	52	50		
Marital Status				
Married or Separated	58%	64%	52%	
Single	21	23	32	
Widowed	15	7	13	
Divorced	6	6	3	
Nativity				
Native born	19%	19%	26%	
Foreign born	81	81	74	
Years of School Completed				
0 - 8 yrs.	45%[4]	35%[4]	52%[5]	
9 - 12 yrs.	23	25	23[5]	
13+ yrs.	32	40	25[5]	
College degree or higher	16%	25%	12%	
Language				
Cannot Speak English	53%	56%		
Speaks English "not well" or "not at all"	53%[6]-70%[7]	56%[6]-82%[7]	41%-68%[8]	

Household Income
(CHHRP data is for 1978, includes family income and personal income of those who live alone)
(Census data is for 1979 and is household income)

Less than $ 5,000	27%	17%	21%	
$ 5,000 - $19,000	56	55	48	
$20,000+	16	27	31	
Median Income	$8,000-$8,999	$9,000-$9,999	$7,475-$20,463[7]	

Table B.3 (*Continued*)

	Chinatown Sample		1980 Census[1]
	Unweighted Data	Weighted Data	
Occupation			
Professional/ Technical	8%	22%	8%
Managers/ Administrators	1%[9]	3%[9]	7%
Sales	4	10	10
Clerical	6	6	10
Craft	3	8	8
Operatives except Transport	15	29	19
Transport Operatives	0	0	2
Farm	0	0	0
Service	18	18	25
Household Work and Protective Services	2	4	1
Mean Household Size			
Gender	--	--	2.82
Core	2.7	2.7	2.57
Noncore	3.0	3.0	2.89

1 "Asian and Pacific Islander Persons" for persons aged 15 years and over.

2 U.S. Census breakdown is 15-19 years, 20-24 years, so it is not possible to calculate 18-24 years from the census data, so the data from the census for 20-24 year olds was used instead.

3 Eliminating 0-14 year olds from the totals, percent for remaining age groups.

4 In the Chinatown survey, this data was collected for persons 18 years and over who were currently employed.

5 U.S. Census: persons 25 years and over.

6 Percent who said they could not speak English.

7 Percent who said they could speak English but "rather poorly."

8 This represents the range by census tracts and not the median.

9 These are "owners of own business." In Chinatown, an owner of own business is normally a small family-owned business (i.e. Chinese restaurant, Chinese grocery store) and is not of the same occupational prestige as "manager or administrator" of a company in the usual meaning of the term.

residing in greater Chinatown in 1980; the proportions of Chinese in Chinatown who resided in each of the areas were 22% for the core, 50% for the residential, and 28% for the expanded. Second, the proportion of the total sample that came from each of these areas was determined to be 71, 23, and 14 for the core, residential, and expanded areas, respectively. The proportions were multiplied by the total sample size, then that figure was divided by the sample size for that area. The result was the weighting factor for the data in each area: core = 23.76; residential = 2.35; expanded = 2.16. This is equivalent to sampling ratios of 1:7:6.5 for the core:residential:expanded areas or 1:6 for core:noncore.

Table B.3 compares demographic data from the 1980 census with both weighted and unweighted data from the Chinatown survey. There were no differences between the two for indices such as gender and nativity distribution; both closely approximated the 1980 census. However, for other indices, the unweighted data more closely approximated the census. Overall, the unweighted data were a very close reflection of the census data. Unweighted data made for more stringent statistical tests of significance due to a larger variance.

References

Acosta, F. X., Yamamoto, J., & Evans, L. A. (1982). *Effective psychotherapy for low income and minority patients*. New York: Plenum.

Allard, W. A. (1975, November). Chinatown: The gilded ghetto. *National Geographic*, pp. 627–643.

Almquist, E. M. (1975). Untangling the effects of race and sex: The disadvantaged status of black women. *Social Science Quarterly, 56,* 127–142.

Alta California. (1851, September 18).

American Institute of Planners Newsletter. (1967, January). *2.*

American Psychiatric Association. (1987). *Diagnostic and statistical manual of mental disorders* (3rd ed.). Washington, DC: Author.

American Psychological Association. (1990). Draft revision of the 1981 ethical principles of psychologists. *APA Monitor, 21,* 28–32.

Anderson, E. N. (1972). Some Chinese methods of dealing with crowding. *Urban Anthropology, 1,* 141–250.

Anderson, P. L. (1982). Self-esteem in the foreign language: A preliminary investigation. *Foreign Language Annals, 15*(2), 109–114.

Anderson, R. (1979). *The Robert Wood Johnson Foundation special report on America's health system: A portrait*. New Brunswick, NJ: Robert Wood Johnson Foundation.

Anderson, R. M., & Anderson, O. W. (1979). Trends in the use of health services. In H. Freeman, S. Levine, & L. G. Reeders (Eds.), *Handbook of medical sociology* (pp. 371–391). Englewood Cliffs, NJ: Prentice Hall.

Andrews, F., & Inglehard, R. F. (1979). The structure of subjective well-being in nine western societies. *Social Indicators Research, 6,* 73–90.

Andrews, F. M., & Withey, S. B. (1976). *Social indicators of well-being*. New York: Plenum.

Appendix to the Report of the Special Health Commissioners, Sacramento. (1900). In *Appendix to Journals of Senate and Assembly of the 35th Session of the Legislature of California,* (Vol. 2, 1901). Sacramento: California State Printer.

Armentrout, L. E. (1976). Conflict and contact between the Chinese and indigenous communities in San Francisco, 1900–1911. In *The life, influence, and the role of the Chinese in the United States, 1776–1960,* Proceedings of the National Conference of the Chinese Historical Society of America (pp. 55–70). San Francisco: Chinese Historical Society of America.

Asian Week. (1985, January 11).

―――. (1988, September 2).

Atkinson, D. R., Morton, G., and Sue, D. W. (1989). *Counseling American minorities: A cross-cultural perspective*. Dubuque, IA: William C. Brown.

Babbie, E. R. (1973). *Survey research methods*. Belmont, CA: Wadsworth.

Baldassare, M. (1979). *Residential crowding in urban America*. Berkeley: University of California Press.

Bales, J. (1985). Minority training falls short. *APA Monitor, 16*(11), 7.

Barth, G. (1964). *Bitter strength: A history of the Chinese in the United States, 1850–1870*. Cambridge, MA: Harvard University Press.

Battle, E., & Rotter, J. B. (1963). Children's feelings of personal control as related to social class and ethnic groups. *Journal of Personality, 31,* 482–490.

Bay Area Social Planning Council. (1971, February). *Chinese newcomers in San Francisco: Report and recommendations of the study committee*. (Available from BASPC, 577 14th St., Oakland, California 94612)

Becker, S. E. W. (1877). Humors of a congressional investigating committee. A review of the report on Chinese immigration. San Francisco. Pamphlet.

Bender, T. (1978). *Community and social change in America*. New Brunswick, NJ: Rutgers University Press.

Bengston, V. L., Grigsby, E., Corry, E. M., & Hruby, M. (1977). Research among racial and cultural minorities: Problems, prospects, and pitfalls. *Journal of Social Issues, 33*(4), 75–92.

Berk, B. B., & Hirata, L. C. (1973). Mental illness among the Chinese: Myth or reality? *Journal of Social Issues, 29,* 149–166.

Bernal, M. E., & Padilla, A. M. (1982). Status of minority curricula and training in clinical psychology. *American Psychologist, 37*(7), 780–787.

Bernard, J. (1973). *The sociology of community*. Glenview, IL: Scott, Foresman.

Bevan, W. (1980). On getting in bed with a lion. *American Psychologist, 35,* 779–789.

Blauner, R. (1971). *Racial oppression in America*. New York: Harper and Row.

Blauner, R., & Wellman, D. (1973). Toward the decolonization of social research. In J. A. Ladner (Ed.), *The death of white sociology* (pp. 310–330). New York: Vintage Books.

Bloodworth, D. (1966). *The Chinese looking glass*. New York: Farrar, Straus, and Giroux.

Bonacich, E. (1972). A theory of ethnic antagonisms: The split labor market. *American Sociological Review, 37,* 547–569.

Booth, A., & Cowell, J. (1976). Crowding and health. *Journal of Health and Social Behavior, 17,* 204–220.

Borthwick, J. D. (1857). *Three years in California*. Edinburgh: Blackwood.

Bottomore, T. (1972). *Sociology: A guide to problems and literature*. New York: Random House, Vintage.

Bourne, P. G. (1973). Suicide among Chinese in San Francisco. *American Journal of Public Health, 63,* 744–750.

Bouvier, L. F., & Gardner, R. W. (1986). Immigration to the United States: The unfinished story. *Population Bulletin, 41,* p. 17.

Brace, C. L. (1869). *The new west*. New York: G. P. Putnam's Sons.

Bracy, J. H. (1976). The quality of life experience of black people. In A. Campbell, P. E. Converse, & W. L. Rodgers (Eds.), *The quality of American life: Perceptions, evaluations, and satisfactions* (pp. 443–464). New York: Russell Sage Foundation.

Bradburn, B. M., & Caplovitz, D. (1965). *Reports on happiness*. Chicago: Aldine.

Brown, R. R., Stein, K. M., Huang, K., & Harris, D. E. (1973). Mental illness and the role of mental health facilities in Chinatown. In S. Sue & N. Wagner (Eds.), *Asian Americans: Psychological perspectives* (pp. 212–231). Palo Alto: Science and Behavior Books.

Burawoy, M. (1976). The functions and reproduction of migrant labor: Comparative material from South Africa and the United States. *American Journal of Sociology, 81,* 1050–1087.

Burgess, E. (1928). Residential segregation in American cities. *The Annals of the American Academy of Political and Social Sciences, 40,* 105–115.

Caen, H. (1980, February 11). *San Francisco Chronicle,* p. 25.

California State Department of Finance. (1988). *Projected total population for California by race/ethnicity.* Sacramento: Author.

California voters information pamphlet: Arguments in favor of and against proposition 38. (1984). Sacramento: Office of the Secretary of State.

Campbell, A., Converse, P. E., & Rodgers, W. L. (1976). *The quality of American life: Perceptions, evaluations, and satisfactions*. New York: Russell Sage Foundation.

Campbell, A., Converse, P. E., Rodgers, W. L., & Marans, R. (1976). The residential environment. In A. Campbell, P. E. Converse, & W. L. Rodgers (Eds.). *The quality of American life: Perceptions, evaluations, and satisfactions* (pp. 212–261). New York: Russell Sage Foundation.

Cantril, H. (1965). *The patterns of human concerns*. New Brunswick, NJ: Rutgers University Press.

Carlson, D. A., Coleman, J. B., Errera, P., and Harrison, R. W. (1965). Problems in treating the lower class psychotic. *Archives of General Psychiatry, 13,* 269–274.

Carp, F. M., & Kataoka, E. (1976). Health care problems of the elderly in San Francisco's Chinatown. *The Gerontologist, 16*(1), 30–38.

Castro, R. (1976). Shifting the burden of bilingualism: The case for monolingual communities. *Bilingual Review, 3,* 3–28.

Chan, S. (1986). *This bittersweet soil*. Berkeley: University of California Press.

Chan, W. (1987, September/October). The Asian American model minority myth. *Unity,* pp. 4–7.

The Chinatown report. (1886). *San Francisco News.*

Chinn, T. W., Lai, H. M., & Choy, P. P. (1969). *A history of the Chinese in California: A syllabus*. San Francisco: Chinese Historical Society of America.

Chiswick, B. (1978). Effects of Americanization on the earnings of foreign-born men. *Journal of Political Economy, 86,* 877–921.

Chiu, P. (1967). *Chinese labor in California, 1850–1880: An economic study,* (2nd ed.). Madison: University of Wisconsin.

Chiu, V. (1958). Marriage laws of the Ching dynasty. *Contemporary China.* Hong Kong.

Choldin, H. M. (1978). Urban density and pathology. *Annual Review of sociology, 4,* 91–113.

Clark, K. (1965). *Dark ghetto: Dilemmas of social power.* New York: Harper & Row.

Cochrane, R. (1977). Mental illness in immigrants to England, Wales: An analysis of mental hospital admissions, 1971. *Social Psychiatry, 12*(1), 25–42.

Cohen, S., & Syme, S. L. (1985). *Social support and health.* New York: Academic Press.

Cohen, S., & Wills, T. A. (1985). Stress, social support, and the buffering hypothesis. *Psychological Bulletin, 98*(2), 310–357.

Cole, N. J., Branch, C. H., & Allison, R. B. (1962). Some relationships between social class and the practice of dynamic psychotherapy. *American Journal of Psychiatry, 118,* 1004–1012.

Coleman, E. (1945). *Chinatown, USA.* New York: John Day.

Commission on Minority Participation in Education and American Life. (1988, May). *One third of a nation.* Washington, DC: American Council on Education.

Committee for Ballots in English. (1983). Arguments in favor of Proposition O. *Opposing Bilingual Ballots,* pp. 72–73. Voting Pamphlet.

Conant, J. E. (1967, August 14). The other face of Chinatown. *San Francisco Examiner,* p. 1.

Coolidge, M. R. (1909). *Chinese immigration.* New York: Henry Holt.

Crandall, D. J., & Dohrenwend, B. P. (1967). Some relations among psychiatric symptoms, organic illness and social class. *American Journal of Psychiatry, 123,* 1527–1537.

Croll, E. (1978). *Feminism and socialism in China.* New York: Schocken Books.

Cronise, T. F. (1868). *The natural wealth of California.* San Francisco: Bancroft.

Cushman, P. (1990). Why the self is empathy: Toward a historically situated psychology. *American Psychologist, 45,* 599–611.

Daniels, R. (1966). Westerners from the East: Oriental immigrants reappraised. *Pacific Historical Review, 35,* 373–383.

Darroch, A. G., & Marston, W. G. (1971). The social class basis of ethnic residential segregation: The Canadian case. *American Journal of Sociology, 77*(3), 491–510.

Davenport, D. (1981). The pathology of racism: A conversation with third world wimmin. In C. Moraga and G. Anzalda (Eds.), *This bridge called my back: Writings by radical women of color* (pp. 85–90). Watertown, MA: Persephone.

DeVries, J. (1974). New effects of language shift in Finland, 1951–1960: A demographic analysis. *Acta Sociological, 17,* 140, 149.

Dillon, R. H. (1962). *The hatchet man.* New York: Coward-McCann.

Dobie, C. C. (1936). *San Francisco's Chinatown.* New York: Appleton-Century-Crofts.

Dohrenwend, B. P., & Dohrenwend, B. S. (1969). *Social status and psychological disorder: A causal inquiry.* New York: John Wiley & Sons.

Dong, C. W. (1979). *Following the dawn.* San Francisco: Chinese Hospital.

Douvan, E., & Walker, A. (1956). The sense of effectiveness in public affairs. *Psychological Monographs, 70,* 429.

Dubos, R. (1965). *Man adapting.* New Haven, CT: Yale University Press.

Duff, D. F., & Arthur, R. J. (1967). Between two worlds: Filipinos in the U.S. Navy. *American Journal of Psychiatry, 123,* 836–843.

Dutton, D. B. (1978). Explaining the low use of health services by the poor: Costs, attitudes, or delivery systems. *American Sociological Review, 43,* 348–368.

East West. (1974, January 16).

———. (1985, January 9 and 16).

———. (1987, August 20).

Fang, J. (1984, March 30). Asians in '84. *Asian Week,* p. 6.

Farwell, W. B. (1885). *The Chinese at home and abroad.* San Francisco: A. L. Bancroft.

Fernandez, R. M., & Kulik, J. C. (1981). A multilevel model of life satisfaction: Effects of individual characteristics and neighborhood satisfaction. *American Sociological Review, 46,* 840–850.

Fishman, D. B., & Neigher, W. D. (1982). American psychology in the '80's: Who will buy? *American Psychologist, 37,* 533–546.

Foley, D. L. (1952). *Neighbors or urbanites: The study of a Rochester residential district* (No. 2). Rochester, NY: University of Rochester Studies of Metropolitan Rochester.

Frank, J. D., Gliedman, L. H., Imber, S. D., Nash, E. H., Jr., & Stone, A. R. (1957). Why patients leave psychotherapy. *Archives of Neurology and Psychiatry, 77,* 283–299.

Freedman, J. (1975). *Crowding and behavior.* San Francisco: W. H. Freeman.

Galagher, E. B., Sharaf, M. R., & Levinson, D. J. (1965). The influence of patient and therapist in determining the use of psychotherapy in a hospital setting. *Psychiatry, 28,* 297–310.

Galton, F. (1908). *Inquiries into human faculty.* London: J. M. Dent.

Gans, H. J. (1962). Urbanism and suburbanism as ways of life: A reevaluation of definitions. In A. M. Rose (Ed.), *Human behavior and social processes: An interactionist approach.* Boston: Houghton Mifflin.

Gergen, K. (1973). Social psychology as history. *Journal of Personality and Social Psychology, 26,* 309–320.

———. (1985). The social constructionist movement in modern psychology, *American Psychologist, 40,* 266–275.

Giorgi, A. (1970). *Psychology as a human science.* New York: Harper and Row.

Glick, B. (1988, May 20). English-Only: America's handicap. *San Jose Mercury News.*

Graves, T. D. (1961). Time perspective and the deferred gratification pattern in a tri-ethnic community (Report No. 5, Tri-Ethnic Research Project). Boulder: University of Colorado, Institute of Behavioral Science.

Grosjean, R. (1982). *Life in two languages.* Cambridge, MA: Harvard University Press.

Guest, A. M. (1971). Retesting the Burgess hypothesis: The location of white collar workers. *American Journal of Sociology, 76,* 1094–1108.

Gurin, G., Veroff, J., & Feld, S. (1960). *Americans view their mental health.* New York: Basic Books.

Gurin, P., Gurin, G., Lao, R., & Beattie, M. (1969). Internal external control in the motivational dynamics of Negro youth. *Journal of Social Issues, 25,* 29–53.

Guzman, R. (1967, October 26–28). Ethics in federally subsidized research—The case of the Mexican American. *The Mexican American: A new focus on opportunity.* Testimony presented at the Cabinet Committee Meeting on Mexican American Affairs, El Paso, Texas. Washington, DC.

Haase, W. (1964). The role of socio-economic class in examiner bias. In F. Riessman, J. Cohen, & A. Pearl (Eds.), *Mental health of the poor.* New York: Free Press.

Haggerty, L. J. (1971). Another look at the Burgess hypothesis: Time as an important variable. *Journal of Sociology, 76,* 1084–1093.

Harre, R. (1984). *Personal being: A theory for individual psychology.* Cambridge, MA: Harvard University Press.

———. (Ed.). (1986). *The social construction of emotions.* Oxford: Basil Blackwell.

Harrison, J., & Howard, W. (1972). The role of meaning in the urban image. *Environment and Behavior, 4,* 389–411.

Hawley, A. (1972). Population density and the city. *Demography, 9,* 521–530.

Heller, K. (1988). *The return to community.* Presidential address, Division 27, presented at the American Psychological Association Convention, Atlanta, GA.

Hessler, R. M., Nolan, M. F., Ogbru, B., & New, P. K. M. (1975). Intraethnic diversity: Health care of the Chinese Americans. *Human Organization, 34,* 253–262.

Hoexter, C. K. (1976). *From Canton to California.* New York: Four Winds Press.

Hollingshead, A. B., & Redlich, F. C. (1954). *Social class and mental illness.* New York: John Wiley & Sons.

Hooks, B. (1984). *Feminist theory from margin to center.* Boston: South End Press.

House, J. S. (1981). *Work stress and social support.* Reading, MA: Addison-Wesley.

Howe, M. (1986, October 19). Racially motivated attacks arouse concern for Asians. *New York Times,* p. 14.

Hsu, F. (1971). *The challenge of the American dream: The Chinese in the United States.* Belmont, CA: Wadsworth.

Huang, J., & Wong, S. Q. (Eds.) (1977). *Chinese Americans: Myths and realities.* San Francisco: Association of Chinese Teachers.

Hunter, D. (1976). Voting rights act and language minorities. *Catholic University Law Review, 2,* 250–270.

Hussein, H. (1985, July 29). Making English mandatory [Letter to the editor]. *Newsweek,* p. 5.

Imber, S. D., Nash, E. H., Jr., & Stone, A. R. (1955). Social class and duration of psychotherapy. *Journal of Clinical Psychology, 11,* 281–284.

Jacobs, J. (1961). *The death and life of great American cities.* New York: Random House.

Jacobs, P., & Landau, S. (1971). *To serve the devil: Colonials and sojourners.* New York: Vintage.

Jemmott, J. B., III, & Locke, S. E. (1984). Psychosocial factors, immunologic mediation, and human susceptibility to infectious diseases: How much do we know? *Psychological Bulletin, 95,* 78–108.

Josephson, E. (1970). Resistance to community surveys. *Social Problems, 18,* 117–129. *Journal of Social Issues.* (1977). (Vol. 33).

Kahn, R. L., Pollack, M., & Fink, M. (1957). Social factors in the selection of therapy in a voluntary mental hospital. *Journal of the Hillside Hospital, 6,* 216–228.

Kantrowitz, N. (1973). *Ethnic and racial segregation in the New York metropolis: Residential patterns among whites, ethnic groups, blacks, and Puerto Ricans.* New York: Praeger.

Kasl, S. V., Evans, A. S., & Neiderman, J. C. (1979). Psychosocial risk factors in the development of infectious mononucleosis. *Psychosomatic Medicine, 41,* 441–466.

Kasschau, R. A., & Kessel, F. (1980). *Psychology and society: In search of symbiosis.* New York: Holt, Rinehart, Winston.

Katz, R., Gutek, B. S., Kahn, R. L., & Barton, E. (1975). *Bureaucratic encounters.* Ann Arbor, MI: Institute of Social Research.

Kelman, H. C. (1972). The rights of the subject in social research: An analysis in terms of relative power and legitimacy. *American Psychologist, 27,* 989–1016.

Kessler, R. C., & McLeod, J. D. (1985). Social support and mental health in community samples. In S. Cohen & S. L. Syme (Eds.), *Social support and health* (pp. 219–240). New York: Academic Press.

Kim, B. L. (1978). *The Asian Americans: Changing patterns, changing needs.* Montclair, NJ: Association of Korean Christian Scholars in North America.

Kim, E. (1982). *Asian American literature.* Philadelphia: Temple University Press.

Kinney, D. G. (1990, September). Reopening the gateway to America. *Life,* pp. 27–35.

Kitano, H. (1969). Japanese-American mental illness. In W. Plog & R. Edgerton (Eds.), *Changing perspectives in mental illness* (pp. 257–284). New York: Holt, Rinehart, Winston.

Kitano, H. C., & Sue, S. (1973). The model minorities. *Journal of Social Issues, 29*(2), 1–9.

Kleinman, A. M. (1977). Depression, somatization and the new cross-cultural psychiatry. *Social Science and Medicine, 11*(1), 3–10.

Kleinman, A. M., & Mechanic, D. (1981). Mental illness and psychosocial aspects of medical problems in China. In A. M. Kleinman & T. Y. Lin (Eds.), *Normal and abnormal behavior in Chinese culture* (pp. 331–356). Dordrecht, Holland: D. Reidel.

Korchin, S. J. (1976). *Modern clinical psychology.* New York: Basic Books.

Kung, S. W. (1962). *Chinese in American life: Some aspects of their history, status, problems and contributions.* Seattle: University of Washington Press.

Kuo, W. H. (1979). On the study of Asian Americans: Its current state and agenda. *Sociological Quarterly, 20,* 290.

Lai, H. M., & Choy, P. P. (1972). *Outline history of the Chinese in America.* San Francisco: Chinese Historical Society of America.

Langner, T. S., & Michael, S. T. (1963). *Life stress and mental health: The Midtown Manhattan study, Vol. 2.* New York: Free Press.

Lee, B. A. (1981). The urban unease revisited: Perceptions of local safety and neighborhood satisfaction among metropolitan residents. *Social Science Quarterly, 62,* 661–629.

Lee, B. A., & Guest, A. M. (1983). Determinants of neighborhood satisfaction: A metropolitan-level analysis. *Sociology Quarterly, 24,* 287–304.

Lee, R. H. (1960). *The Chinese in the United States of America.* New York: Oxford University Press.

Lee, S. D. (1968). Social class bias in the diagnosis of mental illness. *Dissertation Abstracts, 28,* 4758–4759.

Lefcourt, H. M., & Ladwig, G. W. (1961). The effects of reference group upon Negroes' task persistence in a bi-racial competitive game. *Journal of Personality and Social Psychology, 1,* 668–671.

Leong, G. Y. (1936). *Chinatown inside out.* New York: Barrows Mussey.

Leong, R. (1986). Counseling and psychotherapy with Asian Americans: Review of the literature. *Journal of Counseling Psychology, 33,* 196–206.

Levin, D. (1987). Clinical stories: A modern self in the fury of being. In D. Levin (Ed.), *Pathologies of the modern self: Postmodern studies on narcissism, schizophrenia, and depression* (pp. 479–537). New York: New York University Press.

Levine, M., & Perkins, D. Y. (1987). *Principles of community psychology.* New York: Oxford University Press.

Levy, H. S. (1966). *Chinese footbinding: The history of a Chinese erotic custom.* New York: Bell Publishing.

Lewis, O. (1952). Urbanization without breakdown. *Scientific Monthly, 75,* 31–41.

Lieberson, S. (1963). *Ethnic patterns in American cities.* Glencoe, IL: Free Press.

———. (1965). *Language and ethnic relations in Canada.* New York: John Wiley & Sons.

Liebow, E. (1967). *Talley's corner.* Boston: Little, Brown & Co.

Light, I., & Wong, C. C. (1975). Protest or work: Dilemmas of the tourist industry in American Chinatowns. *American Journal of Sociology, 80,* 1342–1368.

Lin, D. M., Tazuma, L., & Masuda, M. (1979). Vietnamese refugees: Health and mental health status. *Archives of General Psychiatry, 36,* 955–961.

Lin, K. M., Kleinman, A. M., & Lin, T. Y. (1981). Overview of mental disorder in Chinese cultures: Reviews of epidemiological and clinical studies. In A. M. Kleinman & T. Y. Lin (Eds.), *Normal and abnormal behavior in Chinese culture* (pp. 233–236). Dordrecht, Holland: D. Reidel.

Lin, T. Y., & Lin, M. C. (1981). Love, denial and rejection: Responses of Chinese families to mental illness. In A. M. Kleinman & T. Y. Lin (Eds.), *Normal and abnormal behavior in Chinese culture* (pp. 387–401). Dordrecht, Holland: D. Reidel.

Lin, T. Y., Tardiff, K., Donetz, G., & Kenny, W. G. (1978). Ethnicity and patterns of help-seeking. *Culture, Medicine and Psychiatry, 2,* 3–13.

Lin, Y. (1936). *My country and my people.* London: Reynal and Hitchcock.

Lloyd, B. E. (1876). *Lights and shades of San Francisco.* San Francisco: A. L. Bancroft.

Lo, W. H. (1976). Urbanization and psychiatric disorders—The Hong Kong scene. *Acta Psychiatrica Scandinavica, 54,* 174–183.

Loo, C. M. (1978). Issues of crowding research, vulnerable participants, assessing perceptions, and developmental differences. *Journal of Population, 1,* 336–348.

———. (1985). The "biliterate" ballot controversy: Language acquisition and cultural shift among immigrants. *International Migration Review, 19,* 493–515.

———. (1986). Neighborhood satisfaction and safety in a low income, ethnic area. *Environment and Behavior, 18,* 109–131.

Loo, C. M., Fong, K., & Iwamasa, G. (1988). Ethnicity and cultural diversity: 1985. An analysis of work published in community psychology journals, 1965–1985. *Journal of Community Psychology, 16,* 332–349.

Loo, C., & Mar, D. (1982). Desired residential mobility in a low income, ethnic community: A case study of Chinatown. *Journal of Social Issues, 3,* 95–106.

———. (1985). Research and Asian Americans: Social change or empty prize? *Amerasia Journal, 12*(2), 85–93.

Loo, C. M., & Ong, P. (1982). Slaying demons with a sewing needle: Feminist issues for Chinatown's women. *Berkeley Journal of Sociology, 18,* 77–88.

———. (1985). Crowding perceptions, attitudes, and consequences among the Chinese. *Environment and Behavior, 16,* 55–87.

Loo, C. M., Tong, B., & True, R. (1989). A bitter bean: Mental health status and attitudes. *Journal of Community Psychology, 17,* 50–60.

Loo, C. M., & Yu, C. (1985). Pulse on San Francisco's Chinatown: Health service utilization and health status. *Amerasia Journal, 11,* 55–73.

Lowe, P. (1937, February). Good life in Chinatown. *Asia,* p. 128.

Lyman, S. M. (1974). *Chinese Americans*. New York: Random House.

Maltzberg, B. (1935). Mental disease in New York State according to nativity and parentage. *Mental Hygiene, 19,* 635–660.

Mar, D. (1985). *Chinese immigrants and the ethic labor market*. Unpublished doctoral dissertation, University of California, Berkeley.

Maracek, J. (1989). Introduction. *Psychology of Women Quarterly, 13,* 367–377.

Marans, R. W., & Rodgers, W. L. (1974). Toward an understanding of community satisfaction. In A. Hawley & V. Rock (Eds.), *Metropolitan America in contemporary perspective*. New York: J. Wiley & Sons.

Marsella, A. J., Kinzie, D., & Gordon, P. (1973). Ethnic variations in the expression of depression. *Journal of Cross-Cultural Psychology, 4,* 435–458.

Marsella, A. J., & Pedersen, R. B. (Eds.). (1981). *Cross-cultural counseling and psychotherapy: Foundations, evaluation, and cultural considerations*. Elmsford, NY: Pergamon Press.

Mathews, L. (1987, July 19). When being best isn't good enough. *Los Angeles Times Magazine*, pp. 23–28.

McCunn, R. L. (1979). *An illustrated history of the Chinese in America*. San Francisco: Design Enterprises of San Francisco.

McLeod, A. (1948). *Pigtails and gold dust*. Caldwell, ID: Caxton Printers.

McWilliams, C. (1969). *Factories in the field: The story of migratory farm labor in California*. New York: Archon Books. (Original work published 1939)

Mears, E. G. (1927). *Resident Orientals on the American Pacific coast*. New York: E. C. Carter for American Group Institute of Pacific Relations.

Mendoza, R. H., & Martinez, J. L. (1981). The measurement of acculturation. In A. Baron, Jr. (Ed.), *Explorations in Chicano psychology* (pp. 71–84). New York: Praeger.

Michelson, W. (1977). *Environmental choice, human behavior, and residential satisfaction*. New York: Oxford University Press.

Miller, G. A. (1969). Psychology as a means of promoting human welfare. *American Psychologist, 24,* 1063–1075.

Miller, S. C. (1969). *The unwelcome immigrant: The American image of the Chinese, 1785–1882*. Berkeley: University of California Press.

Mitchell, R. E. (1971). Some social implications of high density housing. *American Sociological Review, 36,* 18–29.

Montero, D., & Levine, G. N. (Eds.). (1977). Research among racial and cultural minorities: Problems, prospects, and pitfalls. *Journal of Social Issues, 33,* 1–10.

Moore, J. W. (1977). A case study of collaboration: The Chicano Pinto research project. *Journal of Social Issues, 33*(4), 144–158.

Murase, M. (1976). Ethnic studies and higher education for Asian Americans. In E. Gee (Ed.), *Counterpoint: Perspectives on Asian Americans* (pp. 205–223). Los Angeles: Asian American Studies Center, University of California.

Myers, V. (1977). Survey methods for minority populations. *Journal of Social Issues, 33,* 11–19.

Nakanishi, D. (1988). Seeking convergence in race relations research: Japanese Americans and the resurrection of the internment. In P. Katz & D. Taylor (Eds.), *Eliminating racism: Profiles in controversy* (pp. 159–180). New York: Plenum Press.

Nakatsu, P. (1974). Keynote address. In G. Kajiwada, J. Sakai, & G. Lee Davis

(Eds.), *Proceedings of the second Asian American studies conference*. Davis, CA: Association of Asian Studies.

Nandi, P. (1980). *The quality of life of Asian Americans*. Chicago: Pacific/Asian American Mental Health Research Center.

National Center of Health Statistics. (1980). *Health United States 1980*. Washington, DC: U.S. Department of Health, Education, and Welfare, NCHS.

———. (1981). *Health United States 1981*. Washington, DC: U.S. Department of Health, Education, and Welfare, NCHS.

Nee, V., & Nee, B. (1972). *Longtime Californ'*. New York: Pantheon Books.

Newman, O. (1972). *Defensible space*. New York: Collier Books.

Niyakawa, A. M. (1983). Biliteracy acquisition and its sociocultural effects. In M. Chu-Chang & V. Rodriguez (Eds.), *Asian and Pacific-American perspective in bilingual education* (pp. 97–120). New York: Teachers College Press.

Noblit, G. W. & Burcart, J. M. (1975). Ethics, powerless peoples, and methodologist for the study of trouble. *Humboldt Journal of Social Relations, 2*, 20–25.

O'Meara, J. (1884, May). The Chinese in early days. *The Overland Monthly.*

Omi, M., & Winant, H. (1986). *Racial formation in the United States: From the 1960's to the 1980's*. New York: Routledge and Kegan Paul.

Ong, P. (1988, November 25). Asian American community research round table, UCLA. *Asian Week, 10*, p. 17.

Park, P. (1980). A new model for community action research. In A. Murata (Ed.), *Issues in ethnic community research: Asian American perspectives* (pp. 23–24). Chicago: Pacific/Asian American Mental Health Research Center.

Park, R. (1923). A race relations survey. *Journal of Applied Sociology, 8*, 195–205.

———. (1936). Human ecology. *American Journal of Sociology, 42*, 1–15.

Parsons, T. (1960). The principal structures of community. In *Structural processes in modern society* (pp. 250–279). New York: Free Press.

Peters, T. (1988, May 1). How to solve Asian trade problems. *San Jose Mercury News*, p. 1p–5b.

Piore, M. J. (1979). *Birds of passage, migrant labor and industrial societies*. New York: Cambridge Press.

Plant, J. S. (1966). *Personality and the cultural pattern*. New York: Octagon Books. (Original work published 1937)

Platt, J. (1972). Survey data and social policy. *British Journal of Sociology, 23*, 77–92.

Prestowitz, C. (1988, May 1). Japan outwits U.S. in trade talks. *San Jose Mercury News.*

Price, R. H., & Cherniss, C. (1977). Training for a new profession: Research as social action. *Professional Psychology, 8*, 222–231.

Pruitt, I. (1967). *Daughter of Han*. Stanford: Stanford University Press.

Ramirez, A. (1986, November 24). America's super minority. *Fortune*, pp. 150–155.

Reid, D. D. (1975). International studies in epidemiology. *American Journal of Epidemiology, 102*, 469–476.

Reid, P. (1988). Racism and sexism comparisons and conflicts. In P. Katz & D. Taylor (Eds.), *Eliminating racism: Profiles in controversy* (pp. 203–219). New York: Plenum Press.

Report of the San Francisco Chinese community citizens survey and fact finding committee. (1969). San Francisco: H. J. Carle and Sons.

Report of the Senate Committee on Chinese and Chinese immigration. (1887, February 10). 27th Session, Vol. 8. Sacramento: California State Printer.

Report of the Special Health Commissioners, Sacramento, 1901. In *Appendix to journals of Senate and Assembly of the 35th Session of the legislature of California*, Vol. 1. Sacramento: California State Printer, 1903 (pp. 9–11).

Rieff, P. (1966). *The triump of the therapeutic: Uses of faith after Freud*. Chicago: University of Chicago Press.

Riggs, F. W. (1950). *Pressures on Congress: A study of the repeal of Chinese exclusions*. New York: King's Crown.

Rosenthal, D., & Frank, J. D. (1958). The fate of psychiatric clinic outpatients assigned to psychotherapy. *Journal of Nervous and Mental Disease, 127*, 330–343.

Rotter, J. B. (1966). Generalized expectancies for internal versus external control of reinforcement. *Psychological Monographs, 80*, (Whole No. 609).

Rubenstein, E. A., & Lorr, M. A. (1956). A comparison of terminators and remainers in out-patient psychotherapy. *Journal of Clinical Psychology, 12*, 345–349.

Sampson, E. E. (1988). The debate on individualism: Indigenous psychologies of the individual and their role in personal and societal functioning. *American Psychologist, 43*, 15–22.

San Francisco Department of City Planning. (1972). *Chinatown 1970 Census*. San Francisco: Author.

————. (1975, September). *Neighborhood commercial districts*. San Francisco: Author.

————. (1977, February). *Chinatown neighborhood improvement plan*. San Francisco: Author.

————. (1980). *Study on conversion and demolition of residential units*. San Francisco: Author.

————. (1984, February). *Environmental setting of Chinatown: History, people, land use regulations, development trends* (Issue Paper No. 2). San Francisco: Author.

————. (1985, February). *Chinatown plan*. San Francisco: Author.

————. (1987, February 19). *Chinatown plan: A part of the master plan of the city and county of San Francisco and master plan amendment*. San Francisco: Author.

San Francisco Health Department Report. (1977). San Francisco: Department of Health.

San Francisco News. (1950, March 20).

Sarason, S. (1974). *The psychological sense of community: Prospects of a community psychology*. San Francisco: Jossey-Bass.

————. (1976). Community psychology, networks, and Mr. Everyman. *American Psychologist, 31*, 317–328.

Sarason, S. B. (1981). *Psychology misdirected*. New York: Free Press.

————. (1982). *Psychology and social action: Selected papers*. New York: Praeger.

Sawhill, I. V. (1969). The role of social indicators and social reporting in public expenditure decisions. In *The analysis and evaluation of public expenditures: The PPB system*. A compendium of papers submitted to the Subcommittee on Economy in Government of the Joint Economic Committee, Congress of the United States, Vol. 1. Washington, DC: U.S. Government Printing Office.

Saxton, A. P. (1971). *The indispensable enemy: Labor and the anti-Chinese movement in California*. Berkeley: University of California Press.

Schaffer, L., & Myers, J. K. (1954). Psychotherapy and social stratification: An empirical study of practice in a psychiatric outpatient clinic. *Psychiatry, 17*, 83–93.

Schmidt, D., Goldman, R., & Feimer, N. (1976). Physical and psychological factors associated with perceptions of crowding: An analysis of subcultural differences. *Journal of Applied Psychology, 61*(3), 279–289.

Schmitt, R. C. (1963). Implications of density in Hong Kong. *American Institute of Planners Journal, 29,* 210–217.

Schuman, H., & Converse, P. (1971). The effects of black and white interviewers on black response. *Public Opinion Quarterly, 35,* 44–48.

See, C. (1980). Chinese Americans in the San Francisco Bay Area: A survey study. In Y-L. Wu (Ed.) *The economic conditions of Chinese Americans.* Chicago: Pacific Asian American Mental Health Center.

Seiler, L. H. (1973). The 22-item scale used in field studies of mental illness: A question of method, a question of substance, and a question of theory. *Journal of Health and Social Behavior, 14,* 252–264.

Seward, G. F. (1881). *Chinese immigration in its social and economic aspects.* New York: Charles Scribner's Sons.

Sheldon, E. B., & Freeman, H. E. (1972). Notes on social indicators: Promises and potential. *Policy Science, 1,* 97–111.

Shribner, C. (1969). *Financing the California apparel industry.* Thesis for the Graduate School of Credit and Financial Management, School of Business Administration, Harvard University.

Shuy, R. W. (1981). Conditions affecting language learning and maintenance among Hispanics in the U.S. *NABA Journal, 1,* 1–17.

Simmel, G. (1950). The metropolis and mental life. In K. H. Wolfe (Ed.), *The sociology of Georg Simmel* (pp. 409–424). New York: Free Press.

Simon, H. A. (1955). *Models of man.* New York: John Wiley & Sons.

Smith, A. H. (1900). *Village life in China: A study in sociology.* London: F. H. Revell.

———. (1902). *Proverbs and common sayings from the Chinese.* Shanghai: American Presbyterian Mission.

Sommer, R. (1969). *Personal space.* Englewood Cliffs, NJ: Prentice Hall.

Soule, G., Gihon, J. H., & Nisbet, J. (1854). *The annals of San Francisco.* New York: D. Appleton.

Springer, R. (1988, October 20). *East/West News,* p. 4.

Srole, L., Langner, T., Michael, S., Opler, M., & Rennie, T. (1962). *Mental health in the metropolis: The midtown Manhattan study.* New York: McGraw Hill.

Stacey, J. (1983). *Patriarchy and socialist revolution in China.* Berkeley: University of California Press.

Stein, M. (1960). *The eclipse of community: An interpretation of American studies.* Princeton: Princeton University Press.

Stephens, J. W. (1976). A quantitative history of Chinatown, San Francisco. In *The life, influence and the role of the Chinese in the United States, 1776–1960* (pp. 71–87). San Francisco: Chinese Historical Society.

Stokols, D. (1972, March). A social-psychological model of human crowding phenomena. *American Institute of Planners Journal,* pp. 72–83.

Stoller, A. (1966). *New faces: Immigration and family life in Australia.* Melbourne, Australia: Cheshire.

Stoneall, L. (1983). *Country life, city life: Five theories of community.* New York: Praeger.

Success story of one minority group in U.S. (1966, December 26). *U.S. News and World Report,* pp. 6–9.

Sue, D. W. (1981). *Counseling the culturally different: Theory and practice.* New York: John Wiley & Sons.

Sue, D. W., Bernier, J. E., Durran, L. W., Feinberg, L. W., Pedersen, P., Smith, E. J., & Vasquez-Nuttall, E. (1982). Position paper: Cross-cultural counseling competencies. *Counseling Psychologist, 10*(2), 45–52.

Sue, S. (1978). Foreword. In B. L. Kim, *The Asian Americans: Changing patterns, changing needs.* Montclair, NJ: Association of Korean Christian Scholars in North America.

Sue, S., Akutsu, P. D., & Higashi, C. (1985). Training issues in conducting therapy with ethnic minority group clients. In P. Pederson (Ed.), *Handbook of cross-cultural counseling and therapy* (pp. 275–280). Westport, CT: Greenwood Press.

Sue, S., & Kitano, H. (1973). Stereotypes as a measure of success. *Journal of Social Issues, 29,* 83–98.

Sue, S., & McKinney, H. (1975). Asian-Americans in the community mental health care system. *American Journal of Orthopsychiatry, 45,* 111–118.

Sue, S., & Morishima, J. K. (1982). *The mental health of Asian Americans.* San Francisco: Jossey-Bass.

Sue, S., & Sue, D. W. (1971). Chinese American personality and mental health. *Amerasia Journal, 111,* 36–49.

———. (1974). MMPI comparisons between Asian American and non-Asian students utilizing a student health psychiatric clinic. *Journal of Counseling Psychology, 21,* 423–427.

Sue, S., Sue, D. W., & Sue, D. (1975). Asian Americans as a minority group. *American Psychologist, 30,* 906–910.

Sue, S., Wagner, N., Ja, D., Margullis, C., & Lew, L. (1976). Conceptions of mental illness among Asian and Caucasian-American students. *Psychological Reports, 38,* 703–708.

Summers, G. F., Seiler, L. H., & Hough, R. L. (1971). Psychiatric symptoms: Cross-validation with a rural sample. *Rural Sociology, 36,* 367–378.

Surh, J. (1974). Asian American identity and politics. *Amerasia Journal, 2,* 168.

Suzuki, B. H. (1977). Education and the socialization of Asian Americans: A revisionist analysis of the "Model Minority" thesis. *Amerasia Journal, 4,* 23–51.

Takagi, P., & Platt, T. (1978). Behind the gilded ghetto: An analysis of race, class, and crime in Chinatown. *Crime and Social Justice, 9,* 2–25.

Tchen, J. K. W. (1984). *Genthe's photographs of San Francisco's old Chinatown.* New York: Dover.

Toennies, F. (1957). *Community and safety* (C. L. Loomis, Trans. & Ed.). East Lansing: Michigan State University Press. (Original work published 1887)

Tong, B. R. (1971). Ghettos of the mind: Notes on the historical psychology of Chinese America. *Amerasia Journal, 1,* 1–31.

Tow, J. S. (1923). *The real Chinese in America.* New York: Academy.

Trauner, J. B. (1978). The Chinese as medical scapegoats in San Francisco, 1870–1905. *California History, 57,* 70–87.

Trimble, J. E. (1977). The sojourner in the American Indian community: Methodological issues and concerns. *Journal of Social Issues, 33*(4), 159–174.

Tsai, M., Teng, L. N., & Sue, S. (1980). Mental status of Chinese in the United States. In A. M. Kleinman & T. Y. Lin (Eds.), *Normal and deviant behavior in Chinese culture* (pp. 291–307). Hingham, MA: Reidel.

Tseng, W., & Hsu, J. (1969). Chinese culture personality formation and mental illness. *International Journal of Social Psychiatry, 16,* 5–14.

Tudor Engineering. (1979). *Chinatown: Core area traffic circulation study.* San Francisco: Author.

Turner, R. J. (1983). Direct, indirect and moderating effects of social support upon psychological distress and associated conditions. In H. B. Kaplan (Ed.), *Psychosocial stress: Trends in theory and research* (pp. 105–155). New York: Academic Press.

Tuthill, F. (1866). *History of California.* San Francisco: H. H. Bancroft and Co.

U.S. Bureau of the Census. (1970). *Subject Reports.* Washington, DC: U.S. Government Printing Office.

————. (1980a). *1980 Census of population: Asian and Pacific Islander population in the United States: 1980* (Publication No. PC80-2-1E). Washington, DC: U.S. Government Printing Office.

————. (1980b). *1980 Census of Population and Housing.* Washington, DC: U.S. Government Printing Office.

————. (1985). *1985 Statistical abstract of the U.S.* (Publication Nos. 125 and 127). Washington, DC: U.S. Government Printing Office.

————. (1989). *Population estimates by race and Hispanic origin for states, metropolitan areas and selected counties: 1980 to 1985.* Washington, DC: U.S. Government Printing Office.

————. (1990a). *Statistical abstract of the United States: 1990* (110th ed.). Washington, DC: U.S. Government Printing Office.

————. (1990b). *Summary Tape File 1A.* Washington, DC: U.S. Government Printing Office.

U.S. Commission on Civil Rights. (1976). *Using the voting rights act* (Clearinghouse Publication No. 53). Washington, DC: U.S. Government Printing Office.

————. (1978). *Social indicator of equality for minorities and women.* Washington, DC: U.S. Government Printing Office.

————. (1986). *Anti-Asian violence.* Washington, DC: U.S. Government Printing Office.

U.S. Congressional Records. (1975). *H.R. No. 94-196,* 94th Congress, First Session. Washington, DC: U.S. Government Printing Office.

U.S. Department of Health, Education and Welfare. (1969). *Toward a social report.* Washington, DC: U.S. Government Printing Office.

————. (1977, September). *Health of the disadvantaged: Chart book.* Washington, DC: U.S. Government Printing Office.

Van Gulick, R. H. (1974). *Sexual life in ancient China.* Leiden: E. J. Brill.

Vecoli, R. J. (1970). Ethnicity: A neglected dimension of American history. In H. J. Bass (Ed.), *The state of American history* (pp. 70–88). Chicago: Quadrangle Books.

Veltman, C. (1983). *Language shift in the United States.* New York: Mouton Publishers.

Veroff, J., Douvan, E., & Kulka, R. A. (1981). *The inner American.* New York: Basic.

Veroff, J., Kulka, R. A., & Douvan, E. (1981). *Mental health in America: Patterns of help-seeking from 1957–1976.* New York: Basic.

Voting Rights Act of 1965 with 1975 Amendments, Sec. 55, 5 U.S.C. 301, 28 U.S.C. 509, 510, Pub. L. 94-73. (1975). Washington, DC: U.S. Government Printing Office.

Wallston, B. S., Alagna, S. W., DeVellis, B. M., & DeVillis, R. F. (1983). Social support and physical health. *Health Psychology, 4,* 367–391.

Warner, W. L., & Srole, L. (1945). *The social systems of American ethnic groups*. New Haven: Yale University Press.

Warwick, D. P., & Lininger, C. A. (1975). *The sample survey: Theory and practice*. New York: McGraw-Hill.

Weinstock, A. A. (1968). Some factors that retard or accelerate the rate of acculturation, with special reference to Hungarian immigrants. *Human Relations, 17*(4), 321–340.

Williams, J. A., Jr. (1964). Interviewer-respondent interaction: A study of bias in the information interview. *Sociometry, 27*, 338–352.

Williams, R. L. (1981). The death of white research in the black community. In R. L. Jones (Ed.), *Black psychology* (pp. 403–417). New York: Harper and Row.

Williams, S. (1875). *City of the Golden Gate*. New York: Scribner's Monthly.

Wirth, L. (1938). Urbanism as a way of life. *American Journal of Sociology, 44*, 1–24.

Wolf, M. (1974). Chinese women: Old skills in a new context. In M. Z. Rosaldo (Ed.), *Women, culture, and society* (pp. 151–172). Stanford, CA: Stanford University Press.

Wolfe, T. (1969, December). The yellow peril. *Esquire*.

Wright, G. (1983, October 30). Proposition 0. *San Francisco Examiner/Chronicle*.

Yamada, M. (1981). Asian Pacific American women and feminism. In C. Morzaga & G. Anzaldua (Eds.), *This bridge called my back: Writings by radical women of color* (pp. 71–75). Watertown, MA: Persephone.

Yamamoto, E. K. (1990). Efficiency's threat to the value of accessible courts for minorities. *Harvard's Civil Rights Law Review, 25*, 2.

Yamamoto, J., & Goin, M. (1966). Social class factors relevant for psychiatric treatment. *Journal of Nervous and Mental Disease, 142*, 332–339.

Yu, C. Y. (1981). A history of San Francisco Chinatown housing. *Amerasia Journal, 8*(1), 93–109.

Yung, J. (1986). *Chinese women of America: A pictorial history*. Seattle: University of Washington Press.

Zygoskee, A., Strickland, B. B., & Watson, J. (1971). Delay of gratification and internal versus external control among adolescents of low socioeconomic status. *Developmental Psychology, 4*, 93–96.

Index

ABOUT THE AUTHOR

CHALSA M. LOO is visiting associate professor of psychology at the University of Hawaii at Manoa and was associate professor of psychology at the University of California at Santa Cruz and visiting associate professor at the Asian American Studies Research Center at UCLA. She received her Ph.D. in Clinical Psychology at Ohio State University and has since authored over 30 professional articles. Dr. Loo was the principal investigator for the research grant that funded this Chinatown study and was founder of the Chinatown Housing and Health Research Project (CHHRP). She is a Fellow of Division 45 (Society for the Psychological Study of Ethnic Minority Issues) and Division 34 (Environment and Behavior) and was co-president of Division 45 of the American Psychological Association. She also served as an executive council representative for the Association for Asian American Studies. Dr. Loo was the 1991 recipient of the Distinguished Contribution Award presented by the Asian American Psychological Association. She is a licensed psychologist in California and Hawaii and a third-generation Chinese American.